Macintosh® Printer Secrets

Macintosh® Printer Secrets

Larry Pina

HAYDEN BOOKS
A Division of Sams
11711 North College, Carmel, IN 46032 USA

Written and illustrated by Larry Pina
Photos by Larry Pina and Richard Manchester
Test Character Generator software by Larry Pina

FIRST EDITION
FIRST PRINTING-1990

International Standard Book Number: 0-672-48463-3
Library of Congress Catalog Card Number: xxxxxxxx

Aquisitions/Development Editor: *James Rounds*
Copy Editor: *Frank N.Speights*
Graphics Editor: *Tom Emrick*
Cover Illustration: *Ned Shaw*
Indexer: *Hilary Adams*
Technical Reviewer: *Owen Hartnett*
Production: *Jill D. Bomaster, Brad Chinn, Travia Davis, Sharon Hilgenberg, Tami Hughes, Jennifer Matthews, Joe Ramon, Dennis Sheehan, Bruce Steed, Mary Beth Wakefield, Vickie West*

Printed in the United States of America

Overview

Contents

Acknowledgments

Special thanks to Jim Rounds, Acquisitions/Development Editor, Technical Reference Books, Macmillan Computer Publishing, and to the following trade professionals who helped in one way or another to make this a better book:

Hugh Amick, Hewlett-Packard, Margaret Baranowski, Eastman Kodak Company; Bob Cook, Sun Remarketing; Dick Ernst, Eastman Kodak Company; Richard Harold, Shreve Systems; Owen Hartnett, Ohm Software; Bruce Kennedy, Gateway Associates; Michaela Matheson, Entrepreneur Business Machine; Jim McIntosh, GDT Softworks; Ivar Michelsons, Adobe Systems; Pamela Smith, DataPak Software; Roger Smith, Sun Remarketing; Chuck Stegmeir, Les Goldberg Public Relations; Soren Storm, ScanCo.

Trademarks

All terms mentioned in this book that are known to be trademarks or service marks are listed below, In addition, terms suspected of being trademarks or service marks have been appropriately capitalized. SAMS cannot attest to the accuracy of this information. Use of a term in this book should not be regarded as affecting the validity of any trademark or service mark.

Adobe Type Manager, ATM and PostScript are trademarks of Adobe Systems, Inc.

Introduction

Several months ago, I received a letter from someone who'd just bought an elaborate new computer system. Venting his frustration over inadequate user manuals, he explained that it felt like he'd signed on for a long sea voyage, only to find himself stranded on the dock. "The ship has definitely passed me by," he said. "Without going back to school, how are you supposed to learn what every computer manual assumes you already know?"

The beginning of this book is a good place to start. Written for the person who's never been exposed to computer science before, it demystifies terms like baud rate, data bits, handshaking, and so on. Read Chapters 1 through 7, and you'll never feel intimidated by technical terms again.

Chapters 9 through 13 take a similar approach, but concentrate on electromechanical terms. Rather than arguing and complaining about printer malfunctions, you'll be able to correct them yourself.

Then, Chapters 14 to 16 demystify alternatives to ImageWriter serial printers and Mac-to-serial printer connections. With this information, you'll be able to connect any printer you like to a Macintosh. Any printer, any Macintosh.

Test Character Generator

Test Character Generator (TCG), the program included with this book, is both a training aid and a diagnostics tool. Besides standard performance checks, it creates precision alignment patterns which help you to determine what, if anything, is wrong with your printer. Simply running the program does not fix the problem! For that, you need detailed instructions, hand tools, and some test instruments. Detailed instructions about these are in the chapters that follow.

System Requirements

To run this version of Test Character Generator, you need a 512K Mac (or better) and one 400K (or higher capacity) disk drive. TCG also works with Lisa, Mac-XL, Mac-Plus, Mac-SE, and Mac-II computers —everything but the original 128K Macintosh. The 128K Mac is not supported.

The program disk is supplied without System software. To use the disk in a two-drive computer, you have to start the computer with a System disk, and then run the program disk from the second drive.

To use the program on a one-drive computer, you must copy the System software to the disk. Which version of the System software to copy varies according to your hardware configuration. Table I-1 provides a current list of recommendations.

Table I-1. Macintosh System Software

Model	Floppy-Drive Software	SCSI Hard-Drive Software
Mac 512	Finder 4.1/System 2.0	Not applicable
Mac 512E	Finder 5.3/System 3.2	Not applicable
Mac 512E (SCSI upgrade)	Finder 5.3/System 3.2	Finder 4.1/System 5.0
Mac Plus	Finder 6.1/System 6.0.3	Finder 6.1/System 6.0.3
Mac SE/II	Finder 6.1/System 6.0.3	Finder 6.1/System 6.0.3
Lisa/Mac XL (MacWorks XL)	Finder 5.3/System 3.2	Not applicable
Lisa/Mac XL (MacWorks +)	Finder 5.3/System 3.2	Finder 6.1/System 6.0.3

TCG has been extensively tested with these combinations, and is known to work fine, across the board. TCG has not been tested with earlier System software and has not been tested with later System software, such as the forthcoming System 7.

Before running TCG for the first time, it's very important to copy the program disk. The copy (generally called the work disk) is for everyday use; the original disk (generally called the master disk) should be stored as a backup.

For maximum protection, the master disk should be stored in a safe place, preferably somewhere away from the workbench. In rough use, you have to expect disk casualties. If the master disk is nowhere close at hand, you'll always have something to fall back on, in case of an accident.

Starting TCG

To start TCG, double-click the program icon, or simply select it and choose Open from the File menu. As shown in Figure I-1, the first thing you should see is a sign-on screen showing memory and ROM information.

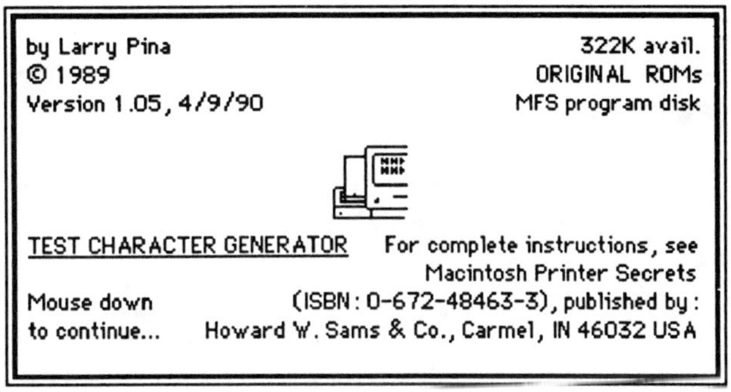

Figure I-1 Test Character Generator sign-on screen.

To dismiss the sign-on screen, click and hold the mouse button down until the sign-on screen disappears, or just press the return key. Assuming the caps lock key is up, the next thing you should see is a list of general instructions, as shown in Figure I-2.

After reading the instructions, you can close the window by clicking the close box, by choosing Close from the File menu, or by typing Command W. You can refer to the list anytime you wish by rechoosing it from the Reference menu. To keep the list of general instructions from reappearing every time you run the program, engage (push down) the caps lock key before you start. You can leave the caps lock key down while you're running the program. It doesn't interfere with command-key short cuts, or with option-key tests.

Indicating the Printer and Port

Next, choose a printer from the Printer menu. As shown in Figure I-3, this version of Test Character Generator supports both Apple-compatible and Epson-compatible printers.

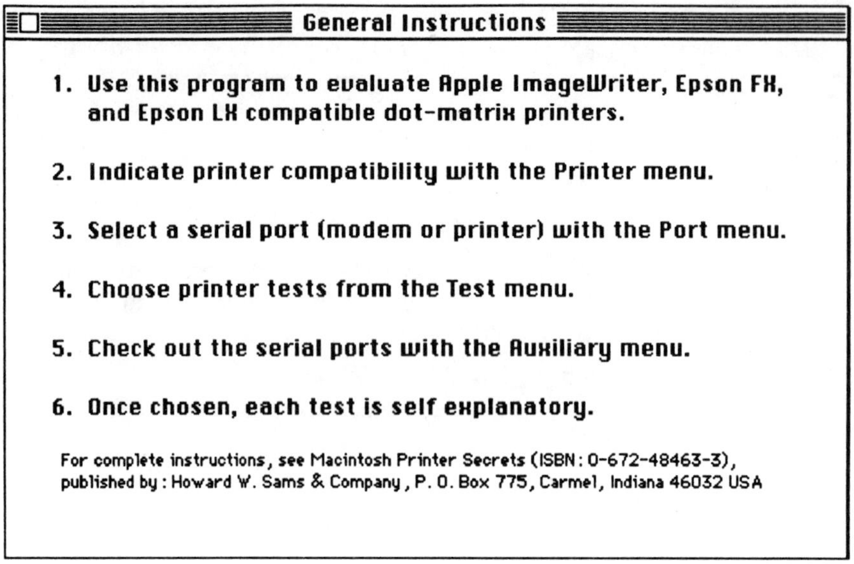

Figure I-2 Test Character Generator General Instructions window.

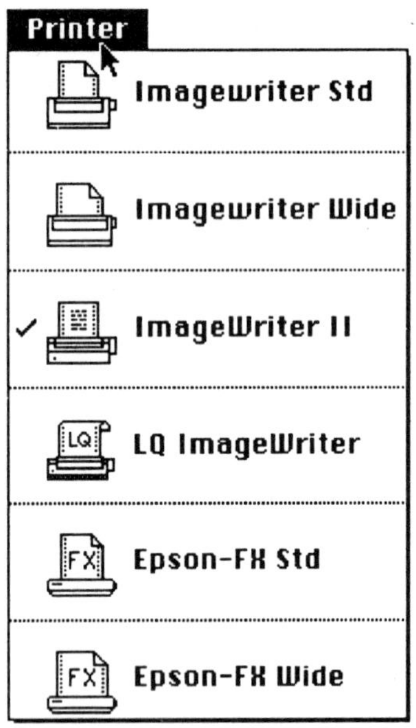

Figure I-3 Test Character Generator Printer menu.

Choosing a printer compatibility from the Printer menu tells the program which code (Apple or Epson) to use, and which baud rate (9600 or 19,200) to set. On startup, the default printer (as indicated by the check mark) is always an ImageWriter II (Apple code, 9600 baud). Don't worry if this is over your head right now. All technical terms are explained in Chapters 1 through 7.

While the program is running, you can change printers as often as you like. Just remember, Apple printers don't run on Epson code, and vice versa. If you try to make an Apple printer run on Epson code, it's going to malfunction. That's to be expected.

After choosing a printer, the next step is to choose a port from the Port menu. As shown in Figure I-4, the test printer can either be connected to the printer port or the modem port. If you indicate the wrong port, nothing is going to happen when you run the printer tests. Under certain circumstances, the program may hang.

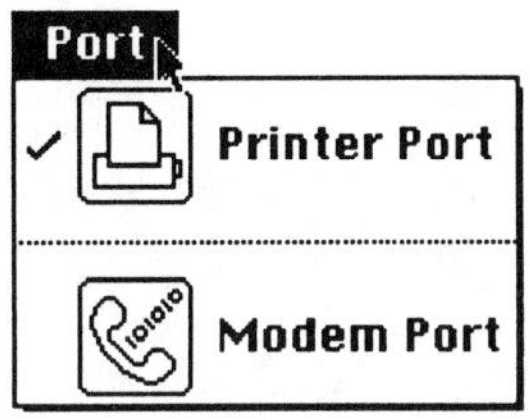

Figure I-4 Test Character Generator Port menu.

TCG's Printer Tests

As shown in Figure I-5, the Test menu contains four printer-hardware tests and four combination tests. Printer-hardware tests check the printer only. Combination tests check the printer-hardware as well as the printer-driver software.

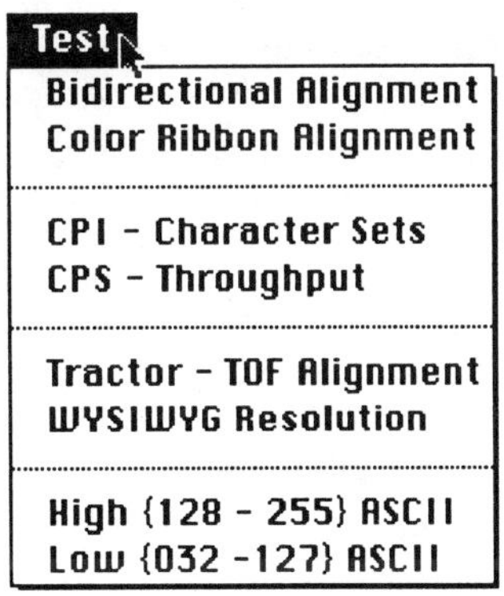

Figure I-5 Test Character Generator Test menu.

The top four items in Figure I-5 are printer-hardware tests. Hardware tests bypass the printer-driver software and print directly to the port selected in the Port menu, using the code selected in the Printer menu. You don't need an ImageWriter driver to run these tests on Apple-compatible printers, nor do you need an Epson-compatible printer driver to run these tests on Epson-compatible printers. TCG's program code drives both printers.

Here's a brief description of each hardware test:

1. Bidirectional Alignment checks for vertical character deviation in the bidirectional print mode. Complete details on this are in Chapters 9 and 11.
2. Color Ribbon Alignment checks for proper color-cam operation. This test is for ImageWriter II and ImageWriter LQ printers only. It's not for Epson printers. If an Epson printer is chosen, the menu item appears dimmed. Instructions are given in Chapters 6, 11, and 13.
3. CPI - Character Sets tests for built-in NLQ character sets. Straight-text printing (on the Macintosh) is generally screen-font specific. If the document's screen fonts don't match the printer's internal character sets exactly, DP (draft quality) may default to ultracondensed; NLQ may not work at all. This test will show you what the printer's built-in character sets look like. It also verifies whether Apple-compatible printers are emulating the correct NLQ codes. Details are given in Chapters 5, 14, and 15.
4. CPS—Throughput measures the printing speed in characters per second (cps) and lines per minute (LPM). Eye-opening revelations are given in Chapters 5 and 10.

The next four items are combination hardware/software tests. Combination tests use the printer driver and port selected in the Chooser DA. You need an ImageWriter driver to run these tests on Apple-compatible printers, and/or an Epson-compatible driver to run these tests on Epson-compatible printers. As usual, the printer drivers have to reside in the System folder of the startup disk.

Here's a brief description of each hardware-/software-combination test:

5. Tractor—TOF Alignment prints a test box with 1-inch margins all around. When the paper is positioned so that the test box is perfectly centered on the page, the headers, footers, and margins set by all other applications should also print perfectly. Full instructions are given in Chapters 7, 8, 10, 12, and 13.
6. WYSIWYG Resolution checks the printer's horizontal and vertical resolution. This test is intended to be a learning tool. Running the test demonstrates the difference between Tall and Tall-Adjusted orientation, and helps to explain the concept of resolution. Instructions are given in Chapter 3.

7. High {128–255} ASCII allows you to compare the printer's high-ASCII assignments to the computer's high-ASCII assignments. This test is useful for checking download-character support. Details are in Chapters 1, 14, and 15.
8. Low {032–127} ASCII allows you to compare the printer's low-ASCII assignments to the computer's low-ASCII assignments. This test is also designed as a learning tool. In every case, the assignments should be identical.

Troubleshooting Hung Computers If you load cut-sheet paper and forget to press the printer's select button (also called the on-line button), running a printer test may or may not "hang up" the computer. If it does hang up, just check the printer's select light. If it's not lit, press the select (or on-line) button on the printer's control panel.

In some cases, the printer may print garbage when it comes back on-line. In other cases, you may have to turn the printer off in order to unhang the computer. Either way, it's the printer's natural response to the error condition. It doesn't mean that there's anything wrong with the printer or the program.

You can avoid this error completely by using pin-feed paper and remembering to check the select light.

TCG's Auxiliary Tests

As shown in Figure I-6, TCG's Auxiliary menu contains two items that indirectly help to solve printer problems.

Figure I-6 Test Character Generator Auxiliary menu.

The first item, Test Serial Port, confirms whether or not the computer's serial port is working. This test requires that a properly constructed loopback plug be inserted into the port prior to testing. Without the plug, the loopback test fails every time. Construction details are given under the Reference menu. Full instructions are given in Chapters 9, 11, and 13.

Decode Hex Dump brings up a handy debugging calculator. Used in conjunction with Appendixes C through F, and similar resources, it simplifies problem solving by helping to identify errant control instructions. To take advantage of this method, the printer has to be run in the hexadecimal-dump mode. Full instructions are given in Chapters 1 and 5.

TCG's Reference-Menu Items

As shown in Figure I-7, TCG's Reference menu contains five on-line reference items. General Instructions is the list shown in Figure I-2. Printer Specifications is the list shown in Figure I-8. DB-9 Loopback, DB-25 Loopback, and Mini-8 DIN Loopback contain the same wiring diagrams as shown in Chapter 11, Figure 11-38.

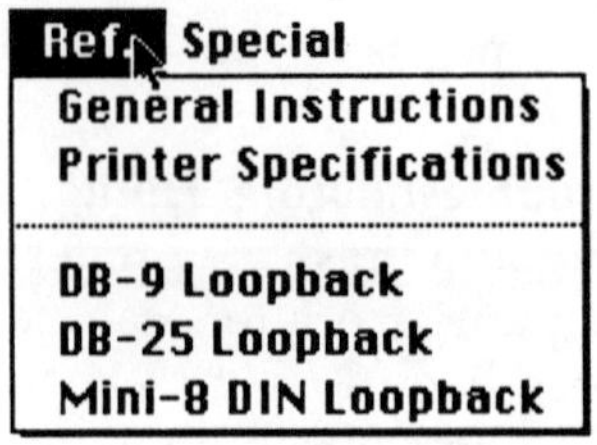

Figure I-7 Test Character Generator Reference menu.

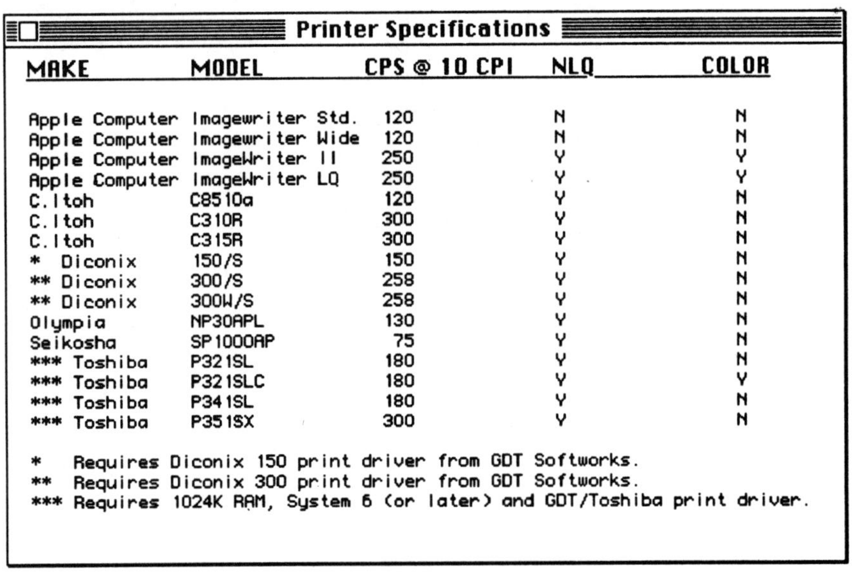

Printer Specifications

MAKE	MODEL	CPS @ 10 CPI	NLQ	COLOR
Apple Computer	Imagewriter Std.	120	N	N
Apple Computer	Imagewriter Wide	120	N	N
Apple Computer	ImageWriter II	250	Y	Y
Apple Computer	ImageWriter LQ	250	Y	Y
C.Itoh	C8510a	120	Y	N
C.Itoh	C310R	300	Y	N
C.Itoh	C315R	300	Y	N
* Diconix	150/S	150	Y	N
** Diconix	300/S	258	Y	N
** Diconix	300W/S	258	Y	N
Olympia	NP30APL	130	Y	N
Seikosha	SP1000AP	75	Y	N
*** Toshiba	P321SL	180	Y	N
*** Toshiba	P321SLC	180	Y	Y
*** Toshiba	P341SL	180	Y	N
*** Toshiba	P351SX	300	Y	N

* Requires Diconix 150 print driver from GDT Softworks.
** Requires Diconix 300 print driver from GDT Softworks.
*** Requires 1024K RAM, System 6 (or later) and GDT/Toshiba print driver.

Figure I-8 Test Character Generator Printer Specifications window.

TCG's Special-Menu Items

As shown in Figure I-9, the Special menu in this version of Test Character Generator contains only one item.

Figure I-9 Test Character Generator Special menu.

In Figure I-10, choosing Shut Down brings out a dialog box which asks whether that's *really* what you want to do. Clicking the yes button ends the program, ejects all disks, and restarts the Mac. When used on old Macs with (slow) 400K drives, choosing Shut Down saves a little time.

Figure I-10 Test Character Generator Shut Down dialog box.

Don't use this command to shut down SCSI drives! With SCSI drives, always choose Quit from the File menu, and use the Finder's Shut Down command instead.

Miscellaneous Files

The program disk contains an assortment of miscellaneous text files that are useful for evaluating printers which have just been repaired. These files can be opened and read at any time by choosing Open... from the File menu.

To create a personal file for use with Test Character Generator, use any word processor, and save the file as TEXT with carriage returns at the end of every line (TEXT with line breaks).

To attach a TCG icon to your file, launch TCG, choose Open... from the File menu, select your file from the standard file selection dialog box, and then choose Save As... (also from the File menu). When you return to the Finder, the file you designated Saved As... will now have the TCG icon. This allows your file to be opened and printed via TCG (no other application necessary), simply by double-clicking on it in the Finder.

When Save As... is chosen and used under MultiFinder, TCG's file icon will be attached, but it won't appear until you restart the Macintosh.

The Color PRN Test.MacWrite2.2 file is exactly what the file name suggests. It's a color-printing test for MacWrite 2.2 that even works with original System software on a 128K Macintosh. It's not for use with TCG. It's included to prove a point. Full details are given in Chapter 6.

The PrinterSpeeds(SS).SYLK file is the spreadsheet shown in Figure 5-10. To use it, you need a program (like Microsoft Excel, Microsoft Multiplan, or Microsoft Works) capable of importing SYLK files. It's included to save a little time, should you decide to compile your own printer-speed data.

The TCG.Help file contains additional information on Test Character Generator. If there are any last minute instructions, that's where you'll find them.

CHAPTER 1

Standard Printing Procedure

This chapter outlines the standard Macintosh® printing procedure. Unlike the printer-specific chapters which appear later in the book, the material presented here applies generally to all printer models. Even if you've worked with computers and computer printers for some time, please read this first chapter for general information, and then turn to the setup and repair chapters for further instructions.

Application-Independent Printing

Printing from the Macintosh is said to be **application independent**. "Independent" means that all applications (programs) are supposed to handle printing in exactly the same way. Whether it's a data base or a word processor, choosing Print... from the File menu should set up a standard Print... dialog box, supplied by the currently selected printer resource. The key phrase is **currently selected**. If there's no printer resource currently selected, no printing can take place.

Installing a Printer Resource

Printer resources (drivers) are programs that allow computers to communicate with a printer. The reason for different printer resources is that various printer ROMs (read-only memory) require different instruction sets. Since the only Apple-compatible graphics printer sold by Apple Computer in 1984, when the Macintosh was introduced, was the

Imagewriter Standard, early Macintosh System disks were supplied with factory installed, Imagewriter printer resources. This was very convenient, because the computer operator did not have to choose from dozens of printer drivers in order to install a printing resource. The appropriate driver (the Imagewriter resource) resided in the System folder along with other important System files, as shown in Figure 1-1.

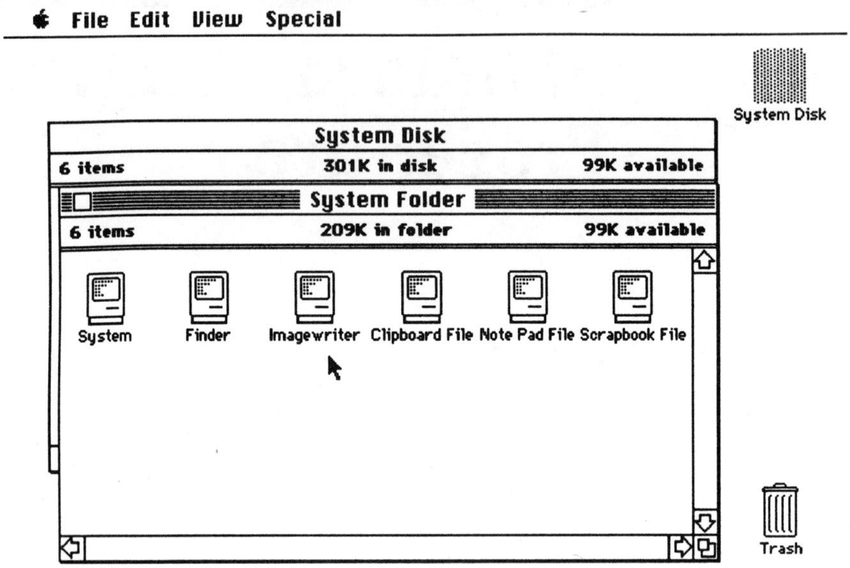

Figure 1-1 Early System disks were supplied with factory installed Imagewriter printer drivers.

Today, Apple Computer sells all kinds of Apple-compatible graphics printers, so the latest System disks are generally supplied without any printer driver. Instead, various printer drivers are supplied on a separate Printing Tools disk, as shown in Figure 1-2.

This requires you to choose the driver most **appropriate** to your particular printer and then **install** it on the startup disk. "Appropriate" means correctly coded for the printer's make and model, while "install" means "copy to the System folder on the startup disk." There's nothing special about copying appropriate printer drivers; printer drivers are copied the same way you copy any other file—by pointing, clicking, and dragging.

To confirm whether there is a printer driver installed on the startup disk, start the computer and open the System folder. Choose By Icon if necessary from the View menu. Assuming you have an Imagewriter

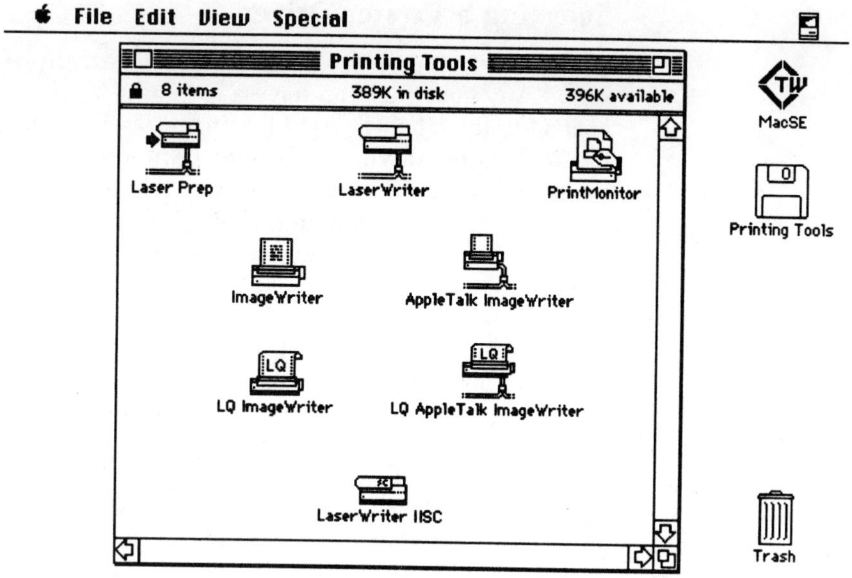

Figure 1-2 Today, various printer drivers are supplied on a separate Printing Tools disk.

(Standard or Wide) or an ImageWriter II printer, you should see an icon named Imagewriter or ImageWriter. Note the difference in capitalization. As shown in Figure 1-3, with the possible exception of version 2.0, Imagewriter icons look like little computers. ImageWriter icons look like little printers.

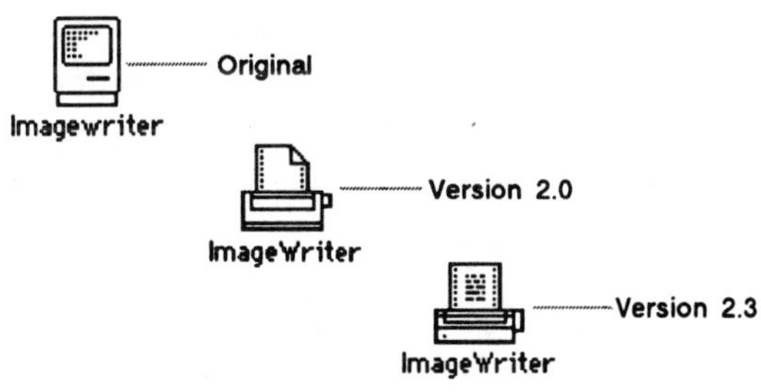

Figure 1-3 With the possible exception of version 2.0, Imagewriter icons look like little computers. ImageWriter icons look like little printers.

The presence of either icon merely indicates that the driver has been installed. Except on the very earliest versions of Macintosh System software, it does not guarantee that the driver is **currently selected**.

Selecting a Printer Driver

Henry Ford, founder of Ford Motor Company, is supposed to have said: "Any customer can have a car painted any color he wants as long as it's black." The original Macintosh designers took a similar approach toward printer drivers. The only printer Apple had available was the Imagewriter, so you could have any printer driver you wanted so long as it was *named* Imagewriter. Only the name was significant. Whatever driver was named Imagewriter became the currently selected printer driver on startup.

In the interest of simplicity, the renaming procedure (from Whatever printer to Imagewriter) was not explained, so most people, including much of the trade press, just assumed that Macs could *only* work with Imagewriters. That was *never* true. Even the earliest operating systems supported other printer drivers.

This misunderstanding is so common, that just for the record, here's how to disprove it using an original 128K Macintosh with System software dated May 2, 1984, and an Epson FX printer driver from GDT Softworks:

1. Turn on the 128K (or 512K) Macintosh.
2. Insert an original System 1.0 disk.
3. Click once on the System folder.
4. Choose Open from the File menu.
5. Choose by Icon (if necessary) from the View menu.
6. Click once on the Imagewriter icon. Note that Imagewriter was originally spelled with a lowercase w, although case is insignificant. Uppercase W works just as well.
7. Select Duplicate from the File menu. The duplicate driver will be named "Copy of Imagewriter."
8. Click once again on the Imagewriter icon.
9. Drag it to the trash. The Copy of Imagewriter should still be in the System folder.
10. Choose Empty Trash from the Special menu.
11. Insert the GDT printer driver disk into the external drive. If you don't have an external drive, choose Eject from the File menu to eject the internal drive.
12. Select the Epson FX driver (or whatever driver is appropriate to the printer that you'd like to use) and drag it on top of the open System 1.0 folder. Swap disks as necessary.
13. Reselect the System 1.0 disk. Click on the Epson FX printer driver to select it. Move the mouse pointer over the name until the arrow cursor changes to the I-beam.

14. Type Imagewriter. Make sure that there are no spaces before the I or after the r. Even one space will stop the renamed driver from working!
15. Tell the Finder to accept the name by clicking anywhere on the desktop.
16. Click the close box to put away the System folder.
17. Choose Eject from the File menu to eject the disk.
18. Turn off the Macintosh.
19. Connect an Epson-compatible printer to the Imagewriter port on the back of the Macintosh, using the printer cable supplied with the GDT driver, and set the printer's DIP (dual in-line package) switches according to GDT's directions.
20. Reboot.

Rebooting automatically selects the renamed driver. To prove it, copy MacWrite (or any other application) to the System disk and try printing. As shown in Figure 1-4, when you choose Print... from MacWrite's File menu, the Epson FX dialog box will appear instead of the familiar Imagewriter dialog box.

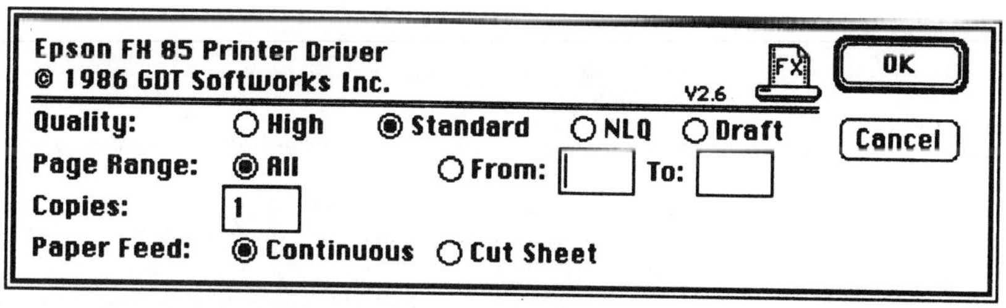

Figure 1-4 Print dialog box from GDT's Epson FX printer driver.

Both dialog boxes work the same way. Clicking the OK button will route text and graphics to the Epson-compatible printer just as it normally would have routed text and graphics to the Imagewriter printer. Assuming that the printer cable is compatible (GDT's is definitely compatible, but not all printer cables are wired the same) and that you set the DIP switches properly, it'll work just fine.

There's a lot more on printer cables and DIP switches in subsequent chapters. But, for now, the important point is that you can use any printer you want on a Macintosh (any Macintosh), as long as you have an appropriate printer driver in the System folder, and as long as the driver is currently selected.

To reselect the Imagewriter driver on the early Macintosh System software disk, trash the FX driver and rename Copy of Imagewriter to Imagewriter. Make sure that there are no spaces before the I or after the r. Note that the W should be lowercase. Tell the Finder to accept the name by clicking anywhere on the desktop. After rebooting, the Imagewriter driver will work just as before.

Exceptions Pertaining to Early Macs Equipped with External Drives

Early Macs were supplied without external disk drives and, consequently, the earliest Macintosh System software requires that the printer driver be on the same disk as the current application. If you have an early Mac *with* an external drive, the most efficient way to use it is to start the computer with a fully loaded System disk (one with a full complement of fonts and desk accessories), and use various workdisks (defined as Printer Driver disks with one or more applications on them) in the external drive. This strategy saves about 180K on each and every workdisk because it eliminates duplicate System folders. You can trash the extra System folders, as long as you leave a printer driver on each and every workdisk. If you trash the print driver along with the extra System folders, attempting to print from an application residing on the workdisk will result in a dialog box similar to Figure 1-5.

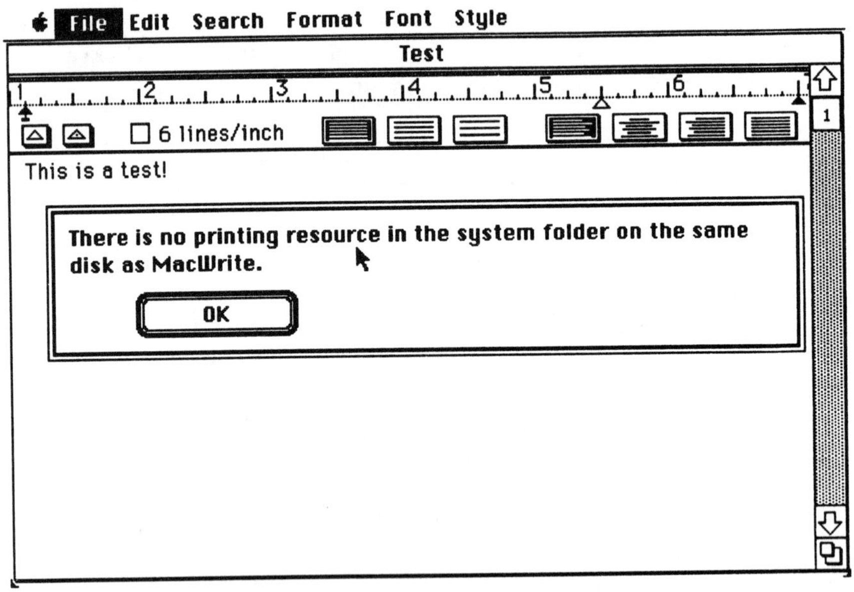

Figure 1-5 If you see this dialog box, copy the printing resource (generally the Imagewriter driver) from the System disk back to the workdisk.

To fix the problem, just copy the printing resource (generally the Imagewriter driver) from the System disk back to the workdisk.

Choosing a Printer Driver

With the release of System software version 2.0, dated April 1985, selecting a printer driver became much easier. The Apple menu included a Choose Printer desk accessory. As shown in Figure 1-6, this desk accessory made it unnecessary to rename drivers in the Finder. You could select any printer driver you wanted simply by pointing and clicking, and the printer driver could be named whatever you wanted (not just Imagewriter).

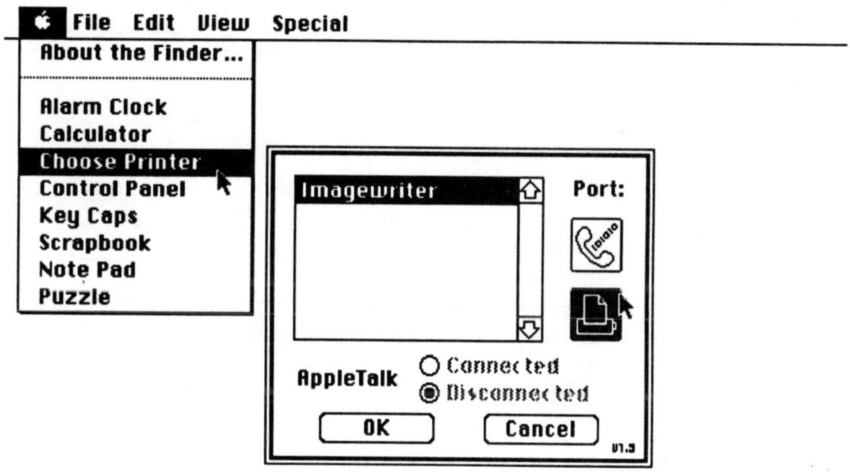

Figure 1-6 The Choose Printer desk accessory.

With the release of System software version 3.2, dated June 2, 1986, the Choose Printer desk accessory was renamed Chooser. The Printer part of the name was dropped. Chooser version 2.3, from System software 3.2, is shown in Figure 1-7.

The current Chooser release from System software version 6.0.3, dated December 9, 1988, is shown in Figure 1-8. Later releases may look different. The important point is that with the exception of very early Macintosh System software, printer driver selection is not automatic. Someone has to select an appropriate driver by pulling out the Chooser, pointing to the driver, and clicking on it. You also have to indicate (by

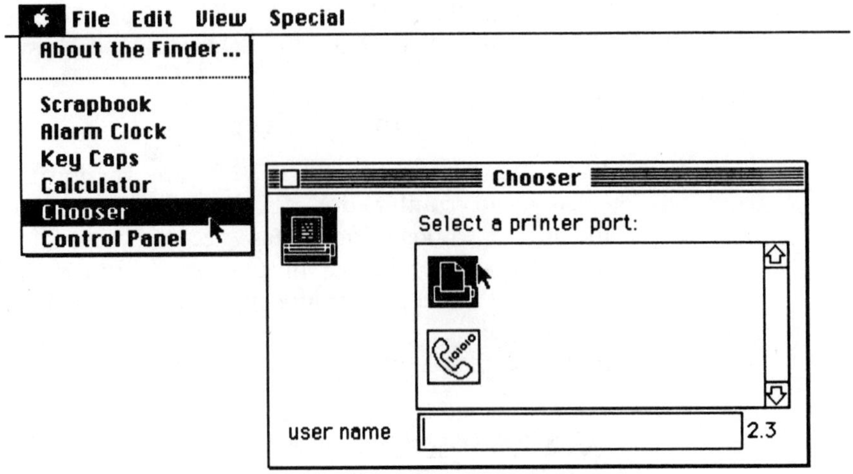

Figure 1-7 The Chooser desk accessory.

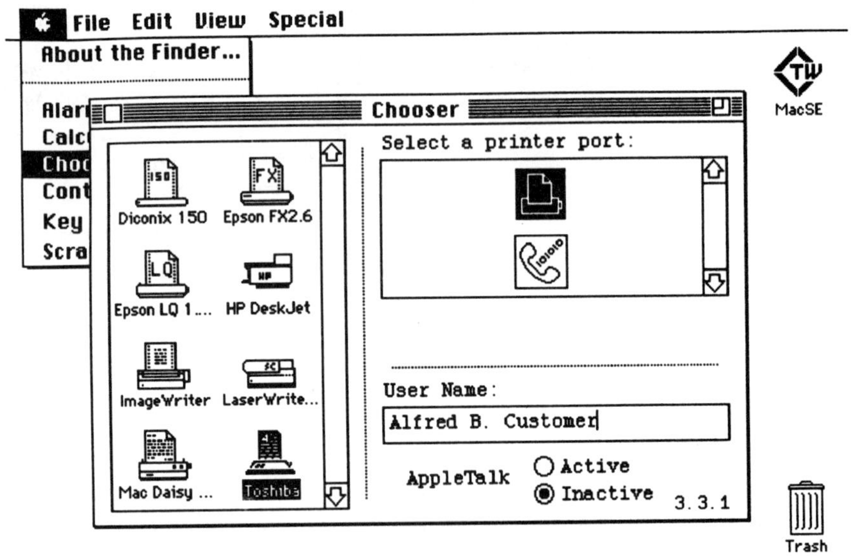

Figure 1-8 Chooser version 3.3.1 from System software version 6.0.3.

pointing and clicking) whether the printer is connected to the printer port or the modem port, otherwise printing will not be successful.

In the next section, we'll take a closer look at what a printer driver does.

Functions of a Printer Driver

Printers, like people, speak different languages and, occasionally, different dialects of the same language. The printer driver functions both as an interpreter and a moderator. It takes text and graphics data supplied by the computer and translates them into commands that can be understood by the printer. The simplest translation involves straight text without any graphics.

Printing Text

Under the American Standard Code for Information Interchange (ASCII, pronounced ASK-ee), every character, every command, and every number that you type on a keyboard is represented (note that the character is represented, not defined) by a numerical code. The code ranges from 0 to 255. Code numbers 0 to 31 represent unprintable standard control instructions, such as line feed (10) and carriage return (13); code numbers 32 to 127 represent printable standard characters, such as lowercase a (97) and lowercase z (122). Code numbers 128 to 255 represent both unprintable control instructions and printable special characters, such as borders, Greek letters, and scientific symbols.

Table 1-1. Low (7-bit) ASCII

<table>
<tr><td>32 =</td><td>48 = 0</td><td>64 = @</td><td>80 = P</td><td>96 = `</td><td>112 = p</td></tr>
<tr><td>33 = !</td><td>49 = 1</td><td>65 = A</td><td>81 = Q</td><td>97 = a</td><td>113 = q</td></tr>
<tr><td>34 = "</td><td>50 = 2</td><td>66 = B</td><td>82 = R</td><td>98 = b</td><td>114 = r</td></tr>
<tr><td>35 - #</td><td>51 - 3</td><td>67 = C</td><td>83 = S</td><td>99 = c</td><td>115 = s</td></tr>
<tr><td>36 = $</td><td>52 = 4</td><td>68 = D</td><td>84 = T</td><td>100 = d</td><td>116 = t</td></tr>
<tr><td>37 = %</td><td>53 = 5</td><td>69 = E</td><td>85 = U</td><td>101 = e</td><td>117 = u</td></tr>
<tr><td>38 = &</td><td>54 = 6</td><td>70 = F</td><td>86 = V</td><td>102 = f</td><td>118 = v</td></tr>
<tr><td>39 = '</td><td>55 = 7</td><td>71 = G</td><td>87 = W</td><td>103 = g</td><td>119 = w</td></tr>
<tr><td>40 = (</td><td>56 = 8</td><td>72 = H</td><td>88 = X</td><td>104 = h</td><td>120 = x</td></tr>
<tr><td>41 =)</td><td>57 = 9</td><td>73 = I</td><td>89 = Y</td><td>105 = i</td><td>121 = y</td></tr>
<tr><td>42 = *</td><td>58 = :</td><td>74 = J</td><td>90 = Z</td><td>106 = j</td><td>122 = z</td></tr>
<tr><td>43 = +</td><td>59 = ;</td><td>75 = K</td><td>91 = [</td><td>107 = k</td><td>123 = {</td></tr>
<tr><td>44 = ,</td><td>60 = <</td><td>76 = L</td><td>92 = \</td><td>108 = l</td><td>124 = |</td></tr>
<tr><td>45 = -</td><td>61 = =</td><td>77 = M</td><td>93 =]</td><td>109 = m</td><td>125 = }</td></tr>
<tr><td>46 = .</td><td>62 = ></td><td>78 = N</td><td>94 = ^</td><td>110 = n</td><td>126 = ~</td></tr>
<tr><td>47 = /</td><td>63 = ?</td><td>79 = O</td><td>95 = _</td><td>111 = o</td><td>127</td></tr>
</table>

NOTE: The blank space after the first equals sign indicates that ASCII 32 = SPACE; the missing equals sign after the last number indicates that ASCII 127 = DELETE.

As shown in Table 1-1, code numbers 32 to 127, known as Low ASCII or 7-bit ASCII, are the same for all computers and all printers. Code numbers from 128 to 255, known as High ASCII or extended 8-bit ASCII, differ. These generally represent accented characters, engineering symbols, foreign language characters, graphics symbols, borders, icons, etc. Test Character Generator (TCG), the diagnostics program included with this book, allows you to check both ASCII character sets. A Low ASCII printout should always be the same. A High ASCII printout depends on DIP switch settings and it varies from printer to printer, even within the Imagewriter family.

It's not necessary to check either printout now. You just need to know that ASCII codes exist and that you can check the characters they represent with Test Character Generator, as shown in Figure 1-9.

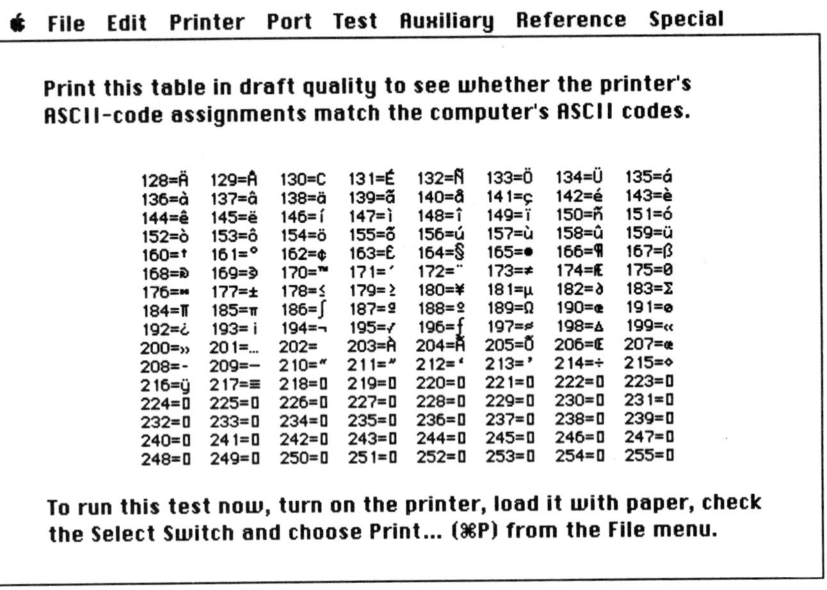

Figure 1-9 Test Character Generator High ASCII {128 – 255} test.

In addition, all printers have unique formatting codes. To commence bold printing on an Apple-compatible printer, the driver has to send code 27, followed by code 33. To commence bold printing on an Epson-compatible printer, the driver has to send code 27, followed by code 69. A primary function of the driver, then, is to interpret the computer's native codes and translate them into printer-compatible codes. If all printers and all computers spoke the same language, then one driver would fit all. Naturally, all printers are different.

Handshaking

Since computers work only with binary digits (1s and 0s), the printer driver has to regulate the flow of bits (bits is a contraction of **bi**nary digi**ts**), just like a policeman regulates automobile traffic at a busy intersection. In computer jargon, traffic control is called *handshaking*. Without some kind of handshaking, data (like traffic) has to move through intersections very slowly or bits will eventually pile up, just like vehicles in a multicar traffic accident.

There are two kinds of handshaking. The first, **Data Terminal Ready (DTR)**, or hardware handshaking, stations an electronic traffic cop (essentially a smart stoplight) on a separate wire of the printer cable. This smart stoplight watches bit traffic, and makes stop-and-go decisions as necessary. DTR traffic control only works if the cable has the necessary extra wire! It does not work if the extra wire is missing. If the extra wire is missing, DTR malfunctions just like real stoplights during a power failure. (If there's no wire, there's no power!)

The second kind of handshaking, **Transmission-ON/Transmission-OFF (X-ON/X-OFF)**, or software handshaking, is more like courteous driving. All vehicles approach every intersection with caution. Drivers look at each other (not at traffic cops or stoplights) and, with an eye signal or a hand signal, they wave (handshake) each other on.

The earliest Imagewriter driver supported both hardware (DTR) and software (X-ON/X-OFF) handshaking. The earliest Imagewriter cables supported only software (X-ON/X-OFF) handshaking. To make up for the missing wire, the earliest Imagewriter printers, which also supported both hardware and software handshaking, were shipped with DIP switch 2-3 set to the X-ON/X-OFF position. Everything worked fine until Macintosh System software version 2.0 was released. On the plus side, Mac users got the Chooser DA. On the minus side, support for X-ON/X-OFF handshaking was dropped. Printing would proceed halfway down the page, and, then, without handshaking to control the flow, there'd be a bit pileup. After that, there would be nothing but gibberish, liberally sprinkled with x (ASCII 120), @ (ASCII 64), and ˆ (ASCII 96) characters. The pileup effect is shown in Figure 1-10.

What grief that handshaking change caused! Most people received regular System software updates along with the new applications they purchased. Invariably, there was no explanation as to why the new software would not drive the original Imagewriter printers. Some people assumed the application was at fault, and returned it. Some people assumed the printer was broken, and scrapped it. Some swapped cables but did not reset the DIP switch 2-3. Others reset DIP switch 2-3, but did not swap cables. Shortly after the System updates appeared, a newer version of the Imagewriter driver was released which reinstated X-ON/X-OFF support. But to this day, service shops continue to see printers which have nothing wrong with them other than an incorrectly positioned DIP switch or an improperly constructed printer cable.

```
                         Gettysburg Address

Fourscore and seven years ago our fathers brought forth on this continent
a new nation, conceived in liberty and dedicated to the proposition that
all men are created equal.

Now we are engaged in a great civil war, testing whether that nation or
any nation so conceived and so dedicated can long endure. We are met on a
great battlefield of that war. We have come to dedicate a portion of that
field, as a final resting place for those who here gave their lives that
that nation might live. It is altogether fitting and proper that we should
do this. [illegible]

But in a larger sense, we ca  not dedicate—we can not consecrate—we can
```

Figure 1-10 Without X-ON/X-OFF handshaking to control the flow, printing would proceed halfway down the page, pile up, and after that, show nothing but gibberish.

We'll have a lot more to say about printer-cable construction and DIP-switch settings in the printer-specific chapters that follow. For now, the important points are that there are two kinds of handshaking (DTR and X-ON/X-OFF), and unless the printer driver, the printer cable, and the printer DIP switches are all set the same, printing will not be successful.

Baud Rate

Baud rate (named for data-communications pioneer, Emile Baudot) is roughly equivalent to bits per second, the speed at which 1s and 0s are sent down the printer cable. The Imagewriter driver is *fixed* at 9600 baud. The Imagewriter printer's baud rate is *selectable,* via DIP switches 2-1 and 2-2.

To work with an Apple Imagewriter driver, Imagewriter-compatible printers must also be set for 9600 baud. Matching the printer's baud rate to the driver's baud rate is like selecting the speed on a record player or a reel-to-reel tape recorder. Unless playback speed is the same as recorded speed, the printed output will be impossible to understand.

The symptom of an incorrectly matched baud rate is one to three lines of gibberish followed by repeated form feeds. The important point is, you can fix it yourself easily, just by resetting the DIP switches. DIP-switch locations and complete details for each of the printers covered in this book are in the printer-specific chapters that follow.

Parity Bits

Even when the handshaking, the cable, and the baud rate are all correct, errors can still occur. When you're dealing with 1s and 0s, it's easy to miss one here and there; miss a single bit and everything becomes garbled. To prevent that, each ASCII code can be summarized with a parity bit. To appreciate the parity bit, you need to have an idea of how ASCII codes are sent down the cable. For that, you need some understanding of binary numbers.

The Binary Numbering System

The numbers we regularly use (in trade and commerce) are called decimal numbers. Since trade and commerce are limited only by human imagination, numerical values in the decimal numbering system range from negative infinity to positive infinity. As suggested by the ASCII code, printers are only concerned with values ranging from 0 to 255. Each of these 256 individual numbers is represented in the binary numbering system with a unique combination of eight individual bits, as shown in Table 1-2.

Table 1-2. Binary-to-Decimal Conversion Table

Binary Number	1	0	0	0	0	0	0	0	=	128
Binary Number	0	1	0	0	0	0	0	0	=	64
Binary Number	0	0	1	0	0	0	0	0	=	32
Binary Number	0	0	0	1	0	0	0	0	=	16
Binary Number	0	0	0	0	1	0	0	0	=	8
Binary Number	0	0	0	0	0	1	0	0	=	4
Binary Number	0	0	0	0	0	0	1	0	=	2
Binary Number	0	0	0	0	0	0	0	1	=	1
Binary Number	0	0	0	0	0	0	0	0	=	0
Decimal Number	128	+64	+32	+16	+8	+4	+2	+1		=255

Note that all binary values from 0 to 255 are eight digits long. As shown by the following, the bit at the extreme left of the eight-digit binary number (shown in bold) is called the *most-significant* bit.

Bit position: **1** 0 0 0 0 0 0 0 = 128

The bit at the extreme right of the eight-digit binary number (shown in bold) is called the *least-significant* bit.

Bit position: 0 0 0 0 0 0 0 **1** = 1

Here's how to remember which is which. The bit position with the lowest decimal value is least significant. (Lowest is least.) The bit position with the highest decimal value is most significant. (Highest is most.)

To convert any number from decimal to binary, all you have to remember are the following relationships:

1. If a bit contains 0, it has 0 value.
2. If a bit contains 1, it has one of eight specific values greater than 0.
3. The value of the least-significant bit is either 0 or 1.
4. The value of the next significant bit is either 0 or 2.
5. The value of the next significant bit is either 0 or 4.
6. The value of the next significant bit is either 0 or 8.
7. The value of the next significant bit is either 0 or 16.
8. The value of the next significant bit is either 0 or 32.
9. The value of the next significant bit is either 0 or 64.
10. The value of the most-significant bit is either 0 or 128.

With Table 1-2, you can easily convert any decimal number from 0 to 255 into binary, simply by breaking it down into one or more of the eight listed values and adding the columns. Here's an example.

As listed in the table, decimal number 128 converts to binary number 10000000; decimal number 1 converts to binary number 00000001. To convert decimal number 129 into binary, just add binary 10000000 (decimal 128) and binary 00000001 (decimal 1). By adding the bit columns from top to bottom, you get the binary number 10000001, which equals decimal 129. The next is a more complex example.

Decimal 67 can be broken down to decimal 64 + decimal 2 + decimal 1. As listed in Table 1-2, decimal number 64 converts to the binary number 01000000; decimal number 2 converts to the binary number 00000010, and decimal number 1 converts to binary number 00000001. By adding the bit columns, binary 01000000 (decimal 64) + binary 00000010 (decimal 2) + binary 00000001 (decimal 1) = binary 01000011, which equals decimal 67. There's nothing the least bit hard about it! No pun intended!

To reconstruct Table 1-2 from memory, all you have to remember are the following associations:

1. There are eight individual bit positions.
2. Any given bit position will either contain 0 or 1.
3. 0s are always zero.
4. 1s double in decimal value from right to left, from decimal 1 to decimal 128, depending on their bit position.

To lock this relationship in memory, think "Two, four, six, eight, who do we appreciate? The binary team, the bit stream...." Even though the six is incorrect, the familiar high school cheer will remind you that binary digits double in value from right to left.

Memorizing material this way is called memorization by association. Trivial details (such as all 256 individual binary numbers) do not have to be memorized. Once you understand *anything,* all you really need to do is make an association while the material is still fresh in your mind. The association becomes the key to that material. Recall the association and, by some miracle, all the details (which are subconsciously linked to it) come right back. Déjà vu!

Make an association now, but only if you want to. Subsequent chapters do not require you to work with binary numbers. All they really expect is that you're generally familiar with the binary numbering system.

Data Bits, Start Bits, and Stop Bits

This section explains how character representations are sent to an ImageWriter. The example uses my initials LP. Afterwards, you can practice the material by working out the same example with your own initials.

To send an uppercase L to the printer, the printer driver has to send ASCII code 76. We know that by looking at Table 1-1. Decimal 76 (broken down to 64 + 8 + 4) = binary 01001100. We determine that by looking at Table 1-2. Binary numbers are always sent from right to left, from least-significant digit to most-significant digit. By reversing the order (not the value) of the bits, so that they read 00110010, we're almost ready to send an uppercase L.

Two other details are involved. The 8 bits that represent the reversed uppercase L character are called **data** bits. In addition, the driver has **frame** the character with **start** and **stop** bits. Without start and stop bits, the printer would have a hard time telling where individual characters begin and where they end. Start bits are 0s. Stop bits are 1s. Framed by start and stop bits, an uppercase L is actually transmitted as 0001100101.

To send an uppercase P to the printer, the printer has to send ASCII code 80. We figure that out by looking at Table 1-1. Decimal 80 (broken down to 64 + 16) = binary 01010000. We figure that out by looking at Table 1-2. With the order reversed, and framed by start and stop bits, ASCII code 80 is transmitted as 0000010101. Both characters together (LP) are transmitted as 00011001010000010101. This particular bit stream is summarized in Figure 1-11.

Note how the bits run together. After a while, that can be hard to follow even for a computer! **Parity** (from the root par, meaning equal) is

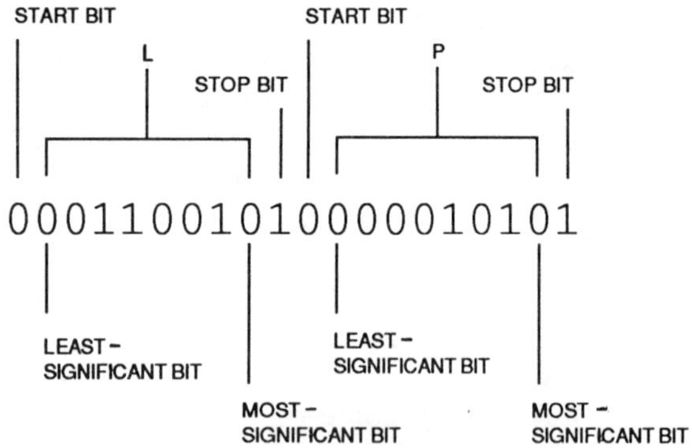

Figure 1-11 Bit-stream representation of the initials LP.

a way of assuring that Low ASCII characters between 0 and 127 are received correctly. There are three kinds of parity: odd, even, and none. Both odd and even parity use the most-significant bit to summarize the character.

If odd parity is in effect, the driver alters the value of the most-significant bit so that every byte contains an odd number of 1s. If even parity is in effect, the driver alters the value of the most-significant bit so that every byte contains an even number of 1s. Odd and even parity are summarized in Figures 1-12 and 1-13.

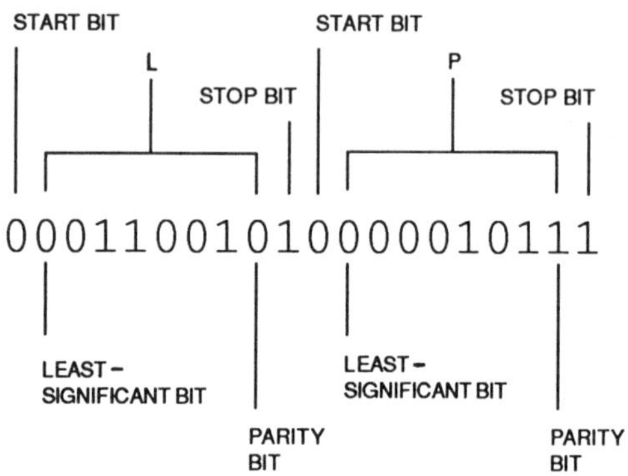

Figure 1-12 Bit-stream representation of the initials LP with odd parity.

For an example of no parity, refer to Figure 1-11. Macintosh printing is generally not concerned with parity, because the most-significant bit is needed to transmit High ASCII characters and it's also needed for printing graphics. When **parity errors** do occur, they usually result in printout peppered with unexpected @ characters. **Framing errors**, which occur when start and stop bits are missed, usually result in unex-

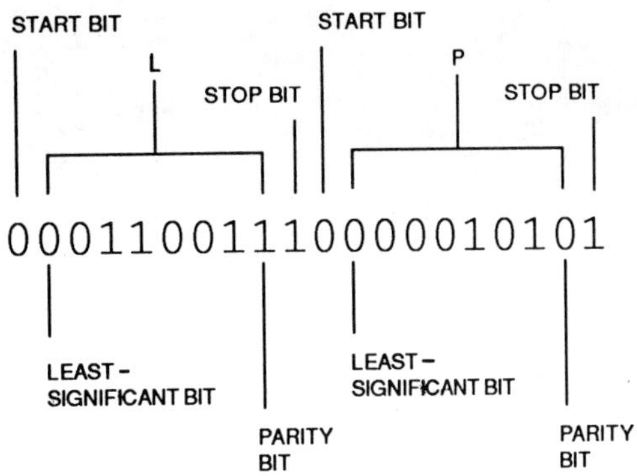

Figure 1-13 Bit-stream representation of the initials LP with even parity.

pected ˆ characters. Other characters often associated with framing errors are x (01111000) and ~ (01111110).

The important point is that when unexpected @, ~, x, or ~ characters permeate the printout, mechanical and/or electrical failures are almost never the cause. The fault is invariably in the printer driver settings, the DIP-switch settings, or in the printer cable.

Dot-Matrix Printing

Assuming that the characters LP are transmitted to the printer correctly, how are they actually printed? Upon receipt of the ASCII code for L, the printer's electronics causes the type head to fire an L-shaped pattern of dots. Upon receipt of the ASCII code for P, the printer's electronics causes the type head to fire a P-shaped pattern of dots. The type head, sometimes referred to as a print head, contains striker wires or pins. Every time a pin fires, it places a dot on the paper. The pattern which defines the horizontal and vertical limits of each character is called a **matrix**. The matrix defines a containment grid, which is made up of regularly spaced, intersecting, parallel lines. The dots which are contained by the matrix always hang down and to the right of the intersections.

Typical matrixes containing fixed-width dot patterns for the uppercase characters L (ASCII 76) and P (ASCII 80) are shown in Figures 1-14 and 1-15.

With a PC-style text-only printer driver, dot-matrix printing starts immediately, because predefined character matrixes similar to the ones shown in Figures 1-14 and 1-15 are stored in the printer's read-only memory (ROM). The ASCII codes sent by the driver only *represent* the matrixes. The advantage is that a single 7-bit code is all you need to print an entire character. The disadvantage is that you're limited to

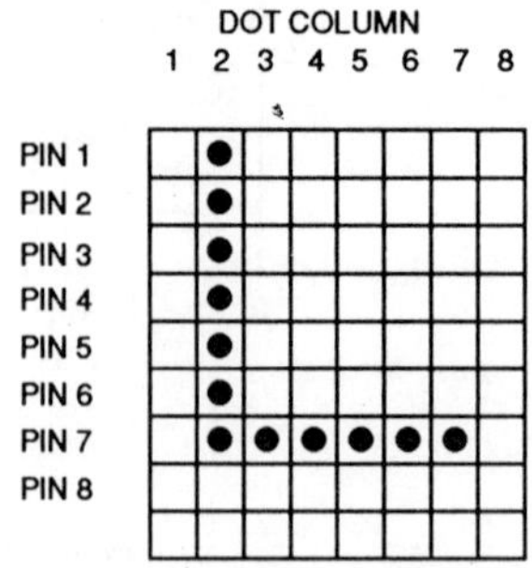

Figure 1-14 A typical matrix containing a fixed-width dot pattern for an uppercase L (ASCII 76).

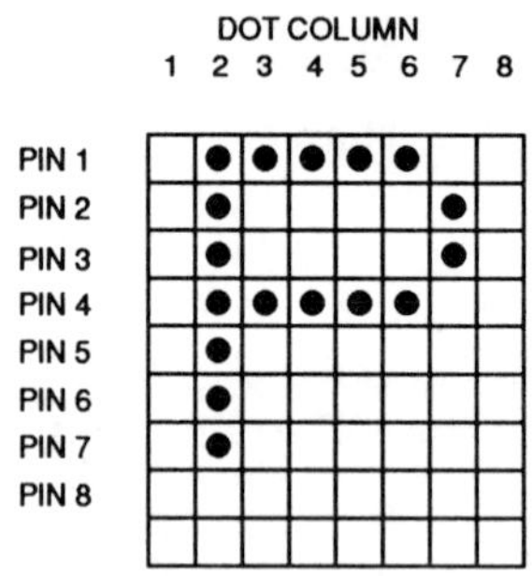

Figure 1-15 A typical matrix containing a fixed-width dot pattern for an uppercase P (ASCII 80).

whatever character matrixes have been hard-coded in the printer's ROM by the printer manufacturer. This difference will become clearer after we look at graphics-mode printing in the next section.

Graphics Mode

In graphics mode, the character matrixes are stored entirely in System software (not in the printer's ROM). As shown in Figure 1-16, each dot column in the matrix is defined by a separate 8-bit binary number. Each of the 8-bit binary numbers and their decimal equivalents is shown below the matrix.

Note that the initials LP require at least 16 bytes to transmit in graphics mode. The same initials require only two bytes under the

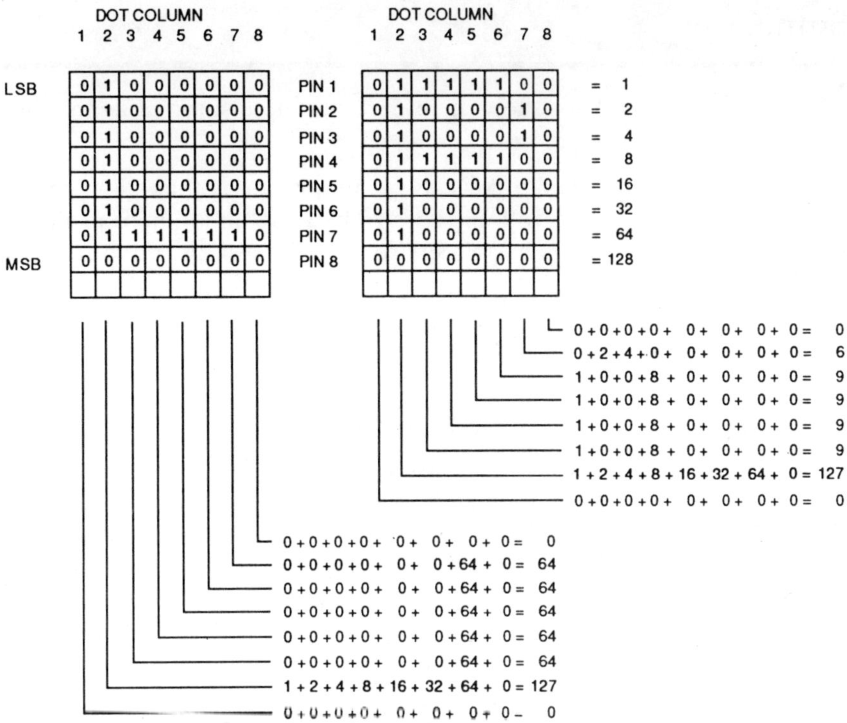

Figure 1-16 In graphics mode, each dot column in the matrix is defined by a separate 8-bit binary number.

ASCII code. That explains why PC printers seem to be so much faster than Macintosh printers. PC printers are almost always driven in ASCII-text mode. Mac printers are almost always driven in graphics mode.

Graphics printing may be slower than text printing, but it provides access to an almost unlimited number of character definitions (type styles). It also allows you to mix graphically defined text with illustrations, and print everything at the same time, all on the same printer!

We take that for granted today. But, when the Macintosh was introduced in 1984, it was a $3000 technological miracle. Such a miracle, that straight text printing has almost been ignored on the Macintosh.

Subsequent chapters show how to take full advantage of both text and graphics printing. Understanding the difference between the two, and knowing when and how to choose one over the other, are among the best-kept Macintosh printer secrets of all.

Summary

The following important points summarize the preliminary material presented in Chapter 1.

1. Printer drivers are programs that allow computers to communicate with a printer. There are all kinds of printer drivers because different printers require differently coded instructions.
2. You can use any printer you want on a Macintosh as long as an appropriate printer driver is installed in the System folder, and as long as it's currently selected.
3. Under the original Macintosh System software, any printer driver named Imagewriter is selected automatically.
4. Under subsequent versions of the System software, printer drivers have to be selected manually.
5. To select a driver, pull out the Chooser (or Choose Printer) Desk Accessory, point to the driver, and click on it. You also have to indicate (by pointing and clicking) whether the printer is connected to the printer port or to the modem port. Otherwise, printing will not be successful.
6. When unwanted form feeds or unexpected @, x, \` , or ^ characters permeate the printout, mechanical- and/or electrical-printer failures are almost never the cause. The fault is invariably in the printer-driver settings, the DIP-switch settings, or in the printer cable.
7. Text printing uses a single 7-bit or 8-bit ASCII code to represent a character matrix which has either been predefined in the printer's ROM or downloaded. It's fast, but limited by hardware.
8. Graphics printing uses multiple 8-bit codes to define custom character matrixes, dot by dot. It's slow but almost unlimited, because new character matrixes can be defined in software.

In the next chapter, we'll explain how to do that. We'll look at standard System fonts, show how to move new fonts into the System, and show how to move old fonts out of the System. In the process, we'll answer the question: "Where do fonts come from?"

CHAPTER 2

Screen Fonts

In Chapter 1, we learned that character sets reside on a ROM chip inside the printer while screen fonts reside in the System file on a startup disk. This chapter looks at screen fonts in greater detail. It's not intended to be a comprehensive guide to screen fonts—just an introduction to screen fonts in general, with an emphasis on font-related printing problems.

Definitions

In the printing business, the word **type** refers to a chiseled block of wood or a cast piece of metal, containing a letter or character carved in relief. **Carved in relief** means that the character projects from the surface of the block. It's not **engraved** (cut) into the block.

Font, as used in the printing business, refers to a complete alphabet of similarly designed characters in a single *size* of type. All available sizes of that type, taken collectively, make up a **typeface**. Variations on that typeface, such as bold, italic, and outline, make up various **type styles**.

These definitions suggest that the ubiquitous Macintosh Font menu is generally misnamed! It's properly a Face menu, because it allows you to choose typefaces, not fonts. In almost every program, fonts are chosen from the Size menu, and type styles are chosen from the Style menu.

It's very important to ignore the menu titles and substitute the correct trade definitions. You may find yourself at a commercial print shop someday. If you consistently misuse the trade terms, the printer may try to correct you. That could lead to an embarrassing disagreement.

Throughout this chapter, the terms typeface, font, and type style are used as they are defined by the printing trade. This usage is also consistent with such English-language dictionaries as Webster, and Funk & Wagnall.

Standard Screen Fonts

While other computers rely on a character-generator ROM (firmware) to draw text on the screen, the Macintosh relies on System software (screen fonts). The standard screen fonts include Chicago 12, Geneva 9, Geneva 12, and Monaco 9.

Chicago 12 is the default menu font. Geneva 12 is the default application font. Geneva 9 is the default icon font. Monaco 9 is a fixed-width special-purpose font. Samples of the four standard screen fonts are shown in Figure 2-1.

This is an example of Chicago 12.

This is an example of Geneva 12.

This is an example of Geneva 9.

This is an example of Monaco 9.

Figure 2-1 The four standard screen fonts.

The four standard screen fonts are the fonts of last resort. Without them, or something to take their place, the Macintosh can't run. Think about it. If there were no Chicago 12 for the Macintosh to draw the menu bar with, how could it draw the menu bar? If there were no Geneva 9 for the Macintosh to label an icon with, how could it label files? If there were no Geneva 12 to display word-processing text with, how could you do any word processing?

Here's another way of looking at it: The standard screen fonts are to the Macintosh what standard bias-ply tires are to an automobile. You can substitute bigger tires. You can substitute radial tires. You can even substitute snow tires, but without at least some tires, you're not going to get anywhere.

Actually, the 512K Enhanced Macintosh and the Macintosh Plus have the Chicago 12 font built into ROM. The Macintosh SE and the Macintosh II have all four of the standard screen fonts in ROM. Technically, you *could* remove these fonts from their respective System files and the computers would still run; but then, the altered system files would be incompatible with earlier Mac models, so it's generally not done.

Font Mover

To continue with the tire analogy, the standard 4-wheel Mac System file can be expanded into an 18-wheel Mac truck. In addition to the four basic fonts (tires) needed just to get rolling, it may contain fonts from other typefaces (extra tires), and other size fonts from within the same typeface. Original 128K Macintosh System files contain all of the fonts listed in Table 2-1. A Fonts file on the original System disks contains the additional fonts listed in Table 2-2.

Table 2-1. Original System-File Fonts

Typeface	Fonts (Type Sizes)
Athens	18
Chicago	12
Geneva	9, 10, 12, 14, 18, 20, 24
London	18
Monaco	9, 12
New York	9, 10, 12, 14, 18, 20, 24
Venice	14

Table 2-2. Original Fonts-File Fonts

Typeface	Fonts (Type Sizes)
Cairo	18
Los Angeles	12, 24
Geneva	9, 10, 12, 14, 18, 20, 24
New York	36
San Francisco	18
Toronto	12, 14, 18, 24

To view the font contents of either file, early Macintosh System disks were supplied with a utility program called Font Mover, as shown in Figure 2-2. Double clicking the Font Mover icon runs the program, which instantly checks the disk for a compatible Fonts file. If it finds one named Fonts, it's automatically opened, as shown in Figure 2-3.

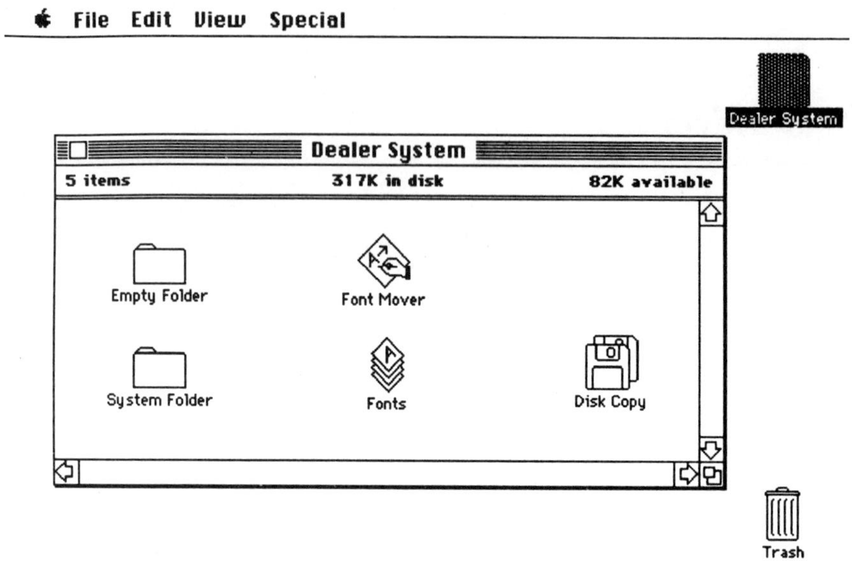

Figure 2-2 Early Macintosh System disks were supplied with a utility program called Font Mover.

Once again, it's the name of the file that's significant. If the file is named something other than Fonts, it's not automatically opened, even if it's perfectly compatible. In addition, Font Mover does not draw a menu bar (there's no File menu to choose Open... from), nor is there an Open (file) button.

Selecting Compatible Files with Font Mover

Just as early System software does not allow you to select printer drivers, except by renaming them from Whatever printer to Imagewriter, as explained in Chapter 1, the original Font Mover program does not allow you to select font files, unless you rename them from whatever they were originally named to Fonts. The *only* other way to open font files with early versions of Font Mover is to double click them in the Finder.

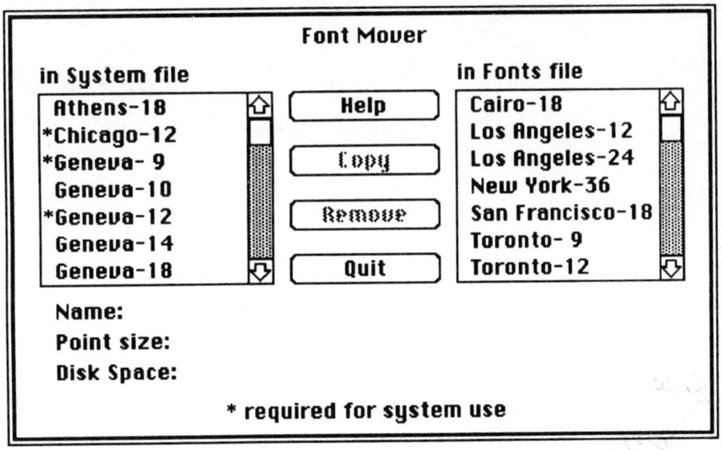

Figure 2-3 Font Mover automatically opens the System file, and any compatible file named Fonts.

Font/DA Mover

With the release of System software version 2.0, dated April 1985, selecting font files became much easier. As shown in Figure 2-4, the Syst Update/85 disk introduced an improved utility program called Font/DAM (Font/DA Mover).

As shown in Figures 2-5 and 2-6, Font / DAM version 2.4 made it unnecessary to rename font files in the Finder. You could select any font file you wanted from within the program simply by clicking the Open button, and the file could be named whatever you wanted (not just Fonts).

Of special interest to English majors and copy editors, Font / DAM also changed the way that font names were punctuated. As shown in Figure 2-3, the original Font Mover put hyphens in font names; beginning with Font / DAM 2.4, subsequent versions do not.

The current Font / DA Mover, version 3.8 from System software version 6.0.3, dated December 9, 1988, is shown in Figure 2-7. Although Font / DA Mover version 3.8 doesn't look any different from Font / DAM

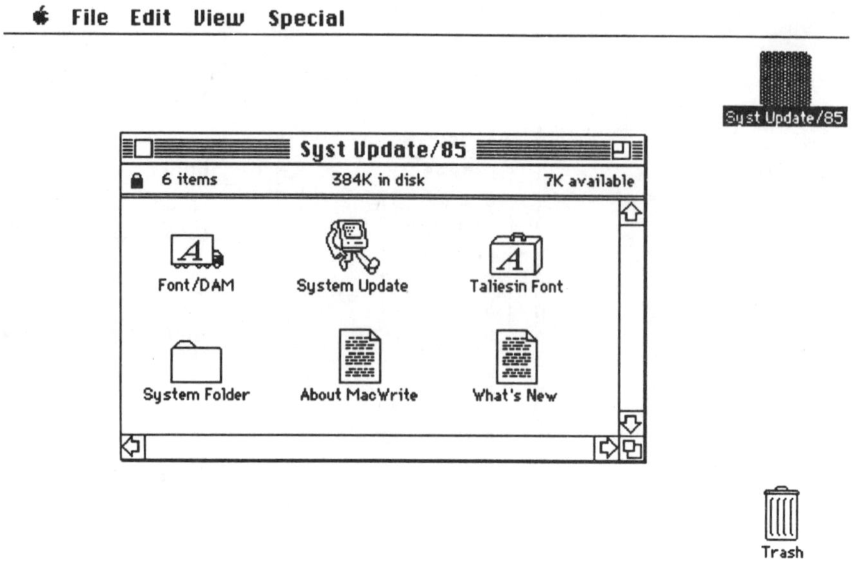

Figure 2-4 The Syst Update/85 disk was supplied with an improved utility program called Font/DAM (Font/DA Mover).

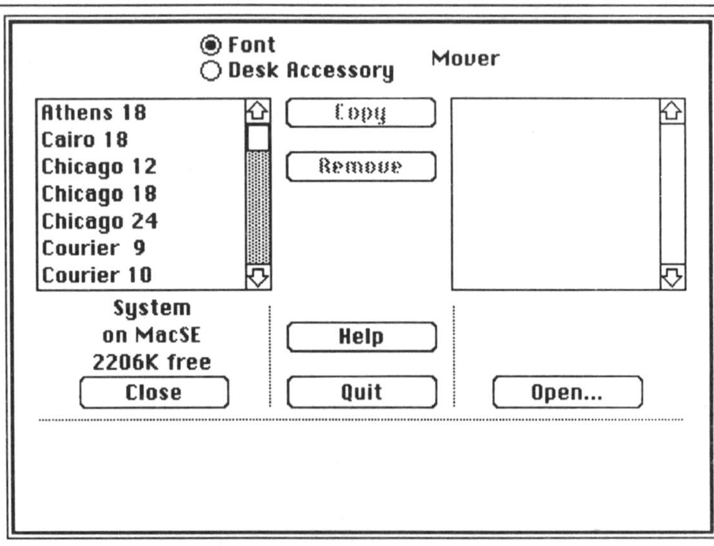

Figure 2-5 Font/DAM version 2.4.

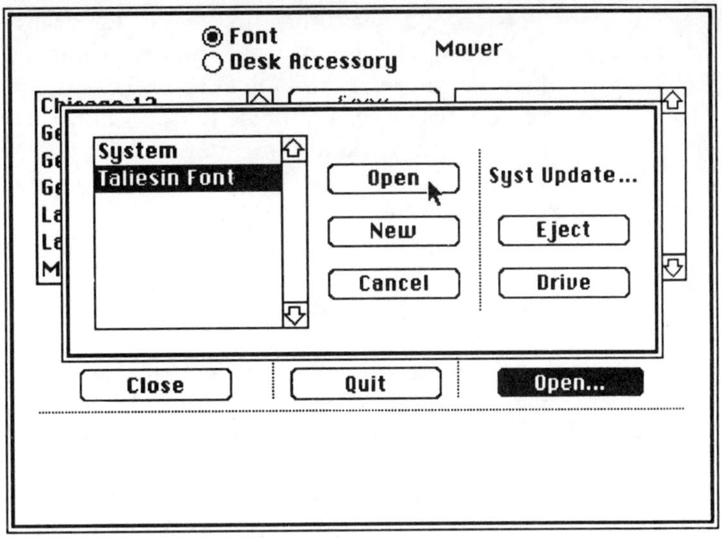

Figure 2-6 Clicking the Open button returns a file selection dialog box.

version 2.4, versions prior to Font/DA Mover 3.2 are notoriously buggy. For that reason, it's important to avoid early versions, even though they appear to be the same, and for reasons explained later, it's best to use Font/DA Mover version 3.8, or greater.

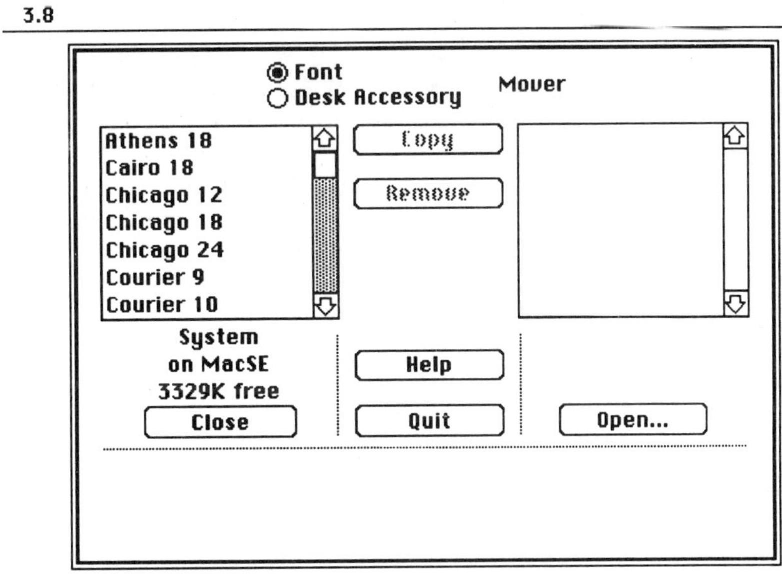

Figure 2-7 Font/DA Mover version 3.8.

FONDs and NFNTs

Version 3.2 was the first Font/DA Mover to work with FOND resources. FOND resources contain a font's fractional-width tables and kerning information. FOND resources are ignored on original 128K and 512K Macs (Macs with 64K ROMS), but software made for later models (Macs with 128K ROMS) may call for that information. If the FOND resource is not there, the results will be unpredictable and it may result in a system error.

Version 3.8 is the first Font/DA Mover to work with NFNT resources. NFNT is an acronym for *New Font Numbering Table*. The original FONT numbering table was limited to 512 ID numbers, of which, only 256 were usable. Of these, 128 were reserved by the manufacturer, so there were only 128 ID's available for third party use. Developers were encouraged to register their fonts, like registering an automobile, and each font would be given a unique ID number—the font equivalent of a license plate.

When the numbers ran out, developers kept right on making fonts, and ID conflicts developed. One person would format a document in one font, and even though that same font might be installed in someone else's System file, it would be numbered differently. When the second person tried to open or print the first person's file, the fonts originally used would not be displayed. This caused margin and page-break problems, and made it risky to use High ASCII characters.

As you recall from Table 1-1 in Chapter 1, Low ASCII printout (32 to 127) is the same for all fonts, but High ASCII (128 to 255) generally contains foreign language characters and special graphics symbols, and differs from font to font. As shown in Figure 2-8, most fonts print box characters (called missing symbols) in place of unassigned High ASCII codes. If you have ever opened a public domain Help file and found lots of little boxes where relevant symbols should have been, an unexpected font substitution is undoubtedly what has happened.

NFNT resources were designed to minimize that. NFNT ID numbers go all the way to 32,768! Presumably, once all the old FONT resources are converted to NFNT resources, FONT ID conflicts should be a thing of the past.

Using Font/DA Mover

As shown in Figures 2-9 and 2-10, on-line help for the Font/DA Mover is fairly complete, with the following exceptions:

1. If the option key is held down while the Open button is clicked, the list box will offer applications as well as files. This option allows you to install fonts and DAs (desk accessories) directly into a program, instead of generally into the System file. Installing DAs

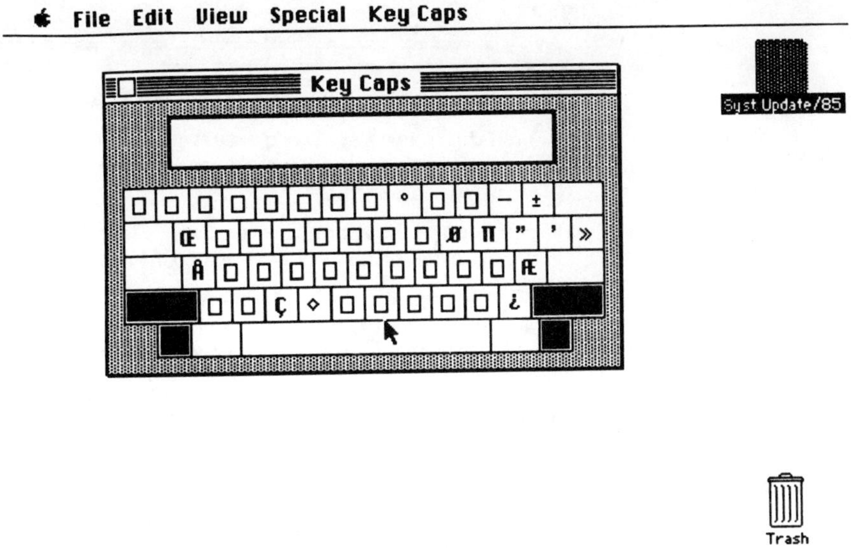

Figure 2-8 Key Caps desk accessory. Many fonts print box characters (called missing symbols) in the place of unassigned High ASCII codes.

and fonts into an application makes them available only when the application is in use.

2. If the option key is held down while the Close button is clicked, the Font / DA file (or the open application) is closed and the disk it resides upon is ejected.
3. If the option key is held down while the Quit button is clicked, Font / DA Mover itself is closed, and *all* inserted floppy disks are ejected.

Two other secret features apply strictly to desk accessories:

4. If the option key is held down while the Font / DAM is double clicked in the Finder, the program will default to desk accessories instead of fonts. This saves a lot of time when all you want to do is remove a desk accessory.
5. If the option key is held down while selecting DAs in the list box, the Font / DA Mover prints size information on the selected DAs code resource, picture resource, and data fork.

Font / DA Mover makes it easy to move fonts in and out of the System file; what's not obvious, other than saving disk space, is why you need to bother.

3.8

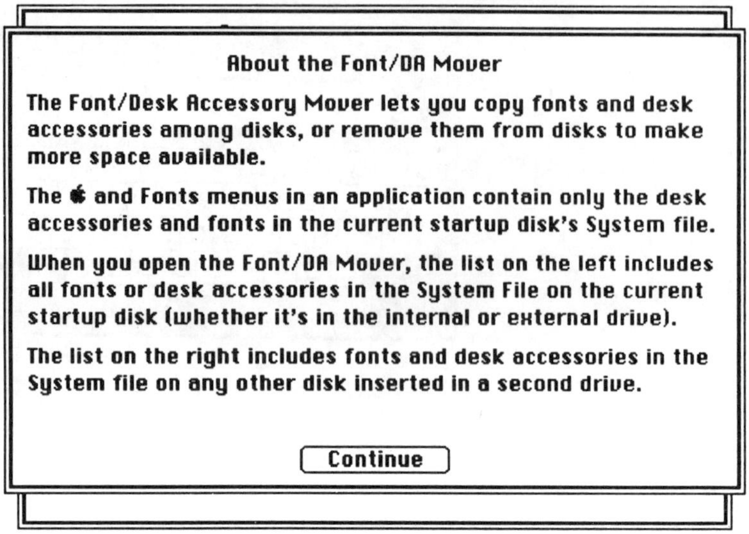

Figure 2-9 On-line help for Font / DA Mover version 3.8.

3.8

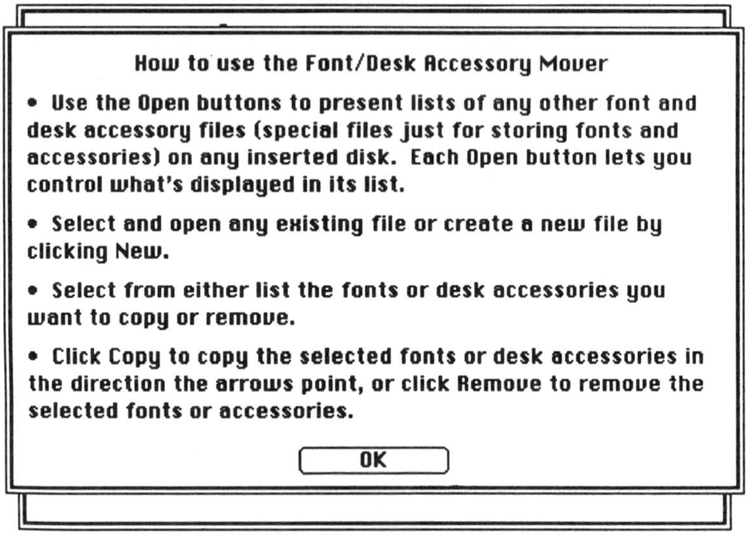

Figure 2-10 More on-line help for Font / DA Mover version 3.8.

When graphics mode is selected, all versions of the ImageWriter driver (through version 2.7) use larger sizes of the screen font to effect high-resolution printing. In the case of the Imagewriter Standard, the Imagewriter Wide, and the ImageWriter II, the printer driver uses a font *twice* the size of the screen font. In the case of the ImageWriter LQ, the printer driver uses a font *three* times the size of the screen font. Even the LaserWriter IISC driver (version 1.0 to 1.1) uses quadruple-size fonts. Exactly how that works is the subject of the next chapter.

For now, the important point to know is that when the larger font sizes are missing from the System file, high-resolution, graphics-mode, text printing is simply not possible. You can still *select* high-resolution printing; you just don't get it. That explains why some System disks print better than others. Some have a full complement of double-size, triple-size, and quadruple-size fonts. Others have just the standard-size fonts.

Whenever you encounter that problem, Font/DA Mover and a handful of System disks are generally all you need to correct it. Here's the complete procedure:

1. Copy Font/DA Mover to the System disk (if necessary) and click once on the Font/DA Mover icon to select it. Once selected, the Font/DA Mover icon should turn black.
2. Choose Get Info from the Finder's File menu. As shown in Figure 2-11, the resulting dialog box will generally contain version information. Use Font/DA Mover version 3.8 (or later) if possible. Avoid Font/DA Mover versions prior to 3.2.
3. Choose Close from the File menu to put away the Get Info dialog box. Then, double click on the Font/DA Mover icon to run the program. All versions of Font/DA Mover (from Font/DAM 2.4 on up) automatically open the System file. As shown in Figures 2-6 and 2-7, fonts currently installed in the System file are displayed in the left-hand list box.
4. Scroll through the list box (if necessary) to identify which fonts are already installed in the System. If the list is very long, it may help to note the installed sizes on scratch paper.
5. If you have an Imagewriter Standard, Imagewriter Wide, or an ImageWriter II, check the fonts you use most often to see whether double sizes are present. If you have an ImageWriter LQ, check for triple sizes. If you have a LaserWriter IISC, check for quadruple sizes. The ones that are frequently missing are Geneva 18, 20, and 24. These are the sizes needed to print Geneva 9 ($2 \times 9 = 18$), Geneva 10 ($2 \times 10 = 20$), and Geneva 12 ($2 \times 12 = 24$) in high resolution on the Imagewriter Standard, the Imagewriter Wide, the ImageWriter II, and most ImageWriter-compatible printers.
6. Note the missing sizes, and insert other disks suspected of containing them into your computer. To open the System files on the other disks, click the Open button, open the System folder on the disk, and then click the Open button again to open the System file. Font/DA Mover will list all the fonts in the new file, in the

right-hand list box. As you find the missing sizes, click on them to select them, and then click the Copy button to copy them into the original System file. When you're done, both disks will have all the necessary sizes. Copying fonts *does not* remove them from the original file. The only way to remove a font is to select it and then click the Remove button. Removing a font by accident is also unlikely. As shown in Figure 2-12, Font / DA Mover always asks whether that's what you really want to do.

7. When you've made all the necessary copies, click the Quit button to exit the program.

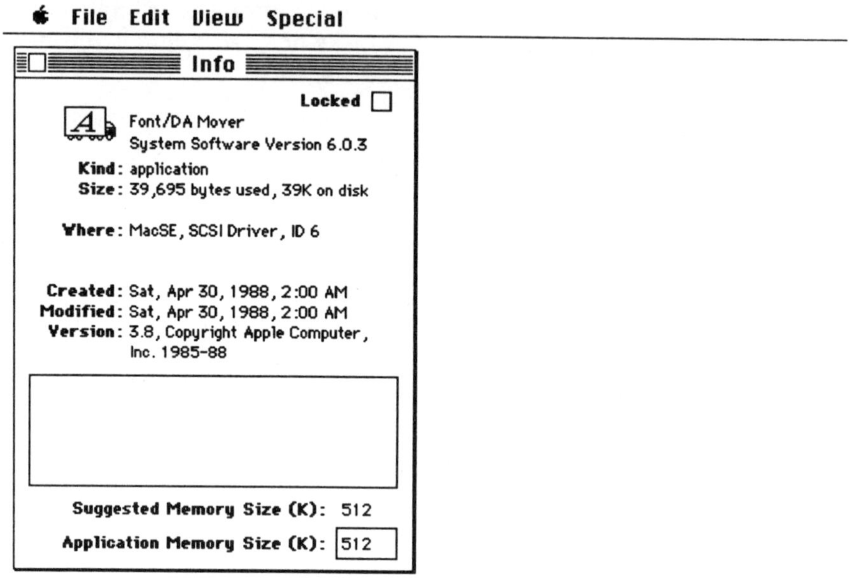

Figure 2-11 Choosing Get Info from the Finder's File menu results in a dialog box which generally contains version information.

Font / DA Mover is a powerful tool used primarily for copying fonts and desk accessories from one file to another. To view individual character matrixes, or to change the way a whole font looks, you need another tool, generally called a Font Editor.

Font Editors

As shown in Figures 2-13 to 2-14, the earliest font editors were more like font-editing *components*. In addition to the editor, you also needed RMover (Resource Mover) to set the FONT ID, plus Set File (a share-

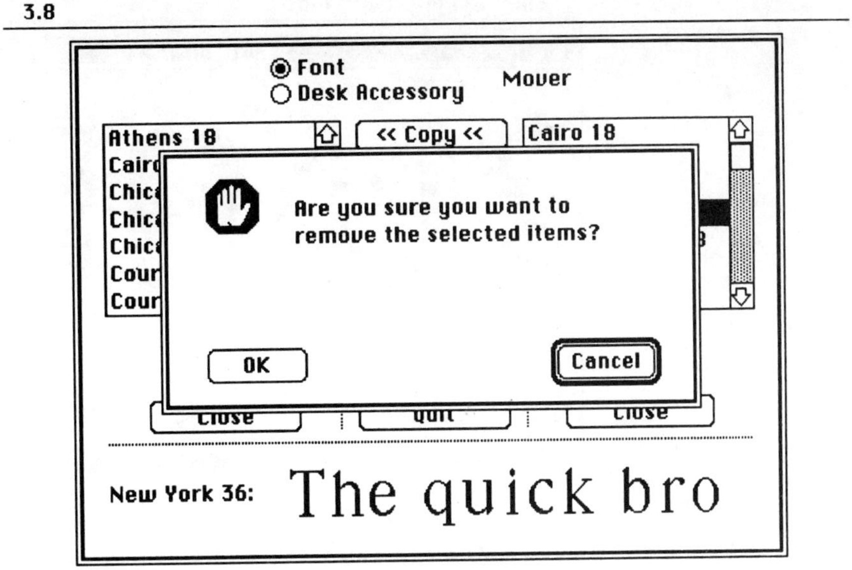

Figure 2-12 "Are you sure?" dialog box from Font / DA Mover version 3.8.

ware program) to set the file's type and creator, and Font Mover (described earlier in this chapter) to move new fonts into the System file. This has made the font-editing process very complicated. Without instructions, all that most people were able to do was bomb the System.

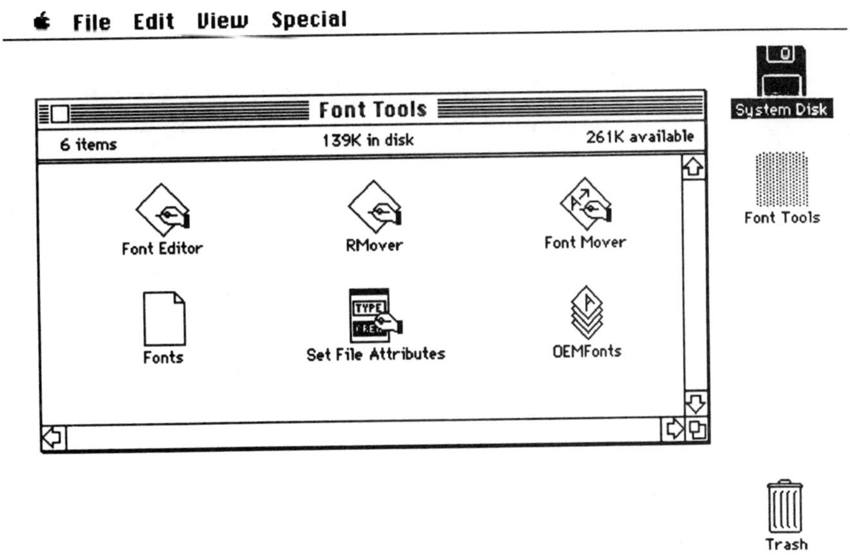

Figure 2-13 The earliest font editors were more like font-editing components.

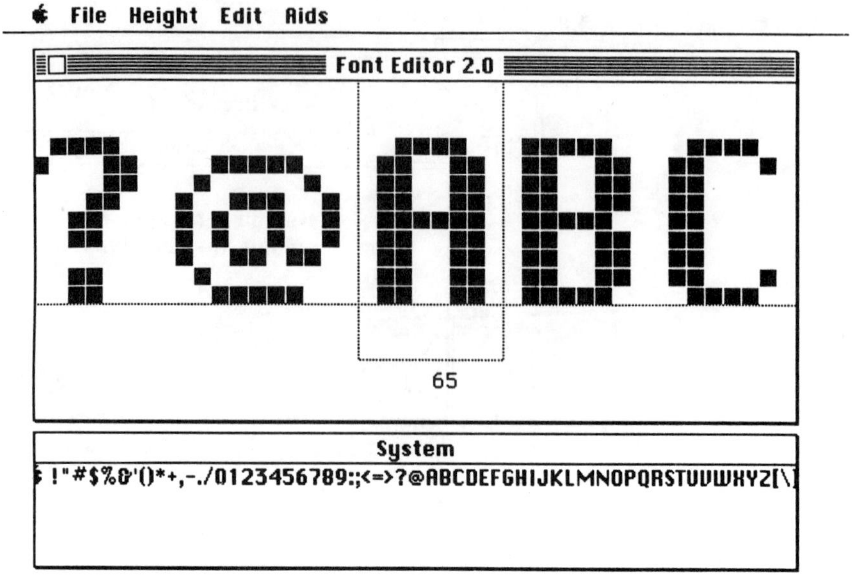

Figure 2-14 Font Edit version 2.0.

With the release of ResEdit (Resource Editor) in 1985, the font-editing process became less complicated. ResEdit combined the functions of Font Editor, RMover, and Set File into a single program. Still, ResEdit was (and still is) widely distributed without documentation. Without documentation, running ResEdit is like attempting to drive without ever having taken a single driving lesson. Most people aren't successful. Figure 2-15 shows the character-editing window from ResEdit version 1.1b3.

Distribution without documentation and the total lack of dealer-level technical support paved the way for commercial font editors. One of the best, Fontastic Plus from Altsys Corporation, is shown in Figure 2-16.

Fontastic Plus can be used to add missing characters to existing fonts, modify existing fonts, and create entirely new fonts from scratch. To understand how that's done, we need to become familiar with font characteristics.

Font Characteristics

Just as a printer's built-in characters are defined by a matrix, Macintosh screen-font characters are also defined by a matrix-like **character rectangle**. As shown in Figure 2-17, the character rectangle is a nonprinting box that limits the height and width of each character.

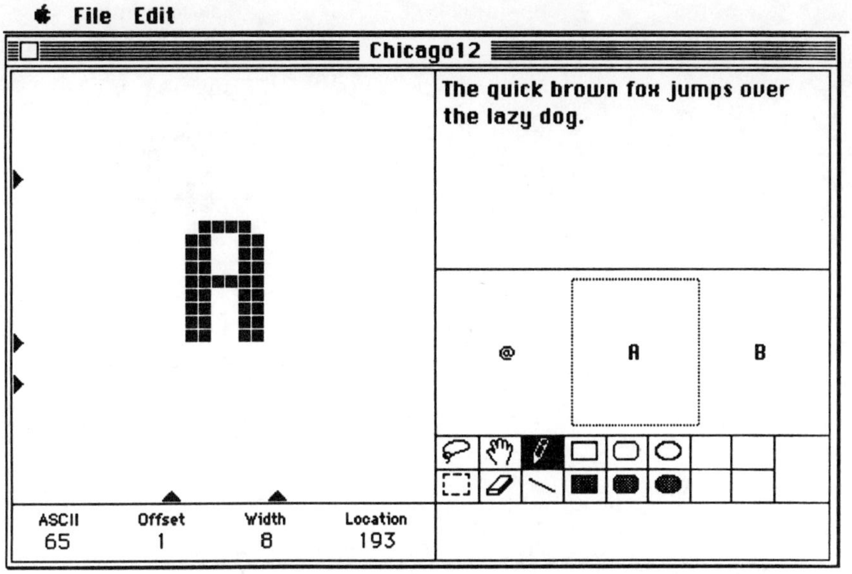

Figure 2-15 Character-editing window from ResEdit version 1.1b3.

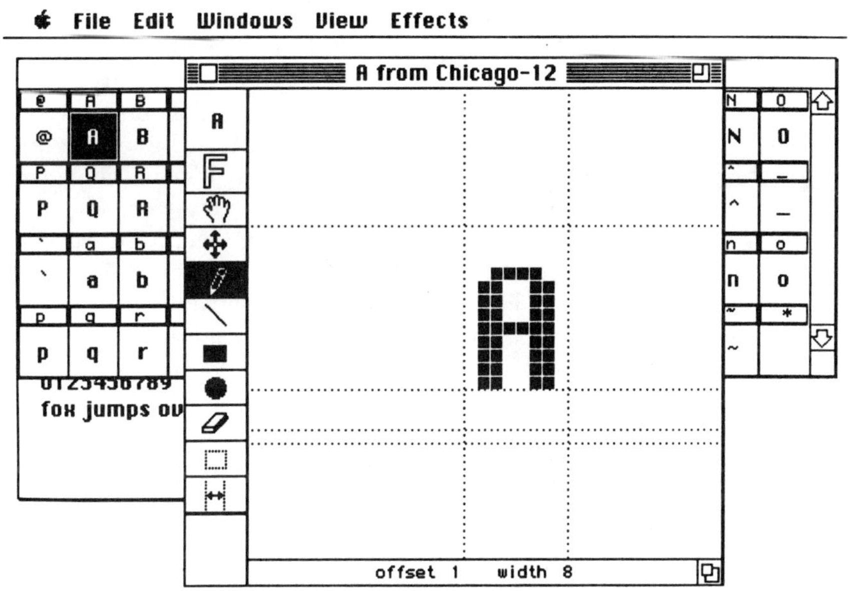

Figure 2-16 Fontastic Plus version 2.0.2.

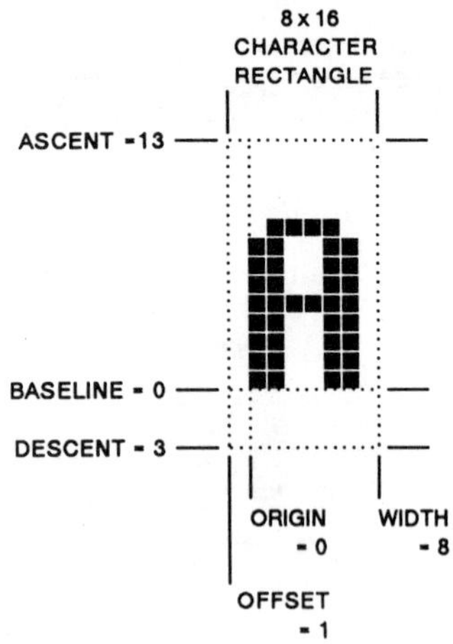

Figure 2-17 Font characteristics.

The term **baseline** refers to the plane from which all uppercase characters ascend. **Ascent** refers to the height of the tallest character. Ascent is measured from the baseline up. Every character has ascent. **Descent** refers to the depth of the lowest character. Descent is measured from the baseline down. Only certain characters (commas, semicolons, g, j, p, q, y, etc.) descend below the baseline.

The term **leading** (pronounced "led-ing") refers to the space between lines. Originally, it was an added space which prevented one line from descending in the next.

Font height can have one of two meanings. In the printing trade, font height refers to the sum of ascent plus descent. That's all. Leading is normally adjusted on the printing press. Way back when, separate thin pieces of lead (shims) were used to adjust line spacing; leading was never carved into the type, so it's not considered a part of the font height.

On the Macintosh, leading is an integral part of the character rectangle. As seen in Figure 2-17, leading exists as empty space above the ascent line (it is not created separately), so in Macintosh context, the term font height does include leading.

The term **origin** refers to the left boundary of a character. Space between the origin and the left boundary of the character rectangle is called **offset**. The space between the left and right boundary of the character rectangle is the **font width**.

Points

All font characteristics are measured in points. In the printing trade, the term **point** refers to 0.0138 inches, or approximately $\frac{1}{72}$ of an inch. Since leading is not included in the font height, a 12-point font should measure approximately 12⁄72 (1⁄6) of an inch high, allowing you to fit 6 lines per inch.

On the Macintosh, the term **point** also refers to 1⁄72 of an inch, but since leading *is* included in the font height, a 12-point font can be several points higher than 12⁄72 of an inch. Geneva 12, for example, is actually 16 points high. That doesn't even allow 5 lines per inch (because 72 ÷ 16 = 4.5)!

A printer will argue that Geneva 12 is properly called a 12⁄16 font—to indicate a 12-point font height with 4 points of leading. Nevertheless, leading is part of the font height on the Macintosh, and since some 12-point fonts contain more leading than others, not including it in the size specification can get very confusing. Table 2-3 compares the indicated point size to the actual font height of the four standard screen fonts.

Table 2-3. Standard Screen Fonts—Point Size vs. Font Height

Screen Font	Point Size	Font Height
Chicago 12	12 points	16 points
Geneva 9	9 points	12 points
Geneva 12	12 points	16 points
Monaco 9	9 points	11 points

In the next chapter, we'll look at other factors affecting font height. We'll compare specified display resolution (theory) to actual display resolution (practice); we'll compare actual display resolution (uncertainty) to printer resolution (reality), and we'll see that it's not just the size of a point that matters, but it's also the shape.

Summary

The following important points summarize the font-related printing problems discussed in Chapter 2.

1. While other computers rely on a character-generator ROM (firmware) to draw text on the screen, the Macintosh relies on System software (screen fonts).
2. Standard screen fonts include Chicago 12, Geneva 9, Geneva 12, and Monaco 9. Without these fonts, the Macintosh can't run.
3. The ImageWriter printer driver requires a font twice the size of the screen font to effect high-resolution, graphics-mode, text printing.

4. The ImageWriter LQ printer driver requires a font three times the size of the screen font to effect high-resolution, graphics-mode, text printing.
5. The LaserWriter IISC printer driver requires a font four times the size of the screen font to effect high-resolution, graphics-mode, text printing.
6. When the larger font sizes are missing from the System file, high-resolution, graphics-mode, text printing can still be chosen, but the file is printed (without any warning or explanation) in low-resolution.
7. Early Macintosh ROMs are susceptible to font-ID conflicts.
8. When font-ID conflicts occur, one font is substituted for another, which causes missing symbols (empty boxes) to be printed in place of relevant characters. NFNT resources (supported by the enhanced Mac Plus ROMs) were designed to eliminate that.
9. Fonts come from font files and from other System files. To view and/or modify the font contents of a font file or a System file, early Macintosh System disks were supplied with a utility program called Font Mover. Versions prior to Font / DA Mover 3.2 are notoriously buggy and should be avoided.
10. Font editors are used to add missing characters to existing fonts, to modify existing fonts, and to create entirely new fonts from scratch.
11. Font characteristics are measured in points, a printer's term for 1/72 of an inch.
12. Leading is a printer's term for the space between lines.
13. 12-point Macintosh fonts are typically 16-points high because leading is an integral part of the font.

CHAPTER 3

Display vs. Printer Resolution

In theory, the Macintosh is said to be a **WYSIWYG** computer. What you see on the screen is supposed to be exactly what you get on paper. In practice, that's almost never true; this chapter explains why.

Points vs. Pixels

In Chapter 2, we learned that font characteristics are measured in **points**, a printer's term for 1⁄72 of an inch. It's important to understand that points are a one-dimensional unit of measurement. They have length, but not width. Points are approximately 1⁄72-inch long, but they are infinitely thin.

Macintosh displays are also measured in points, but they consist of variable-size areas called **pixels** which is short for *picture elements*. Unlike points, which have length only, pixels have both length *and* width. When the display is properly adjusted, each pixel measures 1-point wide and 1-point long.

Just remember that points are fixed units of measurement; pixels are variable-size areas which happen to be measured in points. Pixels and points, though often used interchangeably, refer to completely different things.

Display Resolution

To **re**solve a problem is to **solve** it, by breaking it down into smaller and smaller component parts. In regard to a computer display, the smallest component part is called a pixel, which is a tiny, dot-size, picture element on the face of the display screen.

The term **resolution** generally indicates the number of pixels per square inch. On the 9-inch Macintosh (128K to Mac SE), resolution is specified at 72 × 72 pixels and mathematically, the **solution** to the Macintosh display is 5184 (72 × 72) square pixels.

To comprehend the size of a pixel, run your favorite word processor, select the Geneva 12 screen font, select Normal type style, and enter the following sentence:

The quick brown fox jumps over the lazy dog.

The dot over the *i* in the word quick, the dot over the *j* in the word jump, and the period at the end of the sentence are all single-pixel size. So are the dots and periods in Courier 9, Courier 10, Courier 12, Geneva 9, Geneva 10, Helvetica 9, Helvetica 10, Helvetica 12, Monaco 9, Times 9, Times 10, Times 12, etc. This explains why small fonts don't look good on the Macintosh display. Periods in 9-point fonts are proportionally much larger than periods in 12-point fonts. Periods in 6-point fonts are proportionally twice as large as periods in 12-point fonts! In all sizes below 9 point, periods, dots, and curves overwhelm the characters, making them almost unreadable.

So why not make the periods smaller? Because the periods are already single-pixel size, and a single pixel is the smallest dot-size element on the face of the screen.

Specified vs. Actual Resolution

Resolution can be **specified** or **actual**. Specified resolution is generally stated by equipment manufacturers in **dots per inch (dpi)**. Actual resolution is often reported by technical reviewers in **pixels per inch (ppi)**. How can the two be different?

Pixel size is established by turning the height, width, and voltage controls on the Macintosh analog board. These controls work just like the controls on the back of a television set. Presumably, factory technicians adjust them for 72 × 72 dpi, but unspecified resolutions from 68 × 62 dpi to 144 × 144 dpi (and greater) are also possible.

At 72 dpi, what you see on the screen should approximate what you get on paper. But obviously, if the Mac's built-in monitor is out of adjustment, then what you see on the screen won't even be close to what you get on paper.

If the display is stretched (less than 72 dpi), what you see on the screen is going to be much larger than what you get on paper. If the display is shrunken (greater than 72 dpi), what you see on the screen is going to be much smaller than what you get on paper. Consequently, the concept of a WYSIWYG (what you see is what you get) Macintosh presumes a perfectly adjusted 72-dpi monitor displaying perfectly square $\frac{1}{72}$-inch pixels. In practice, that's almost *never* the case.

Checking Display Resolution

Display resolution on standard-size 9-inch Macs (512K, 512K Enhanced, Macintosh Plus, and Macintosh SE) can be checked by choosing WYSIWYG resolution from Test Character Generator's test menu. TCG's WYSIWYG Resolution test is shown in Figure 3-1. Assuming a properly adjusted, 9-inch, standard Macintosh (128K to Macintosh SE), the on-screen T-squares should measure exactly 7.11 ($\frac{512}{72}$) inches wide and 4.47 ($\frac{322}{72}$) inches high.

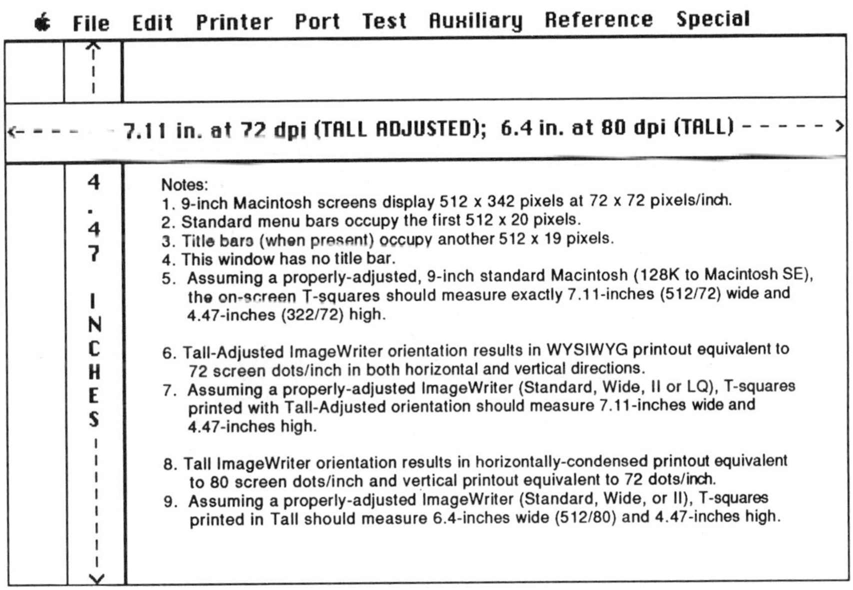

Figure 3-1 Test Character Generator's WYSIWYG Resolution test.

It's important to understand that TCG's on-screen T-squares do not reveal actual display measurements. They merely indicate what the display specifications are. More often than not, the actual display measurements are much shorter than specified. The only way to tell is to pick up a ruler and measure the T-squares yourself.

Correcting the Display Resolution

Correcting the display resolution is the subject of several chapters in a prior Howard W. Sams & Company book, titled *Macintosh Repair & Upgrade Secrets* (ISBN 0-672-48452-8). Basically, the Macintosh is taken apart as illustrated in Figure 3-2, and the analog board is readjusted, as suggested in Figure 3-3.

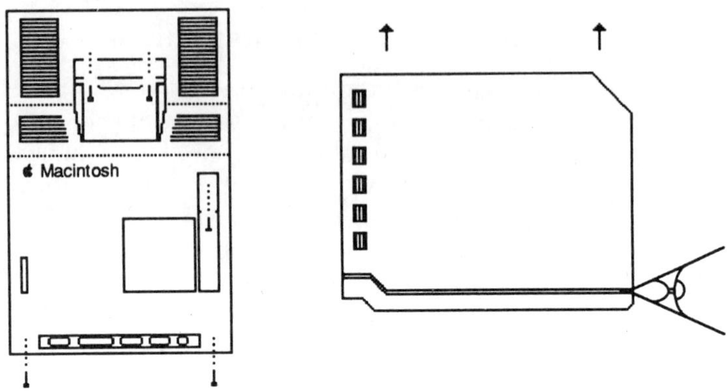

Figure 3-2 Macintosh take-apart.

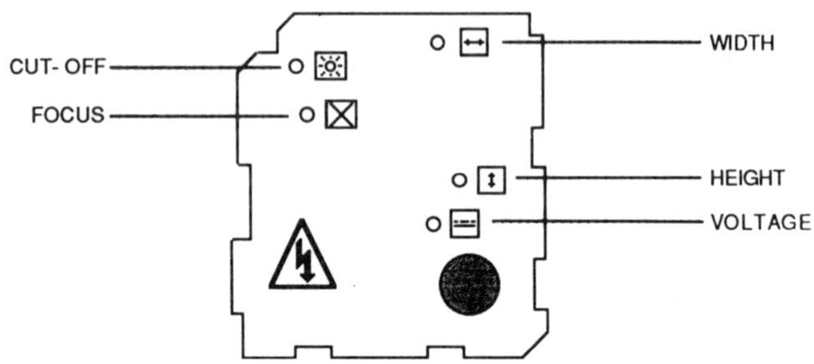

Figure 3-3 Macintosh analog board adjustments.

Maladjusted displays are often the result of component-level problems which should be taken care of at the same time. Repairs and adjustments can get quite involved. For complete instructions, refer to the *Macintosh Repair & Upgrade Secrets*.

PPI vs. DPI

As suggested earlier, technical reviewers often ignore the manufacturer's dpi (dots per inch) specification and report actual ppi (pixels per inch) figures. Ppi is determined exactly the same as dpi—by measuring the display with a ruler, and then dividing the measurements into the display's horizontal and vertical specifications. If the monitor is set up properly, ppi and dpi will be the same. If the monitor is not set up properly, ppi and dpi will not be the same.

The important point here is that when ppi is given without dpi, ppi is meaningless. Dpi states the specification; ppi confirms alignment. Generally speaking, the terms are *not* synonymous. More important, unless ppi equals dpi, and unless both equal 72, you can forget about WYSIWYG. What you see on the Macintosh will never be what you get on paper.

In that case, servicing the ImageWriter won't accomplish anything, because WYSIWYG problems are never in the ImageWriter. They're always in the Macintosh.

Pixels vs. Printer Dots

While the Macintosh display consists of adjustable-size pixels (squares) that are approximately 1/72-inch wide × 1/72-inch high, the Imagewriter printout consists of fixed-size dots (circles) that are approximately 1/72-inch in diameter. Essentially, it's a classic example of square pegs and round holes. Take a moment to dwell on the differences:

1. Macintosh pixels are square; ImageWriter dots are round.
2. Macintosh pixels are adjustable; ImageWriter dots are fixed.

Another difference between the screen and the printer has to do with overlapping dots. The Macintosh cannot display overlapping pixels. The ImageWriter can print overlapping dots. By overlapping dots, the ImageWriter can produce output that comes very close to the original computer display.

Printer Resolution

As stated earlier, **re**solving a problem involves solving it by breaking it down (over and over) into smaller and smaller component parts. In regard to ImageWriter printout, the smallest component parts are called **dots** (not pixels). These dots are circular impressions made by cylindrical striker wires in the printer's type head.

The expression **printer resolution** refers to the number of circular impressions per square inch. On the Imagewriter Standard, the Imagewriter Wide, and the ImageWriter II, dot size is fixed (at 1/72 inch to 1/80 inch) by the design of the type head, but the printer resolution is user-selectable. The lowest printer resolution is 72 × 72 dpi, exactly the same as the Mac's built-in monitor. The highest printer resolution is

160 × 144 dpi, more than twice the resolution of the Mac's built-in monitor!

Printer resolutions are chosen from the Page Setup... and Print... dialog boxes, and they vary slightly from one version of the ImageWriter driver to the next. These variations are covered in Chapter 4. The important point right now is that Macintosh display resolution (128K to Mac SE) is fixed on the assembly line (or on the repair bench) in hardware, but the ImageWriter resolution is user-selectable with software.

Low-Resolution, WYSIWYG Graphics Printing

As shown in Figures 3-4 and 3-5, when low-resolution, WYSIWYG graphics printing is selected (Standard quality with Tall-Adjusted orientation or Faster quality with Tall-Adjusted special effect), every pixel in the Macintosh display is reproduced by a single printer dot, just as if a **bit map** of the screen were overlaid on the paper.

Actual terms used in the Page Setup... boxes change, depending on which version of the ImageWriter driver happens to be in use. All of these terms are explained completely in Chapter 4, but here's a quick conversion chart.

The term	is equivalent to
Tall	Portrait
Tall-Adjusted	Tall-Adjusted special effect
Wide	Landscape

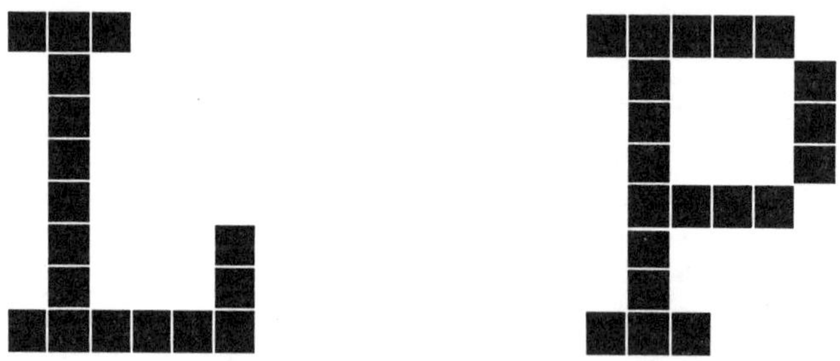

Figure 3-4 Fixed-resolution Macintosh display.

Note the loss of detail. Without square edges, the ImageWriter printout looks much worse than the built-in Macintosh display, even though resolution (72 × 72 dpi) is exactly the same.

Figure 3-5 Low-resolution, WYSIWYG graphics printout.

> The pixels depicted in Figure 3-4 are separated by broad white lines for clarity. In reality, whatever space there is between pixels is infinitely thin. For all practical purposes, pixels are not separated by lines but actually touch each other.

Low-Resolution, NonWYSIWYG Graphics Printing

As shown in Figure 3-6, when low-resolution, nonWYSIWYG graphics printing is selected (Standard quality with Tall orientation or Faster quality without Tall Adjusted special effect), horizontal printer dots are packed 11% closer together. Vertical dots are packed the same as in low-resolution, WYSIWYG graphics printing.

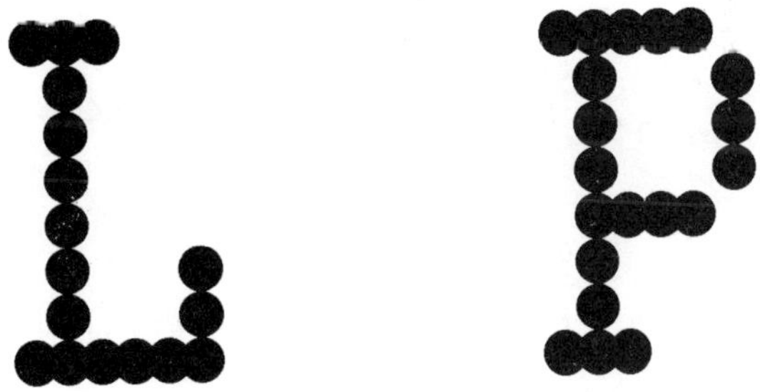

Figure 3-6 Low-resolution, nonWYSIWYG graphics printout.

This method is known as low-resolution, nonWYSIWYG graphics printing, because the resulting number of dots per inch (80 horizontal × 72 vertical) is slightly denser than the 72 × 72 dots per inch displayed on the screen. At 80 × 72 dpi, the printout looks less jagged, but WYSIWYG display proportions are lost. Characters are 11% narrower (80 dpi − 72 dpi = 8 dots; 8 dots/72 dpi = 11%) than they appear on the computer display. Consequently, they seem taller. Circles are also 11% narrower; they print out like footballs on a kicking tee. Squares look like macaroni boxes.

High-Resolution, WYSIWYG Graphics Printing

As shown in Figure 3-7, when high-resolution, WYSIWYG graphics printing is selected (High quality with Tall-Adjusted orientation or Best quality with Tall-Adjusted special effect), every pixel in the display is reproduced by two to four printer dots.

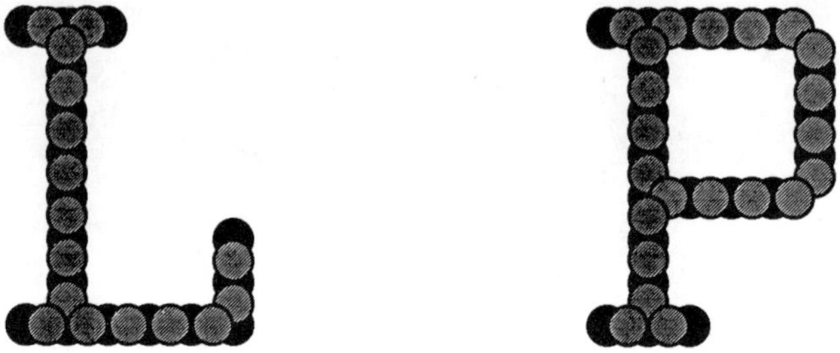

Figure 3-7 High-resolution, WYSIWYG graphics printout.

This method is called high-resolution, WYSIWYG graphics printing, because the resulting number of dots per inch (144 × 144 dpi) is twice as high as the 72 × 72 dots per inch displayed on the screen.

The overstrike dots depicted in Figure 3-7 are colored gray for clarity. In reality, overstrike dots are just as dark as the dots underneath them.

High-Resolution, NonWYSIWYG Graphics Printing

As shown in Figure 3-8, when high-resolution, nonWYSIWYG graphics printing is selected (High quality with Tall orientation or Best quality without Tall-Adjusted special effect), horizontal printer dots are packed 11% closer together. Vertical dots are packed the same as in high-resolution, WYSIWYG graphics printing.

This method is called high-resolution, nonWYSIWYG graphics printing because the resulting number of dots per inch (160 horizontal × 144 vertical) is *more* than twice as high as the 72 × 72 dots per inch displayed on the screen. At 160 × 144 dpi, the printout looks very good, but WYSIWYG proportions are lost, the same as in low-resolution, nonWYSIWYG graphics. Individual characters are *much* less jagged, but are still 11% narrower ((160 dpi/2) − 72 dpi = 8 dots; 8

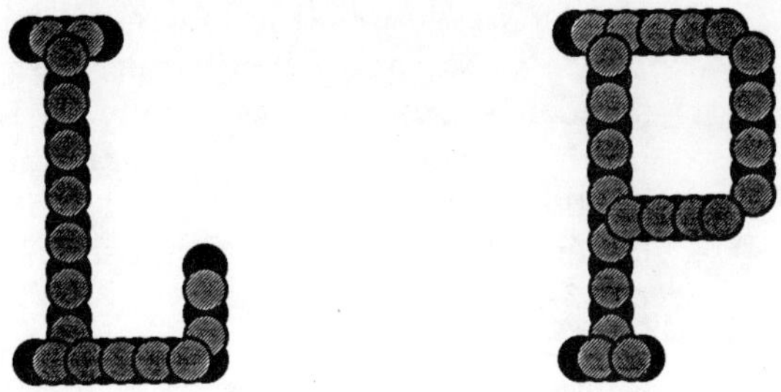

Figure 3-8 High-resolution, nonWYSIWYG graphics printout.

dots/72 dpi = 11%) than they appear on the computer display. Circles are also 11% narrower, as are squares.

High-resolution, nonWYSIWYG graphics printing is often preferred over high-resolution, WYSIWYG graphics printing, especially for text, because the greater the number of dots per inch, the greater the detail. This can be seen by comparing Figures 3-5, 3-6, 3-7, and 3-8. Also, thin (Tall) dots, like sharpened pencils, provide greater detail than thick (Tall Adjusted) dots (like dull pencils).

Printer Fonts vs. Screen Fonts

On an ImageWriter, the thickness of the dots is determined by the diameter of the type head's striker wires. Striker-wire thickness varies from model to model of the ImageWriter, but dot placement is determined by the availability (or absence) of double-size fonts in the System file. If the double-size fonts are missing, you still get twice as many dots, but they don't necessarily print in all the right places. This effect is illustrated in Figure 3-9.

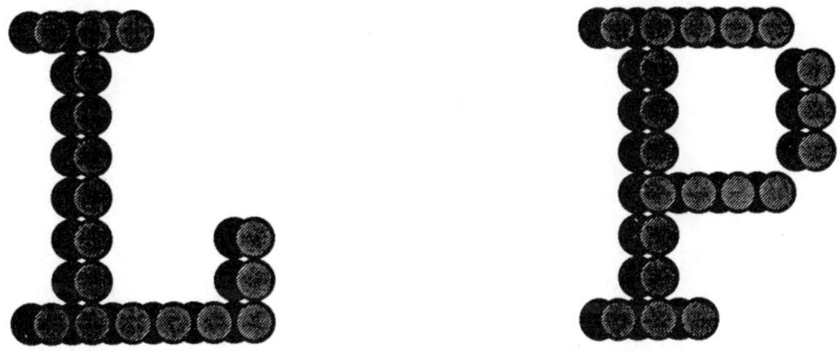

Figure 3-9 High-resolution, WYSIWYG graphics without double-size printer font.

Figure 3-9 illustrates an important difference between screen fonts and the so-called printer fonts: Only the standard-size fonts (9 to 12 points) are designed to look good on the screen. The other sizes (18 to 24, 36 to 48, and 72 to 96) are designed to be exact multiples of the standard sizes (not necessarily to look good on-screen), so that the printer driver will be able to scale them properly. If you were to touch up the larger-font sizes with a font editor, they would certainly look better on-screen, but their appearance would be worse (resembling Figure 3-9) on paper.

This leads us to an interesting conclusion: *Under the current OEM method of scalable (bitmapped) printer fonts, text display on the Macintosh is compromised to satisfy ImageWriter printout.* With standard Macintosh System software, you can either have a great-looking Imagewriter printout, or a great-looking Macintosh display, but not both.

Outline Fonts

One way around that limitation is with **outline** fonts. Outline fonts don't rely on the presence of double-size, triple-size, or quadruple-size fonts in the System file. Instead, they rely on mathematical font definitions which are stored in special outline-font files on the startup disk. Not only do font outlines produce a superior printout, but the matching screen fonts can be optimized for the Macintosh display.

Whether or not a printer uses outline fonts is a function of the printer driver. Version 2.7 of the ImageWriter driver does not, but several alternative printer drivers do use outline fonts, including the Toshiba P321SLC driver described in Chapter 16.

Whether or not the printer *and* the computer display use outline fonts is a function of the System software. System version 6.0.4 does not, but you can add that capability (inexpensively) with Adobe Type Manager.

Adobe Type Manager

Adobe Type Manager is a control device (CDEV) that adds outline-font technology to *existing* Macintosh System software (versions 6.0.2 to 6.0.4) and to *existing* Macintosh printer drivers. With Type Manager, you can have a great-looking ImageWriter printout, *as well as* a great-looking Macintosh display. As shown in Figure 3-10, Adobe Type Manager consists of various items supplied on disk.

The ~ATM icon represents the Adobe Type Manager CDEV. It goes in the System folder of every start-up disk. The ~ATM 68000 and ~ATM 68020/68030 icons represent different versions of the Adobe outline-font printer driver. The ~ATM 68000 driver is for older Macs with MC-68000 processors. Machines in this category include:

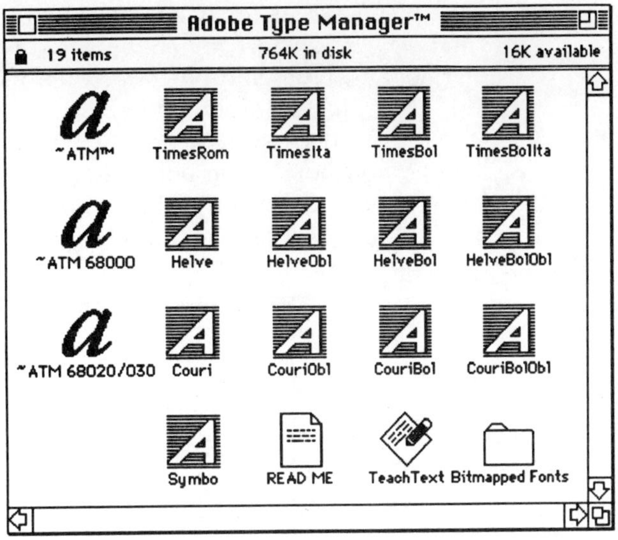

Figure 3-10 Adobe Type Manager disk contents.

1. 128K and 512K Macs with 800K disk-drive/128K ROM upgrade, and a minimum 1024K RAM upgrade.
2. 512K Enhanced Mac with a minimum 1024K RAM upgrade.
3. Stock-configuration Macintosh Plus.
4. Stock-configuration Macintosh SE.
5. Stock-configuration Macintosh SE with 20-Meg drive.
6. Lisa's and Mac XL's with 800K disk-drive/ROM upgrade, MacWorks Plus v1.1, and a minimum 1024K RAM.

The ~ATM 68020/030 is for newer Macs with MC-68020 or MC-68030 processors. Machines in this category include:

1. Stock-configuration Macintosh II.
2. Stock-configuration Macintosh SE/30.
3. Stock-configuration Macintosh IIx, IIcx, IIci.

In order for ATM to be used with any Mac on the first list that is equipped with an accelerator card, *both* drivers go in the System folder!

The icons labeled TimesRom, TimesIta, TimeBol, and TimesBolita are the outline fonts for the Times typeface. The icons labeled Helve, HelveObl, HelveBol, and HelveBolObl are the outline fonts for the Helvetica typeface. The icons labeled Couri, CouriObl, CouriBol, and CouriBolObl are the outline fonts for the Courier typeface. The Symbo icon is an outline font for the Symbol typeface. These files go in the System folder, as appropriate. If you only use Courier and Helvetica typefaces, copy just the Couri and Helve fonts. Skip the others.

Obl is short for oblique (slanted) type, *Bol* is short for bold type, and *BolObl* is short for bold-oblique type. Note how Adobe uses the terms font, type, and typeface. Their usage is consistent with the printing trade, just as it should be.

TeachText is there to open the READ ME file, which contains application notes. The notes should be read, but neither file has to be copied to your startup disk.

Figure 3-11 shows the contents of the Bitmapped-Fonts folder.

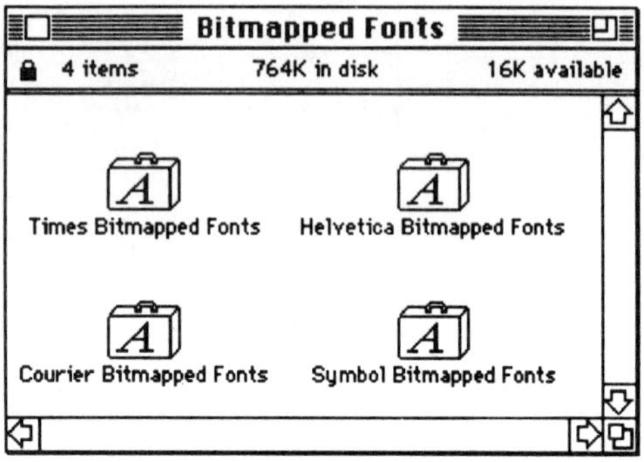

Figure 3-11 Adobe Type Manager contents of the Bitmapped-Fonts folder.

The supplied-screen fonts differ from the OEM versions. These have to be moved into the System file on every startup disk, using Font / DA Mover 3.8 (or later). Remember that Font / DA Mover versions prior to v3.8 do not support new font numbering tables (NFNTs). A discussion of NFNTs along with complete details on how to use Font / DA Mover v3.8 was given in Chapter 2.

If you only use Courier and Helvetica typefaces, move just the Couri and Helve fonts. Skip the Times and Symbol fonts. The matching B Courier Bold, I Courier Oblique, BI Courier BoldOblique, B Helvetica Bold, I Helvetica Oblique, and BI Helvetica BoldOblique bit-mapped fonts are not *absolutely* necessary, but should also be moved. These greatly enhance the ImageWriter printout as well as the Macintosh display, and they don't take very much room in the System file. Unlike the OEM-display driver and the OEM-Macintosh printer drivers that scale 2×, 3×, and 4× bit-mapped fonts, Adobe's outline-font driver only requires the installation of 10- and 12-point bit-mapped font sizes. All of the others, with the exception of the standard-screen fonts defined in Chapter 2 (Chicago 12, Geneva 9, Geneva 12, and Monaco 9), can be trashed. Even when you consider the size of the Adobe outline-font files, the net disk-storage savings is enormous. The entire ATM package requires only 500K of disk space. The minimum configuration requires only 100K!

Display Improvement

Figure 3-12 shows the Adobe Type Manager control panel. The 96K (48K × 2) default cache allows two fonts (10 and 12 point) to be held completely in memory for maximum display speed. Increasing the cache size (memory permitting) allows ATM to hold more fonts in memory, which makes it run faster when elaborately formatted documents are displayed. For maximum speed, the cache size should be increased by 48K for every font you use. If you never display more than 2 fonts, 96K is fine.

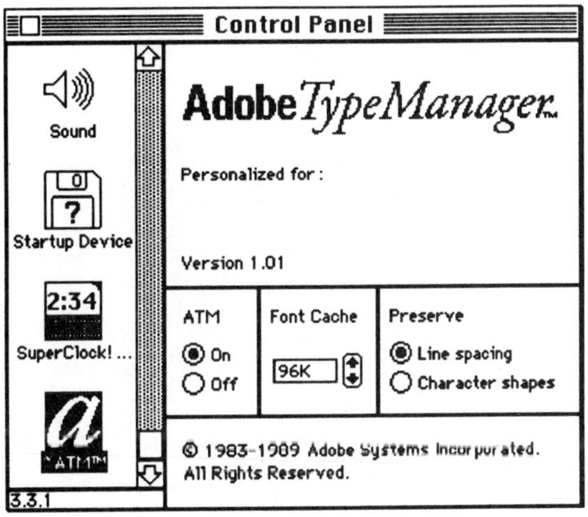

Figure 3-12 Adobe Type Manager Control Panel.

The improvement in the Macintosh display is just incredible. Figure 3-13 shows the standard Mac System software rendition of 127-point Times. It's terrible. Figure 3-14 shows Adobe Type Manager's outline-font rendition of the same display. It speaks for itself.

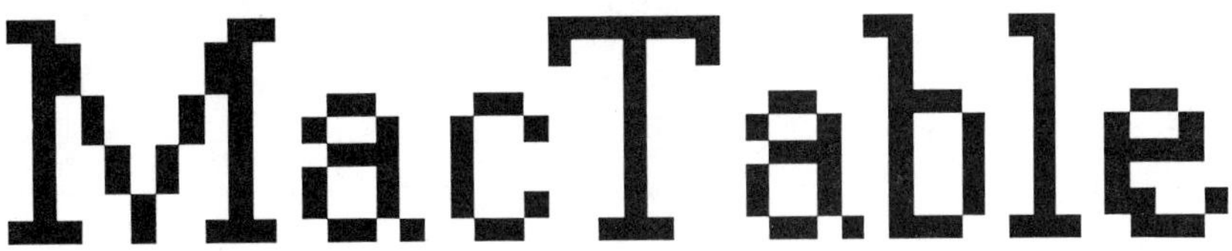

Figure 3-13 Macintosh System software bitmapped-font display of 127-point Times.

Why would anyone want to display type in 127 point? Figures 3-13 and 3-14 are based on a real-life example recently brought to my attention by Soren Storm, the president of ScanCo, makers of *MacTable*.

As shown in Figure 3-15, *MacTable* is an ergonomically designed workstation for Macintosh computer systems. Note the details pertain-

MacTable

Figure 3-14 Adobe Type Manager outline-font display of 127-point Times.

ing to printer support and paper delivery. The half-round molding on the printer shelf is much more than a decoration. Its roundness minimizes line squashing and paper jams, two common ImageWriter problems.

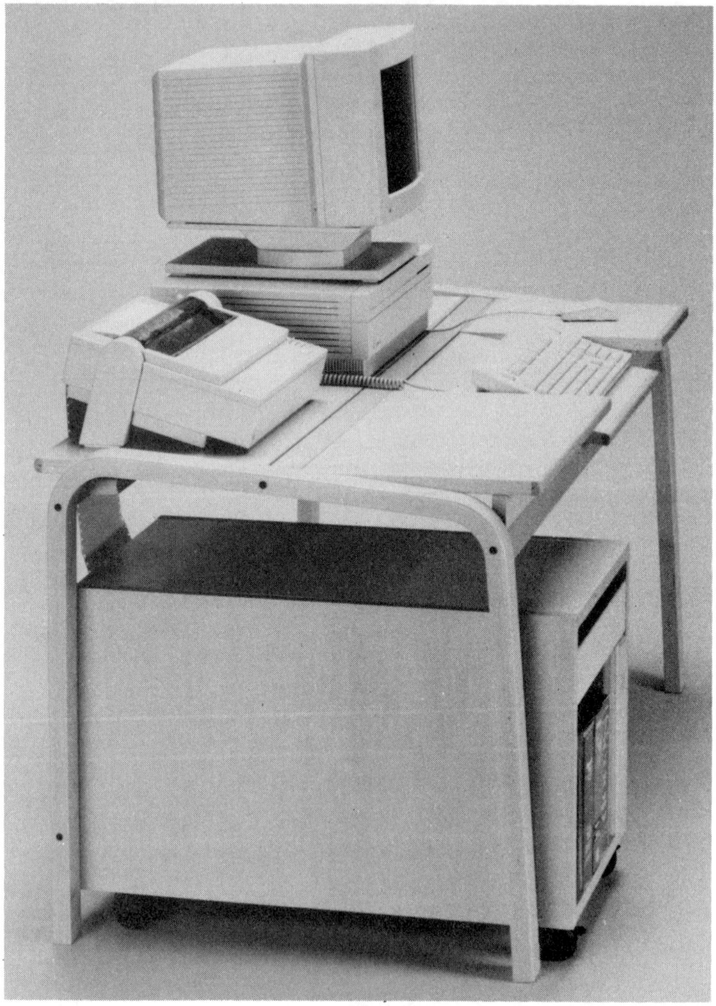

Figure 3-15 MacTable workstation. *(Courtesy ScanCo.)*

Right now, the point has to do with ScanCo's media advertising. The company's ads are outstanding, but computer screens, even Macintosh computer screens, never look very exciting when the display is blank. Ideally, ScanCo would like to display their trademark on the screen, but the standard Macintosh System software (Figure 3-13) just can't handle it. With Adobe Type Manager (Figure 3-14), perfect trademarks (headlines, etc.) are just a mouse click away.

Since the Macintosh already does a fine job of displaying 9- to 12-point screen fonts, there's little or no improvement in the standard sizes. ATM's main impact is on large-size printer fonts (14 point and above). Even though display resolution (72 dpi) never varies, the *quality* of the display is dramatically improved. Unlike the bit-mapped characters shown in Figure 3-9, each and every dot is drawn in exactly the right place.

Note: Figures 3-14 and 3-15 were printed at 75% Reduction on a LaserWriter IISC. When displayed on the computer screen, proportions are identical, but both figures are actually 33% larger.

Printout Improvement

Printout improvement is even more dramatic. Not only is every character drawn to perfection, but every character is printed at the maximum resolution of the display device. Table 3-1 provides maximum-resolution figures for some popular Macintosh printers.

Table 3-1. Resolution Figures for Popular Macintosh Printers

OEM	Printer Model	Maximum WYSIWYG Resolution
Apple	Imagewriter Standard	160 dpi × 144 dpi
Apple	Imagewriter Wide	160 dpi × 144 dpi
Apple	ImageWriter II	160 dpi × 144 dpi
Apple	ImageWriter LQ	320 dpi × 216 dpi
Apple	LaserWriter IISC	300 dpi × 300 dpi
Kodak	M150 Plus	192 dpi × 192 dpi
HP	DeskWriter	300 dpi × 300 dpi
Olympia	NP 30 APL	160 dpi × 144 dpi
Seikosha	SP-1000AP	160 dpi × 144 dpi
Toshiba	P321SL	360 dpi × 360 dpi
Toshiba	P321SLC	360 dpi × 360 dpi
Toshiba	P341SL	360 dpi × 360 dpi
Toshiba	P351SX	360 dpi × 360 dpi

In general, Adobe Type Manager is a lot like light beer: "It works great, and it's less filling." After trashing all of the bit-mapped (2×, 3×, and 4×) printer fonts in the *Macintosh Printer Secrets* System file and replacing them with ATM, our development hard drive was 4Mb lighter.

Without ATM, the LaserWriter IISC printout quality shown in Figure 3-14 would have required a 528-point (4 × 127-point) bitmapped font. God knows how many kilobytes that would require. The operating system couldn't handle it, anyway.

Most important, at least as far as *Macintosh Printer Secrets* readers are concerned, Adobe Type Manager makes the information in the ImageWriter repair chapters even more valuable. Align your printer to perfection as instructed, install Adobe Type Manager, and you won't believe the difference!

Summary

The following important points summarize the material presented in Chapter 3.

1. Points are a one-dimensional unit of measurement. They have length, but not width.
2. Points are approximately 1/72-inch long, but they are infinitely thin.
3. Pixels are variable-size areas which happen to be measured in points. Pixels have length and width.
4. Macintosh pixels are squares measuring approximately 1/72-inch long × 1/72-inch wide.
5. ImageWriter dots are circles measuring approximately 1/72 inch in diameter.
6. Macintosh resolution refers to the number of pixels per square inch.
7. ImageWriter resolution refers to the number of dots per square inch.
8. 128K to Macintosh SE resolution is fixed (in the hardware) at 72 × 72 pixels per inch.
9. ImageWriter resolution is user-selectable via the ImageWriter driver's Page setup... and Print... dialog boxes.
10. WYSIWYG is an acronym for "What You See Is What You Get."
11. Low-resolution, WYSIWYG graphics printing is 72 × 72 dots per inch, the same as the Mac's built-in monitor.
12. Low-resolution, nonWYSIWYG graphics printing is 80 × 72 dots per inch, slightly denser than the Mac's built-in monitor.

13. High-resolution, WYSIWYG graphics printing is 144 × 144 dots per inch, exactly twice as dense as the Mac's built-in monitor.
14. High-resolution, nonWYSIWYG graphics printing is 160 × 144 dots per inch, more than twice as dense as the Mac's built-in monitor.
15. Higher resolutions are accomplished by overlapping dots, a printer-specific feature not available on computer displays.
16. Only the standard-size fonts (9 to 12 points) are designed to look good on the screen.
17. Fonts that look good on the screen are called screen fonts.
18. Larger font sizes (18 to 24, 36 to 48, and 72 to 96) are designed to be exact multiples of the standard sizes, not necessarily to look good on-screen.
19. Fonts that look less than perfect on the screen but scale perfectly when printed are called printer fonts.
20. If you were to touch up the larger font sizes with a font editor, they would certainly look better on-screen, but their appearance would be worse when printed.
21. Under the current OEM method of scalable, bit-mapped, printer fonts, text display on the Macintosh is compromised to satisfy ImageWriter printout.
22. With standard System software, through version 6.0.4, you can either have a great-looking Imagewriter printout, or a great-looking Macintosh display, but not both.
23. Outline fonts don't rely on the presence of double-size, triple-size, or quadruple-size fonts in the System file. Instead, they rely on mathematical font definitions which are stored in special outline-font files on the startup disk.
24. Adobe Type Manager is a control device (CDEV) that brings outline-font technology to standard Macintosh System software, versions 6.0.2 to 6.0.4.
25. With Adobe Type Manager, you *can* have a great-looking ImageWriter printout, as well as a great-looking Macintosh display.

CHAPTER 4

The ImageWriter Driver

In Chapter 3, we learned that high-resolution graphics printing is accomplished by overlapping dots, a printer-specific feature not available on computer displays. This chapter relates that information to the ImageWriter's Page Set-up... and Print... dialog boxes. If you've ever wondered what the differences between High vs. Best, Standard vs. Faster, or Tall vs. Tall Adjusted printing were, you'll find complete explanations here.

The Original Imagewriter Driver

Figure 4-1 shows the Page Setup... dialog box provided by the original Imagewriter driver. Four **papers** can be selected—US Letter, US Legal, A4 Letter, and International Fanfold, and three **orientations**—Tall, Tall Adjusted, and Wide.

Figure 4-1 Page Setup... dialog box from the original Imagewriter driver.

Papers

Most of the labels in the Page Setup... dialog box completely miss their marks. First, the *paper* options do not allow you to select paper (defined as a substance made from rags, straw, wood, or other fibrous material). All they allow you to do is *indicate* a paper size (the numerical proportions of the paper). Unfortunately, the paper sizes are not shown! How large is A4 Letter? How large is International Fanfold?

For reference, Table 4-1 lists various Imagewriter papers and their sizes. Even to this day (through ImageWriter driver version 2.7), the various paper sizes are still not shown!

Table 4-1. Paper Sizes

Paper	Size
US Letter	8½ inches × 11 inches
US Legal	8½ inches × 14 inches
A4 Letter	210 millimeters × 297 millimeters
International Fanfold	210 millimeters × 305 millimeters
Computer Paper	14 inches × 11 inches

Orientations

Likewise, **Tall** and **Tall Adjusted** are not **orientations** (derived from the word *orientate*, which means to turn or to face east, toward Mecca, in the Orient). Tall and Tall Adjusted are both horizontal **resolutions**. Tall Adjusted indicates low-resolution graphics at 72 × 72 dpi, or high-resolution graphics at 144 × 144 dpi. Tall indicates a low-resolution, nonWYSIWYG graphics at 80 × 72 dpi, or a high-resolution, non-WYSIWYG graphics at 160 × 144 dpi.

As illustrated in Figures 3-6 and 3-8, Tall results in a graphics-mode text printout that is slightly less jagged than WYSIWYG. **Tall** (80-dpi horizontal resolution) also matches the ImageWriter's built-in Pica 10 character set. In theory, Tall should make it possible to print perfectly spaced, high-speed, draft-mode text and perfectly spaced, ImageWriter II NLQ characters at 80 cpi (characters per inch), just as if the ImageWriter II were a PC-compatible office printer connected to a PC-compatible computer running an 80-column monitor. In practice, the ImageWriter *driver* doesn't allow it. The reason has to do with Draft Quality printing. Complete details on this are in Chapter 5.

Wide orientation prints from top to bottom, up and down the page (instead of from left to right across the page), and treats the paper width as though it was the paper length. When US Letter paper is used, the resulting printout is 11-inches wide × 8½-inches long instead of the usual 8½-inches wide by 11-inches long. Wide orientation is similar to a landscape painting, while Tall and Tall Adjusted both resemble portraits.

Most people never take advantage of Wide orientation, but if you need to print out a big spreadsheet on an 8-inch Imagewriter or an 8-inch ImageWriter II, Wide orientation with "No breaks between pages selected" (this assumes Imagewriter driver version 1.1 or greater) is exactly the way to do it.

Understanding Printer Orientations

To understand how the ImageWriter responds to Tall Adjusted orientation, follow this procedure:

1. Start your Macintosh in the normal way and run Test Character Generator. Hold the mouse button down or hit the return key to dismiss the startup screen.
2. Choose Page Setup... from the File menu, and select Tall Adjusted (72 dpi × 72 dpi) from the Page Setup... dialog box. Click the OK button.
3. Choose WYSIWYG Resolution from the Test menu. This brings up TCG's T-squares test, as shown in Figure 3-1.
4. Check for paper in the printer and turn it on.
5. Choose Print... from the File menu, and select either Standard, Faster, High, or Best quality. Click the OK button. After a brief delay, the Imagewriter will begin printing the T-squares.

The printout should measure 7.11 ($^{512}/_{72}$) inches by 4.47 ($^{322}/_{72}$) inches, exactly the same as the Macintosh display. In Tall Adjusted, what you see on the screen should be exactly what you get on paper.

To check resolution in the Tall orientation, follow the same steps but select Tall (80 dpi × 72 dpi) instead of Tall Adjusted from the Page Setup... dialog box. At 80-dpi horizontally (Tall), the printed T-squares should measure 6.40 ($^{512}/_{80}$) inches by 4.47 ($^{322}/_{72}$) inches, exactly 0.71-inches *shorter* than the screen display. With Tall selected, what you see on the screen should be exactly 11% (80 ÷ 72 = 1.11) *wider* than what you get on paper.

To check resolution in the Wide orientation, follow the same steps but select Wide from the Page Setup... dialog box. The printed T-squares should measure 7.11 ($^{512}/_{72}$) inches by 4.47 ($^{322}/_{72}$) inches, oriented exactly the same as if the Macintosh had been rotated to the right and set down on its side.

Metric System

If you'd rather measure using the metric system, hold down the option key while selecting WYSIWYG Resolution. Holding down the option key tells TCG to measure in centimeters rather than inches. TCG's metric T-squares are shown in Figure 4-2.

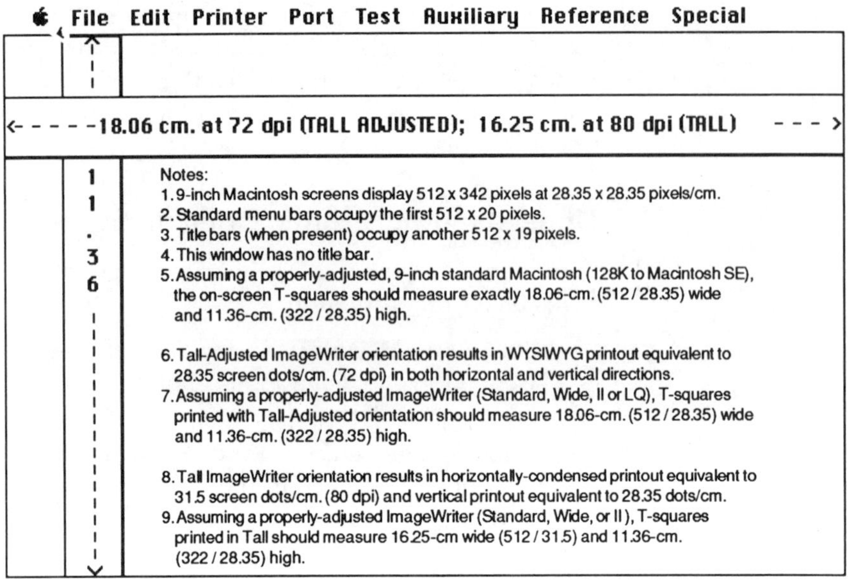

Figure 4-2 Test Character Generator metric T-squares.

With the metric system in effect, Tall Adjusted printout should measure 18.06 centimeters (512/28.35) by 11.36 centimeters (322/28.35), exactly the same as the Macintosh display.

With Tall ImageWriter orientation, the printed T-squares should measure 16.25 centimeters (512/31.5) by 11.36 centimeters, exactly 1.81 centimeters *shorter* than the screen display. Once again, what you see on the screen should be exactly 11% ($80 \div 72 = 1.11$) *wider* than what you get on paper.

Orientation Games

To look better on paper, early applications usually default to Tall orientation. In an effort to maintain the illusion of WYSIWYG, some applications, like MacWrite versions 2.2 to 4.5, play games with their rulers. Even when the Macintosh display is perfectly adjusted for 7.11 inches × 4.75 inches, MacWrite's ruler (versions 2.2 to 4.5) does not agree with a tape measure held up to the screen! Instead, every inch on the ruler measures just under 1⅛-inches long (exactly 1.11 inches) in order to ultimately agree with the Tall orientation printout. Since the excess accumulates, MacWrite's 7-inch marker (versions 2.2 to 4.5) is actually 0.66 inch longer than indicated ($(7 - 1) \times 1.11 = 6.66$)!

That information is *not* in the manual. If you just assume that an inch is an inch, and print mixed text and graphics using Tall-Adjusted orientation (so that circles and squares print proportionally), your margins come out lopsided.

MacWrite's oversize ruler is illustrated in Figure 4-3. There's nothing to be done about the oversize ruler. The only solution is to use MacWrite version 4.6 or later, or switch to a completely different word processor.

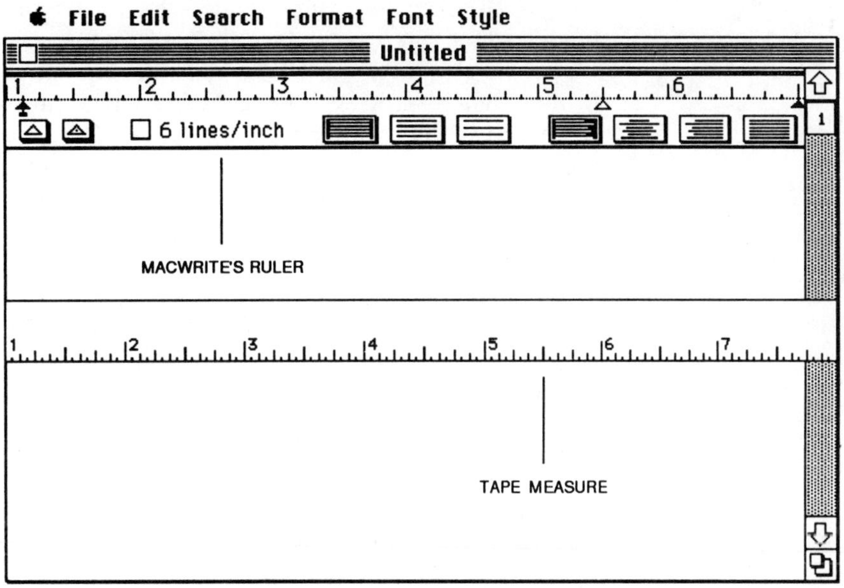

Figure 4-3 When the Macintosh display is properly adjusted, every inch on MacWrite's ruler (versions 2.2 to 4.5) measures 1.11 inches long!

The Original Print... Dialog Box

Figure 4-4 shows the Print... dialog box provided by the original Imagewriter driver. Three **qualities** can be selected—High, Standard, and Draft, and two **paper feeds**—Continuous and Cut Sheet.

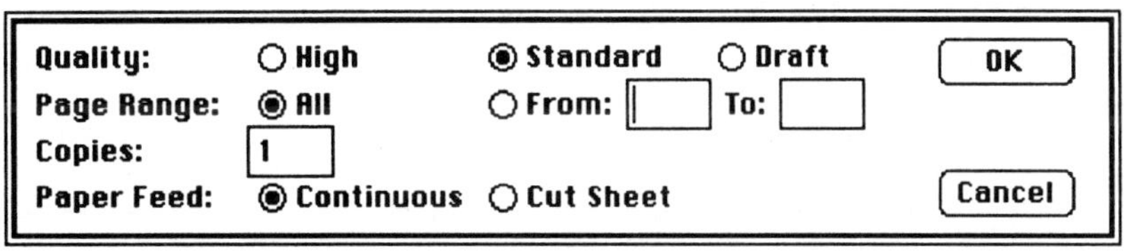

Figure 4-4 Print... dialog box from the original Imagewriter driver.

Qualities

High printout quality doubles the current graphics resolution (originally selected via the Page Setup... dialog box) from 72 dpi (or 80 dpi) to 144 dpi (or 160 dpi). **Standard** printout quality halves the current graphics resolution from 144 dpi (or 160 dpi) to 72 dpi (or 80 dpi).

High accurately suggests a better than Standard quality printout, but **Draft**, suggesting a less than Standard quality printout, is completely misleading. In Draft, dot density is entirely dependent on printer-switch settings. If the printer switches are set to **NLQ** (assuming NLQ is available), and if the computer's screen font exactly matches the printer's built-in character set, then Draft quality produces a near letter quality printout which is substantially *higher* than High quality!

Paper Feeds

Continuous, of course, is not a paper feed. Continuous refers to the type of paper which is fed. When Continuous is selected, it's assumed that the friction clutch (just like the friction clutch on a typewriter) is disengaged, and the pin-feed sprockets are engaged. The friction clutch is engaged and disengaged with the paper-release lever on the printer. If it's in the wrong position and you forget to check, the print job will jam after just a few pages.

Likewise, **Cut Sheet** is also not a paper feed. Cut Sheet refers to paper that has been precut to one of the standard sizes. When Cut Sheet is selected, it's assumed that the sprockets are disengaged, and the friction clutch is engaged.

On any other printer, sprockets would be known as tractors. Continuous would be known as tractor-feed paper, and Cut Sheet would be known as friction-feed paper.

The inappropriate ImageWriter driver labels may be part of the reason that the business world failed to perceive the early Macs as real computers, and may explain why many people still feel that Macintosh users are virtual computer illiterates. When you can't speak the language, you don't earn any respect.

ImageWriter Driver Version 1.1

Figure 4-5 shows the Page Setup... dialog box provided by ImageWriter driver version 1.1. This driver adds one new paper (Computer Paper), two **paginations** (Normal pages and No breaks between pages), and two **reductions** (None, and 50 percent).

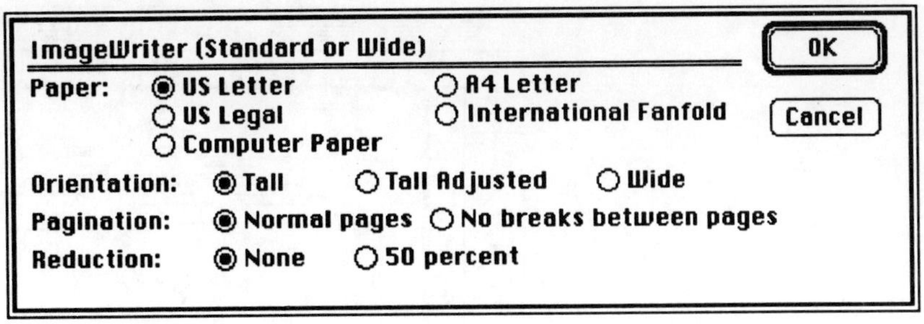

Figure 4-5 Page Setup... dialog box from ImageWriter driver version 1.1.

Paginations

Normal pages indicates that at least a ½-inch margin will appear at the top of each and every page, even when margins are not specifically set by the current application. Normal pages allows you to load the paper under the paper bail, the same as on a typewriter, and print without having to waste the first sheet of paper.

No breaks between pages indicates that no margin should appear at the top of every page. In order to accomplish that, the first sheet of paper is wasted, and page one of the print job is printed from the top of the second sheet.

For consistency with the reductions discussed in the next section, think of paginations as top margins, and think of the choices as None and ½ inch.

Reductions

50 percent reduction is accomplished the same as high-resolution graphics printing, with one interesting twist. Instead of scaling a double-size font to produce the screen size, the screen size is used as-is, and scaled to produce a high-resolution 50 percent reduction.

As simple as this is to understand, some users never grasp the implications. 50 percent reduction means that there *is* a way to get high-resolution bit-mapped graphics and an alternate way to get high-resolution graphics-mode text.

Instead of working on actual-size layouts, where 5-, 6-, and 7-point details are impossible to implement on-screen, 50 percent reduction allows you to work 400% oversize (with 12-, 10-, and 14-point details on-screen), and then reduce the layout to the desired size at print time. This concept is illustrated in Figures 4-6 and 4-7, using MacDraw, version 1.95.

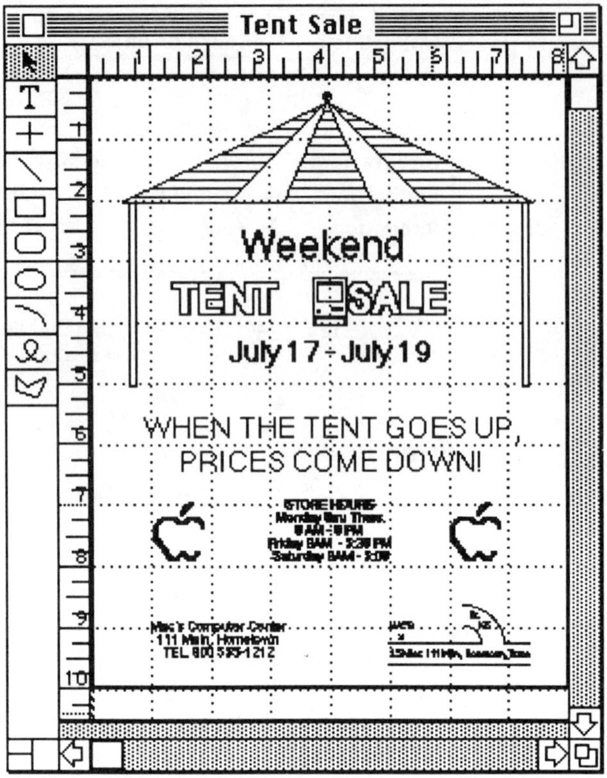

Figure 4-6 8-inch × 10-inch Macintosh layout.

Note that the original layout measures 8 inches × 10 inches (80 square inches), while the final layout measures 4 inches × 5 inches (20 square inches). Thus, 80 square inches is 400% (4×), not 200% (2×) larger than 20-square inches.

With 50 percent reduction, low-resolution 8-inch × 10-inch layouts can be used in comfort (with much less eye strain), to provide high-resolution, 4-inch × 5-inch printouts. Not only that, but you don't need to clutter up the System file with double-size fonts; even bit-mapped graphics print at 144 dpi!

Recreating the Tent-Sale Ad

400-percent layouts are more easily prepared with a full-page monitor, but are no more impossible with a standard-size Mac monitor than any other task. To recreate the tent-sale ad, select MacDraw's rectangle tool (or SuperPaint's rectangle tool, etc.), and draw a border 8-inches wide × 10-inches deep. Fill should be none. Use the polygon tool to draw the tent top. Fill alternating sections with the broader of MacDraw's two

Figure 4-7 4-inch × 5-inch ImageWriter results.

horizontal line patterns. The broader pattern gives the impression that lines will be spaced too far apart, but ImageWriter printing reduces the layout to 25% of actual size, resulting in four times as many lines in the same relative space.

The top ornament is a perfect circle, drawn with the oval tool by holding down the shift key. Fill is black. Tent poles are drawn with the rectangle tool and filled with none or medium-density gray. Weekend is set in plain Helvetica 48. Tent Sale is set in bold, outline, Helvetica 48. The Mac itself and both Apples are in oversized, retouched, Taliesin 18. The tiny font in the road map is actually Helvetica 10, which 50-percent printing reduces to a very legible Helvetica 5!

All this may sound complicated, but it really isn't. Once you install the fonts in your System file (for details, refer to Chapter 2) and get some practice, similar ads will take only a half hour or so to produce. This not only reduces labor costs when compared to manual preparation, but you get exactly the ad you want without having to worry whether the copy will fit the allotted layout size.

No one is going to mistake 50-percent reductions for laser printing, but few people will identify the reduction as ImageWriter printing. Figure 4-7 is reproduced here, unretouched, exactly as it came out of my ImageWriter II. Figure 4-7 should be equivalent to the results you might expect if you were to hand a similar printout to a display-advertising representative for publication in the local newspaper.

Version 1.1 of the Print... Dialog Box

Figure 4-8 shows the Print... dialog box provided by ImageWriter driver version 1.1. Note that the word ImageWriter (which had been spelled with a lowercase W) is spelled with an uppercase W, and that the wide-carriage ImageWriter is recognized.

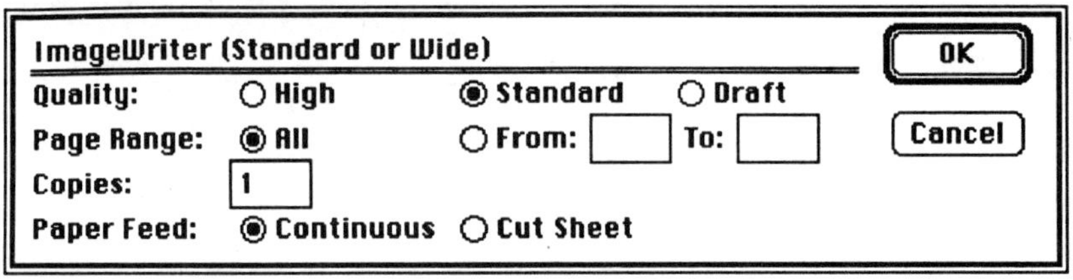

Figure 4-8 Print... dialog box from ImageWriter driver version 1.1.

ImageWriter Driver Version 2.0

Figure 4-9 shows the Page Setup... dialog box provided by ImageWriter driver version 2.0. This driver is provided on the official April, 1985, System Update disk, and it's still recommended by most sources as the driver to use if you own an original 128K or 512K Macintosh with 400K disk drives. That recommendation is incorrect.

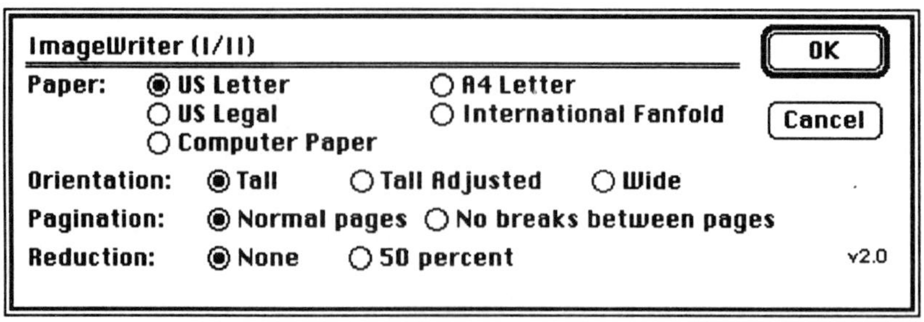

Figure 4-9 Page Setup... dialog box from ImageWriter driver version 2.0.

If you recall from Chapter 1, this version mysteriously dropped support for X-ON/X-OFF (software) handshaking. Switching to version 2.0 as part of the recommended update, or along with a new application disk, will cause quite a few Imagewriters (equipped with official Apple-brand cables) to malfunction.

There's nothing to be done about the driver. Whenever you encounter the problem (shown in Figure 1-9), the fix is to replace version 2.0 of the ImageWriter driver with version 1.1, or with version 2.3. Version 2.3 is preferred, because it's reliable, relatively small, and it supports multicolor printing on the ImageWriter II.

Version 2.0 of the Print... Dialog Box

Figure 4-10 shows the Print... dialog box provided by ImageWriter driver version 2.0. Note that a printer which had originally been named Imagewriter, and then renamed ImageWriter (Standard or Wide), is renamed again, this time to ImageWriter I.

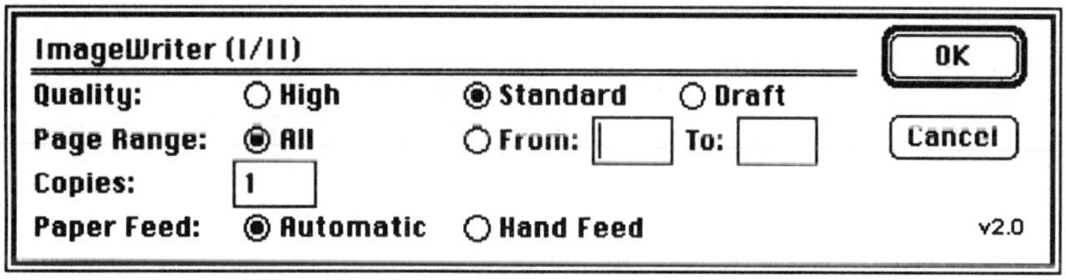

Figure 4-10 Print... dialog box from ImageWriter driver version 2.0.

The ImageWriter II is also listed, and the driver's version number is conveniently printed in the lower right-hand corner of the dialog box.

ImageWriter Driver Version 2.3

Figure 4-11 shows the Page Setup... dialog box provided by ImageWriter driver version 2.3. This is the driver provided on the original Mac Plus System Tools disk and it's still all right to use if you own an older 128K or 512K Mac with 400K disk drives.

Note that Tall orientation is gone, Wide orientation is gone, and Tall Adjusted orientation is now called a special effect! In place of Tall and Wide orientations, this driver offers portrait and landscape printing, which are selected by clicking on icons in the lower left-hand corner of the dialog box. Without any label indicating "Click to select...", some people never quite figure that out!

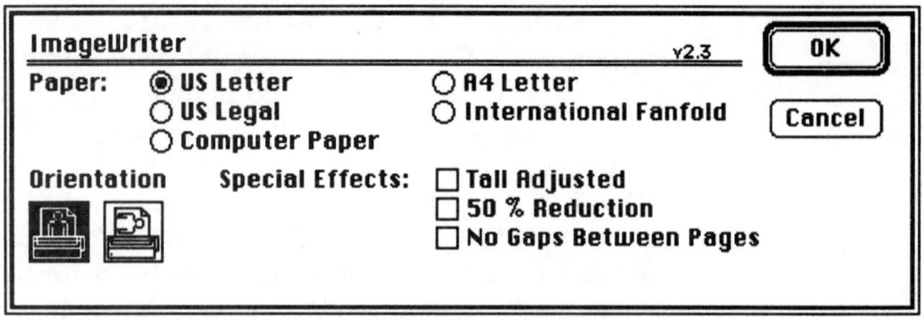

Figure 4-11 Page Setup... dialog box from ImageWriter driver version 2.3.

The problem with these seemingly senseless changes is that they make it very difficult to document precise page setup/printer procedures. Imagine having to say: "If you have the original Imagewriter driver, then do it this way; if you have ImageWriter driver 1.1, do it that way; if you have ImageWriter driver version 2.0, do it another way; but if you have ImageWriter driver 2.3, then do it this way." Few developers bother. Instead, you get a description of whatever driver they happen to be using, which is often inappropriate to the driver that you're currently using.

Another change has to do with reductions. The Reduction category is completely gone, and what had been "Reduction: 50 percent" is now "50 % Reduction."

Multicolor Printing Support

There is an unapparent but very important change that has to do with multicolor printing and the ImageWriter II. Prior versions of the ImageWriter driver do not support multicolor ribbons. With older versions, only the black band is used, even when you create color graphics and print them using a color-graphics program.

If you've never been able to print in color with your ImageWriter II, it's not likely that the printer or the ribbon is at fault. Install ImageWriter driver version 2.3 (or later), reinstall the multicolor ribbon, and everything should be fine.

Color printing is covered in Chapter 6.

Version 2.3 of the Print... Dialog Box

Figure 4-12 shows the Print... dialog box provided by ImageWriter driver version 2.3. Note that the ImageWriter (I/II) designation is gone, and the location of the version number has been moved from the lower right corner of the dialog box to the upper right corner of the box!

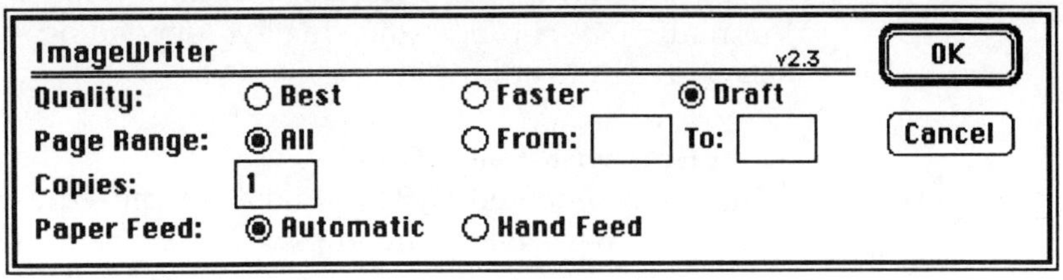

Figure 4-12 Print... dialog box from ImageWriter driver version 2.3.

Both Paper Feeds have been renamed. Continuous is now called Automatic; Cut Sheet is now called Hand Feed. In addition, High and Standard print qualities are completely gone. In their places are two brand-new print qualities: Best and Faster.

Best and Faster Quality

Best quality is similar to High quality, but as shown in Figure 4-13, **Faster** is actually a boldface version of Standard quality. Because Faster prints extra horizontal dots (standard boldface), Faster is noticeably slower than Standard, but it's still faster than High and Best, both of which print twice as many vertical dots as well. In addition, Best is certainly not the very best, because Best quality is still not as good as Draft NLQ.

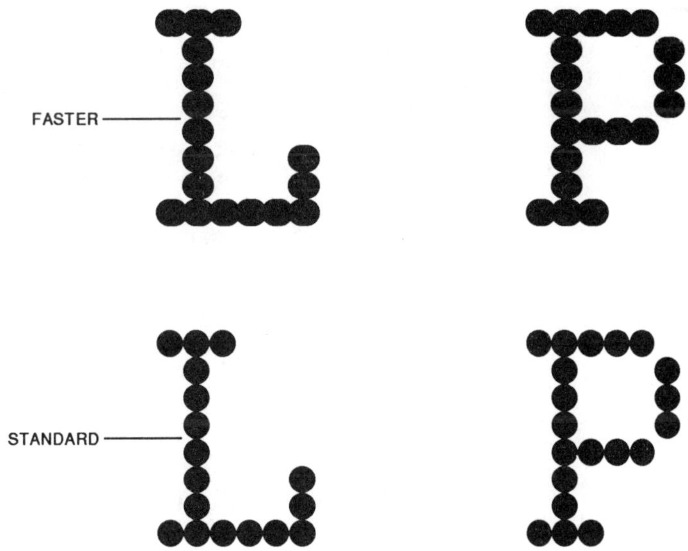

Figure 4-13 Faster vs. Standard quality.

To straighten out the print-quality confusion, think of Best as high-resolution graphics; think of Faster as medium-resolution graphics; and think of Draft as either higher-resolution Near Letter Quality, or lower-resolution data-processing quality, depending on the printer's front-panel control settings.

Problems with Faster Quality

The undocumented switch to boldface caused a problem that lingers to this day, particularly among owners of older 128K and 512K floppy-drive Macs. As explained previously, most people receive regular System software updates along with new applications. As a result, different Macintosh application disks come with different versions of the ImageWriter driver. Switching from Standard quality (ImageWriter driver 2.0 and below) to boldfaced Faster Quality (ImageWriter driver 2.3 and above) causes intermittent light and dark printing. Sometimes (whenever you use ImageWriter driver 2.0 and below) printout is light, and sometimes (ImageWriter driver 2.3 and above) printout is dark.

Because it's not obvious that the ImageWriter driver is at fault, many people just assume there's something wrong with the application disk and/or the printer. It's neither the application disk nor the printer. The problem is definitely in the driver. The fix is to replace all prior versions of the driver with ImageWriter driver version 2.3 or later. Then, every print job will be dark.

Later Versions of the ImageWriter Driver

Later versions of the ImageWriter driver (through version 2.7) are functionally identical to ImageWriter driver version 2.3, with one noticeable difference. Older versions of the ImageWriter driver locate their Page Setup... and Print... dialog boxes at fixed display coordinates. The fixed coordinates place the dialog boxes at the center of a 9-inch monitor, but place them way-off-to-the-left on larger monitors. With ImageWriter driver version 2.7, the Page Setup... and Print... dialog boxes appear in the middle of the display regardless of monitor size. That's inconsequential on a 9-inch Mac, but a welcome improvement on larger models.

For reference, the Page Setup... and Print... dialog boxes for ImageWriter driver 2.7 (part of System software 6.0.3, dated 1989) are shown in Figures 4-14 and 4-15. That's it for the ImageWriter driver. In Chapter 5, we'll explain the mysteries of Draft-quality printing, and show how to print in NLQ using the ImageWriter II.

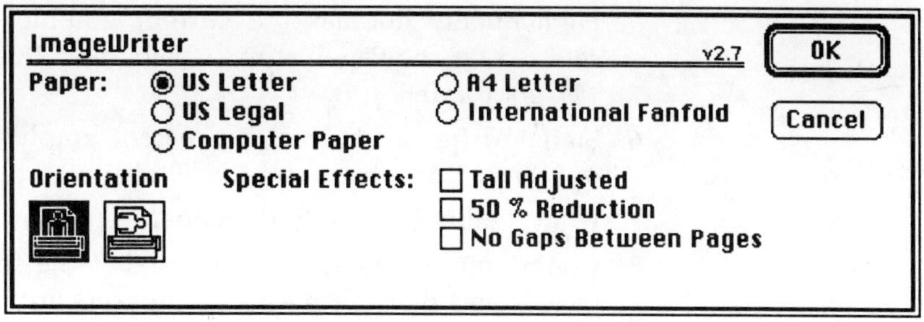

Figure 4-14 Page Setup... dialog box from ImageWriter driver version 2.7.

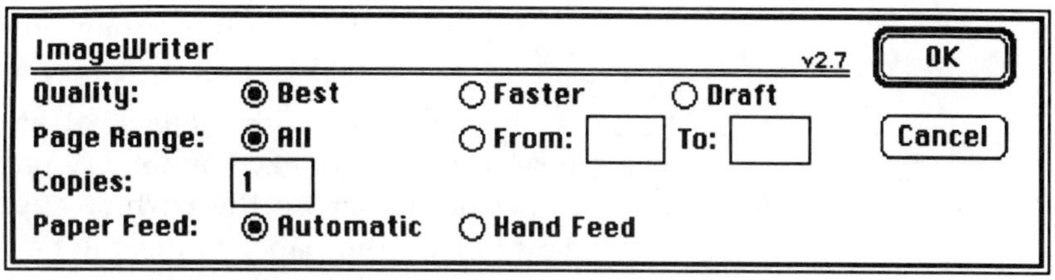

Figure 4-15 Print... dialog box from ImageWriter driver version 2.7.

Summary

The following important points summarize the concepts discussed in Chapter 4.

1. Tall Adjusted orientation indicates low-resolution graphics at 72 × 72 dpi, or high-resolution graphics at 144 × 144 dpi. With Tall-Adjusted orientation, what you see on the screen should be exactly what you get on paper.
2. Tall orientation indicates low-resolution nonWYSIWYG graphics at 80 × 72 dpi, or high-resolution nonWYSIWYG graphics at 160 × 144 dpi. Tall orientation results in a graphics-mode text printout that is slightly less jagged than WYSIWYG, but what you see on the screen is 11% (80 ÷ 72 = 1.11) *wider* than what you get on paper.
3. Wide orientation resembles a wide-angle photograph.
4. Word-processing rulers in MacWrite (versions 2.2 to 4.5) do not agree with tape measures that are held up to the screen! Even when the display is properly adjusted, MacWrite's 7-inch marker is approximately ⅔-inch too long!

5. High quality doubles the current graphics resolution (originally selected via the Page Setup… dialog box) from 72 dpi (or 80 dpi) to 144 dpi (or 160 dpi).
6. Standard quality halves the current graphics resolution from 144 dpi (or 160 dpi) to 72 dpi (or 80 dpi).
7. Draft quality is entirely dependent on printer-switch settings.
8. Continuous paper feed assumes that the friction clutch is disengaged, and that the pin-feed sprockets are engaged.
9. Cut Sheet paper feed assumes that the sprockets are disengaged, and that the friction clutch is engaged.
10. The friction clutch is engaged and disengaged with the printer's paper-release lever. If it's in the wrong position and you forget to check, the print job will jam after just a few pages.
11. Normal-pages pagination indicates that at least a ½-inch margin will appear at the top of each and every page, even when margins are not specifically set by the current application. Normal pages allows you to load the paper under the paper bail, the same as on a typewriter, and print without having to waste the first sheet of paper.
12. No breaks between pages pagination indicates that no margin should appear at the top of every page. In order to accomplish that, the first sheet of paper is wasted, and page one of the print job is printed from the top of the second sheet.
13. With 50-percent reduction, low-resolution, 8-inch × 10-inch layouts can be used in comfort, with much less eyestrain, to provide high-resolution 4-inch × 5-inch printouts.
14. Faster quality is a boldface version of Standard quality.
15. Faster quality is slower and darker than Standard quality.

CHAPTER 5

Draft Printing

When a computer printer malfunctions, the first question to ask is whether the problem is hardware-related or software-related. So far, we've looked at software-related problems that most people improperly blame on the hardware. In Chapter 1, we learned that a printout which garbles halfway down the page is often due to a handshaking problem in the ImageWriter driver. The driver is software. In Chapter 2, we learned that an intermittently jagged, Best quality (or High quality) printout is generally due to the absence of double-size fonts in the System file. The System file is software. In Chapter 4, we learned that an inconsistent light and dark printing is due to boldface printing differences between old and new versions of the ImageWriter driver—another software-related problem. While all very common, none of these problems has anything to do with circuit boards, gears, or other mechanical parts. None of them can be fixed by taking your printer into a repair shop.

In this chapter, we'll examine yet another software-related problem that can't be fixed in a repair shop—the bizarre word spacing which results whenever documents are printed in draft quality using the OEM ImageWriter driver. First we'll look at why that happens, and then we'll learn about a little-known method for working around it.

Finally, we'll examine printer speed ratings. We'll look at the mathematical definitions of characters per second (cps) and lines per minute (LPM) and show how to take both measurements with Test Character Generator.

The Symptoms of Bizarre Word Spacing

To view the bizarre word spacing which occurs whenever documents are printed in Draft quality with the OEM ImageWriter driver, you can use Test Character Generator, any Macintosh text editor, or any Macintosh word processor. To use Test Character Generator:

1. Load the ImageWriter with paper (if necessary) and turn it on.
2. Start your Macintosh, using a TCG startup disk.
3. Open the Miscellaneous folder (on the TCG startup disk), select a text file, and choose Open... from the File menu.
4. When the file is displayed, choose Print... from the File menu.
5. When the ImageWriter driver's print dialog box appears, click the Draft button, and then click the OK button.

As shown in Figure 5-1, the printout will typically consist of tiny, 15-cpi (characters per inch) type with unacceptably large spacing between words. When you hold the printout up to the screen, it won't look anything at all like the computer display.

The Cause of Bizarre Word Spacing

To view the cause of this problem, you can use the Imagewriter's built-in debugging mode, also known as the **hexadecimal-dump** mode. To enter the hex-dump mode:

1. SWITCH OFF—If it's already on, switch the printer off.
2. LOAD PAPER—Verify that 8½-inch-wide cut-sheet paper (or 9½-inch-wide pin-feed paper) is loaded into a standard-size printer. Verify that 14-inch-wide cut-sheet paper (or 14⅞- to 15-inch-wide pin-feed paper) is loaded into a wide-carriage printer. Load whatever the printer's maximum-size paper is, as necessary.
3. ENGAGE HEX-DUMP MODE—The next step varies from printer to printer. If the printer is an original Imagewriter (Standard or Wide), hold down the LINE FEED button, and, while keeping the LINE FEED button down, press the ON/OFF button. If the printer

> WARNING! Regarding step 2, nearly all built-in printer tests (a.k.a. Self-Tests) assume maximum-size paper. Use anything less than maximum-size paper, and printing may continue right past the edge of the paper and impact the platen!

Gettysburg Address

Fourscore and seven years ago our fathers brought forth on this continent a new nation, conceived in liberty and dedicated to the proposition that all men are created equal.

Now we are engaged in a great civil war, testing whether that nation or any nation so conceived and so dedicated can long endure. We are met on a great battlefield of that war. We have come to dedicate a portion of that field, as a final resting place for those who here gave their lives that that nation might live. It is altogether fitting and proper that we should do this.

But, in a larger sense, we can not dedicate-we can not consecrate-we can not hallow-this ground. The brave men, living and dead, who struggled here, have consecrated it, far above our poor power to add or detract. The world will little note, nor long remember, what we say here, but it can never forget what they did here. It is for us the living, rather, to be dedicated here to the unfinished work which they who fought here have this far so nobly advanced.

It is rather for us to be here dedicated to the great task remaining before us-that from these honored dead we take increased devotion to that cause for which they gave the last full measure of devotion-that we here highly resolve that these dead shall not have died in vain-that this nation, under God, shall have a new birth of freedom-and that government of the people, by the people, for the people shall not perish from the earth.

Figure 5-1 Typical Draft quality printout consists of tiny, 15-cpi type with unacceptably large spacing between words.

is an ImageWriter II, hold down the *select* button, and, while keeping the *select* button down, press the *on/off* button.

4. OPEN TEST FILE—Assuming that TCG is still running, choose Open... from the File menu, open the TCG Misc folder (on the TCG startup disk), select the TIAT.text (This is a test.) file, and click the Open button. As shown in Figure 5-2, the TIAT.text file contains a single sentence: This is a test.
5. BRING OUT PRINT... DIALOG BOX—When the TIAT.text file appears, choose Print... from the File menu.
6. ENTER PRINT... COMMANDS—When the ImageWriter driver's print dialog box appears, click the Draft button, and then click the OK button.

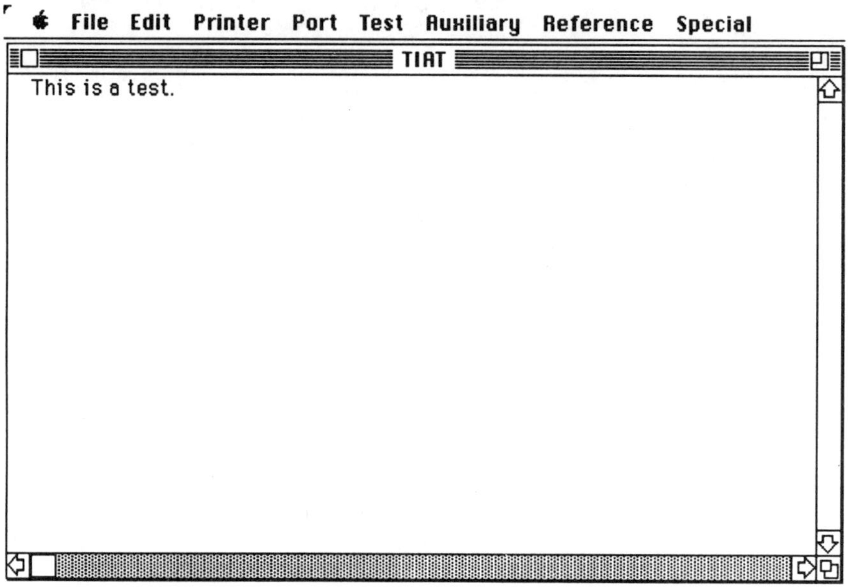

Figure 5-2 The TIAT.text file contains a single sentence: This is a test.

As shown in Figure 5-3, a hex-dump printout consists entirely of hexadecimal numbers. Unlike the previous printout, which only contains text, hex-dump printouts contain every instruction sent to the printer, as well as the text, including the mystery instruction which causes the word-spacing problem. To identify the instruction and solve the problem, all you have to do is decode the hex dump.

```
1B 3F 1B 6F 1B 3C 1B 66 1B 54 39 39 0A 1B 54 30 35 0A 1B 4E
1B 46 30 30 36 30 1B 71 0F 1B 22 1B 59 54 68 69 73 1B 4E 1B
46 30 30 39 31 1B 71 0F 1B 22 1B 59 69 73 1B 4E 1B 46 30 31
30 37 1B 71 0F 1B 22 1B 59 61 1B 4E 1B 46 30 31 31 38 1B 71
0F 1B 22 1B 59 74 65 73 74 2E 1B 3C 1B 66 1B 54 39 39 0A 0A
0A 0A 0A 0A 0A 0A 0A 0A 0A 0A 0A 1B 54 34 39 0A 1B 4E 1B 46
30 32 39 35 1B 71 0F 1B 22 1B 59 50 61 67 65 1B 4E 1B 46 30
33 32 38 1B 71 0F 1B 22 1B 59 2D 1B 4E 1B 46 30 33 33 39 1B
71 0F 1B 22 1B 59 31 1B 66 1B 54 39 39 0A 1B 54 34 35 0A 1B
59 0F 1B 5A 07 00 1B 54 32 34 1B 45 1B 3C 1B 22
```

Figure 5-3 The hex-dump printout of the TIAT file consists entirely of hexadecimal numbers.

Hexadecimal Numbers

The word decimal is derived from the Latin prefix **dec**, which means ten. December was originally the tenth month. (Prior to Pope Gregory, March was the first month). A decade is still ten years long.

Hexadecimal is derived from the Latin prefix **hex**, meaning six. A hexagram is a six-pointed star. A hexagonal window has six angles. Logically, the word hexadecimal indicates 6 (hex) plus (a) ten (dec) numerals (imals). Hexadecimal, 6 + 10, or base 16, works the same as decimal, (base 10), except that you count by 16s instead of by 10s.

Rather than counting 10, 20, 30, 40, 50, 60, 70, 80, 90, 100, 110, 120, 130, 140, 150, and 160, hexadecimal (translated into decimal) uses 16, 32, 48, 64, 80, 96, 112, 128, 144, 160, 176, 192, 208, 224, 240, and 256.

The digits representing the values 0 through 9 are the same in both numbering systems. In both decimal and hexadecimal, a 0 (zero) indicates the absence of quantity, and the digits from 1 to 9 indicate identical quantities. The big difference lies in how the decimal values 10 through 16 are represented in hexadecimal.

In hexadecimal:

1. Decimal 10 is represented by A.
2. Decimal 11 is represented by B.
3. Decimal 12 is represented by C.
4. Decimal 13 is represented by D.
5. Decimal 14 is represented by E.
6. Decimal 15 is represented by F.
7. Decimal 16 is represented by 10 (1×16).

Table 5-1 provides a decimal-to-hexadecimal conversion chart for the numbers 0 to 255. It's worth studying the table, so you can see how hexadecimal notation works.

Table 5-1. Decimal-to-Hexadecimal Conversion Chart

Dec	Hex	Dec	Hex	Dec	Hex	Dec	Hex	Dec	Hex	Dec	Hex
0 =	00	39 =	27	78 =	4E	117 =	75	156 =	9C	195 =	C3
1 =	01	40 =	28	79 =	4F	118 =	76	157 =	9D	196 =	C4
2 =	02	41 =	29	80 =	50	119 =	77	158 =	9E	197 =	C5
3 =	03	42 =	2A	81 =	51	120 =	78	159 =	9F	198 =	C6
4 =	04	43 =	2B	82 =	52	121 =	79	160 =	A0	199 =	C7
5 =	05	44 =	2C	83 =	53	122 =	7A	161 =	A1	200 =	C8
6 =	06	45 =	2D	84 =	54	123 =	7B	162 =	A2	201 =	C9
7 =	07	46 =	2E	85 =	55	124 =	7C	163 =	A3	202 =	CA
8 =	08	47 =	2F	86 =	56	125 =	7D	164 =	A4	203 =	CB
9 =	09	48 =	30	87 =	57	126 =	7E	165 =	A5	204 =	CC
10 =	0A	49 =	31	88 =	58	127 =	7F	166 =	A6	205 =	CD
11 =	0B	50 =	32	89 =	59	128 =	80	167 =	A7	206 =	CE
12 =	0C	51 =	33	90 =	5A	129 =	81	168 =	A8	207 =	CF
13 =	0D	52 =	34	91 =	5B	130 =	82	169 =	A9	208 =	D0
14 =	0E	53 =	35	92 =	5C	131 =	83	170 =	AA	209 =	D1
15 =	0F	54 =	36	93 =	5D	132 =	84	171 =	AB	210 =	D2
16 =	10	55 =	37	94 =	5E	133 =	85	172 =	AC	211 =	D3
17 =	11	56 =	38	95 =	5F	134 =	86	173 =	AD	212 =	D4
18 =	12	57 =	39	96 =	60	135 =	87	174 =	AE	213 =	D5
19 =	13	58 =	3A	97 =	61	136 =	88	175 =	AF	214 =	D6
20 =	14	59 =	3B	98 =	62	137 =	89	176 =	B0	215 =	D7
21 =	15	60 =	3C	99 =	63	138 =	8A	177 =	B1	216 =	D8
22 =	16	61 =	3D	100 =	64	139 =	8B	178 =	B2	217 =	D9
23 =	17	62 =	3E	101 =	65	140 =	8C	179 =	B3	218 =	DA
24 =	18	63 =	3F	102 =	66	141 =	8D	180 =	B4	219 =	DB
25 =	19	64 =	40	103 =	67	142 =	8E	181 =	B5	220 =	DC
26 =	1A	65 =	41	104 =	68	143 =	8F	182 =	B6	221 =	DD
27 =	1B	66 =	42	105 =	69	144 =	90	183 =	B7	222 =	DE
28 =	1C	67 =	43	106 =	6A	145 =	91	184 =	B8	223 =	DF
29 =	1D	68 =	44	107 =	6B	146 =	92	185 =	B9	224 =	E0
30 =	1E	69 =	45	108 =	6C	147 =	93	186 =	BA	225 =	E1
31 =	1F	70 =	46	109 =	6D	148 =	94	187 =	BB	226 =	E2
32 =	20	71 =	47	110 =	6E	149 =	95	188 =	BC	227 =	E3
33 =	21	72 =	48	111 =	6F	150 =	96	189 =	BD	228 =	E4
34 =	22	73 =	49	112 =	70	151 =	97	190 =	BE	229 =	E5
35 =	23	74 =	4A	113 =	71	152 =	98	191 =	BF	230 =	E6
36 =	24	75 =	4B	114 =	72	153 =	99	192 =	C0	231 =	E7
37 =	25	76 =	4C	115 =	73	154 =	9A	193 =	C1	232 =	E8
38 =	26	77 =	4D	116 =	74	155 =	9B	194 =	C2	233 =	E9

Table 5-1. *(continued)*

Dec Hex	Dec Hex	Dec Hex	Dec Hex	Dec Hex	Dec Hex
234 = EA	238 = EE	242 = F2	246 = F6	250 = FA	254 = FE
235 = EB	239 = EF	243 = F3	247 = F7	251 = FB	255 = FF
236 = EC	240 = F0	244 = F4	248 = F8	252 = FC	
237 = ED	241 = F1	245 = F5	249 = F9	253 = FD	

Looking at numerical conversions from the other direction, Table 5-2 provides a hexadecimal-to-decimal conversion chart. Hexadecimal-to-decimal conversion for the numbers 0 to FF is actually quite simple. Only two digits are involved. All you have to do is multiply the left (most-significant) hex digit by decimal 16 and add the decimal value of the right (least-significant) hex digit to the product (of the most-significant digit multiplied by decimal 16).

Table 5-2. Hexadecimal-to-Decimal Conversion Chart

Dec Hex	Dec Hex	Dec Hex	Dec Hex	Dec Hex	Dec Hex
00 = 0	15 = 21	2A = 42	3F = 63	54 = 84	69 = 105
01 = 1	16 = 22	2B = 43	40 = 64	55 = 85	6A = 106
02 = 2	17 = 23	2C = 44	41 = 65	56 = 86	6B = 107
03 = 3	18 = 24	2D = 45	42 = 66	57 = 87	6C = 108
04 = 4	19 = 25	2E = 46	43 = 67	58 = 88	6D = 109
05 = 5	1A = 26	2F = 47	44 = 68	59 = 89	6E = 110
06 = 6	1B = 27	30 = 48	45 = 69	5A = 90	6F = 111
07 = 7	1C = 28	31 = 49	46 = 70	5B = 91	70 = 112
08 = 8	1D = 29	32 = 50	47 = 71	5C = 92	71 = 113
09 = 9	1E = 30	33 = 51	48 = 72	5D = 93	72 = 114
0A = 10	1F = 31	34 = 52	49 = 73	5E = 94	73 = 115
0B = 11	20 = 32	35 = 53	4A = 74	5F = 95	74 = 116
0C = 12	21 = 33	36 = 54	4B = 75	60 = 96	75 = 117
0D = 13	22 = 34	37 = 55	4C = 76	61 = 97	76 = 118
0E = 14	23 = 35	38 = 56	4D = 77	62 = 98	77 = 119
0F = 15	24 = 36	39 = 57	4E = 78	63 = 99	78 = 120
10 = 16	25 = 37	3A = 58	4F = 79	64 = 100	79 = 121
11 = 17	26 = 38	3B = 59	50 = 80	65 = 101	7A = 122
12 = 18	27 = 39	3C = 60	51 = 81	66 = 102	7B = 123
13 = 19	28 = 40	3D = 61	52 = 82	67 = 103	7C = 124
14 = 20	29 = 41	3E = 62	53 = 83	68 = 104	7D = 125

(continued)

Table 5-2. *(continued)*

Dec	Hex	Dec	Hex	Dec	Hex	Dec	Hex	Dec	Hex	Dec	Hex
7E	= 126	94	= 148	AA	= 170	C0	= 192	D6	= 214	EC	= 236
7F	= 127	95	= 149	AB	= 171	C1	= 193	D7	= 215	ED	= 237
80	= 128	96	= 150	AC	= 172	C2	= 194	D8	= 216	EE	= 238
81	= 129	97	= 151	AD	= 173	C3	= 195	D9	= 217	EF	= 239
82	= 130	98	= 152	AE	= 174	C4	= 196	DA	= 218	F0	= 240
83	= 131	99	= 153	AF	= 175	C5	= 197	DB	= 219	F1	= 241
84	= 132	9A	= 154	B0	= 176	C6	= 198	DC	= 220	F2	= 242
85	= 133	9B	= 155	B1	= 177	C7	= 199	DD	= 221	F3	= 243
86	= 134	9C	= 156	B2	= 178	C8	= 200	DE	= 222	F4	= 244
87	= 135	9D	= 157	B3	= 179	C9	= 201	DF	= 223	F5	= 245
88	= 136	9E	= 158	B4	= 180	CA	= 202	E0	= 224	F6	= 246
89	= 137	9F	= 159	B5	= 181	CB	= 203	E1	= 225	F7	= 247
8A	= 138	A0	= 160	B6	= 182	CC	= 204	E2	= 226	F8	= 248
8B	= 139	A1	= 161	B7	= 183	CD	= 205	E3	= 227	F9	= 249
8C	= 140	A2	= 162	B8	= 184	CE	= 206	E4	= 228	FA	= 250
8D	= 141	A3	= 163	B9	= 185	CF	= 207	E5	= 229	FB	= 251
8E	= 142	A4	= 164	BA	= 186	D0	= 208	E6	= 230	FC	= 252
8F	= 143	A5	= 165	BB	= 187	D1	= 209	E7	= 231	FD	= 253
90	= 144	A6	= 166	BC	= 188	D2	= 210	E8	= 232	FE	= 254
91	= 145	A7	= 167	BD	= 189	D3	= 211	E9	= 233	FF	= 255
92	= 146	A8	= 168	BE	= 190	D4	= 212	EA	= 234		
93	= 147	A9	= 169	BF	= 191	D5	= 213	EB	= 235		

Once you understand the rules, hexadecimal 20 ((2 × 16) + 0) easily becomes decimal 32. Hexadecimal 1B ((1 × 16) + 11, *because hexadecimal B is decimal 11*) becomes decimal 27, and so on. All you need to remember in order to make hexadecimal-to-decimal conversions are three simple facts:

1. The decimal values of hex digits A through F are 10 through 15.
2. The most-significant (left) hex digit is multiplied by decimal 16.
3. The value of the least-significant (right) hex digit is added to the product of the most-significant digit that was multiplied by decimal 16.

On-line Conversion Calculator

As shown in Figure 5-4, TCG's Auxiliary menu contains a hexadecimal-to-decimal conversion calculator. This calculator makes it relatively simple to decode hex dumps. To use the calculator:

1. Start your Macintosh using a TCG startup disk.
2. Select the TCG icon and choose Open from the File menu.
3. When TCG's startup screen appears, click and hold down the mouse button, or press the return key to dismiss it.
4. Choose Decode Hex Dump from the Auxiliary menu.
5. Enter the number to convert.
6. Hit the return key.
7. Note the answer.
8. Enter a new number *and* hit the return key to continue; hit *just* the return key, without entering a new number, to quit.

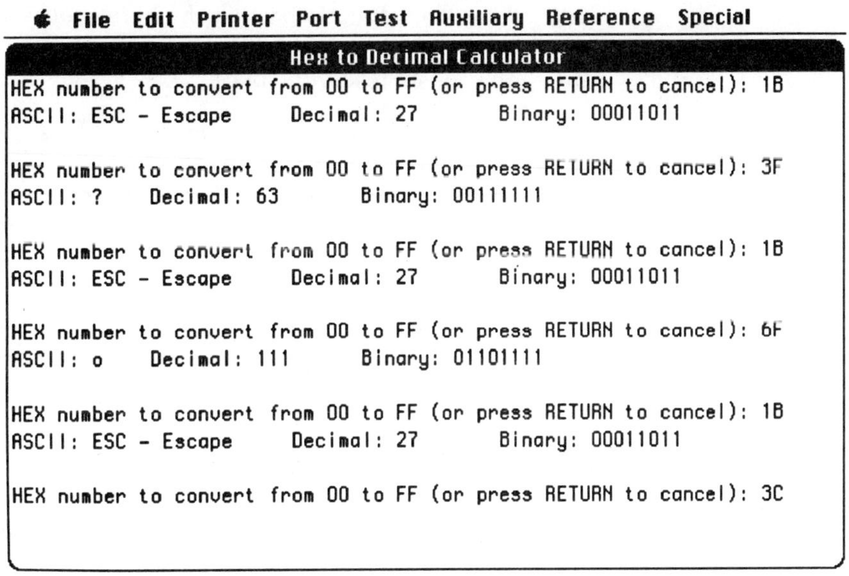

Figure 5-4 Test Character Generator Hex-to-Decimal Calculator.

As shown in Figure 5-4, the Hex-to-Decimal Calculator uses a PC-style command-line interface. Command-line interfaces are common in the PC world, but using one in a Macintosh program is just short of heresy. Instead, party-line programmers are expected to simulate real calculators by programming mouse-clickable buttons around a simulated numerical readout. There's nothing wrong with that, but I chose a command-line hex calculator for TCG because the command line is easier to program, it works just as well, and it's *much* faster to use. Try it and see for yourself!

Decoding a Hex Dump

Whether you do it mentally, look up the numbers in a chart, or use TCG's hexadecimal-to-decimal conversion calculator, decoding a hex dump is a simple, straightforward process:

1. First, the hex numbers have to be converted to decimal.
2. Next, the decimal numbers have to be converted to ASCII.
3. Finally, the ASCII characters have to be converted to printer codes.

Technically, you could bypass step 2 and go directly from hex to ASCII, but without familiar decimal numbers in the middle, it's easy to get confused. Table 5-3 provides the familiar decimal-to-ASCII conversion chart given in Chapter 1. Table 5-4 lists pertinent control codes. With all the conversion charts right here, you should be able to work through the hex-dump decoding exercise without having to flip pages and continuously lose your place.

Table 5-3. Decimal-to-ASCII Conversion Chart

32 =	48 = 0	64 = @	80 = P	96 = `	112 = p
33 = !	49 = 1	65 = A	81 = Q	97 = a	113 = q
34 = "	50 = 2	66 = B	82 = R	98 = b	114 = r
35 = #	51 = 3	67 = C	83 = S	99 = c	115 = s
36 = $	52 = 4	68 = D	84 = T	100 = d	116 = t
37 = %	53 = 5	69 = E	85 = U	101 = e	117 = u
38 = &	54 = 6	70 = F	86 = V	102 = f	118 = v
39 = '	55 = 7	71 = G	87 = W	103 = g	119 = w
40 = (	56 = 8	72 = H	88 = X	104 = h	120 = x
41 =)	57 = 9	73 = I	89 = Y	105 = i	121 = y
42 = *	58 = :	74 = J	90 = Z	106 = j	122 = z
43 = +	59 = ;	75 = K	91 = [	107 = k	123 = {
44 = ,	60 = <	76 = L	92 = \	108 = l	124 = |
45 = -	61 = =	77 = M	93 =]	109 = m	125 = }
46 = .	62 = >	78 = N	94 = ^	110 = n	126 = ~
47 = /	63 = ?	79 = O	95 = _	111 = o	127

NOTE: The blank space after the first equal sign indicates that ASCII 32 = SPACE; the missing equal sign after the last number indicates that ASCII 127 = DELETE.

Table 5-4. Selected Control Codes

Decimal	ASCII
9	HT (Horizontal Tab)
10	LF (Line Feed)
11	VT (Vertical Tab)
12	FF (Form Feed
13	CR (Carriage Return)
17	X-ON (Transmission On)
19	X-OFF (Transmission Off)
27	ESC (Escape—allows use of numerical codes > 31)

Step 3, where you have to convert ASCII characters into printer-control codes, is always the hardest part of the decoding process. As explained in Chapter 1, printer control codes vary from printer to printer. Epson control codes are different from Apple control codes. ImageWriter II codes are different from ImageWriter LQ codes.

Generally, a list of model-specific control codes is given in the owner's manual. In the event that your printer didn't come with a manual, or in case it's been misplaced, there's a comprehensive list of printer codes for the Imagewriter (Standard and Wide), the ImageWriter II, the LQ ImageWriter, and for Epson FX-compatible printers in Appendixes C through F.

You don't need to look in these appendixes right now. Table 5-5 contains all the information you need to decode Figure 5-3, and ultimately solve the bizarre word-spacing problem.

Table 5-5. Figure 5-3 Decoded

Hex	Decimal	ASCII	ImageWriter Meaning
1B 3F	27 63	ESC ?	Send printer ID
1B 6F	27 111	ESC .	Paper-out sensor ON
1B 3C	27 60	ESC <	Bidirectional ON
1B 66	27 102	ESC f	Forward line feed ON
1B 54 39 39	27 84 57 57	ESC T 99	$^{99}/_{144}$-inch distance between lines
0A	10	LF	Line feed
1B 54 30 35	27 84 48 53	ESC T 05	$^{05}/_{144}$-inch distance between lines
0A	10	LF	Line feed
1B 4E	27 78	ESC N	10 cpi Pica
1B 46	27 70	ESC F	Place print head

(continued)

Table 5-5. *(continued)*

Hex	Decimal	ASCII	ImageWriter Meaning
30 30 36 30	48 48 54 48	0 0 6 0	60 dots from left margin
1B 71	27 113	ESC q	15 cpi condensed
0F	15	CTRL-O	Double width OFF
1B 22	27 34	ESC "	Boldface OFF
1B 59	27 89	ESC Y	Underline OFF
54	84	T	Print T
68	104	h	Print h
69	105	i	Print i
73	99	s	Print s
1B 4E	27 78	ESC N	10 cpi Pica
1B 46	*27 70*	*ESC F*	*Place print head*
30 30 39 31	*48 48 57 49*	*0 0 9 1*	*91 dots from left margin*
1B 71	27 113	ESC q	15 cpi condensed
0F	15	CTRL-O	Double width OFF
1B 22	27 34	ESC "	Boldface OFF
1B 59	27 89	ESC Y	Underline OFF
69	105	i	Print i
73	99	s	Print s
1B 4E	27 78	ESC N	10 cpi Pica
1B 46	*27 70*	*ESC F*	*Place print head*
30 31 30 37	*48 49 48 55*	*0 1 0 7*	*107 dots from left margin*
1B 71	27 113	ESC q	15 cpi condensed
0F	15	CTRL-O	Double width OFF
1B 22	27 34	ESC "	Boldface OFF
1B 59	27 89	ESC Y	Underline OFF
61	97	a	Print a
1B 4E	27 78	ESC N	10 cpi Pica
1B 46	*27 70*	*ESC F*	*Place print head*
30 31 31 38	*48 49 49 56*	*0 1 1 8*	*118 dots from left margin*
1B 71	27 113	ESC q	15 cpi condensed
0F	15	CTRL-O	Double width OFF
1B 22	27 34	ESC "	Boldface OFF
1B 59	27 89	ESC Y	Underline OFF
74	100	t	Print t
65	86	e	Print e
73	99	s	Print s
74	100	t	Print t
2E	46	.	Print .
1B 3C	27 60	ESC <	Bidirectional ON

Table 5-5. *(continued)*

Hex	Decimal	ASCII	ImageWriter Meaning
1B 66	27 102	ESC f	Forward line feed ON
1B 54 39 39	27 84 57 57	ESC T 99	$^{99}/_{144}$-inch distance between lines
0A	10	LF	Line feed
0A	10	LF	Line feed
0A	10	LF	Line feed
0A	10	LF	Line feed
0A	10	LF	Line feed
0A	10	LF	Line feed
0A	10	LF	Line feed
0A	10	LF	Line feed
0A	10	LF	Line feed
0A	10	LF	Line feed
0A	10	LF	Line feed
0A	10	LF	Line feed
0A	10	LF	Line feed
1B 54 34 39	27 84 52 57	ESC T 49	$^{49}/_{144}$-inch distance between lines
0A	10	LF	Line feed
1B 4E	27 78	ESC N	10 cpi Pica
1B 46	27 70	ESC F	Place print head
30 32 39 35	48 50 57 53	0 2 9 5	295 dots from left margin
1B 71	27 113	ESC q	15 cpi condensed
0F	15	CTRL-O	Double width OFF
1B 22	27 34	ESC "	Boldface OFF
1B 59	27 89	ESC Y	Underline OFF
50	80	P	Print P
61	97	a	Print a
67	103	g	Print g
65	101	e	Print e
1B 4E	27 78	ESC N	10 cpi Pica
1B 46	*27 70*	*ESC F*	*Place print head*
30 33 32 38	*48 51 50 56*	*0 3 2 8*	*328 dots from left margin*
1B 71	27 113	ESC q	15 cpi condensed
0F	15	CTRL-O	Double width OFF
1B 22	27 34	ESC "	Boldface OFF
1B 59	27 89	ESC Y	Underline OFF
2D	45	-	Print -
1B 4E	27 78	ESC N	10 cpi Pica

(continued)

Table 5-5. *(continued)*

Hex	Decimal	ASCII	ImageWriter Meaning
1B 46	*27 70*	*ESC F*	*Place print head*
30 33 33 39	*48 51 51 57*	*0 3 3 9*	*339 dots from left margin*
1B 71	27 113	ESC q	15 cpi condensed
0F	15	CTRL-O	Double width OFF
1B 22	27 34	ESC "	Boldface OFF
1B 59	27 89	ESC Y	Underline OFF
31	49	1	Print 1
1B 66	27 102	ESC f	Forward line feed ON
1B 54 39 39	27 84 57 57	ESC T 99	99/144-inch distance between lines
0A	10	LF	Line feed
1B 54 34 35	27 84 52 53	ESC T 45	45/144-inch distance between lines
0A	10	LF	Line feed
1B 59	27 89	ESC Y	Underline OFF
0F	15	CTRL-O	Double width OFF
1B 5A 07	27 90 7 0	ESC Z BEL	Ring Bell
00	0	NUL	
1B 54 32 34	27 84 50 52	ESC T 24	24/144-inch distance between liness
1B 45	27 69	ESC E	12 cpi Elite
1B 3C	27 60	ESC <	Bidirectional ON
1B 22	27 34	ESC "	Boldface OFF

The Reason for the Tiny Type

The reason for the tiny type is found in line 12 of Table 5-5. Even though TCG displays all text files in the recommended Macintosh application font, Geneva 12, and even though the ImageWriter II is equipped with beautifully formed, near letter quality Pica 10 and Elite 12 character sets (both fixed-width and proportional), the ImageWriter driver substitutes ugly, 15-cpi, condensed characters. Appropriate or not, tiny type (1B 71) is what the driver code calls for.

The Reason for the Bizarre Word Spacing

The reason for the bizarre word spacing can be seen by examining the italicized lines in Table 5-5. Even though the TIAT file contains but four words (This is a test.), and even though the first three words are clearly separated by space characters (ASCII 32), the ImageWriter driver *ignores the space characters* (which were properly entered by pressing the space bar) and substitutes unwanted, inappropriate, graphics coordinates. This can be seen by examining the italicized lines immediately following the last letter in each of the first three words (This is a).

Presumably, the substitution of graphics coordinates for ASCII 32 space characters assures that field data will line up properly on a business form, even when you don't use a monospaced screen font. But what about NLQ business correspondence? Since the Mac's default, Geneva 12 screen font, is relatively large, while the ImageWriter's 15 CPI-Condensed character set is relatively small, the uneven spacing which occurs between words is completely unacceptable.

Fixing this problem would be simple. The ImageWriter driver's Page Setup.. dialog box simply needs a user-selectable draft option labeled: "Treat spaces as spaces." Until that happens (if ever), there are two known work-arounds.

The Usually Recommended Work-Around

The usually recommended work-around involves formatting the entire document in Monaco 12 or Courier 12. Unlike Geneva 12 which has a preprogrammed, variable-width, character rectangle, both Monaco 12 and Courier 12 have preprogrammed, uniform-width, character rectangles. Each Monaco 12 character rectangle measures 7-points wide × 16-points high. Each Courier-12 character rectangle measures 7-points wide × 12-points high. Both fonts work better than Geneva 12, but neither yields a 100% satisfactory draft-quality printout. The first objection has to do with line spacing.

Line-Spacing Problems Since the 16-point font height of Monaco 12 is 33% taller than the 12-point font height of Courier 12 (16 points − 12 points = 4 points; 4 points ÷ 12 points = 0.33), Courier 12 results in single-spaced draft printout at 6 lines per inch (72 dots per vertical inch ÷ 12 points per line = 6 lines per inch), while Monaco 12 results in 1.5-spaced draft printout at 4.5 lines per inch (72 dots per vertical inch ÷ 16 points per line = 4.5 lines per inch).

Since 1.5-spaced draft printout is usually not what you want, the fix (assuming Courier 12 is unavailable) is to format the document with 6 lines-per-inch spacing. If the program you happen to be using doesn't support 6 lines-per-inch spacing (some programs don't), the fix is to install Courier 12 into the System file using Font/DA Mover.

Word-Spacing Problems If you print in Tall (80-dpi) orientation, both screen fonts will cause 12-cpi Elite to be used in place of 15-cpi Condensed. The resulting word spacing is much better. The typical variation is less than 1 mm.

If you print in Tall-Adjusted (72-dpi) orientation, either screen font will still cause 12-cpi Elite to be used in place of 15-cpi Condensed, but the resulting word spacing is much worse. In Tall-Adjusted orientation, typical variation increases to 3 mm. That's to be expected. Tall-Adjusted (72 dpi) orientation is 11% wider than Tall orientation (80 dots per horizontal inch ÷ 72 dots per horizontal inch = 1.11); each line is 11% longer; individual words are that much further apart.

The Little-Known Work-Around

The only 100% satisfactory work-around involves typing the document in Monaco 12, carefully editing it, and then just before printing, switching to Monaco 10.

Unlike Monaco 12, Monaco 10 is not a real screen font. It doesn't exist, and it's not to be found on-disk anywhere. The scaled version which appears on the Macintosh display is also not a monospaced font. Nor is it a preprogrammed proportional font. Instead, what you get is a dynamic (continuously changing), variable-width font. In Monaco 10, character widths continuously change as you type! One moment, a character measures 7-points wide; the next moment, the same character measures 6-points wide.

The net result is that when you stop typing, each word, in every line, contains the correct mix of 6-point and 7-point characters for perfect draft-mode word spacing, provided you print using Tall-Adjusted orientation. In addition, Monaco-10 draft printout is always single spaced, even when applications do not support 6 lines per inch!

So, if Monaco 10 fixes the spacing problem, why not select Monaco 10 in the first place and just type away? There are two reasons. First, as can be seen in Figure 5-5, the simulated Monaco-10 screen font looks unattractive. Second, it's distracting to have previously entered words expand and contract as you type. Dynamic font width also slows down the computer display.

Nevertheless, as given in Table 5-6, the simulated Monaco-10 screen font is the only font that provides even draft-quality word spacing each and every time you print.

Further Experimentation

Table 5-7 provides ImageWriter II printer codes for the printer's other built-in character sets. To experiment with other screen fonts, print the TIAT.text (This is a test.) file from your favorite word processor using the ImageWriter's hex-dump mode, and then note the code locations circled in Figure 5-6.

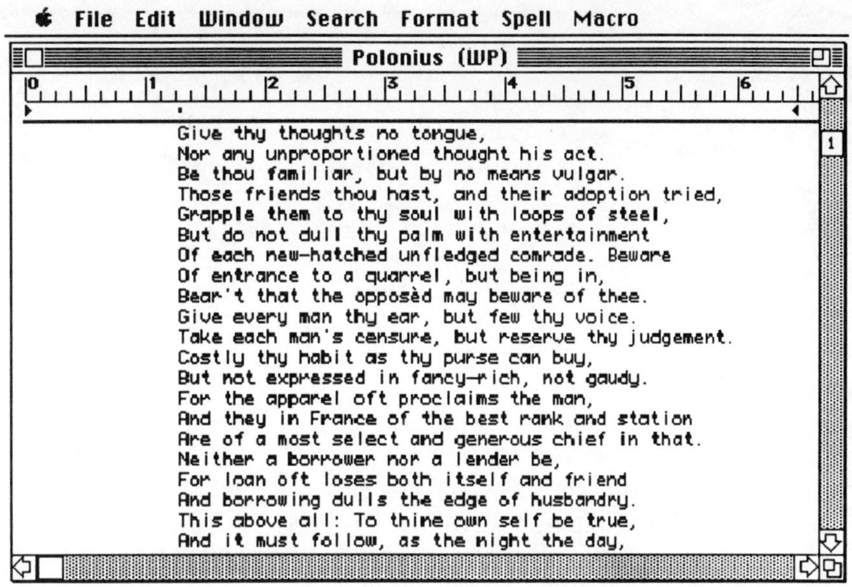

Figure 5-5 The simulated Monaco-10 screen font looks unattractive, but it provides a perfectly spaced, draft-quality printout.

Table 5-6. Macintosh Screen Font-to-ImageWriter Character Set Conversion Chart

Screen Font	Orientation	Character-Set CPI	Typical Word Spacing
Courier 9	Tall	Ultracondensed 17	1 to 2 mm (varies)
Courier 9	Tall Adjusted	Ultracondensed 17	1 to 4 mm (varies)
Courier 10	Tall	Condensed 15	2 to 4 mm (varies)
Courier 10	Tall Adjusted	Condensed 15	2 to 6 mm (varies)
Courier 12	Tall	Elite 12	2 to 3 mm (varies)
Courier 12	Tall Adjusted	Elite 12	3 to 6 mm (varies)
Monaco 9	Tall	Condensed 15	2 to 4 mm (varies)
Monaco 9	Tall Adjusted	Condensed 15	2 to 6 mm (varies)

(continued)

Table 5-6. *(continued)*

Screen Font	Orientation	Character-Set CPI	Typical Word Spacing
Monaco 10	Tall	Condensed 15	2 to 4 mm (varies)
Monaco 10	Tall Adjusted	Elite 12	2 mm (consistent)
Monaco 12	Tall	Elite 12	2 to 3 mm (varies)
Monaco 12	Tall Adjusted	Elite 12	3 to 6 mm (varies)

Table 5-7. Hexadecimal Codes for ImageWriter II Character Sets

Hex	Character Set	Pitch
1B 6E	Extended	9 cpi
1B 4E	Pica	10 cpi
1B 45	Elite	12 cpi
1B 70	Pica Proportional	Varies
1B 50	Elite Proportional	Varies
1B 65	Semicondensed	13.4 cpi
1B 71	Condensed	15 cpi
1B 51	Ultracondensed	17 cpi

```
1B 3F 1B 6F 1B 3C 1B 66 1B 54 39 39 0A 1B 54 30 35 0A 1B 4E
1B 46 30 30 36 30 1B 71 0F 1B 22 1B 59 54 68 69 73 1B 4E 1B
46 30 30 39 31 1B 71 0F 1B 22 1B 59 69 73 1B 4E 1B 46 30 31
30 37 1B 71 0F 1B 22 1B 59 61 1B 4E 1B 46 30 31 31 38 1B 71
0F 1B 22 1B 59 74 65 73 74 2E 1B 3C 1B 66 1B 54 39 39 0A 0A
0A 0A 0A 0A 0A 0A 0A 0A 0A 0A 0A 1B 54 34 39 0A 1B 4E 1B 46
30 32 39 35 1B 71 0F 1B 22 1B 59 50 61 67 65 1B 4E 1B 46 30
33 32 38 1B 71 0F 1B 22 1B 59 2D 1B 4E 1B 46 30 33 33 39 1B
71 0F 1B 22 1B 59 31 1B 66 1B 54 39 39 0A 1B 54 34 35 0A 1B
59 0F 1B 5A 07 00 1B 54 32 34 1B 45 1B 3C 1B 22
```

Figure 5-6 The first circled code selects the orientation (Tall vs. Tall Adjusted). The second circled code selects a built-in character set.

The first circled code indicates orientation. Tall (80 × 72 dpi) is always indicated by 1B 6E (9-cpi Extended), while Tall Adjusted (72 × 72 dpi) is always indicated by 1B 4E (10-cpi Pica). The second circled code selects a built-in character set. By experimenting with different screen fonts, you'll get varying results.

Identifying Built-in Character Sets To positively identify each character set, run TCG, select the appropriate printer from the Printer menu, select the appropriate port from the Port menu, and choose CPI - Character Sets from the Test menu. As shown in Figures 5-7 and 5-8, choosing Print... from the File menu will cause TCG to step through each of the printer's native character sets and accurately print out the results. Use the test printout for reference when experimenting with other screen fonts and/or testing other ImageWriter drivers.

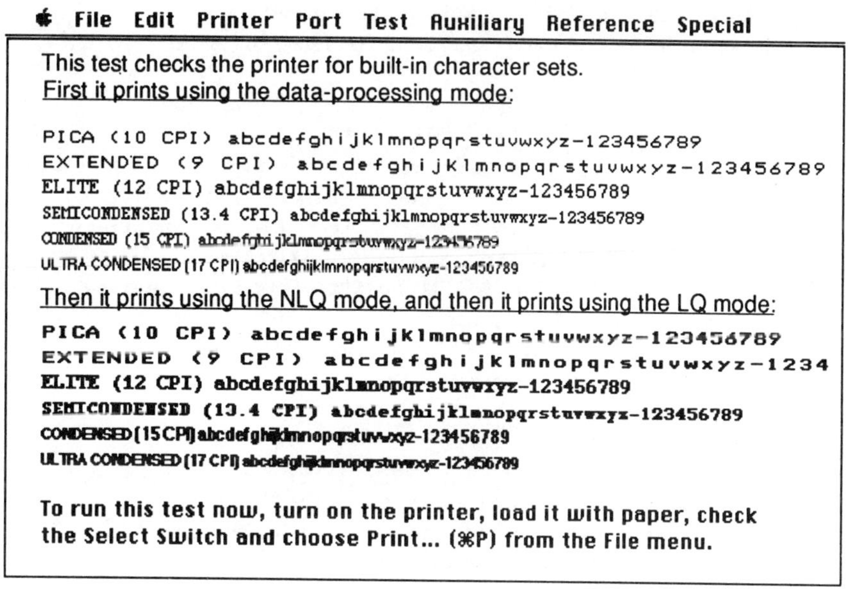

Figure 5-7 Test Character Generator CPI - Character Sets test.

Troubleshooting ImageWriter Compatibility Problems The hex-dump mode is a powerful general-purpose diagnostics tool. In addition to troubleshooting printer-driver problems, it can also be used to track down ImageWriter compatibility problems.

At least one so-called ImageWriter-compatible printer does not support **download characters**. As explained in Chapter 1, low-ASCII characters are the same for all printers and all computers, but high-ASCII characters differ, even within the Imagewriter family. The

CONTROL SECTION - DP (DATA PROCESSING)
PICA (10 CPI) abcdefghijklmnopqrstuvwxyz-123456789
EXTENDED (9 CPI) abcdefghijklmnopqrstuvwxyz-123456789
ELITE (12 CPI) abcdefghijklmnopqrstuvwxyz-123456789
SEMICONDENSED (13.4 CPI) abcdefghijklmnopqrstuvwxyz-123456789
CONDENSED (15CPI) abcdefghijklmnopqrstuvwxyz-123456789
ULTRA CONDENSED (17 CPI) abcdefghijklmnopqrstuvwxyz-123456789

TEST SECTION - NLQ (NEAR LETTER QUALITY)
PICA (10 CPI) abcdefghijklmnopqrstuvwxyz-123456789
PICA PROPORTIONAL (144 DPI) abcdefghijklmnopqrstuvwxyz-123456789
EXTENDED (9 CPI) abcdefghijklmnopqrstuvwxyz-123456789
ELITE (12 CPI) abcdefghijklmnopqrstuvwxyz-123456789
ELITE PROPORTIONAL (160 DPI) abcdefghijklmnopqrstuvwxyz-123456789
SEMICONDENSED (13.4 CPI) abcdefghijklmnopqrstuvwxyz-123456789
CONDENSED (15CPI) abcdefghijklmnopqrstuvwxyz-123456789
ULTRA CONDENSED (17 CPI) abcdefghijklmnopqrstuvwxyz-123456789

TEST SECTION - LQ (LETTER QUALITY)
PICA (10 CPI) abcdefghijklmnopqrstuvwxyz-123456789
PICA PROPORTIONAL (144 DPI) abcdefghijklmnopqrstuvwxyz-123456789
EXTENDED (9 CPI) abcdefghijklmnopqrstuvwxyz-123456789
ELITE (12 CPI) abcdefghijklmnopqrstuvwxyz-123456789
ELITE PROPORTIONAL (160 DPI) abcdefghijklmnopqrstuvwxyz-123456789
SEMICONDENSED (13.4 CPI) abcdefghijklmnopqrstuvwxyz-123456789
CONDENSED (15CPI) abcdefghijklmnopqrstuvwxyz-123456789
ULTRA CONDENSED (17 CPI) abcdefghijklmnopqrstuvwxyz-123456789

HOW TO INTERPRET THE TEST RESULTS:
Where NLQ is available, character sets in the NLQ-TEST section will be dark
and well formed, much darker than the same character sets in the CONTROL section.
Where LQ is available, character sets in the LQ-TEST section will be even
darker than the same character sets in the NLQ-TEST section.
If neither NLQ nor LQ is available, all character sets will appear to be the same.

Figure 5-8 Typical CPI test results from an ImageWriter LQ.

ImageWriter II contains high-ASCII, Mouse-Text characters for use with Apple II computers. The Imagewriter Standard, the Imagewriter Wide, and the ImageWriter LQ do not. None of the four ImageWriters contain high-ASCII characters compatible with the standard Macintosh System fonts.

To compensate, some programs (mostly desk accessories) download Mac-compatible high-ASCII characters into the printer's memory area prior to printing. The characters extend the ImageWriter's built-in ASCII character sets, making them compatible with standard Mac System fonts.

When download characters are not supported, 1B 49, the commence-download instruction, causes the printer to malfunction. How can you verify that it's the commence-download instruction and not some other problem? First, print out the file; then, print a matching hex dump. As shown earlier in this chapter, if you compare the two printouts, you'll find an 1B 49 (commence-download) instruction immediately preceding the problem.

In some cases, there's nothing to be done about it. In other cases, download support may be temporarily switched OFF. To turn it back ON, all you have to do is throw the appropriate DIP switch. "Which switch?" It should be marked on the printer, or listed in the owner's manual.

Measuring Printer Speed

Printer speed is always rated in cps (Characters Per Second), using a built-in character set, but most OEM's (Original Equipment Manufacturers) grossly exaggerate speed ratings, a curiosity you can easily prove by running Test Character Generator and choosing CPS - Throughput from the Test menu. TCG's CPS - Throughput test is shown in Figure 5-9.

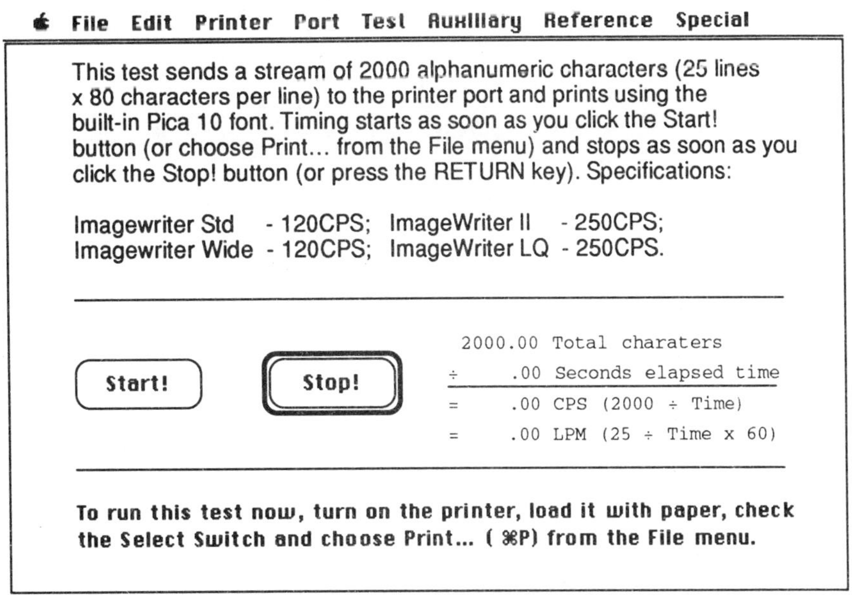

Figure 5-9 Test Character Generator CPS - Throughput test.

TCG's CPS - Throughput test bypasses the printer driver and sends a stream of 2000 alphanumeric characters (25 lines × 80 characters per line) to the selected printer port (whichever one is selected under the Port menu), using the printer's built-in Pica-10 font.

TCG's timer starts as soon as you click the Start! button (or choose Print... from the File menu) and stops as soon as you click the Stop! button (or press the return key). Pressing the return key seems to be a few hundredths of a second faster.

Because TCG has no way of knowing when the printer mechanism stops, you have to pay attention and count the lines as they go by. Click the Stop! button as soon as you hear the print head complete the twenty-fifth (last) line. Within normal reaction times, TCG's posted scores (cps = 2000 alphanumeric characters ÷ elapsed time) are accurate to about 1 character per second.

To confirm the scores, you might want to run the test a second time. Each test prints only 25 lines, so you can easily fit two tests on a single sheet of paper. To average the results, bring out the Mac's calculator desk accessory, add the scores, and divide by 2. Sometimes, there's a substantial difference between the first and second test. The reasons are explained below.

Note: In calculating printer speed, TCG's CPS - Throughput test does not count line feeds. Since the line feed (CHR$(10)) is a character, and since 25 line feeds are generated (one for each line) during the test, you may want to add that figure to the total number of alphanumeric characters (25 + 2000 = 2025) and divide the elapsed time into 2025.

Characters Per Second

Recalculating may increase the test score slightly—even so, many Imagewriter-compatible printers and many Epson-compatible printers test well below their published specifications!

Most OEM specifications are based on the time it takes to print a single line of 80 characters. Since printing a single line does not require the print head to reverse and drop to the next line (both of which take time), a single-line speed score is considerably higher. It's also completely irrelevant. People use printers for correspondence and reports. When was the last time you printed a report containing a single line of text?

Without taking the line feed into account, single-line scores above 80 cps are also illogical. The Pica-10 character set prints 10 characters to the inch. 10-inch-wide printer carriages are limited to an 8-inch line width; an 8-inch line width × 10-characters per inch = 80 characters per line *maximum*. So, if the printer has an 8-inch line width, and if it's rated at 240 characters per second, then, mathematically, it needs to execute 2 line feeds during that second as well. The first line feed occurs between the 80th and 81st characters; the second line feed occurs between the 160th and 161st characters. Ignore the time it takes to execute the line feeds and you don't have a logical characters-per-second rating. All you have is a characters-per-*fractional*-second rating.

The fact that almost every manufacturer does ignore line feeds doesn't make it right. Cps ratings based on fractional seconds (instead of whole seconds) are just as misleading as the theoretical instantaneous-peak-power (IPP) ratings that plagued the audio industry back in the 1970s. There are no two ways about it. If the published speed rating can't be sustained for at least one entire second, then it does not indicate characters per second.

Another factor that manufacturers tend to ignore has to do with built-in bidirectional-printing delays. When you load a fresh sheet of paper into an ImageWriter (II or LQ), or if you've just turned the printer on, you'll notice that bidirectional printing may be delayed for several lines. The reason for the delay is to improve registration at the top of the page. Nevertheless, the bidirectional-printing delay does slow down the printer, and because it does, it *must* be taken into account.

Some testing labs pretend that built-in bidirectional printing delays don't exist. Whenever I find one, I prefer to factor it in by running a second test and taking the average of the two scores. The two-test output (4000 characters) for 8½-inch wide paper is roughly equivalent to a one-page business letter. The average score gives a good indication of actual-use printer speed.

Lines Per Minute

TCG's other posted speed score, LPM (lines per minute), divides 25 total lines by the elapsed time to figure lines per second, and then multiplies by 60 (because there are 60 seconds in a minute) to figure lines per minute. The formula for LPM looks like this:

$$\text{LPM} = (25 \text{ total lines} \div \text{elapsed time in seconds}) \times 60$$

Thus, 25 total lines divided by elapsed time in seconds gives lines per second, and lines per second multiplied by 60 seconds per minute gives lines per minute.

In OEM literature, LPM is often listed as Throughput. The terms, LPM and Throughput, are generally synonymous. Either way, TCG's posted score is usually within one line of the manufacturer's specifications.

Running TCG's CPS - Throughput test and proving the scores on paper shows that OEM cps ratings are generally meaningless. Everyone refers to them, but they are unverifiable. The original Imagewriter, for example, has a 10-inch (standard size) carriage with an 8-inch print line. At 10 characters per inch, the built-in Pica-10 font can only fit 80 characters per line. According to page 101 of the "Apple Imagewriter Owner's Manual, Part I: Reference," cps is stated at 120 and LPM is stated at 72. Now, let's prove (or disprove) the statements, using figures right out of the OEM manual.

72 LPM × 80 characters per line = 5760 characters per minute

5760 characters per minute ÷ 60 seconds per minute = 96 cps

96 characters per second? The very same (OEM) manual specifies cps at 120 characters per second! Which is correct, the manual or the math? Run TCG and you'll *see* that the math is correct. 96 cps (plus or minus 1 cps for reaction time) is all the speed that it's got.

The fact that OEM math doesn't work out *proves* that something is wrong. You can't point the finger at any one manufacturer. They all do it. When you really want to know which is the fastest printer, take TCG into the store with you and measure cps for yourself, or go by the manufacturer's LPM ratings. If the OEM doesn't publish LPM ratings, run TCG and double-check the test scores on paper. Why double-check? Because TCG is just a program, and programmers make mistakes.

> For all of the above reasons, if you only remember one thing from this book, it should be this: *Always* confirm specifications by making your own calculations.

Optional Speed Tests

Holding down the option key while choosing CPS - Throughput from the Test menu will select the printer's built-in Elite 12 font (rather than the default Pica 10 font). Sometimes Elite 12 is actually faster than Pica 10, although, usually, it's just the opposite.

To switch back to Pica 10, reselect CPS - Throughput from the Test menu without holding down the Option key. In either case, if you press the Select button (to deselect the printer) and then press the printer's LQ button (to turn on LQ), or the NLQ button (to turn on NLQ), and then press the Select button again (to reselect the printer), the CPS - Throughput test will measure LQ or NLQ speed rather than Draft speed.

By varying character sets with the option key, you can measure six different printer speeds: Draft Pica 10, NLQ Pica 10, LQ Pica 10, Draft Elite 12, NLQ Elite 12, and LQ Elite 12.

Notes:

1. TCG issues a software reset after every CPS - Throughput test. The software reset restores the printer's standard instructions, so that the current instructions don't adversely affect other tests.
2. The data-processing mode is usually part of the printer's standard instructions. When running back-to-back NLQ or LQ tests, make sure that you reselect NLQ or LQ, as necessary, between trials.
3. On the ImageWriter II and the ImageWriter LQ, NLQ and LQ are selected with a *print-quality* button, not with NLQ and LQ buttons. There are no NLQ or LQ buttons on these models.
4. If the computer appears to hang on subsequent tests, check the printer's Select button! Chances are, you forgot to press it.
5. Remember, this is a hardware-level test. It assumes that a printer is directly connected to the specified serial port. It does not support Apple Talk and/or LocalTalk network adapters. The only thing that should be between the printer and the computer is a direct-connect printer cable.

Measuring Epson FX-Compatible Printer Speed

TCG's CPS - Throughput test works just as well with Epson FX compatible printers as it does with ImageWriter-compatible printers. Parallel Epson-compatible printers require a Mac-to-Imagewriter-Standard cable, a serial-to-parallel converter, and a Centronics-compatible parallel cable. Serial/parallel Epson-compatible printers only require a Mac-to-ImageWriter-Standard cable.

TCG turns any 512K Macintosh into an *informal* laboratory test instrument. You can use it to compare PC-compatible printers, even if you don't normally work with Macintoshes. Configuration and connection details (for hooking up serial-to-parallel converters to a Macintosh) are covered in Chapter 15.

Charting the Results

Figures 5-10 and 5-11 compare draft-mode cps and draft-mode LPM results for the Imagewriter Standard, the ImageWriter II, and the ImageWriter LQ. All tests were run with 8½-inch × 11-inch paper.

Figures 5-12 and 5-13 show how to format the data using Microsoft Works so that you can create your own charts.

To speed things up, a preprogrammed spreadsheet named PrinterSpeeds(SS).SYLK is included on the TCG disk. Originally created

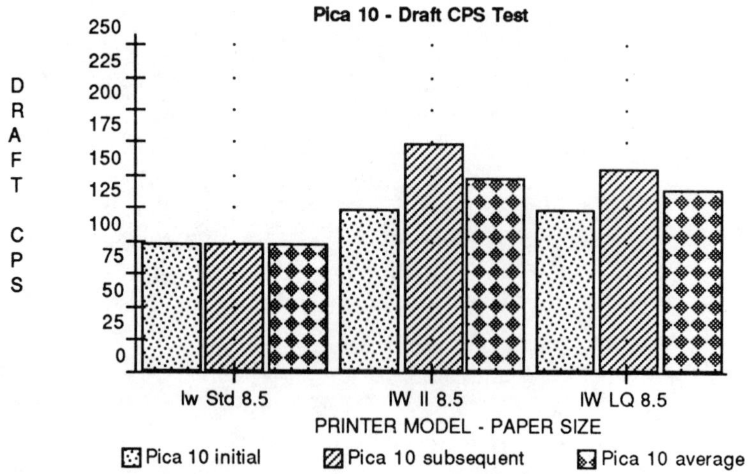

Figure 5-10 Draft cps test results. Microsoft Works chart indicates initial, subsequent, and average Pica-10 scores for the ImagewriterStandard, the ImageWriter II, and the ImageWriter LQ.

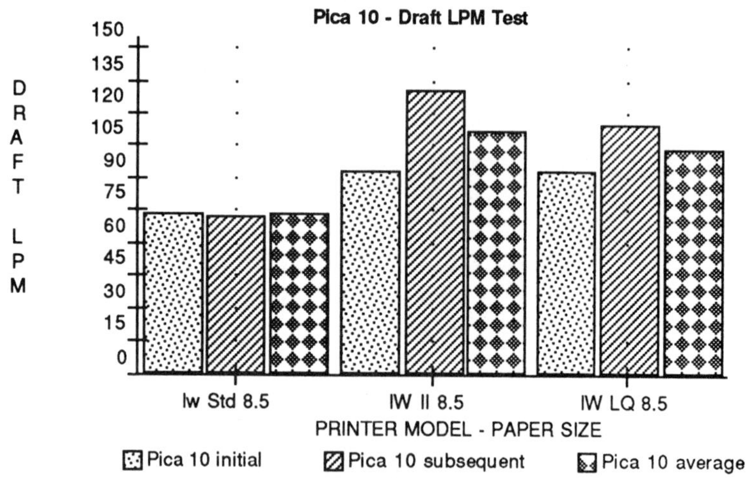

Figure 5-11 Draft LPM test results. Microsoft Works chart indicates initial, subsequent, and average Pica-10 scores for the Imagewriter Standard, the ImageWriter II, and the ImageWriter LQ.

		Imagewriter PRINTER SPEEDS			
DRAFT CPS	Iw Std 8.5	IW II 8.5	IW LQ 8.5	Iw Std 14	IW LQ 14
Pica 10 initial	96.71	121.73	121.95	0.00	144.74
Pica 10 subsequent	96.06	172.86	152.32	0.00	172.96
Pica 10 average	96.39	147.29	137.14	0.00	158.85
Elite 12 initial	66.07	120.85	123.84	0.00	145.70
Elite 12 subsequent	65.94	160.90	147.93	0.00	172.05
Elite 12 avg. CPS	66.01	140.88	135.89	0.00	158.88
DRAFT LPM	Iw Std 8.5	IW II 8.5	IW LQ 8.5	Iw Std 14	IW LQ 14
Pica 10 initial	72.53	91.30	91.46	0.00	65.79
Pica 10 subsequent	72.05	129.65	114.24	0.00	78.62
Pica 10 average	72.29	110.48	102.85	0.00	72.21
Elite 12 initial	49.55	90.63	92.88	0.00	66.23
Elite 12 subsequent	49.46	120.68	110.95	0.00	78.21
Elite 12 average	49.51	105.66	101.92	0.00	72.22
LQ CPS	Iw Std 8.5	IW II 8.5	IW LQ 8.5	Iw Std 14	IW LQ 14
Pica 10 initial	N/A	26.95	62.27	N/A	69.14
Pica 10 subsequent	N/A	28.74	67.16	N/A	74.64
Pica 10 average	0.00	27.85	64.72	0.00	71.89
Elite 12 initial	N/A	27.21	60.64	N/A	68.79
Elite 12 subsequent	N/A	29.13	65.10	N/A	74.04
Elite 12 average	0.00	28.17	62.87	0.00	71.42
LQ LPM	Iw Std 8.5	IW II 8.5	IW LQ 8.5	Iw Std 14	IW LQ 14
Pica 10 initial	N/A	20.21	46.70	N/A	31.43
Pica 10 subsequent	N/A	21.56	50.37	N/A	34.38
Pica 10 average	0.00	20.89	48.54	0.00	32.91
Elite 12 initial	N/A	20.41	45.48	N/A	31.27
Elite 12 subsequent	N/A	21.85	48.83	N/A	33.65
Elite 12 average	0.00	21.13	47.16	0.00	32.46
TECHNICIAN DATA					
Set tested by:	Larry P.	Larry P.	Larry P.		Larry P.
Using:	TCG 1.02a	TCG 1.01a	TCG 1.01a		TCG 1.02a
Date:	2/4/90	1/31/90	2/1/90		2/5/90

Figure 5-12 PrinterSpeeds(SS).SYLK. Note that the printer ID's (horizontal titles) start in column B and occupy the third row. Test ID's (data legends) start in the third row and occupy column A.

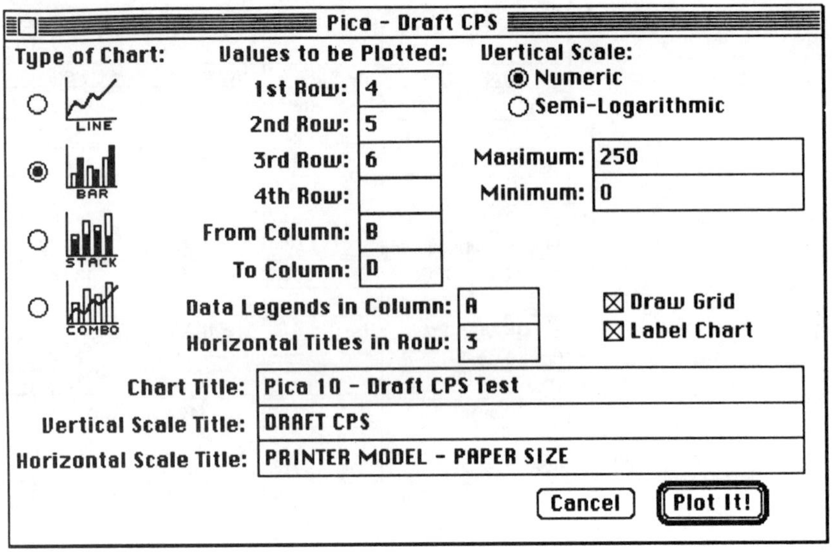

Figure 5-13 Use this chart definition for a graph similar to Figure 5-10.

using Microsoft Works v2.0a, it's provided in SYLK format for numerical compatibility with Microsoft Excel, Microsoft Multiplan, and earlier versions of Works. Even though you'll have to recreate the bar charts, starting from the supplied spreadsheet is a lot easier than starting from scratch!

> Note: The supplied SYLK file contains formatting information only. It's not a stand-alone spreadsheet program! Although you can open this file with Test Character Generator, you need Microsoft Excel, Microsoft Multiplan, Microsoft Works, or some other program capable of importing Microsoft.SYLK files to make use of it.

The charts shown in Figures 5-10 and 5-11 suggest that the ImageWriter II is the fastest of all the ImageWriter models. That's no mistake! In draft mode, it scores much higher than the original Imagewriter (Standard and Wide) and slightly higher than the ImageWriter LQ.

But, let's not sell the ImageWriter LQ short. Presumably, the main reason for buying an LQ printer is to print letter-quality documents. That's what the LQ was designed to do. As shown in Figures 5-14 and 5-15, the ImageWriter LQ scores twice as high as the ImageWriter II in letter-quality mode.

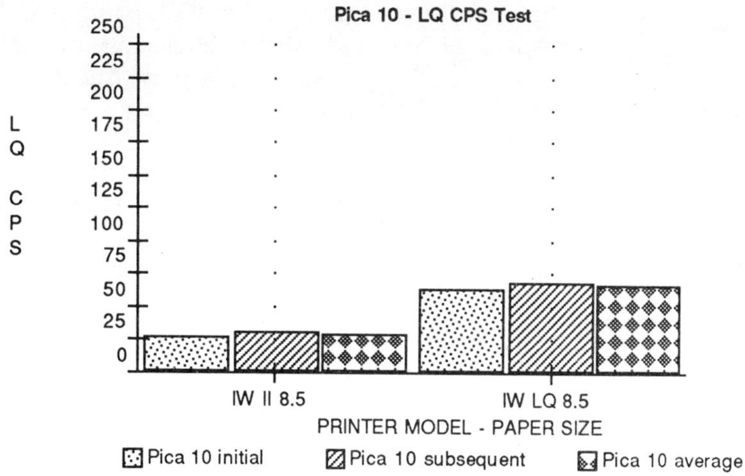

Figure 5-14 Letter-quality cps test results. Microsoft Works chart indicates initial, subsequent, and average Pica-10 scores for the ImageWriter II and the ImageWriter LQ.

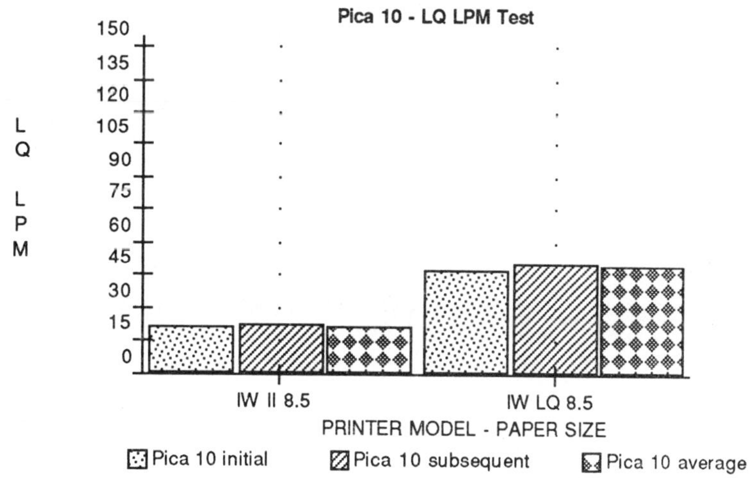

Figure 5-15 Letter-quality LPM test results. Microsoft Works chart indicates initial, subsequent, and average Pica-10 scores for the ImageWriter II and the ImageWriter LQ.

Effects of Baud Rate on Printer Speed

As explained in Chapter 1, baud rate (named for data-communications pioneer, Emile Baudot) is roughly equivalent to bits per second, the speed at which 1s and 0s are sent down the printer cable. The

Imagewriter driver is *fixed* at 9600 baud. The ImageWriter LQ driver is *fixed* at 19,200 baud. Many people assume that the faster the baud rate, the faster the printer. That's only true for speeds below 1200 baud. Above 1200 baud, the limiting factor is the top speed of the printer's carrier mechanism.

None of the ImageWriters released to date have carrier mechanisms that can work any faster than 1200 baud, so it doesn't matter how high the baud rate is set. The ImageWriter LQ tests no faster at 19,200 baud than it does at 9600 baud. Neither the ImageWriter LQ nor the ImageWriter II test any faster at 9600 baud than they do at 1200 baud!

The math behind these statements is explained in Chapter 10 under the heading "ImageWriter II to PC-compatible Setup Secrets," so we won't duplicate it here. There's an easy way to prove it to yourself though, using Test Character Generator.

As explained in Chapter 13, the baud rate on the ImageWriter LQ is *selectable*, using DIP switches 2-1 and 2-2. The default setting for use with the ImageWriter LQ driver (and TCG's ImageWriter LQ Printer-menu selection) is 19,200 baud. The alternate setting for use with ImageWriter driver v2.3 and above (and TCG's ImageWriter II Printer-menu selection) is 9600 baud.

Set the DIP switches to 9600 baud, and the ImageWriter LQ essentially becomes a wide-carriage ImageWriter II. To test the ImageWriter LQ's speed at 9600 baud, select ImageWriter II from TCG's Printer menu and run the CPS - Throughput test. The 9600-baud scores will be almost identical to the 19,200-baud scores. As usual, variations of ±2 cps can be attributed to human reaction times and should be disregarded.

So what's the advantage of higher baud rates? Aside from the possibility of faster carrier mechanisms, the higher the baud rate, the faster the data transfer. Assuming a large enough printer buffer (data-holding area), and printer-driver software designed to take advantage of large printer buffers, higher baud rates simply mean you'll get the computer back sooner. That's all. In general, Mac printer drivers do not take advantage of large printer buffers, so it's usually much ado about nothing.

> TCG.Pro (an enhanced version of TCG designed for testing labs) allows you to reconfigure the baud rate for each Printer menu selection. With TCG.Pro, you can speed-test the ImageWriter II all the way down to 300 baud. TCG.Pro contains many other advanced features. See Appendix B for a list of vendors.

Wide-Carriage Testing

Whenever you select a wide-carriage printer from the Printer menu, TCG returns a dialog box asking whether to configure tests for 14-inch-wide paper or 8½-inch-wide paper. As indicated in Figure 5-16, clicking the Yes button sets up all tests for 14-inch-wide paper; clicking the No button sets up the tests for 8½-inch-wide paper.

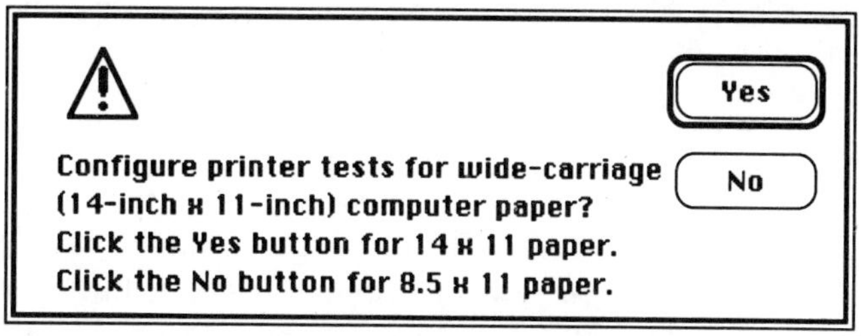

Figure 5-16 Whenever you select a wide-carriage printer from the Printer menu, TCG returns a dialog box asking whether to configure tests for 14-inch-wide paper or 8½-inch-wide paper.

This dialog box uses cut-sheet paper sizes. The corresponding pin-feed paper sizes are ⅞-inch to 1-inch wider than the cut-sheet paper sizes—14⅞-inches wide to 15-inches wide for a 15-inch (wide-carriage) printer, and 9⅜-inches wide to 9½-inches wide for a 10-inch (standard-size) printer.

In general, pin-feed paper widths are always an inch larger than cut-sheet paper widths. In addition, carriage widths are generally ½-inch larger than the maximum pin-feed paper width. These relationships can be summarized as follows:

1. The maximum-size paper for a 10-inch printer is 9½ inches.
2. The maximum-size paper for a 15-inch printer is 14½ inches.
3. Maximum-size paper is invariably sold as pin-feed paper.
4. Pin-feed paper is approximately 1 inch wider than cut-sheet paper.
5. A 10-inch carriage minus 1 inch for the pin-feed stubs minus ½ inch for the printer's hardware margins equals an 8-inch (80 column) print line.
6. A 15-inch carriage minus 1 inch for the pin-feed stubs minus ½ inch for the printer's hardware margins equals a 13½-inch (135 column) print line.

When you indicate 14-inch-wide paper, TCG uses 132 columns (not 135) for compatibility with industry-wide display standards.

Never indicate 14-inch-wide paper (132 columns) when you intend to use 8½-inch-wide paper! On a standard-size (80 column) printer, the extra 52 characters (132 − 80 = 52) wrap and overprint harmlessly, but on a wide-carriage (132 column) printer, they'll print right past the edge of the paper and impact the platen. That can damage the print head and the platen!

Other than annoying "Are-you-sure?" dialog boxes, there's no way for TCG to verify paper size. There's no sensor inside the printer that it can check. Indicate 14-inch paper and you'll get 132 columns every time, even when 80-column (8½ inch) paper is in the printer.

Interpreting Wide-Carriage Scores Cps scores pick up substantially when speed tests are run on 14-inch-wide paper, but LPM scores go down. In other words, 132-character lines result in *more* characters per second but *less* lines per minute. If you think about it, you'll see that it's an obvious, inverse relationship.

As a result of that relationship, wide-carriage printers generally test *much* faster than standard-carriage printers, but only when 14-inch-wide (132 column) paper is used. If you plan to use 8½-inch (80 column) paper most of the time, the speed difference between otherwise equivalent models (i.e., Imagewriter Standard vs. Imagewriter Wide) might be irrelevant. Bear that in mind when reporting and/or evaluating cps scores.

Summary

The following important points summarize the concepts discussed in Chapter 5.

1. When there is a computer/printer malfunction, the first question to ask is whether the problem is hardware related or software related.
2. Software-related problems cannot be fixed by taking your printer into a repair shop!
3. To pin-point software-related problems, most printers have a built-in debugging mode, also known as the hexadecimal-dump mode.
4. To enter the ImageWriter's hexadecimal-dump mode, switch off the power, hold down the ImageWriter's *select* button, and while keeping pressure on the ImageWriter's *select* button, switch the power back on.
5. To identify the particular software instruction causing a problem, all you have to do is decode the hex dump.
6. The tiny type which results when ImageWriter documents are printed in Draft quality is a software problem. Instead of default-

ing to Elite 12 or Pica 10, the printer driver usually substitutes ugly 15-cpi Condensed.

7. The bizarre word spacing which results whenever ImageWriter documents are printed in draft quality is also a software problem. Instead of printing properly entered space characters (ASCII 32) as space characters, the printer driver substitutes unwanted graphics coordinates.
8. The work-around for both problems is to set type in Monaco 12, and then, just before printing, select the entire document and switch typefaces to Monaco 10.
9. The hexadecimal-dump mode can also be used to track down ImageWriter-compatibility problems. At least one so-called Image-Writer-compatible printer is incompatible with desk accessories which rely on download characters.
10. Printer speed is always rated in cps (Characters Per Second), using a built-in character set, but most OEMs (Original Equipment Manufacturers) grossly exaggerate speed ratings.
11. If a published speed rating can *only* be sustained for a fraction of a second, then, logically, it does not indicate characters per whole second.
12. Unlike cps ratings, published LPM (Lines Per Minute) ratings are generally verifiable. TCG can usually verify them to within one LPM.
13. OEM LPM ratings are sometimes listed under Throughput. The terms LPM and Throughput are generally synonymous.
14. If you really want to know which is the fastest printer, take TCG into the store with you and measure CPS/LPM for yourself, or go by the manufacturer's published LPM (Throughput) ratings.

CHAPTER 6

Color Printing

This chapter examines monochrome and color printing, tells how various colors are mixed, identifies the seven standard colors, and shows how to print out a labeled color-identification chart. In the process, we uncover massive color confusion within the development community, and show how to print color graphics with any Macintosh from the 128K on up, using ImageWriter driver v2.3 (or later) and an ImageWriter II.

At this point, the instructions assume that you've made a TCG/System disk, and that you're generally familiar with printer drivers. If necessary, please review Chapter 4 before proceeding.

Monochrome Printing

In order to understand what color printing is all about, it's important to understand how the words *color* and *monochrome* are used in connection with computer equipment. Both words are used as adjectives. The word monochrome, is from the Greek roots *monos*, meaning one, and *chroma*, meaning color. **Monochrome** simply means one color. There are no restrictions on the one color. Monochrome can mean any color you like, as long as it doesn't mean more than one color at a time.

Monochrome Ribbons

The most common monochrome ribbon color is black. But solid-red, solid-green, and solid-blue ribbons are also popular. Simply by installing various solid-color (monochrome) ribbons in an original Imagewriter (Standard or Wide), you can vary the output color.

A solid-red business letter would be inappropriate, but red or green holiday mailing labels look very nice. So does blue ink on a light-gray paper. For a personal (feminine) touch, try violet ink on light-blue paper.

Fitting an original Imagewriter (Standard or Wide) with a monochrome ribbon is no substitute for an ImageWriter II or an ImageWriter LQ equipped with a multicolor ribbon, but provided your monochrome choices are coordinated to the paper color, they can liven up routine correspondence, and add a whole new dimension to the personal computer experience. Drive your printer with Adobe Type Manager™ as described in Chapter 3, periodically adjust the bidirectional alignment as described in Chapter 9, and you'll get surprisingly crisp output.

Monochrome ribbons cost only slightly more than regular black ribbons. Check Appendix B for a list of vendors.

Color Printing

While monochrome refers to one color, the adjective color without any prefix implies **multicolor**. Multicolor printers like ImageWriter II, ImageWriter LQ, and the Toshiba P321SLC allow you to switch colors *without* having to change ribbons. Even then, monochrome printing is the default mode. In order to switch colors on-the-run, you also need:

1. *ImageWriter II*—ImageWriter driver v2.3, a 4-color ribbon, any Mac from the original 128K on up, and a color-graphics program.
2. *ImageWriter LQ*—ImageWriter driver v2.3, a 4-color ribbon, any Mac from the original 128K on up, and a color-graphics program.
3. *ImageWriter LQ*—LQ ImageWriter driver v2.0, a 4-color ribbon, any Mac from the Mac Plus (or equivalent) on up, and a color-graphics program.
4. *Toshiba P321SLC*—Toshiba MacMatrix Printer driver v1.0, 4-color ribbon, any Mac from the Mac Plus (or equivalent) on up, and a color-graphics program.

In addition, both the LQ ImageWriter printer driver and the Toshiba MacMatrix printer driver require Macintosh System software

6.0, or later. In both cases, this is a driver requirement, not a printer requirement. As noted above, the ImageWriter LQ is fully compatible with ImageWriter driver v2.3, which is, in turn, compatible with every Mac ever made, including the original 128K. All you need to do is reset the printer's baud rate from 19,200 baud to 9600 baud. Baud rate on the ImageWriter LQ is selected via DIP switches SW2-1 and SW2-2. Full details are in Chapter 13.

Color Ribbons

Figure 6-1 shows monochrome (1-color) and 4-color ribbons designed for the ImageWriter II. Note how much larger the 4-color ribbon is. The 4-color ribbon *only* fits the ImageWriter II. The monochrome ribbon fits in the Imagewriter Standard, the Imagewriter Wide, *and* the ImageWriter II. As shown by the ribbons in Figure 6-2, neither ribbon fits an ImageWriter LQ.

Figure 6-1 Monochrome and 4-color ribbons for the ImageWriter II.

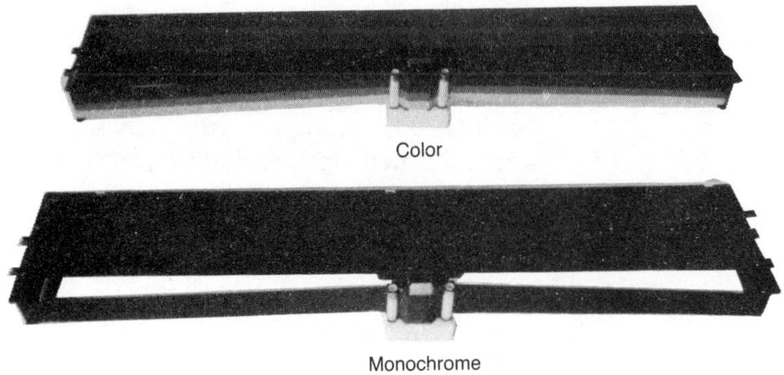

Figure 6-2 Monochrome and 4-color ribbons for the ImageWriter LQ.

By studying these pictures, we can conclude that:

1. Monochrome Imagewriter ribbons fit the original Imagewriter (Standard), the Imagewriter Wide, *and* the ImageWriter II.
2. The 4-color ImageWriter ribbons *only* fit the ImageWriter II.
3. ImageWriter LQ ribbons (monochrome or color) are ImageWriter LQ specific. They don't fit *any* of the earlier ImageWriters.

Mixing Colors

As shown in Figures 6-1 and 6-2, 4-color ImageWriter ribbons contain discrete color bands. Starting from the top, the four colors are black, cyan, magenta, and yellow. Based on visual observation, it's logical to assume that the printer can *only* produce these colors, but that's not true. By mixing yellow and magenta, both the ImageWriter II and the ImageWriter LQ produce orange. By mixing yellow and cyan, both printers produce green. Purple is produced by mixing magenta and cyan.

Black, yellow, magenta, cyan, orange, green, and purple are called the seven **standard colors**, because they're supported at the printer's hardware level. To use them, programs don't have to do anything but ask the printer for them.

Additional colors are also possible, but they have to be mixed under software control. In every case, the lightest color is always printed first, followed by a carriage return with no line feed. Then, darker colors are overprinted, one at a time. That explains why color printing takes so much longer than monochrome printing. It takes a lot of passes to mix exotic colors!

TCG's Color Ribbon Alignment Test

To view the seven standard colors (assuming an ImageWriter II or an ImageWriter LQ equipped with a color ribbon), TCG provides a Color Ribbon Alignment test. This test prints a repeating text pattern in the seven standard colors.

This test is normally used to check color-ribbon alignment and to reposition broken color cams, but it can also be used to print out a color-identification chart. Unlike the Imagewriter II's built-in test (which leaves you guessing), TCG's test identifies the seven standard colors by listing their most-recent proper names. To print a color chart:

1. Start your Macintosh in the normal way and run TCG.
2. Hold the mouse button down (or press the return key) to dismiss the startup screen.

3. Click the close box (or choose Close from the File menu) to dismiss the General Instructions window.
4. Select a printer from the Printer menu.
5. Indicate the current printer port with the Port menu.
6. Choose Color Ribbon Alignment from TCG's Test menu.
7. Turn on the printer, load it with paper, check the select switch, and choose Print... from the File menu.
8. When TCG asks you to "Repeat this test?", click the No button. Since we're not actually aligning the printer right now, all we need is one pass. Clicking the No button stops the test, returns you to TCG, and ejects the paper.

Don't worry if the colors overlap slightly on character descenders and underlines. This indicates that the color cam is out of alignment. It's a common problem and is easily repaired. Full details are given in Chapter 11. The only purpose for this exercise right now is to print out a labeled color-identification chart.

Believe it or not, with the exception of occasional red accents, the ImageWriter II Owner's Guide is printed entirely in black and white. It doesn't contain a color chart! There's also no color chart in the ImageWriter II Technical Reference Manual! With no color chart built into the ImageWriter II's self test, and no color charts in either manual, how do you tell which color is which?

The omission of labeled color charts, combined with the editing of previously established color names, has resulted in a massive color confusion, not just among customers, but also within the entire development community.

Color Confusion

An eye-opening color cross-reference chart for the ImageWriter II and the ImageWriter LQ is provided on the card inserted in this book. Columns 1, 2, and 3 compare the OEM Owner's Guides for the ImageWriter II and the ImageWriter LQ to their corresponding Reference manuals. Columns 4 to 7 compare the OEM literature to the actual implementation, using SuperPaint v1.1MS, Microsoft Works v2.0a, Microsoft Word v4.0, and TCG v1.0a as examples.

Rationale Behind the Program Choices

SuperPaint v1.1MS (MS for Microsoft) was chosen because it's bundled with Microsoft Word 4.0. Both SuperPaint and Word are best-selling, color graphics programs. Every graphic in Sams book, *Macintosh Repair & Upgrade Secrets*, was drawn with SuperPaint. Only two of the graphics in this book were not.

Microsoft Works 2.0a was chosen because it's another best seller from the same software house as Microsoft Word. *Macintosh Repair & Upgrade Secrets* was written entirely in Microsoft Works, enhanced by Lundeen and Associates' WorksPlus Spell. So was *Macintosh Printer Secrets*. Test Character Generator was chosen because I'm the author, and it's the color-diagnostics program bundled with *Macintosh Printer Secrets*.

Before we go any further, let me say that Microsoft Word, Microsoft Works, and SuperPaint are three of my favorite programs. Even though the color-printing secrets about to be revealed are completely bizarre, nothing you're about to read is intended to discredit these programs in any way. I chose them because I'm familiar with them, and I use them every day.

Interpreting the Chart

By comparing columns 1, 2, and 3 (on the insert card), you'll see that two of the original seven standard colors listed in the ImageWriter II Owner's Guide (p. 114) were arbitrarily renamed in the ImageWriter II Technical Reference Manual (p. 204). Red became magenta; blue became cyan. Note that the colors themselves did not change, only their names changed. So if you're a developer, what labels do you choose for *your* red and blue items? Do you agree with the ImageWriter II Owner's Guide, or the ImageWriter II Technical Reference Manual?

Comparing column 4 to column 1 (on the insert card), we see that SuperPaint v1.1MS agrees with the ImageWriter II Owner's Guide. That's a wise decision. Presumably, everyone gets an Owner's Guide. Relatively few owners buy the Technical Reference Manual. The logic is good. It's the kind of decision I would have made. I'm glad it wasn't mine to make, though. Microsoft Word v4.0 (which comes in the very same package as part of the Word/SuperPaint bundle) agrees with the ImageWriter II Technical Reference Manual.

As a result of the color name changes, Red in SuperPaint is the same as Magenta in Word, Red in Word is the same as Orange in SuperPaint, and Blue in SuperPaint is the same as Cyan in Word. Blue in Word is the same as Purple in SuperPaint.

Note that Word's substitution of blue for purple is completely unique. It agrees neither with the ImageWriter II Owner's Guide, nor the ImageWriter II Technical Reference Manual. Word only agrees with Works.

In deciding what labels to use for TCG's Color Ribbon Alignment test, I examined all of the manuals listed in columns 1 and 2, and I examined the card insert chart. I finally decided to agree with the ImageWriter II Technical Reference Manual. It agrees with both the ImageWriter LQ Owner's Guide, and the ImageWriter LQ Reference manual. All three were published subsequent to the ImageWriter II Owner's Guide. I saw three out of four and went with the percentages.

Frustration Unless you've actually tried to produce color graphics, you can't possibly imagine how frustrating the color inconsistency is. Standard 9-inch Macintosh monitors are black-and-white. They don't display colors, nor do Mac programs display color-formatting information at the bottom of the screen like their PC-compatible counterparts. Instead, you've got to take color consistency on faith. Logically, you *should* be able to do that. Unfortunately, you can't.

If you still can't relate to this, imagine having ordered the car of your youthful dreams—a new red convertible. You always see red convertibles in car ads. Now, imagine that the car that they tried to deliver was bright orange. Would you take it? When was the last time you saw bright orange paint on a new convertible? Not on a new car, lately!

Color-Printing Test for Older Software

One of the files on the TCG disk is a color-printing test for MacWrite v2.2 and above. Figure 6-3 shows the file icon. If you view this file on a standard black-and-white Macintosh (MacWrite-compatible software required), the lines appear to be standard black. But if you print the file to an ImageWriter II or an ImageWriter LQ equipped with a 4-color ribbon, the lines print in color!

Figure 6-3 File icon for Color PRN Test.MacWrite 2.2.

This test proves that even though there are no color options on the MacWrite 2.2 Style menu, the program does support color. So do many of the other early Macintosh programs. All you generally need is ImageWriter driver v2.3 (or later), a 4-color ribbon for your ImageWriter II, and a color-graphics program to create the artwork.

That's it for color printing. Next we'll look at margins.

Summary

The following important points summarize the concepts discussed in Chapter 6.

1. **Monochrome** is from the Greek roots monos, meaning one, and chroma, meaning color.
2. Monochrome can mean any color you like, as long as it doesn't mean more than one color at a time.
3. By simply installing various monochrome ribbons in an original Imagewriter (Standard or Wide), you can vary the output color.
4. Color, when used as an adjective, generally implies **multicolor**.
5. ImageWriter monochrome ribbons fit the Imagewriter Standard, the Imagewriter Wide, *and* the ImageWriter II.
6. ImageWriter 4-color ribbons *only* fit the ImageWriter II.
7. ImageWriter LQ ribbons (monochrome or color) are ImageWriter LQ specific. They don't fit *any* of the earlier ImageWriters.
8. ImageWriter 4-color ribbons contain discrete color bands. Starting from the top of the ribbon, the four colors are black, cyan, magenta, and yellow. These colors can be mixed to provide additional colors.
9. Black, yellow, magenta, cyan, orange, green, and purple are called the seven **standard colors**, because they're supported at the printer's hardware level.
10. Color names are inconsistent from one program to another.
11. Red in SuperPaint v1.1MS is the same color identified as Magenta in Word v4.0.
12. Red in Word v4.0 is the same color identified as Orange in SuperPaint v1.1MS.
13. Blue in SuperPaint v1.1MS is the same color identified as Cyan in Word 4.0.
14. Blue in Word v4.0 is the same color identified as Purple in SuperPaint v1.1MS.
15. Even though there are no color options on the MacWrite 2.2 Style menu, the program does support color. All you generally need is ImageWriter driver v2.3 (or later), a 4-color ribbon for your ImageWriter II, and a color-graphics program to create the artwork.

CHAPTER

7

Margins

This chapter looks at Macintosh margins. If you've ever been frustrated by page creep on the original Imagewriter, if you've ever wondered why sometimes margins start further to the left, further to the right, further up, or further down than other at times, you'll find definitive explanations here. We also show how to stop rollback on the ImageWriter II, and we document TCG's unique Tractor—TOF (Top of Form) Alignment test.

At this point, the instructions assume that you've made a TCG/System disk, that you're generally familiar with printer drivers, and that you understand the difference between Tall and Tall-Adjusted orientation. If necessary, please review Chapters 3 and 4 before proceeding.

Definitions—Paper, Page, and Margins

As used throughout this book, **paper** is defined as a substance made from rags, straw, wood, or other fibrous material. All papers have physical size (width and height). Inset on the paper is the page. **Page** refers to the printed part of the paper—the *printed* page. Unprinted areas which fall *between* the paper and the page are called **margins**. These terms (as defined by the original Imagewriter driver) are illustrated in Figure 7-1.

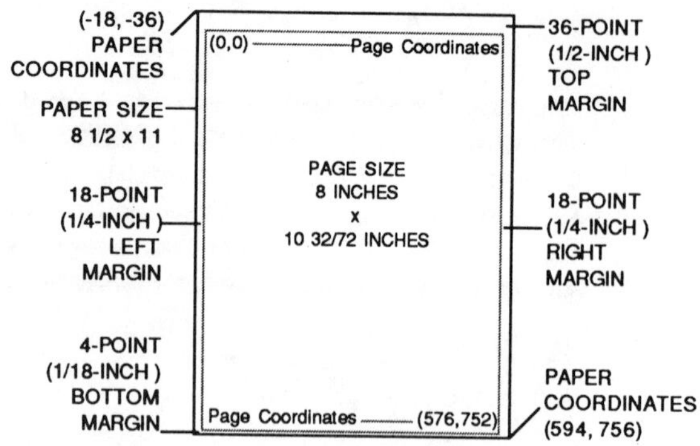

Figure 7-1 Margins, paper size, and page size as defined by the original Imagewriter driver.

Paper Coordinates vs. Page Coordinates

Paper is normally measured in inches (8½ × 11, for US Letter-size paper) and/or millimeters (210 × 297, for A4 Letter-size paper), but Macintosh printer drivers measure paper in terms of resolution (at 72 dpi or 80 dpi), using algebraic (x, y) – (xx, yy) coordinates.

Since all drawing takes place on the page, and since it's easier to plot exact positions relative to position zero, the upper left corner of the page is given the coordinates (0, 0). The upper left corner of the paper, where no drawing takes place, is given negative coordinates (−x, −y), which vary.

As illustrated in Figure 7-2, the minimum value of the negative paper coordinates is determined by the hardware margins of the printer.

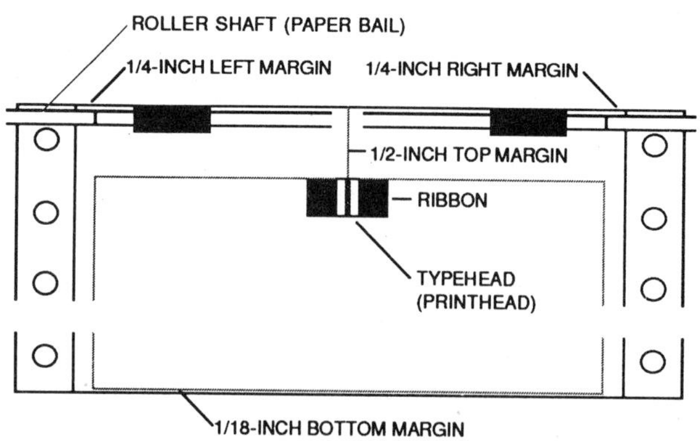

Figure 7-2 Hardware margins of the Imagewriter Standard printer.

Hardware Margins

The expression "hardware margins" refers to the physical relationship between a single sheet of maximum-size paper and the printer itself. No printer can completely cover a single sheet of maximum-size paper. The maximum paper size is always bigger than the maximum page size. The difference between the maximum paper size and the maximum page size is called the **hardware margin**.

At 72 dpi (dots per inch), the coordinates (−18, −36) shown in Figure 7-1 tell us that the default left margin for the original Imagewriter is ¼ inch (18/72 = 0.25), and that the default top margin for the original Imagewriter (Standard) is ½ inch (−36/72 = −0.50). In other words, assuming Tall-Adjusted orientation, and assuming that 8½ × 11-inch paper has been properly loaded into the printer, there'll be at least a ¼-inch white space to the left of the page, and at least a ½-inch white space at the top of the page.

Notice where the ½-inch top margin comes from: the top of the type head (print head), which is hardware, is approximately ½ inch below the top of the roller shaft (paper bail), which is also hardware. If the default top margin were any less than ½ inch, printing would have to take place on continuous paper (not cut paper), and the first sheet of paper would have to be wasted. This situation is illustrated in Figure 7-3.

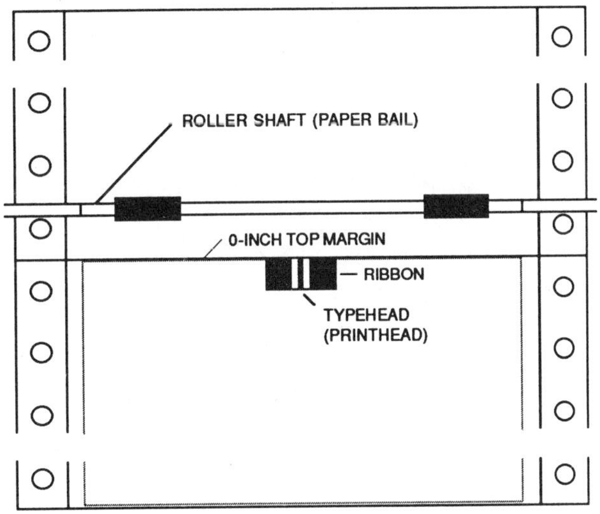

Figure 7-3 For the Imagewriter Standard, if the default top margin were any less than ½ inch, printing would have to take place on continuous paper (not cut paper), and the first sheet of paper would have to be wasted.

The Macintosh designers did not want to waste the first sheet of paper, so they set the printing routines such that the hardware margins were taken care of by default. This brings us to the lower sets of coordinates.

The lower right corner of the page is given an xx coordinate equal to the paper width multiplied by 72 dpi (or 80 dpi, if Tall orientation is in effect) minus the left and right hardware margins, and a yy coordinate equal to the paper height multiplied by 72 dpi (or 80 dpi, if Tall orientation is in effect) minus the top margin, and *minus an unapparent 4-point bottom margin*. That 4-point bottom margin also has to do with the hardware. When using a cut sheet of paper, the printer's friction clutch can't position the type head any closer to the bottom edge of the paper than that.

Problems with the Bottom Margin

Unfortunately, some of the early Macintosh programmers weren't aware of the 4-point bottom margin and set up their applications as though the **page rectangle**, which is defined as the area described by the page coordinates, went all the way to the bottom edge of the paper. In effect, their printing algorithms assumed that every page was 4 points longer than it really was. This error (or some variation of it) was frequently masked by software margins (footers), but was predictably compounded by 4 points (one way or the other) with every succeeding page. In other words, when the page rectangle is not calculated correctly, it gradually creeps along the paper as shown in Figure 7-4.

Page creep, whenever it occurred, was invariably thought to be hardware related. Reviewer after reviewer condemned the Imagewriter printer. They generalized and said that the Macintosh did not handle long documents very well. In fact, the page-creep problem had nothing to do with the Imagewriter or the Macintosh. It was 100% software related.

When those same early Imagewriters were connected to PC-compatible computers and run under PC-software control, page registration was fine—page after page after page. If the printer was faulty, then, logically, it should have malfunctioned on PC-compatible computers as well. Unfortunately, few reviewers thought to run that test.

Today, it's not necessary to use a PC-compatible computer. If you connect those very same Imagewriters to the very same Macs, but use up-to-date software, the page registration problem completely disappears, something you can easily prove for yourself.

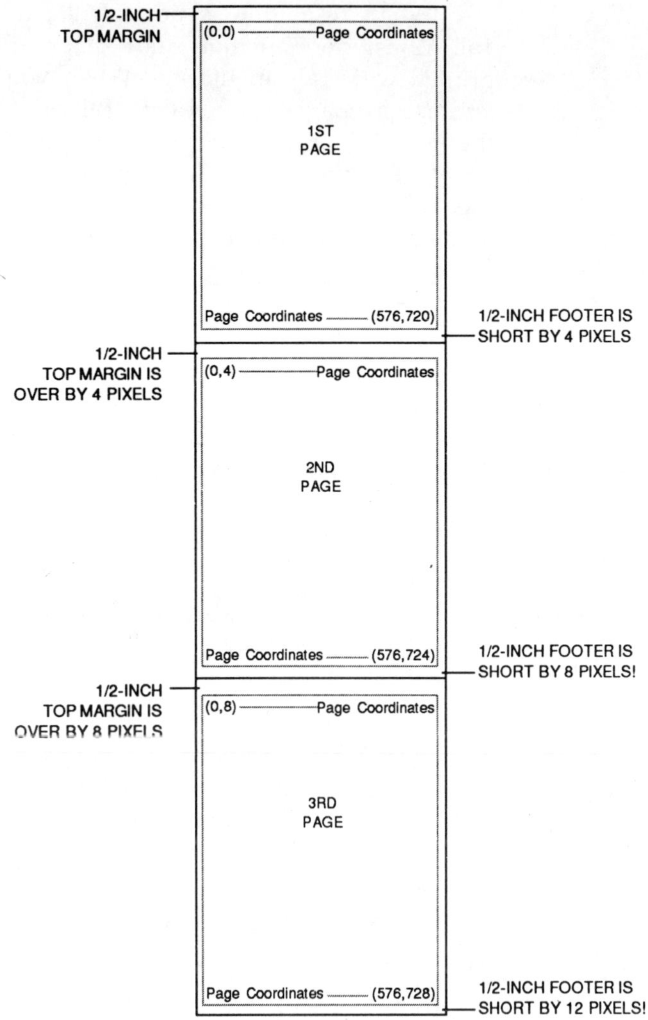

Figure 7-4 When the page rectangle is not calculated correctly, it gradually creeps along the paper.

Problems with the Size of the Left Margin

The 4-point bottom margin wasn't the only margin misunderstood by early Mac programmers. There were (and still are) big problems with the left margin as well.

The first problem has to do with the *size* of the left margin. If the programmer fails to consider that there's an 8-dpi difference between Tall (80 dpi) and Tall-Adjusted (72 dpi) orientation, the size of the left margin varies accordingly.

When resolution is not calculated correctly, pages printed with Tall-Adjusted orientation start 11% further to the right than pages printed with Tall orientation. When you adjust the rulers for a 1-inch left margin, pages printed with Tall orientation start exactly 1 inch from the left edge of the paper (assuming the tractors are properly aligned), but pages printed with Tall-Adjusted orientation start 1.11 inches from the left edge of the paper. This effect is shown in Figure 7-5. Try hitting fields on a form under those circumstances!

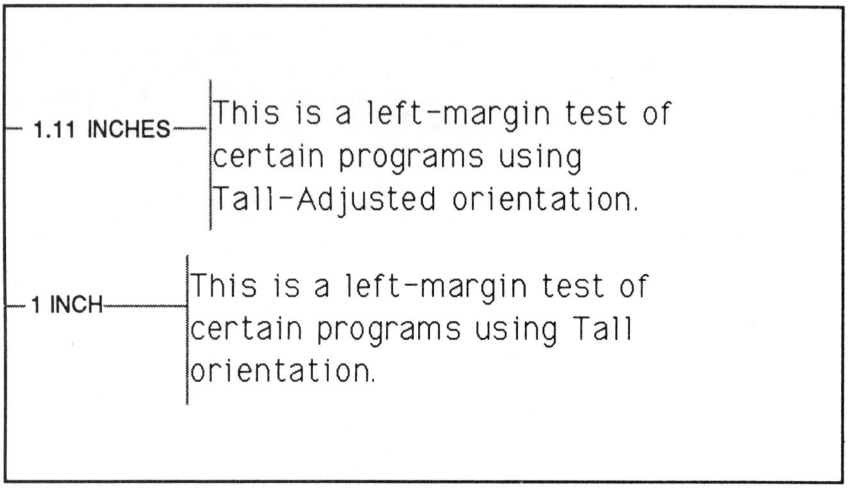

Figure 7-5 When resolution is not calculated correctly, pages printed with Tall-Adjusted orientation start 11% further to the right than pages printed with Tall orientation.

Problems with Inch Measurements

The expanding and contracting left margin is another manifestation of the miscalibrated ruler problem we ran into earlier. In the Macintosh world, there seems to be continuing confusion over how long an inch is. There shouldn't be.

Inches are internationally accepted units of measurement. They are constants, not program variables subject to alteration. By definition, each and every inch has to measure exactly 1-inch long, no more, no less. Otherwise, it's *not* an inch. "Inches" that sometimes measure 1 inch and other times measure 1.11 inches are a complete absurdity.

Problems with the Start of the Left Margin

The second problem has to do with *where* the left margin starts. If you're the programmer, do you write the printing code so that it starts from the paper rectangle, or the page rectangle? Most customers (the people who are going to buy your software) aren't aware of the difference between the paper rectangle and the page rectangle, so they *naturally* assume that margins start from the extreme left edge of the paper. In other words, customers start from the paper rectangle. That being the case, it's up to the printing code to subtract the hardware margin from the software margin. But, supposing the customer sets up a 0-inch left margin? Because of the default ¼-inch hardware margin, nothing can be printed in the first ¼-inch, so how should the program handle it?

With Microsoft Works (all versions through 2.0a), 0.0-inch and 0.25-inch left margins are considered the same. All measurements are taken from the paper rectangle, but printing *always* begins at the page rectangle. In addition, Works always defaults to Tall-Adjusted printing, so what you see is always what you get.

With Microsoft Word (version 4.0), 0.0-inch and 0.25-inch left margins are considered different. All measurements are taken from the paper rectangle, and printing also *begins* at the paper rectangle. Since *nothing* can be printed in the first ¼ inch (because of the printer's hardware margin), anything that lies within that area (assuming the tractors have been aligned correctly) doesn't print. Word doesn't warn you about that. Instead, Word starts printing from the paper rectangle and the first few characters in every line are truncated by the printer's hardware margin. This effect is shown in Figure 7-6.

```
LONIUS' SPEECH TO LAERTES

ve thy thoughts no tongue,
r any unproportioned thought his act.
 thou familiar, but by no means vulgar.
ɔse friends thou hast, and their adoption
ied,
apple them to thy soul with loops of steel,
t do not dull thy palm with entertainment
 each new-hatched unfledged comrade. Beware
 entrance to a quarrel, but being in,
ar't that the opposèd may beware of thee.
ve every man thy ear, but few thy voice.
```

Figure 7-6 When the left margin is set to 0.0 inches, Microsoft Word 4.0 starts printing from the paper rectangle and the first few characters in every line are truncated by the printer's hardware margin.

The fact that the Microsoft Works' printing code handles 0.0-inch left margins transparently by always printing from the page rectangle, while the Microsoft Word 4.0 printing code truncates the entire left $\frac{1}{4}$ inch of the page by always printing from the paper rectangle, suggests that Macintosh margin handling is still as inconsistent as it ever was. Margins continue to vary from one program to the next, even within the same software house. To help you make sense out of that, Test Character Generator contains a powerful Get (Page Setup...) Info routine.

TCG's Get (Page Setup...) Info Routine

As shown in Figure 7-7, choosing Get Info... from TCG's File menu opens a Page Setup... Information window and brings out the standard Page Setup... dialog box.

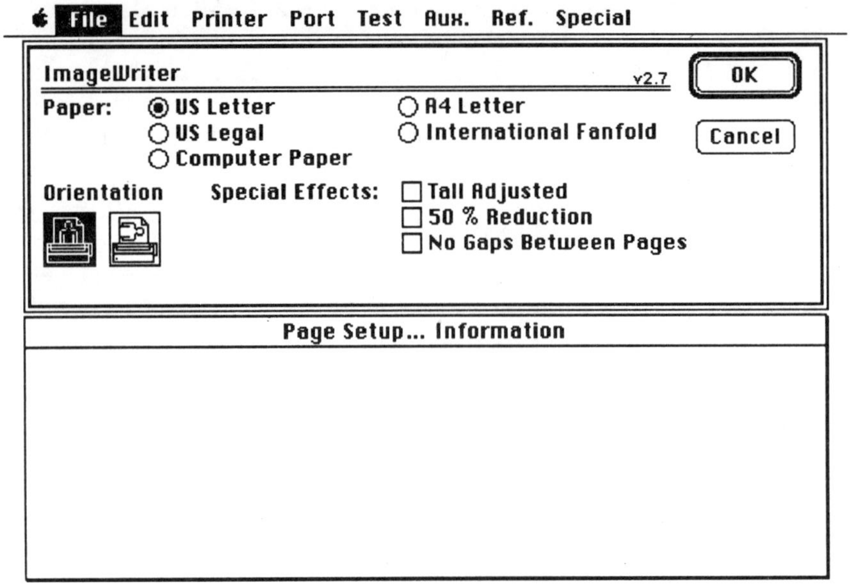

Figure 7-7 Test Character Generator. Choosing Get Info... from TCG's File menu opens a Page Setup... Information window and brings out the standard Page Setup... dialog box.

As soon as you click the OK button, the Page Setup... Information window translates the current Page Setup... jargon (Tall vs. Tall-Adjusted, Breaks vs. No Breaks, Gaps vs. No Gaps, etc.) into common-sense math expressions.

Page Setup... Info for US Letter Paper with (Tall) Portrait Orientation

A mathematical description of US Letter paper with (Tall) Portrait Orientation is shown in Figure 7-8. To reproduce Figure 7-8 exactly as it appears here, choose Get Info... (from the File menu) a second time. This brings out the Page Setup... dialog box again. With the current selections in view, it's easy to prove the math:

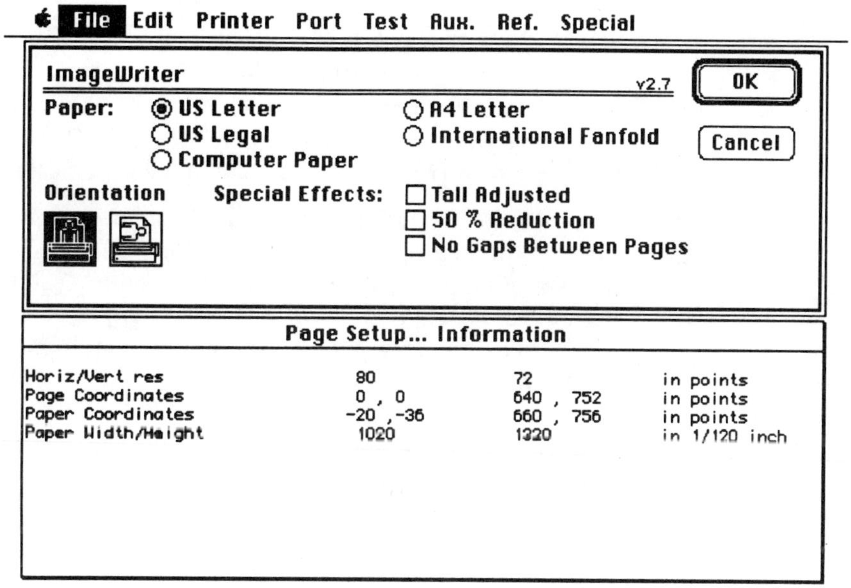

Figure 7-8 ImageWriter Driver v2.7 Page Setup Information for US Letter Paper with (Tall) Portrait Orientation.

1. On the first line, we see that the default horizontal resolution for (Tall) Portrait orientation is 80 dpi (not 72 dpi, like the WYSIWYG Macintosh display), while the default vertical resolution is 72 dpi.
2. The 80-dpi horizontal resolution is also reflected in the page coordinates. Divide the 640-point xx coordinate by 80 dpi and the answer indicates an 8-inch wide page.
3. The 80-dpi horizontal resolution is reflected again in the paper coordinates. Divide the −20-point x coordinate by 80 dpi and the answer indicates a −¼-inch left margin.

4. To obtain the paper width, add the unsigned value of the −20-point left margin to the 660-point xx coordinate and divide the sum (680) by 80 dpi. The answer indicates 8½-inch wide paper.
5. The y and yy coordinates are all divisible by 72 dpi, the default vertical resolution.
6. Divide the 752-point yy coordinate by 72 and the answer indicates a 10.44-inch (not 10½-inch) page length. The 0.06-inch difference is the elusive 4-point (4/72-inch) bottom hardware margin associated with the page-creep problem described earlier.
7. Divide the −36-point y coordinate by 72 dpi and the answer indicates a −½-inch top margin.
8. To determine the paper length, add the unsigned value of the −36-point top margin to the 756-point yy coordinate and divide the sum (792) by 72 dpi. The answer indicates 11-inch-long paper.

It's worth pulling out a calculator to prove the math. If you're at the computer, you can use the Macintosh desk-accessory calculator. Desk-accessory calculators work fine with Test Character Generator. Otherwise, use a hand-held, battery operated model, and work through every calculation for yourself. Remember, authors are frequently wrong. In general, never take an author's word for anything!

Page Setup... Info for US Letter Paper with (Tall-Adjusted) Portrait Orientation

Figure 7-9 shows the Page Setup... Information for US Letter paper with Tall-Adjusted (not Tall) orientation.

1. On the first line, we see that both the horizontal and vertical resolutions are 72 dpi (not 80 dpi), just like the WYSIWYG Macintosh display.
2. Note that the 72-dpi horizontal resolution is now reflected in the page coordinates. At 80 dpi, the xx coordinate was 640. Now it reads 576. Divide 576 by 72 dpi, however, and the answer still indicates an 8-inch-wide page.
3. The 72-dpi horizontal resolution is also reflected in the paper coordinates. At 80 dpi, the x coordinate was −20. Now it reads −18. Divide −18-point by 72 dpi, however, and the answer still indicates a ¼-inch left margin.
4. To obtain the paper width, add the unsigned value of the −18-point left margin to the 594-point xx coordinate and divide the sum by 72 dpi. The answer indicates 8½-inch-wide paper.
5. The y and yy coordinates are all divisible by 72 dpi, the same as before. Neither coordinate has changed.

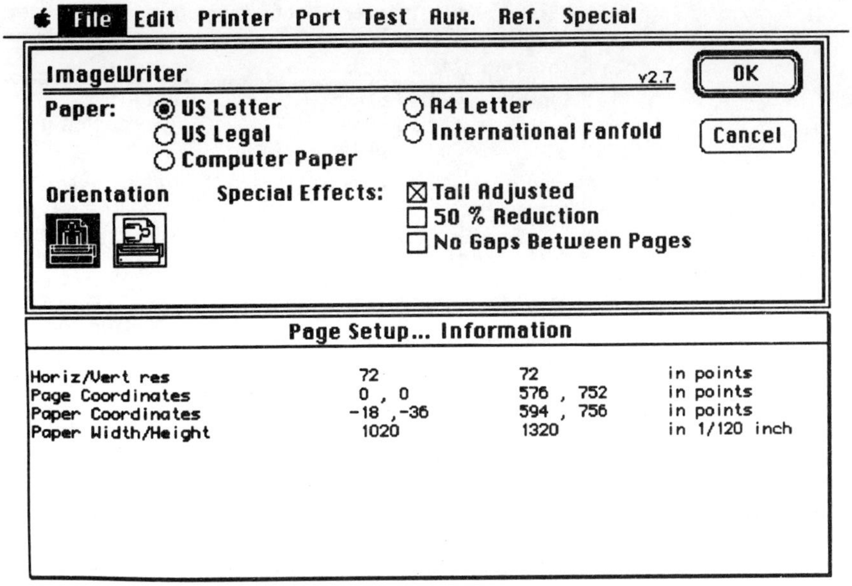

Figure 7-9 ImageWriter Driver v2.7 Page Setup... Information for US Letter Paper with (Tall-Adjusted) Portrait Orientation.

6. Divide the 752-point yy coordinate by 72 and the answer indicates a 10.44-inch (not 10½-inch) page length. The 0.06-inch difference is the 4-point (4/72-inch) bottom hardware margin described earlier.
7. Divide the −36-point y coordinate by 72 dpi and the answer indi cates a ½inch top margin.
8. To determine the page length, add the absolute value of the −36-point top margin to the 756-point yy coordinate and divide the sum by 72 dpi. Just as before, the answer indicates an 11-inch paper length.

Page Setup... Info for US Letter Paper with (Tall) Portrait Orientation and No Gaps (Breaks) Between Pages

Figure 7-10 shows the Page Setup... Information for US Letter paper with (Tall) Portrait Orientation and No Gaps (Breaks) Between Pages.

1. On the first line, we see once again that the default horizontal resolution for (Tall) Portrait orientation is 80 dpi (not 72 dpi, like the WYSIWYG Macintosh display), while the default vertical resolution is 72 dpi.
2. The 80-dpi horizontal resolution is also reflected in the page coordinates. Divide the 640-point xx coordinate by 80 dpi and the answer indicates an 8-inch-wide page.

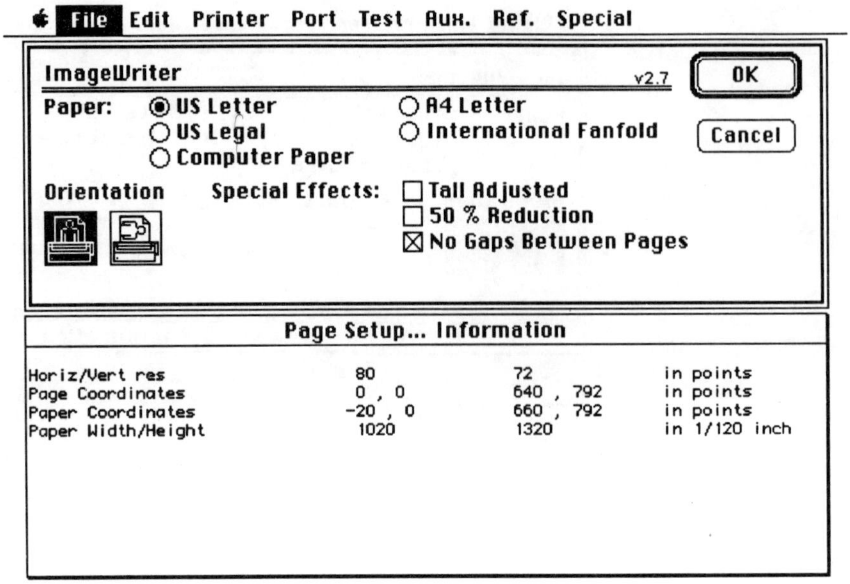

Figure 7-10 ImageWriter Driver v2.7 Page Setup... Information for US Letter Paper with (Tall) Portrait Orientation and No Gaps (Breaks) Between Pages.

3. The 80-dpi horizontal resolution is reflected again in the paper coordinates. Divide the −20-point x coordinate by 80 dpi and the answer indicates a −¼-inch left margin.
4. To obtain the paper width, add the unsigned value of the −20-point left margin to the 660-point xx coordinate and divide the sum by 80 dpi. The answer indicates 8½-inch-wide paper.
5. The y and yy coordinates are all divisible by 72 dpi, the default vertical resolution.
6. Divide the 792-point yy coordinate by 72 and the answer indicates an 11-inch (not a 10.94-inch) page length. With No Gaps (Breaks) Between Pages selected, the 4-point (4/72-inch) hardware margin associated with the page-creep problem disappears!
7. The 0-point y coordinate indicates no top margin.
8. To determine the paper length, divide the 792-point yy coordinate by 72. The answer indicates 11-inch-long paper.

Page Setup... Info for US Letter Paper with Tall-Adjusted Portrait Orientation and No Gaps (Breaks) Between Pages

Figure 7-11 shows the Page Setup... Information for US Letter paper with Tall-Adjusted (not Tall) Portrait Orientation and No Gaps (Breaks) Between Pages.

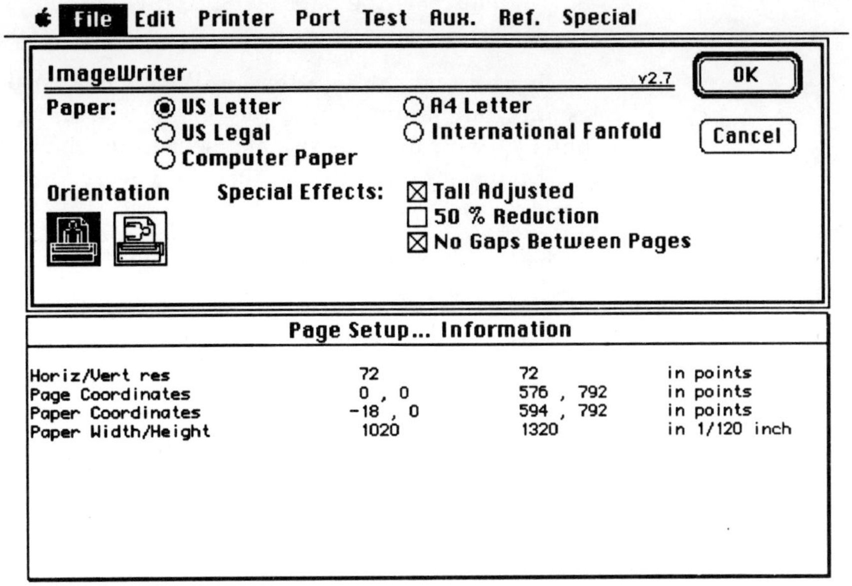

Figure 7-11 ImageWriter Driver v2.7 Page Setup... Information for US Letter Paper with Tall-Adjusted Portrait Orientation and No Gaps (Breaks) Between Pages.

1. On the first line, we see that both the horizontal and vertical resolutions are 72 dpi (not 80 dpi), just like the WYSIWYG Macintosh display.
2. Note that the 72-dpi horizontal resolution is once again reflected in the page coordinates. At 80 dpi, the xx coordinate was 640. Now it reads 576. Divide 576 by 72 dpi, however, and the answer still indicates an 8-inch-wide page.
3. The 72-dpi horizontal resolution is once again reflected in the paper coordinates. At 80 dpi, the x coordinate was −20. Now it reads −18. Divide −18-point by 72 dpi, however, and the answer still indicates a ¼-inch left margin.
4. To obtain the paper width, add the unsigned value of the −18-point left margin to the 594-point xx coordinate and divide the sum by 72 dpi. The answer indicates 8½-inch-wide paper.
5. The y and yy coordinates are all divisible by 72 dpi, the same as before. Neither coordinate has changed.
6. Divide the 792-point yy coordinate by 72 and the answer indicates an 11-inch (not a 10.94-inch) page length. With No Breaks Between Pages, the 4-point (4/72-inch) hardware margin associated with the page-creep problem disappears!
7. The 0-point y coordinate indicates no top margin.

8. To determine the paper length, divide the 792-point yy coordinate by 72. The answer indicates 11-inch-long paper.

By working through the No Breaks (Gaps) Between Pages examples and comparing them to the previous Breaks (Gaps) Between Pages examples, we can start to make sense out of the Page Setup... dialog box by translating its cryptic labels into everyday math and English. For example:

1. Gaps (Breaks) Between Pages means:
   A. Insert a ½-inch top margin.
   B. Insert a 1/18-inch (4-point) bottom margin.
2. No Gaps (Breaks) Between Pages means:
   A. Don't insert a ½-inch top margin.
   B. Don't insert a 1/18-inch (4-point) bottom margin.

Now that we know that gaps and/or breaks between pages refers to the automatic insertion of a ½-inch top margin and a 1/18-inch bottom margin, we can apply that information to the ImageWriter II and stop the annoying ½-inch rollback.

Applied Page Setup... Information—How to Stop the ½-Inch Rollback on an ImageWriter II

As previously explained, the top of the type head (print head) on an Imagewriter Standard is approximately ½-inch below the top of the roller shaft (paper bail). Without at least a ½-inch top margin, printing would have to take place on continuous paper (not cut-sheet paper) and the first sheet of paper would have to be wasted. This situation was illustrated in Figure 7-3.

On the ImageWriter II, the top of the print head is approximately 1-inch (not ½-inch) below the top of the paper bail. By necessity, we now need 1-inch (not ½-inch) gaps between pages to avoid wasting the first sheet of paper. We also need at least 1-inch gaps to print on cut-sheet paper. This situation is illustrated in Figure 7-12.

The difference in the default hardware margin amounted to a major incompatibility problem. To avoid wasting the first sheet of paper, the original Imagewriter requires a ½-inch default margin. The ImageWriter II requires a 1-inch default margin. This requirement was *easily* met by programs that allowed you to *adjust* the top margin. In general, all you had to do was pull out their custom Page Setup... dialog boxes and increase the distance.

Early versions of MacWrite and MacPaint, however, did not allow you to adjust margins. As originally designed, Macintosh margins were supposed to be preset by the ImageWriter driver. So how best to deal with the new 1-inch margin requirement? Among the available options may have been:

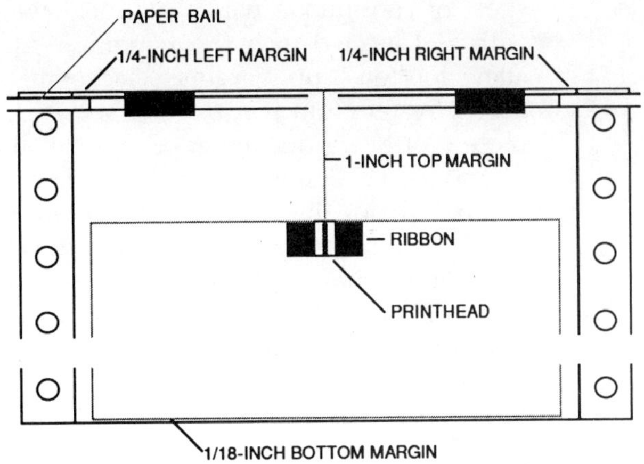

Figure 7-12 For the ImageWriter II, the top of the print head is approximately 1 inch (not ½ inch) below the top of the paper bail. By necessity, we now need 1-inch (not ½-inch) gaps between pages to avoid wasting the first sheet of paper.

1. Release an ImageWriter II specific driver with default gaps (breaks) measuring 1 inch instead of ½ inch.
2. Add a new Special Effect to the ImageWriter driver's Page Setup... dialog box. Possibly label it: Bigger Gaps (Breaks) Between Pages.
3. Have the gap-size increase automatically from ½ inch to 1 inch in response to an ID query.
4. Build in a plastic paper guide (card holder) and instruct the printer to roll back every sheet of paper ½ inch, unless No Gaps Between Pages is selected.

For better or worse, the ½-inch rollback "feature" was implemented. There's been no end of problems with it. Multipart forms generally derail when rolled back. Mailing labels tend to peel off and stick to the platen. Stuck materials jam the paper-out sensor, which bends and subverts the auto paper-feed option. To say that the ½-inch rollback has been the biggest source of complaints, and the feature least-liked about the ImageWriter II, would be an understatement.

The amazing thing is that just like the page-registration problem examined earlier, the ½-inch rollback has nothing to do with the ImageWriter II! In this case, it's a printer driver problem. The problem (or feature, depending on your point of view) is 100% software related.

Canceling ImageWriter II Rollback for Letter-Size Paper Rollback is incredibly easy to stop. As suggested in option 4 above, selecting No Gaps (Breaks) Between Pages completely cancels the rollback command. To allow printing on cut-sheet paper and/or avoid wasting the first sheet of continuous paper, all you have to do is to set up documents with at least a 1-inch top margin. With older applications that don't allow you to set up margins, select 6 lines-per-inch spacing (or the Monaco 12 System font with regular spacing), and type 6 carriage returns at the top of every document. Generally, that's *all* there is to it.

If you'd rather not have to bother with pulling out the Page Setup... dialog box and selecting No Gaps (Breaks) Between Pages, another way to stop the rollback is to set up documents with at least a 1½-inch top margin. With older applications that don't allow you to set up margins, select 6 lines-per-inch spacing (or the Monaco 12 System font with regular spacing), and type 9 (not 6) carriage returns at the top of every document.

Whichever method you use, the rollback will definitely stop!

Canceling ImageWriter II Rollback for Mailing Labels To stop 3.5 × 1 mailing labels from rolling back on the ImageWriter II, set up a 1-inch custom page size, with no (0.0 inch) top or bottom margins, and select No Breaks (Gaps) Between Pages. After choosing Print... from the File menu, etc., the first label will advance (be wasted), and printing will start from the second label.

Although the rollback "feature" has resulted in countless complaints (most of which are improperly leveled at the ImageWriter II), the cancel procedure is relatively simple. Still an even better solution might be to release an ImageWriter driver where No Gaps Between Pages is selected by default. Every major Macintosh application released for the past *several years* allows you to set margins in software. Those that don't, like TCG, *preset* their margins to an inch. Developers are fully aware that you need to leave an inch at the top of every page to prevent wasting the first sheet of paper. At this point in time, there seems to be little (if any) reason for printer drivers to assume otherwise.

Page Setup... Info for US Letter Paper with (Tall) Portrait Orientation and 50 % Reduction

Figure 7-13 shows the Page Setup... Information for US Letter paper with (Tall) Portrait Orientation and 50 % Reduction.

1. On the first line, we see once again that the default horizontal resolution for (Tall) Portrait Orientation is 80 dpi (not 72 dpi, like the WYSIWYG Macintosh display), while the default vertical resolution is 72 dpi. Note that even with 50 % Reduction in effect, the Mac's display resolution does not double. Only the printer resolution doubles, from 80 × 72 dpi to 160 × 144 dpi.
2. With 50 % Reduction in effect, the page coordinates have doubled. To scale these, the same as they're scaled for printing, first divide

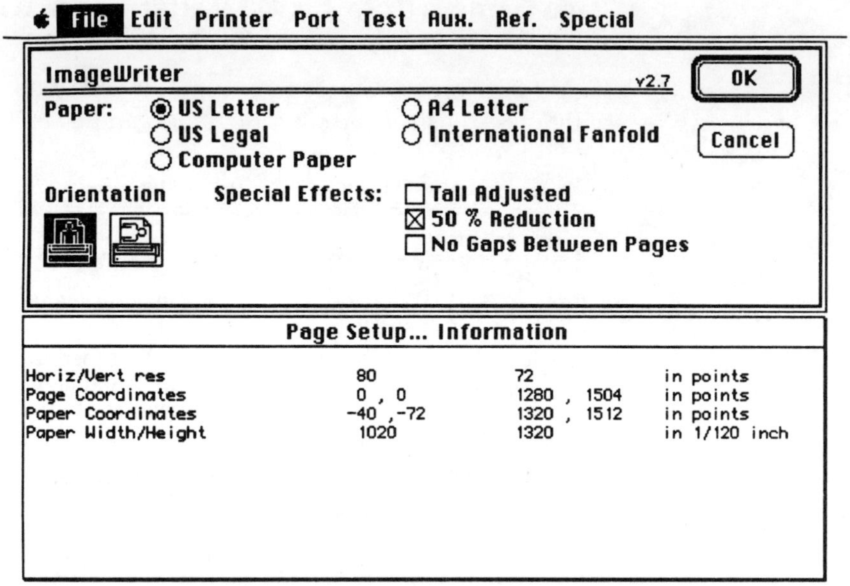

Figure 7-13 ImageWriter Driver v2.7 Page Setup... Information for US Letter Paper with (Tall) Portrait Orientation and 50 % Reduction.

the 1280-point xx coordinate by 2, and then divide the quotient by 160 dpi. The answer indicates a 4-inch-wide page.

3. The 160-dpi horizontal printer resolution is reflected again in the paper coordinates. Divide the −40-point x coordinate by 160 dpi and the answer indicates a −¼-inch left margin.
4. To obtain the paper width, add the unsigned value of the −40-point left margin to the 1320-point xx coordinate and divide the sum by 160 dpi. The answer indicates 8½-inch-wide paper.
5. The y and yy coordinates are all divisible by 144 dpi, the printer's increased vertical resolution.
6. Divide the 1504-point yy ordinate by 2, and then divide the quotient by 144; the answer indicates a 5.22-inch page length. Note that a 5.22-inch page is exactly half (50%) the length of a 10.44-inch page.
7. Divide the −72-point y coordinate by 144 dpi and the answer indicates a −½-inch top margin.
8. To determine the paper length, add the unsigned value of the −72-point top margin to the 1512-point yy coordinate and divide the sum (1584) by 144 dpi. The answer indicates 11-inch-long paper.

Page Setup... Info for US Letter Paper with Tall-Adjusted Portrait Orientation and 50 % Reduction

Figure 7-14 shows the Page Setup... Information for US Letter paper with Tall-Adjusted Portrait Orientation and 50 % Reduction.

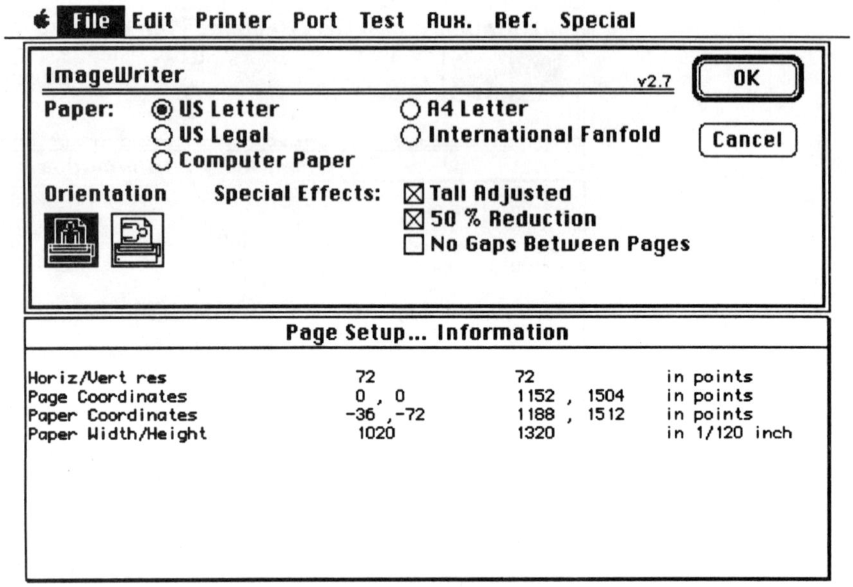

Figure 7-14 ImageWriter Driver v2.7 Page Setup... Information for US Letter Paper with Tall-Adjusted Portrait Orientation and 50 % Reduction.

1. On the first line, we see that both the horizontal and vertical resolutions are 72 dpi (not 80 dpi), just like the WYSIWYG Macintosh display.
2. Note that the 72-dpi horizontal resolution is now reflected in the page coordinates. At 80 dpi, the xx coordinate was 640. Now it reads 576. Divide 576 by 72 dpi however, and the answer still indicates an 8-inch-wide page.
3. The 72-dpi horizontal resolution is also reflected in the paper coordinates. At 80 dpi, the x coordinate was −20. Now it reads −18. Divide −18-point by 72 dpi however, and the answer still indicates a ¼-inch left margin.
4. To obtain the paper width, add the unsigned value of the −18-point left margin to the 594-point xx coordinate and divide the sum by 72 dpi. The answer indicates 8½-inch-wide paper.
5. The y and yy coordinates are all divisible by 72 dpi, the same as before. Neither coordinate has changed.

6. Divide the 752-point yy coordinate by 72 and the answer indicates a 10.44-inch (not 10½-inch) page length. The 0.06-inch difference is the 4-point (4/72-inch) bottom hardware margin described earlier.
7. Divide the −36-point y coordinate by 72 dpi and the answer indicates a ½-inch top margin.
8. To determine the page length, add the absolute value of the −36-point top margin to the 756-point yy coordinate and divide the sum by 72 dpi. Just as before, the answer indicates an 11-inch paper length.

By repeating this process with Wide orientation, other Paper sizes, and/or other printer drivers, you'll soon become master of the Page Setup... dialog box. Instead of wondering what's going to happen, you'll know exactly what to expect. And if you ever do get unexpected results, you can pull out TCG again and work through the coordinates to find out exactly where you miscalculated.

Bear in mind that precise margins depend on precision paper alignment. If the paper is loaded incorrectly, or if it's loaded inconsistently, then margin size will vary.

TCG's Tractor - TOF Alignment Test

As shown in Figure 7-15, TCG's Tractor - TOF (Top of Form) Alignment test prints a test page which is always surrounded by 1-inch margins, regardless of orientation or paper size.

To run the test, choose Page Setup... from the File menu and select No Gaps (Breaks) Between Pages. Click the OK button. This step cancels the rollback on an Imagewriter II. You don't need to bother if you don't care about the rollback, nor is this step necessary when printing to an Imagewriter Standard or an Imagewriter Wide.

Next choose Tractor - TOF Alignment from the Test menu, and then choose Print... from the File menu. Select Faster (Standard) or Best (High) quality (not Draft quality) and then click the OK button. TCG will print a test box, which may or may not be centered. Here's how to interpret the results:

1. If the top margin is greater than 1 inch, it means you loaded the paper too high. Advance the paper a little less and try again.
2. If the top margin is less than 1 inch, it means you loaded the paper too low. Advance the paper a little more and try again.
3. If the left margin is greater than 1 inch, it means the tractors are too far to the left. Move them one half the distance of the error to the right and try again.

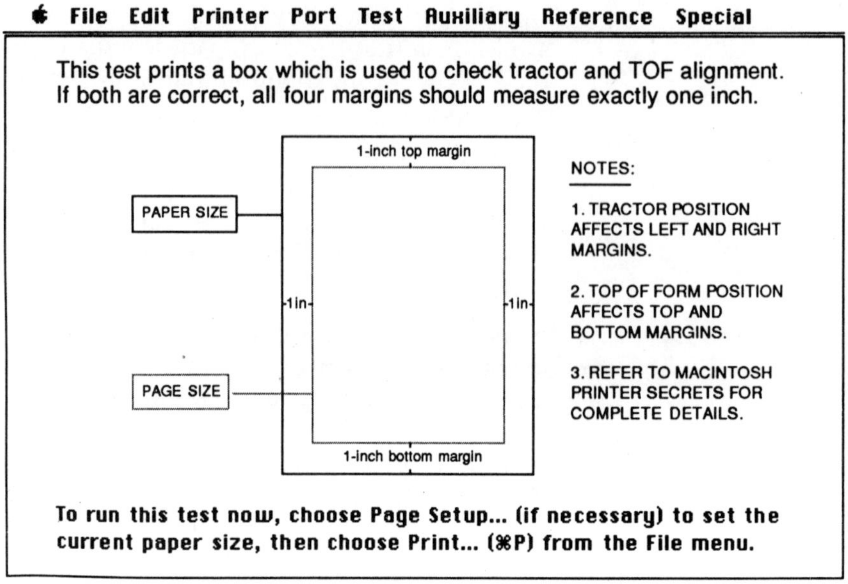

Figure 7-15 Test Character Generator Tractor - TOF Alignment test.

4. If the left margin is less than 1 inch, it means the tractors are too far to the right. Move them one half the distance of the error to the left and try again.

Combination errors can be solved the same way. If the margins are narrow at the left and narrow on the top, move the paper up and to the left. If the margins are wide at the left and wide on the top, move the paper down and to the right.

In many cases, you can move the tractors while the test box is printing. If so, you can quickly eyeball the left and right margins into place. Setting the TOF (Top of Form, where form equals paper) is generally harder. You may have to run several sheets, noting exactly where each sheet was loaded beneath the paper bail.

Once you've established the correct tractor and TOF positions, subsequent test boxes should be perfectly centered. From then on, your document margins will also be perfectly centered, provided you load the paper exactly the same way.

By running this test, you may be surprised to discover that the alignment marks (if any) on your printer are wrong. Sometimes the error is only one sixteenth of an inch. Other times, they're off by as much as an eighth of an inch. In that case, you can either believe your eyes and go by the test results, or you can close your eyes and follow the alignment marks.

Follow the alignment marks and your margins may never come out right. Go by the test results and they should come out perfectly, each and every time you print.

Summary

The following important points summarize the concepts discussed in Chapter 7.

1. Unprinted areas which fall *between* the paper and the page boundries are called margins.
2. Macintosh printer drivers measure margins in terms of resolution (at 72 dpi or 80 dpi), using algebraic (x, y) – (xx, yy) coordinates.
3. No printer can completely cover a single sheet of maximum-size paper.
4. The maximum paper size for any given printer is always larger than its maximum page size.
5. The difference between the maximum paper size and the maximum page size is called the printer's hardware margin.
6. The left hardware margin for all models of the Imagewriter (and most other printers as well) is ¼ inch.
7. Nothing can be printed in the left hardware margin. If an application tries to print in the left hardware margin, the first few characters on every line are truncated.
8. The top hardware margin for the original Imagewriter is ½ inch.
9. The top hardware margin for the ImageWriter II is 1 inch.
10. The ImageWriter II ½-inch rollback is a response to the printer driver's built-in Gaps (Breaks) Between Pages feature.
11. To stop the ½-inch rollback, select No Gaps (Breaks) Between Pages and set up documents with at least a 1-inch top margin.
12. Precise margins depend on precision paper alignment. If the paper is loaded incorrectly, or if it's loaded inconsistently, then margin size will vary.

That's it for the software-related problems. In the following chapters, we'll concentrate on hardware.

CHAPTER 8

Imagewriter Setup Secrets

This chapter provides a Macintosh-specific Imagewriter (Standard and Wide) owner's guide. The ImageWriter Standard, identified by model number A9M0303, is a light-duty printer with a 10-inch carriage. The Imagewriter Wide, identified by model number A9M0305, is a somewhat heavier-duty printer with a 15-inch carriage. Cosmetically, both printers are identical. Figure 8-1 shows the Imagewriter Standard.

Figure 8-1 Imagewriter Standard, model number A9M0303.

Cabinet Parts and Setup Controls

Figure 8-2 identifies the Imagewriter's major cabinet parts and Figure 8-3 the major setup controls.

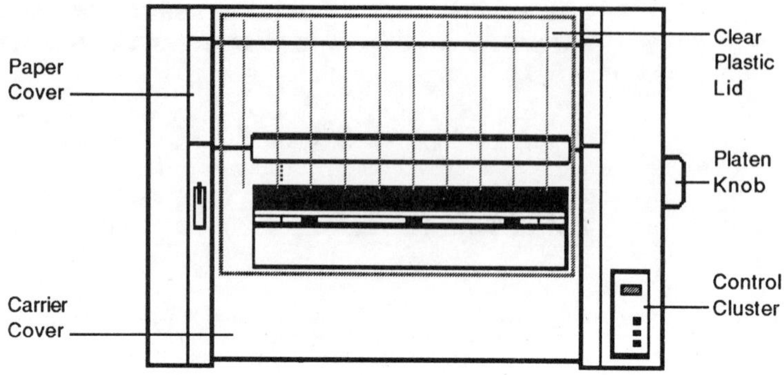

Figure 8-2 Imagewriter Standard cabinet parts.

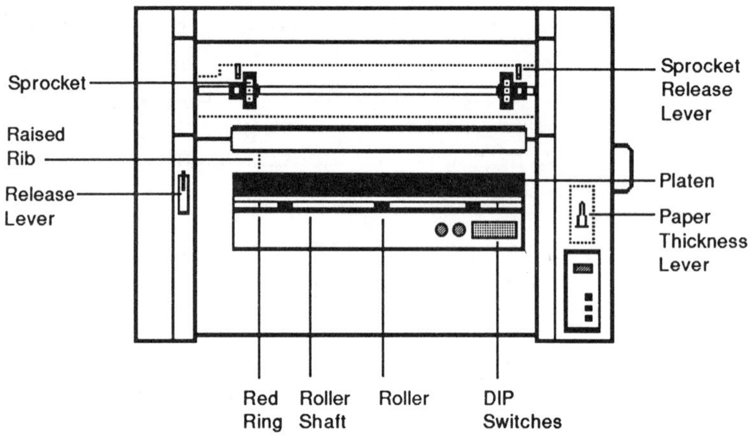

Figure 8-3 Imagewriter Standard setup controls.

The cabinet parts and setup controls shown in Figures 8-2 and 8-3 are labeled (and spelled) exactly as they were in the *Apple Imagewriter User's Manual, Part I: Reference*. Unfortunately, these same parts are labeled and spelled differently from Imagewriter model to ImageWriter model. They are also labeled and spelled differently from printer manufacturer to printer manufacturer.

To minimize confusion, Table 8-1 provides an Imagewriter cabinet part and setup control cross-reference guide.

Table 8-1. Imagewriter Cabinet-Part and Setup-Control Cross-Reference Guide

Imagewriter Std	ImageWriter II	ImageWriter LQ
Carrier Bar	Carrier Rod	Carrier Rod
Carrier Cover	Front cover	Front cover
Clear Plastic Lid	Front cover window	Clear plastic window
Control Cluster	Control panel	Control panel
N/A	Mini-circular plug	Minicircular plug
N/A	Mini-circular socket	Minicircular socket
Paper Cover	Back cover	Rear cover
Paper Cover Slot	Unnamed	Single-sheet guide
Release Lever	Paper-feed selector	Paper-feed lever
Ribbon Cassette	Ribbon cartridge	Ribbon cartridge
Ribbon Deck	Ribbon cartridge deck	N/A
Roller Shaft	Paper bail	Paper bail
Sprocket	Tractor	Tractor
Type Head	Print head	Print head

If you ever asked a printer-related question and thought that no one knew what they were talking about, study Table 8-1 and you'll begin to understand why. Intelligent conversation is very difficult when you can't agree on the language.

Cabinet Parts

As shown in Figure 8-2, there are three top covers on the Imagewriter. The frontmost cover is called the **carrier cover**. It covers the carrier track, referring to the steel bar directly beneath.

The rearmost cover is called the **paper cover**. It covers the pin-feed paper stock. Made of smooth plastic, it reduces friction and helps to keep the pin-feed stock from interfering with the printed pages. Some people remove the cover (when they're loading paper) and never replace it. That's a mistake. The paper cover should be kept in place at all times, *and* it should be waxed from time to time. Figure 8-4 shows the paper exit path. A slippery (waxed) paper cover reduces exit friction and minimizes jamming.

The third cover is made from clear plastic. It pivots on hinges attached to the front carrier cover. The *Apple Imagewriter User's Manual, Part I: Reference* refers to it simply as a **clear plastic lid**. In theory, the lid's functions are to:

1. Hold printer noise down.
2. Keep dust and pollen from falling into the printer.
3. Keep hands and fingers away from rapidly moving parts.

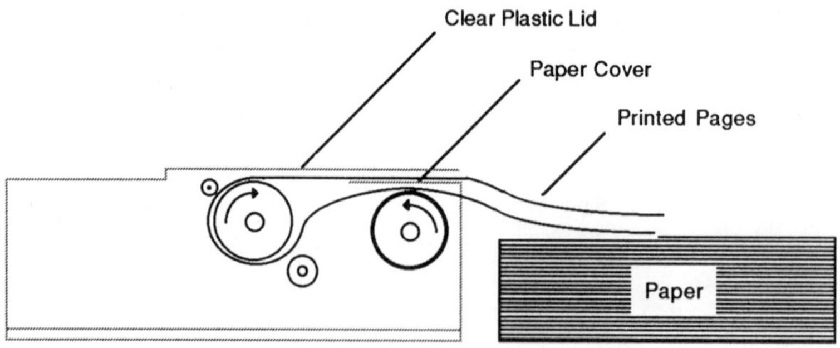

Figure 8-4 Imagewriter Standard paper exit path.

In practice, the clear plastic lid traps heat inside the printer causing all kinds of problems. In addition, it's awkward to use. Instead of rotating 180° and laying flat, it rotates only 135° and props open. Instead of getting out of the way, it opens directly into your way. As a result, many clear plastic lids have either broken off or been removed.

On the plus side, this helps to keep the type head cool, and extends lubricant life. As detailed in Chapter 9, dried-up, sticky grease and burned-out print heads are two common repair problems. On the minus side, the missing lid creates a safety hazard: curious users might stick their fingers into the printer and suffer serious physical injury.

Setup Controls

The **platen knob** extends from the right side of the printer. It's attached to a steel shaft which runs lengthwise through the black-rubber drive **platen**. When loading single sheets of paper, you turn the platen knob to advance the paper by hand, the same as on a typewriter.

Three plastic **rollers** are attached to a metal **roller shaft**. As shown in Figure 8-5, the roller shaft is under light spring tension. You pull back on the shaft to get a single sheet of paper started, then you push it forward to press the paper against the drive platen. The roller shaft curls the paper which causes it to exit on top of the paper cover. If you forget to engage the roller shaft, the paper climbs straight up and jams against the clear plastic lid. These effects are shown in Figures 8-6 and 8-7.

As their names imply, the rollers are supposed to *rotate* on the roller shaft. When new, you can spin the rollers like a top. Over a period of time, the roller bearings get clogged with paper dust. Clogged rollers barely make a single revolution. The increased bearing friction resists the initial line feed and eventually it becomes so great that the first few millimeters of paper buckle. Instead of slipping beneath the rollers, the stock actually has to lift the roller shaft up and out of the way. In the meantime, the paper fails to advance and the printout squashes. These effects are shown in Figure 8-8.

Figure 8-5 The roller shaft is under light spring tension.

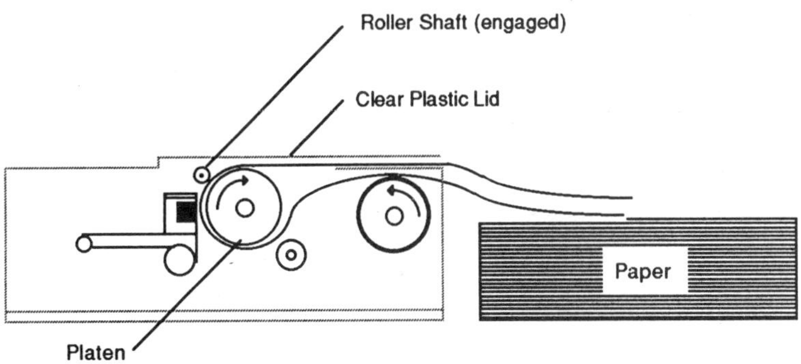

Figure 8-6 Push the roller shaft forward to keep the paper lightly pressed against the platen.

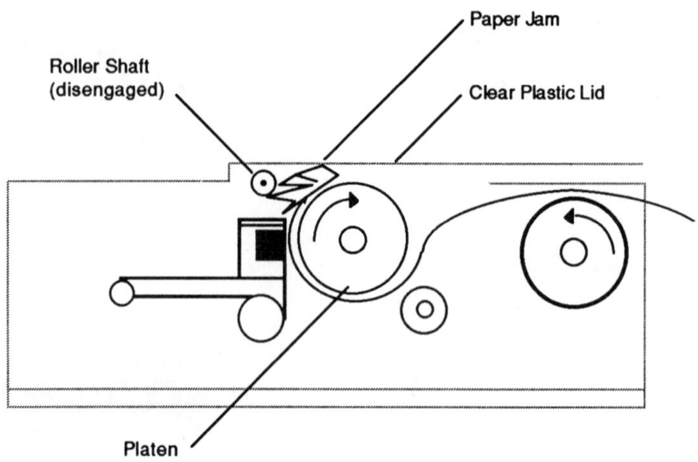

Figure 8-7 If you forget to engage the roller shaft, the paper climbs straight up and jams against the clear plastic lid.

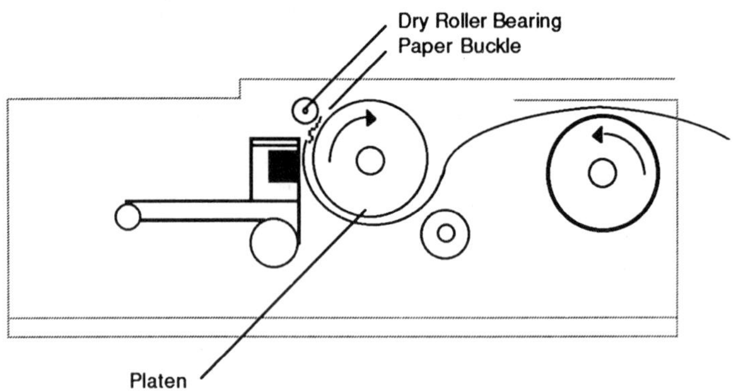

Figure 8-8 Dry roller bearings cause the first few millimeters of paper to buckle.

Squashed lines at the top of the page due to dry roller bearings is a common problem with all push-tractor printers, not just Imagewriters. Maintaining the bearings is, or at least it should be, part of routine maintenance. The complete procedure is described in Chapter 9.

Release Lever The **release lever** controls a second roller shaft underneath the platen. When the release lever is pushed toward the back of the printer as shown in Figure 8-9, the second roller shaft (underneath the platen) is released. This clears the way for single sheets of paper to feed manually, and also clears the path for pin-feed paper to feed automatically. The lower roller shaft functions as a clutch. The release lever functions as a clutch pedal. Pushing it back as shown in Figure 8-10, disengages the clutch. Pulling it forward as shown in Figure 8-11, engages the clutch, exactly the same as on an automobile.

Figure 8-9 Imagewriter Standard release lever.

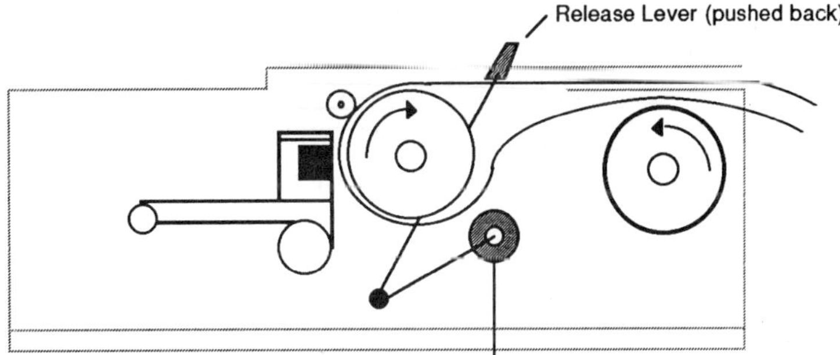

Figure 8-10 Push back to disengage the clutch.

The manual clutch-release lever has caused a lot of problems. To clutch something means to hold it close. In mechanical context, clutch implies a friction device. Unlike the upper roller shaft which is supposed to apply minimal friction, the lower roller shaft is supposed to apply considerable friction. Considerable friction between the lower rollers and the drive platen is just what you need to advance cut sheets of paper, but exactly the opposite of what you need to advance continuous pin-feed paper. *The platen drive is not synchronized to the tractor drive.* The tractor drive seems to be a little faster. When platen friction opposes the sprockets, the invariable result is a paper jam.

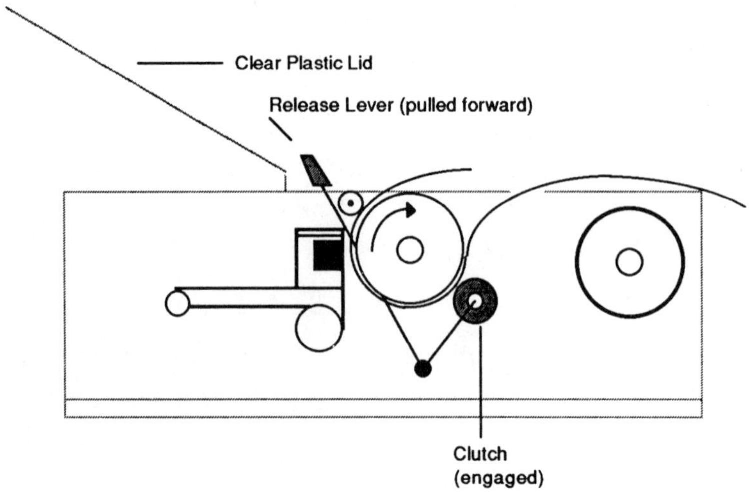

Figure 8-11 Pull forward to engage the clutch.

To avoid paper jams, push the release lever towards the back of the printer for pin-feed paper, and push it towards the front of the printer for cut-sheet paper.

The correct positions are suggested by icons etched onto the cabinet next to the release lever, but the icons are the same color as the cabinet, so they're easily overlooked. To make them more noticeable, trace the icons with a red, fine-point marker as shown in Figure 8-12. Red naturally suggests stop, which draws attention to the lever.

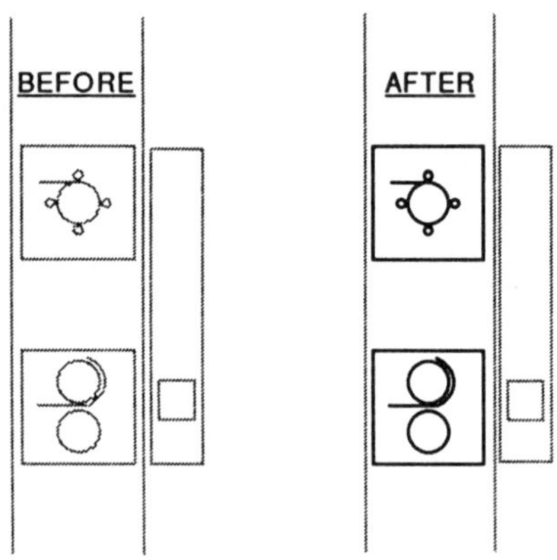

Figure 8-12 Release lever. To make them more noticable, trace the icons with a red, fine-point marker.

Paper-Thickness Lever The **paper-thickness lever** is located inside the cabinet, just in front of the control cluster, along the right side of the printer. The paper-thickness lever moves the position of the carrier bar in relation to the platen in four distinct stages. Each of the four stages corresponds to a specific paper thickness:

1. When the paper-thickness lever is pulled all the way toward the back of the printer, as shown in Figure 8-13, the type head is positioned correctly for 1 sheet of paper.
2. When the paper-thickness lever is pushed one click away from the back of the printer (counting from top to bottom), the type head is positioned correctly for 2 sheets of paper, and 2-part business forms.
3. When the paper-thickness lever is pushed two clicks away from the back of the printer (counting from top to bottom), the type head is positioned correctly for 3 sheets of paper, 3-part business forms, and most mailing labels.
4. When the paper-thickness lever is pushed three clicks away from the back of the printer (counting from top to bottom), the type head is positioned correctly for 4 sheets of paper, 4-part business forms, and very thin envelopes.

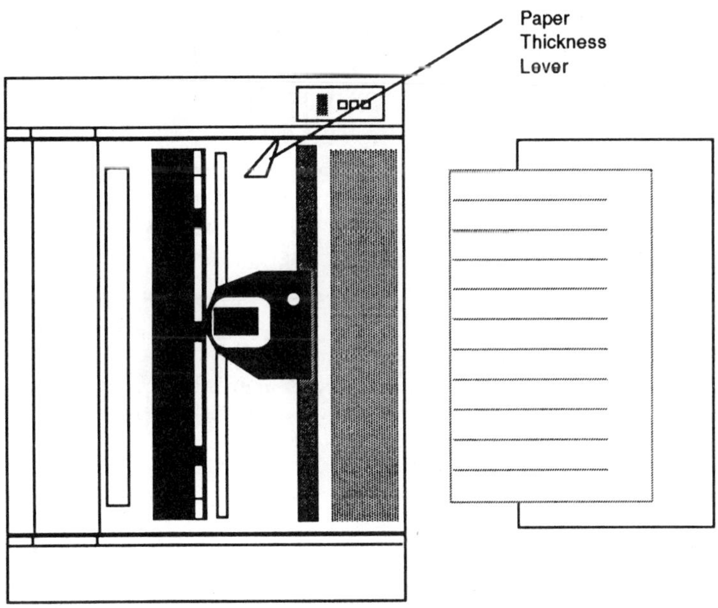

Figure 8-13 Imagewriter Standard paper-thickness lever.

Hiding the paper-thickness lever has caused a lot of problems. The location is not obvious. Some Imagewriters were sold without manuals;

consequently, many Imagewriter owners are not even aware of its existence.

When the paper thickness lever is not set correctly, mailing labels, business forms, and envelopes jam; single sheets print lighter than normal. The lion's share of Imagewriter complaints are directly related to incorrectly positioned release levers and incorrectly positioned paper-thickness levers. To remind you to check the paper-thickness lever, mark the cabinet with a red, fine-point marker as shown in Figure 8-14. Red naturally suggests "stop," which draws attention to the lever.

Figure 8-14 Paper-thickness lever. Mark the cabinet with a red, fine-point marker to remind yourself to check it.

Only the thinnest (cheapest) envelopes should be used with an Imagewriter (Standard or Wide). Thick (expensive) envelopes invariably jam, even in the fourth paper-thickness position. Other than that, envelope printing is intuitive. You load and fill out the envelope exactly the same as you would on a typewriter.

Control Cluster As shown in Figure 8-15, the **control cluster** contains the ON/OFF, SELECT, LINE FEED, and FORM FEED buttons. The **on/off** button applies AC power. The **select** button selects on-line status and off-line status. When the printer is on-line, as evidenced by a green light, it's under computer control. When it's off line, as evidenced by no light, it's under manual control.

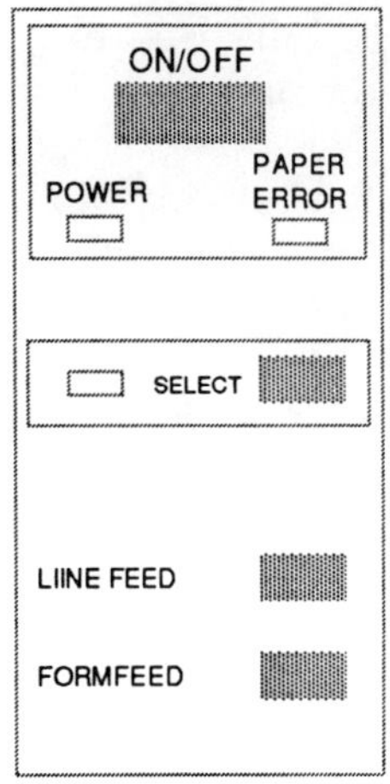

Figure 8-15 Imagewriter Standard control cluster.

The printer has to be under manual control (off-line) in order to work the line feed and form feed buttons. The **line feed** button *always* advances the paper $\frac{1}{6}$ inch. The **form feed** button advances the paper by 11 or 12 inches, measured from the current **top-of-form** setting, minus however many line feeds have been executed, depending on the setting of DIP switch 1-4. In other words, line feeds accumulate.

Whenever you turn the printer on, wherever the top of the paper happens to be is recorded as the top-of-form position. If DIP switch 1-4 is set for 11-inch (66-line) paper, and you press the select button to take the printer off line, then press the line feed button 6 times to advance the paper by 6 lines. Pressing the form feed button will advance the paper another 60 lines (66 lines $-$ 6 lines $=$ 60 lines) to the top of the next form.

As far as the line feed button is concerned, all lines are $\frac{1}{6}$-inch high. *The line feed button does not consider bitmapped font heights.* Even when you chose a 36-point font (approximately $\frac{1}{2}$-inch line height), taking the printer off-line and pressing the line feed button only advances the paper by $\frac{1}{6}$ inch. Typical manuals never tell you that!

Likewise, the form feed button does not consider custom paper sizes. Even when you set up an $8\frac{1}{2}$-inch $\times$ 7-inch paper size (for working with imprinted checks, invoices, statements, and purchase orders), taking the printer off-line and pressing the form feed button always advances the paper by either 11 inches or 12 inches, depending on the current setting of DIP switch 1-4. Instead of advancing to the next 7-inch business form, the stock overshoots 4 to 5 inches. The same thing happens with 1-inch mailing labels. Press the form feed button and 11 (or 12) labels advance, not one!

The only way to use the line feed button effectively is to set up your programs for 6 lines-per-inch spacing. If a program doesn't support 6 lines-per-inch spacing, choose either the Courier 10 or the Monaco 12 font. As explained in Chapter 5, both fonts automatically give 6 lines-per-inch spacing.

To use the form feed button effectively, you have to use 8½-inch × 11-inch US letter paper, 14-inch × 11-inch computer paper (and an Imagewriter Wide), or 8¼-inch × 12-inch international fanfold paper. In all three cases, DIP switch 1-4 has to be set to match. DIP switches settings are covered next.

As designed, there's no way to get the form feed button to recognize 210-mm × 297-mm A4 letter paper or 8½-inch × 14-inch US legal paper. The only two lengths supported by the Imagewriter (Standard and Wide) are 11 inch and 12 inch.

DIP Switches DIP is an acronym for dual in-line package. Dual means that there are two rows of pins on the switch. In-line means that both rows are straight.

The Imagewriter's DIP switches are marked SW 1 and SW 2. As shown in Figure 8-3, these switches are located under the carrier cover, below the drive cabling, and slightly to the left of the paper-thickness lever. Tables 8-2 through 8-6 contain DIP-switch function details. Figure 8-16 shows the recommended US-Macintosh settings.

Table 8-2. Imagewriter (Standard and Wide) DIP Switch 1 Functions

Switch	Function	CLOSED	OPEN	US-Mac Setting
1-1	Alphabet	See Table 8-4		Open
1-2	Alphabet	See Table 8-4		Open
1-3	Alphabet	See Table 8-4		Open
1-4	Paper length	12 inch	11 inch	Open
1-5	Data bits	7 bits	8 bits	Open
1-6	CPI	See Table 8-5		Open
1-7	CPI	See Table 8-5		Open
1-8	CR code	CR + LF	CR	Open

Table 8-3. Imagewriter (Standard and Wide) DIP Switch 2 Functions

Switch	Function	CLOSED	OPEN	US-Mac Setting
2-1	Baud rate	See Table 8-6		Closed
2-2	Baud rate	See Table 8-6		Closed
2-3	Handshaking	X-ON/X-OFF	DTR	Open*
2-4	Not used	N/A	N/A	N/A

* Exceptions:

1. SW 2-3 should be closed (X-ON/X-OFF) for use with 128K/512K/512K Enhanced Macs connected via 590-0121 or 590-0169-B cables.
2. 590-0121 and 590-0169-B cables do not work in either position with Imagewriter driver v2.0.

Table 8-4. Imagewriter (Standard and Wide) DIP Switch 1-1 through 1-3 (Alphabet Selection) Settings

SW 1-1	SW 1-2	SW 1-3	Alphabet Selection
Open	Open	Open	American English
Closed	Closed	Open	European English
Open	Open	Closed	German
Open	Closed	Closed	French
Closed	Open	Closed	Swedish
Closed	Open	Open	Italian
Closed	Closed	Closed	Spanish
Open	Closed	Open	Danish

Table 8-5. Imagewriter (Standard and Wide) DIP Switch 1-6 and 1-7 (Character Set) Settings

SW 1-6	SW 1-7	Character Set/CPI
Open	Open	Pica 10
Closed	Open	Elite 12
Open	Closed	Ultracondensed 17
Closed	Closed	Elite Proportional

Table 8-6. Imagewriter (Standard and Wide) DIP Switch 2-1 and 2-2 (Baud Rate) Settings

SW 2-1	SW 2-2	Baud Rate
Open	Open	300 baud
Closed	Open	1200 baud
Open	Closed	2400 baud
Closed	Closed	9600 baud

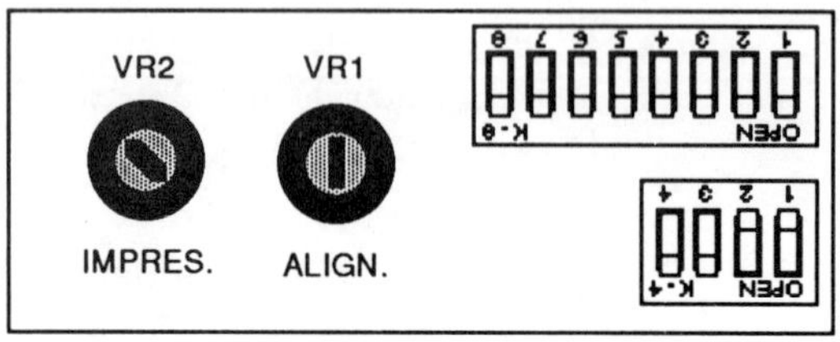

Figure 8-16 Imagewriter Standard recommended DIP-switch settings.

The recommendations given in Figure 8-16 differ from those given in other sources. Most sources recommend the Elite 12 font. That pitch almost never works with business forms. They also recommend X-ON/X-OFF (software) handshaking, but as previously explained in Chapters 1 and 4, software handshaking doesn't work with version 2.0 of the Imagewriter driver, and software handshaking doesn't work in general with PC-compatible computers. Elite 12 is also incorrect for PC-compatible use. So is the usually recommended 7 data-bit setting.

In other words, if you don't ever want the printer to work on PC-compatible computers, set the switches any way you want, but if you want the printer to work on all computers (not just Macintosh), set the switches according to Figure 8-16.

The only exception to that statement has to do with 128K, 512K, and 512K Enhanced Macs connected via OEM cables numbered 590-0121 or 590-0169-B. Because *neither cable works* with DTR handshaking, DIP switch SW 2-3 has to be closed (set to X-ON/X-OFF). That makes the whole computer system incompatible with Imagewriter driver 2.0 which *only works* with DTR handshaking.

One widely quoted source recommends scrapping the cable in that case. A much less-expensive alternative is to use another version of the Imagewriter driver. Every driver version *but* 2.0 works fine with OEM cable #590-0121 (provided SW 2-3 is closed). As explained in Chapter 4, the correct driver to use with older 400K-floppy-drive Macs is version 2.3.

Pin-Feed Paper Handling

When 9½-inch × 11-inch pin-feed paper (8½-inch × 11-inch without the stubs) is properly loaded into an Imagewriter, the release lever should be towards the back of the printer, the paper-thickness lever should be *all the way* toward the back of the printer (set for one-sheet thickness), the top edge of the first sheet of paper should just be visible under the roller shaft, and the left and right perforations should be centered ¼ inch beyond the red rings on the roller shaft. Single-thickness 9½-inch × 7-inch computer forms load in exactly the same way. There's no need to readjust the sprockets, the paper-thickness lever, or anything at all when switching from stationery to single-thickness computer forms.

When switching from stationery to multipart forms, you have to reset the paper-thickness lever. As shown in Figure 8-3, the paper-thickness lever is located under the front carrier cover just in front of the power switch. Be sure to set the paper-thickness lever for a two-sheet thickness when printing two-part forms, for a three-sheet thickness when printing three-part forms, and for a four-sheet thickness (all the way toward the front of the printer) when printing four-part forms.

Pin-feed form files generally assume a fixed ¼-inch hardware margin. That means, regardless what form you're loading, the left perforation should always be aligned ¼ inch to the left of the red ring on the roller shaft. In other words, most developers lay out their printing files so that the left Imagewriter sprocket, once properly adjusted for 9½-inch × 11-inch stationery, becomes an anchor point fixing the alignment point for both stationery and forms. In practice, this makes it very easy changing from one form to another. To load narrow forms, like 7-inch × 7-inch monthly statements or 1-inch × 3½-inch mailing labels, leave the left anchor tractor where it is and simply move the right, traveler tractor towards the left.

Wide-Carriage Exceptions

The procedure for wide-carriage printers is identical to the one just described, except the Imagewriter Wide doesn't have red rings on the roller shaft to mark the left and right edges of the printable page. Instead, there's a single raised rib on the left side of the front-carrier cover, just in back of the roller shaft. The raised rib is the same color as the top cabinet, so it's easy to overlook. If there's a red fine-point marker handy, the rib can be traced to make it stand out.

Once the rib is traced, the left perforation of the pin-feed stock should be positioned ⅜ inch to the left of the mark (not ¼ inch). In other words, there's generally an ⅛-inch difference in the left hardware margin between the Imagewriter Standard and the Imagewriter Wide.

To determine exactly where the left margin starts, run TCG's Tractor - TOF Alignment Test as explained in Chapter 7.

If you fail to take the extra ⅛-inch hardware margin into account, fields printed on business forms will always hit ⅛ inch to the left of where they should hit. If you assume a ¼-inch hardware margin just like the Imagewriter Standard, your left margins will invariably come out an ⅛-inch short.

Printer Stands

Successful printing of multipart pin-feed computer forms on the Imagewriter (Standard and Wide) requires a printer stand. Otherwise, the heavily folded paper feeds back into itself and jams. Without a printer stand, it is unlikely that business forms will print successfully on either machine.

Check Appendix B for vendors, or make an inexpensive, do-it-yourself printer stand from two 1-foot lengths of ordinary 4 × 4 framing lumber. With a printer stand, you can tuck the paper stock underneath the printer, instead of having to place it in back of the printer. As shown in Figure 8-17, this saves desk space, and clears an exit path for printed pages.

> Note: At most lumber yards, 4 × 4 lumber actually measures closer to 3⅜ inches × 3⅜ inches.

Figure 8-17 A do-it-yourself printer stand.

Cable Requirements

Tables 8-7 through 8-9 show DB-9S, DB-25S, and 8-pin minicircular socket Mac to Imagewriter (Standard and Wide) connector functions.

Table 8-7. 128K/512K/512K Enhanced Macintosh (RS-422) DB-9S Functions

Pin	Function	Description	Direction
1	FG	Frame ground	
2	+5 V DC	Positive five volts	
3	SG	Signal ground	
4	TxD+	Transmitted data +	Output to printer
5	TxD−	Transmitted data −	Output to printer
6	+12 V DC	Positive twelve volts	
7	HSKi	Handshake input	Input from printer
8	RxD+	Received data +	Input from printer
9	RxD−	Received data −	Input from printer

Table 8-8. Imagewriter (Standard and Wide) DB-25S Functions

Pin	Function	Description	Direction
1	FG	Frame ground	
2	TxD	Transmitted data	Output to computer
3	RxD	Received data	Input from computer
4	RTS	Request to send	Output to computer
5	NC	Not connected	
6	NC	Not connected	
7	SG	Signal ground	
8	NC	Not connected	
9	NC	Not connected	
10	NC	Not connected	
11	NC	Not connected	
12	NC	Not connected	
13	NC	Not connected	
14	FAULT		Output to computer
15	NC	Not connected	
16	NC	Not connected	
17	NC	Not connected	
18	NC	Not connected	
19	NC	Not connected	
20	DTR	Data terminal ready	Output to computer
21	NC	Not connected	
22	NC	Not connected	
23	NC	Not connected	
24	NC	Not connected	
25	NC	Not connected	

Table 8-9. Mac Plus and SE/II 8-pin Mini-circular Socket Functions

Pin	Function	Description	Direction
1	DTR	Data terminal ready	Output to printer
2	DSR	Data set ready	Input from printer
3	TxD−	Transmitted data −	Output to printer
4	SG	Signal ground	
5	RxD−	Received data −	Input from printer
6	TxD+	Transmitted data +	Output to printer
7	NC	Not connected	
8	RxD+	Received data +	Input from printer

Figures 8-18 through 8-20 are wiring diagrams for various Macintosh-to-Imagewriter (Standard and Wide) cables. The dotted lines between pin numbers indicate a connection. NC between pin numbers indicates no connection.

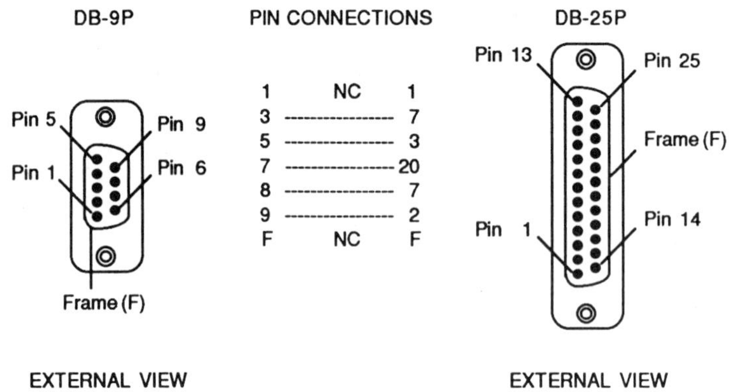

Figure 8-18 Wiring diagram for OEM part number 590-0069-A, Mac (128K/512K/512K Enhanced) to Imagewriter (Standard and Wide) cable.

Figure 8-21 is the wiring diagram for a Lisa/Mac XL modem cable. Figure 8-22 is the wiring diagram for a Lisa/Mac XL modem-eliminator cable. The modem-eliminator cable is only 10-inches long. When joined to the modem cable, it makes an OEM-recommended Lisa/Mac XL to Imagewriter (Standard and Wide) cable.

If you're making up a Lisa/Mac XL to Imagewriter (Standard and Wide) cable from scratch, you can skip the modem cable. All you really need to make is a long modem-eliminator cable.

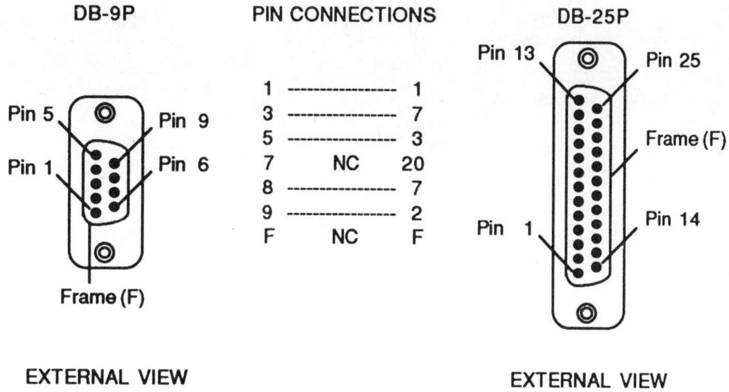

Figure 8-19 Wiring diagram for OEM Part-Number 590-0069-B, Mac (128K/512K/512K Enhanced) to Imagewriter (Standard and Wide) cable.

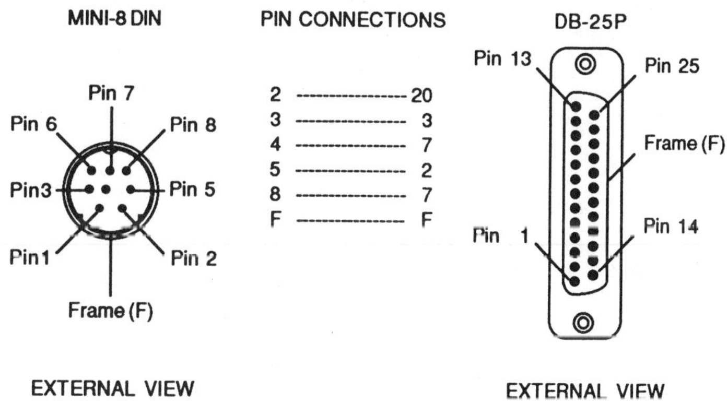

Figure 8-20 Wiring diagram for Mac (Plus and SE/II) to Imagewriter (Standard and Wide) cable.

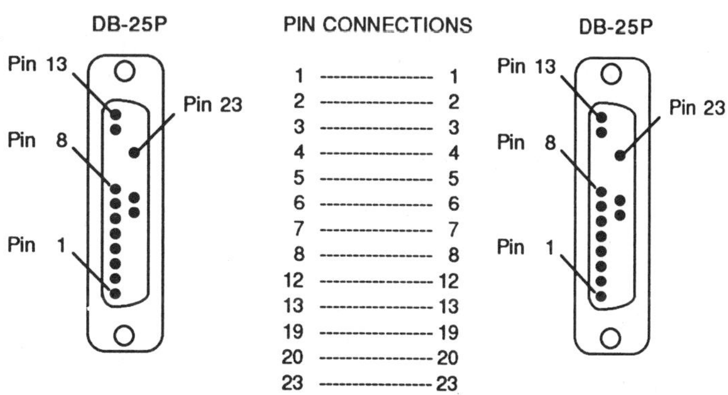

Figure 8-21 Wiring diagram for OEM part number 590-0037-B, Lisa/Mac XL modem cable.

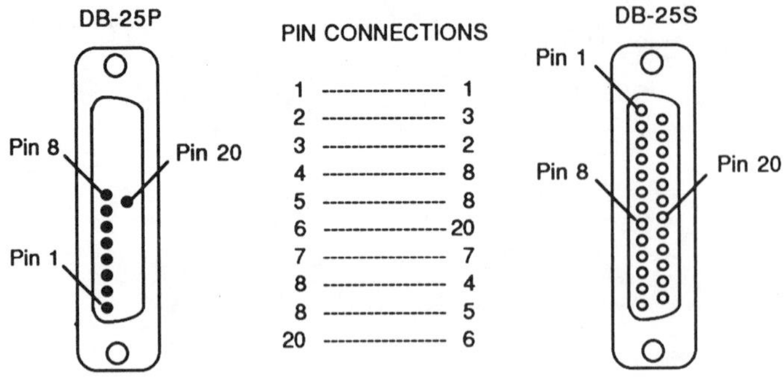

Figure 8-22 Wiring diagram for OEM part number 590-0029-00, Lisa/Mac XL modem-eliminator cable.

PC-Compatible Cable Requirements

Ask the typical Macintosh dealer how to connect an Imagewriter printer to a PC-compatible computer and more than likely the answer will be, "It can't be done." The truth is it *can* be done, very easily. This section shows you how.

Figure 8-23 shows the wiring diagram for connecting an Imagewriter (Standard and Wide) to PC/XT-compatible computer cable. This diagram assumes a standard PC/XT (eXtra Technology) computer fitted with a DB-25P (P for plug) serial connector. Some PC/XT computers have DB-25S (S for socket) serial connectors. In that case, you can make the same cable with two female connectors, or you could use the specified cable together with a gender changer.

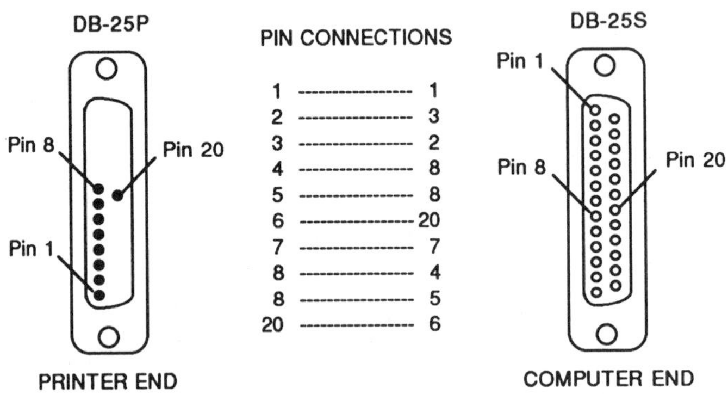

Figure 8-23 Wiring diagram for Imagewriter (Standard and Wide) to PC/XT-compatible computer cable.

Gender changers come in plug-to-plug (male-to-male), which converts female connections to male connections, and socket-to-socket (female-to-female), which converts male connections to female connections. The required gender changer should have two DB-25P (plug) connectors in order to change the female connection to a male connection.

AT-class (Advanced Technology) computers generally have DB-9P connectors. In that case, you also need a DB-9S to DB-25P (AT to XT) adapter in order to change the 9-pin male AT serial port into a 25-pin male XT serial port.

Prewired gender changers and prewired AT to XT serial adapters are both inexpensive and readily available. Check Appendix B for vendors.

PC-Compatible DIP Switch Settings As previously mentioned, PC-compatible computers do not support X-ON/X-OFF (software) handshaking so the Imagewriter (Standard and Wide) has to be configured for DTR (hardware) handshaking. In other words, DIP switch SW 2-3 has to be open. If DIP switch 2-3 is closed for X-ON/X-OFF handshaking, there'll be garbage and/or missing characters in the printout, after just a few pages.

In order for the printout to match the computer display, DIP switches SW 1-6 and SW 1-7 have to be open. These positions enable the Pica 10 character set, which prints 80 characters per line.

Finally, DIP switch SW 1-5 has to be open, for 8-bit data length. Otherwise, the printout will be peppered with unwanted characters.

PC-Compatible MS-DOS MODE Commands Once the cables and the DIP switches are correct, you need to enter two MS-DOS MODE commands on the PC-compatible computer. At the DOS prompt, type:

```
MODE COM1: 9600,N,8,1,P
MODE LPT1: = COM1:
```

The first MODE command configures the specified COM<n>: port (COM1: or COM2:) for 9600 baud, no parity, 8 data bits, and 1 stop bit. These terms were explained in Chapter 1. The P (at the end of the command) indicates that the device is a serial printer. If the Imagewriter (Standard and Wide) is plugged into COM2:, specify COM2: instead of COM1:. If the baud rate is stepped down to 1200, specify 1200 instead of 9600.

The second MODE command redirects LPT1: (the usually designated line printer) to the specified COM<n>: port. With this command in place, output from any program expecting a parallel printer on the parallel port (LPT1:) is automatically redirected to the Imagewriter.

To avoid having to enter these commands every time you switch on the PC-compatible computer, you can create a batch file. At the PC-compatible drive prompt, type:

```
COPY CON IW.BAT
ECHO OFF
MODE COM1: 9600,N,8,1,P
MODE LPT1: = COM1:
ECHO COM1: is now set for the Apple Imagewriter
ECHO ON
```

Type the instructions exactly as shown. Don't edit the instructions, add spaces, or change the punctuation. When you're finished, hold down the Control key and while keeping it down, type a Z. Let up the Control key and press the Return key. "1 File(s) copied" will appear on the display, followed by the usual drive prompt (A>).

From now on, whenever you want to set up for Imagewriter printing, all you'll have to do is type IW at the drive prompt (A>), and press the Return key.

PC-Compatible Imagewriter Printer Drivers Text printing from MS-DOS is automatic. Text printing from an application requires a TTY (teletypewriter) print driver. Graphics printing from an application requires a C.ITOH 8510a driver. The C.ITOH 8510a printer is 95% code-compatible with Imagewriter printers. To use the C.ITOH 8510a on a Mac, all you need is an ImageWriter driver. Conversely, to use an Imagewriter on a PC-compatible computer, all you need is a C.ITOH 8510a driver.

With the 8510a driver selected, the Imagewriter will print mixed text and graphics on a PC exactly the same as when it's connected to a Macintosh. Under Microsoft Windows, Microsoft Windows Write works pretty much like MacWrite. Microsoft Windows Paint works a lot like MacPaint. As far as the Imagewriter is concerned, there's no difference.

Apple II Cable Requirements

Table 8-10 shows the DIN-5 connector functions of the Apple IIc. Figure 8-24 shows the wiring diagram for an Imagewriter (Standard and Wide) to Apple IIc-compatible computer cable.

Table 8-10. Apple IIc DIN-5 Connector Functions

Pin	Function	Description	Direction
1	DTR	Data terminal ready	Output to printer
2	TxD	Transmit data	Output to printer
3	SG	Signal ground	
4	RxD	Receive data	Input from printer
5	DSR	Data set ready	Input from printer

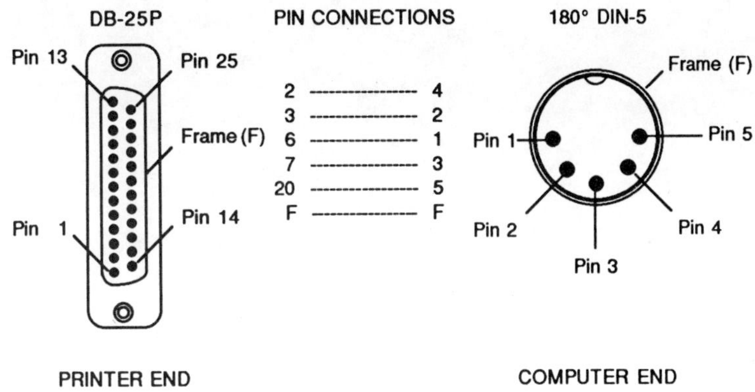

Figure 8-24 Wiring diagram for Imagewriter (Standard and Wide) to Apple IIc-compatible computer cable.

The Imagewriter (Standard and Wide) can also be used with an Apple II, Apple II+, or Apple IIe, provided the computer is fitted with an optional Super-Serial Card (OEM #661-91067 or equivalent). Connection is made using the Lisa/Mac XL modem (Apple Serial) cable shown in Figure 8-21; the modem/terminal jumper block on the Super-Serial Card has to be rotated toward the terminal (away from modem). For use with an Apple IIe, DIP-switch SW1-5 on the Imagewriter has to be closed.

Tables 10-10 through 10-13 (given at the end of Chapter 10) contain Apple II Super-Serial Card DIP-switch function details. Figure 10-23 (also given at the end of Chapter 10) shows the recommended Apple II Super-Serial Card DIP-switch settings for use with the ImageWriter II. These settings apply equally well to the Imagewriter (Standard and Wide); as far as the Apple II Super-Serial card is concerned, the settings are the same for all three printers.

That's it for Imagewriter setup secrets. Next, we'll look at repairs and maintenance.

CHAPTER

9

Imagewriter Repair Secrets

This chapter covers Imagewriter (Standard and Wide) repair and maintenance. Primarily concerned with mechanical repairs, it also shows how to remove stuck mailing labels, tells what to do about missing dots in the printout, tells how to spot bad ribbons, shows how to correct deviated (uneven) printout, and tells how to deal with completely dead sets.

Stuck Mailing Labels—Routine Maintenance

There's an old saying: "If it ain't broke, don't fix it." As a result, most people neglect their Imagewriters until there's a work-stopping mechanical problem. By far and away, the most common work-stopping mechanical problem is a stuck mailing label.

This section shows how to remove the label. In the process, we'll clean and lubricate the various mechanical parts, and generally restore the printer mechanism to like-new condition.

Imagewriter (Standard and Wide) Take-Apart Procedure

As shown in Figure 9-1, the cabinet top is hinged, and fastened by two hidden Phillips-head screws.

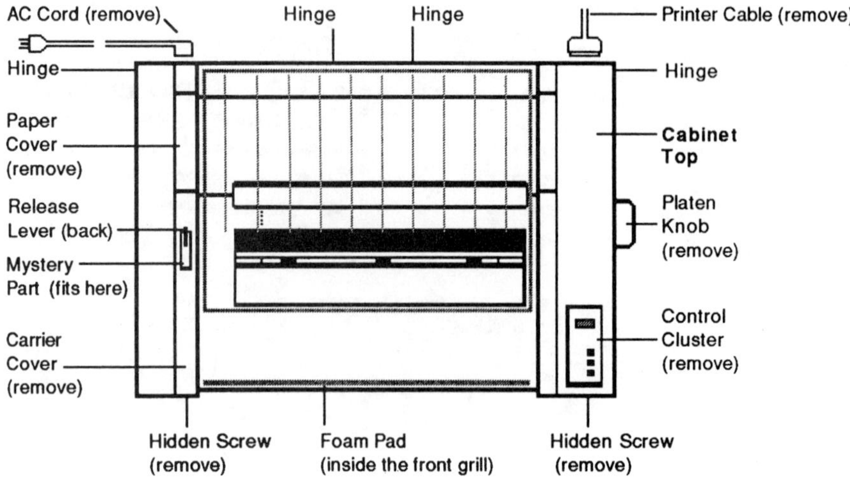

Figure 9-1 Imagewriter (Standard and Wide) take-apart procedure. The cabinet top is hinged, and fastened by two hidden Phillips-head screws.

For safety, always start the Imagewriter take-apart procedure by disconnecting the AC power cord. Disconnect means to physically separate it from the printer. Simply switching off the power is not enough. As long as the power cord is connected, every component between the power socket and the power switch is still alive. Taking the printer apart is hard enough as it is, without having to worry about live electrical connections. Be smart. Play it safe. Disconnect the power cord before beginning!

With electrical safety in mind, here's the complete take-apart procedure:

1. Disconnect the AC power cord from the wall outlet.
2. Disconnect the AC power cord from the printer.
3. Unscrew the Mac to Imagewriter cable from the DB-25S connector at the back of the printer.
4. Pull off the platen knob and put it aside.
5. Lift off the carrier and paper covers. Refer to Figure 9-1, if necessary for part identification. Put the paper and carrier covers aside.
6. As shown in Figure 9-2, there are two barbed latches at the front of the control cluster. The barbed latches hook the control cluster to the cabinet top. In this photo, the completely removed cabinet top is shown from the inside out as it lays on its right side. The control cluster has been reinstalled for clarity. When the cabinet top is attached to the Imagewriter, you can't see the latches. You have to feel for them.

Figure 9-2 There are two barbed latches at the front of the control cluster.

7. Make absolutely sure that the AC power cord is disconnected from the printer, then reach inside the cabinet top and feel for the control cluster latches. Release the barbed latches one at a time, then push the cluster upwards to separate it from the cabinet top.

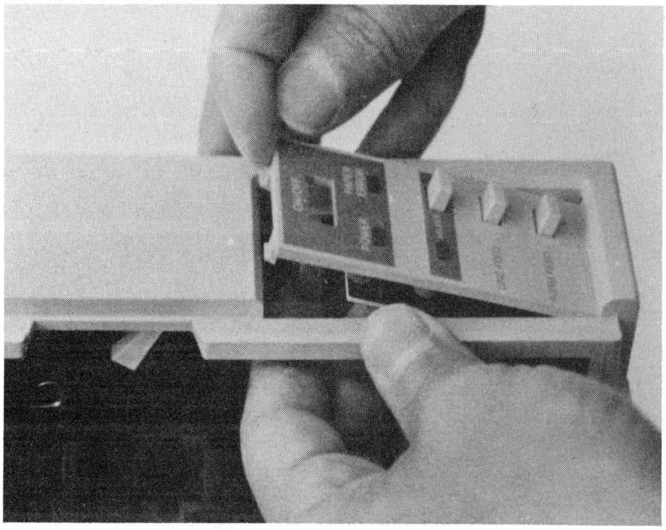

Figure 9-3 Release the barbed latches one at a time, then push the cluster upwards to separate it from the cabinet top.

8. As shown in Figure 9-4, disconnect the control-cluster wiring harness. Put the control cluster aside.

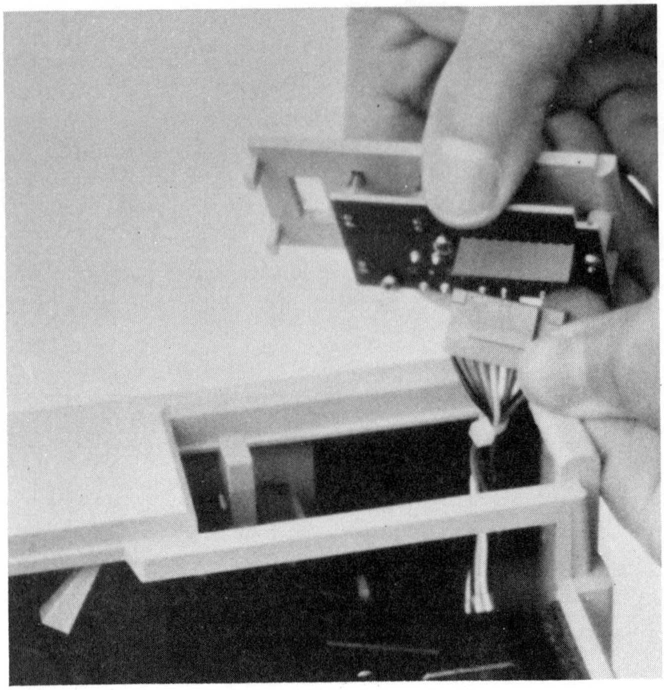

Figure 9-4 Disconnect the control-cluster wiring harness.

9. As shown in Figures 9-1 and 9-5, remove the two hidden cabinet-top screws (one screw in each front corner) using a magnetic screwdriver fitted with a #1 Phillips-head bit. If possible, use a magnetic screwdriver with a 4⅛-inch long shaft. Magnetic screwdrivers with 3⅛-inch short shafts fit through the control-cluster opening, but they are too short for use on the opposite side of the cabinet top. Note that both screws have flat tips. The platen-retaining screws removed later are exactly the same size and color, except they have pointed tips.
10. Refer to Figure 9-1. Push the release lever towards the back of the printer (into the pin-feed position).
11. Refer to Figure 9-1. Grip the foam pad which runs along the inside of the front grill, lift 1 inch or so, and rotate the cabinet top on its rear hinges. After an inch or so, two plastic eyelets (which were secured by the hidden screws) will snag on hidden obstructions, preventing the cabinet top from lifting any higher. The right-front eyelet snags on the control-cluster wiring harness. The left-front

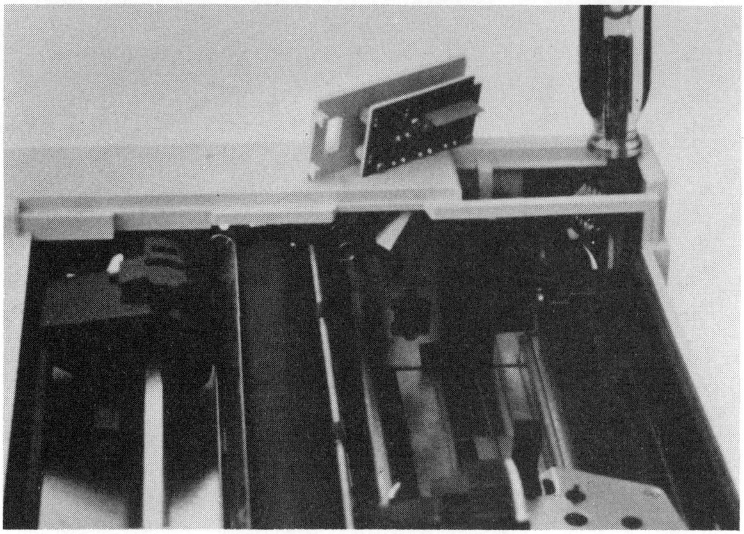

Figure 9-5 Remove the hidden cabinet-top screws using a magnetic screwdriver fitted with a #1 Phillips-head bit.

eyelet snags on the front carrier bar. Reach under the 1-inch clearance and pull the front of the cabinet towards you (pull out). Bend the cabinet plastic just enough to clear the obstructions and push up slightly (another ¼ inch or so).

12. Lift and rotate the cabinet top another 2 inches toward the back. Stop when the mystery part identified in Figure 9-6 falls out. At this point the front of the cabinet top should be approximately 3 inches above the table. The mystery part is a plastic trim piece for the release lever. It's called a mystery part, because once it falls out, its decorative function is not obvious. If you didn't know what it was, you'd probably have the whole printer back together again before you realized where it went.
13. Put the mystery part aside and rotate the cabinet top (backward) just enough to separate it from the rear hinges.
14. Rotate the unhinged cabinet 90° to the left. As shown in Figure 9-7, reach under the release lever and disconnect the carrier-cover switch.
15. The cabinet top is now completely disconnected. Lift it away and put it aside.

Clean the Cabinet Parts As shown in Figure 9-8, some Imagewriter cabinets are marred by packing-tape residue. Believe it or not, the original plastic bags were not large enough to completely enclose the printer, so they were taped (along with cardboard strips) directly to the cabinet.

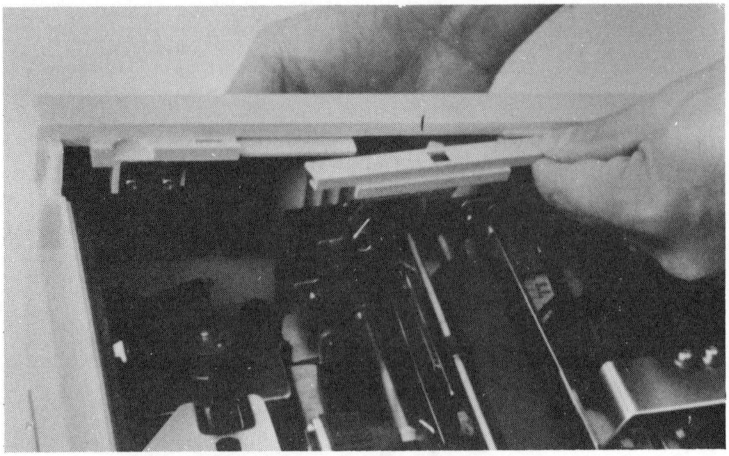

Figure 9-6 Mystery part.

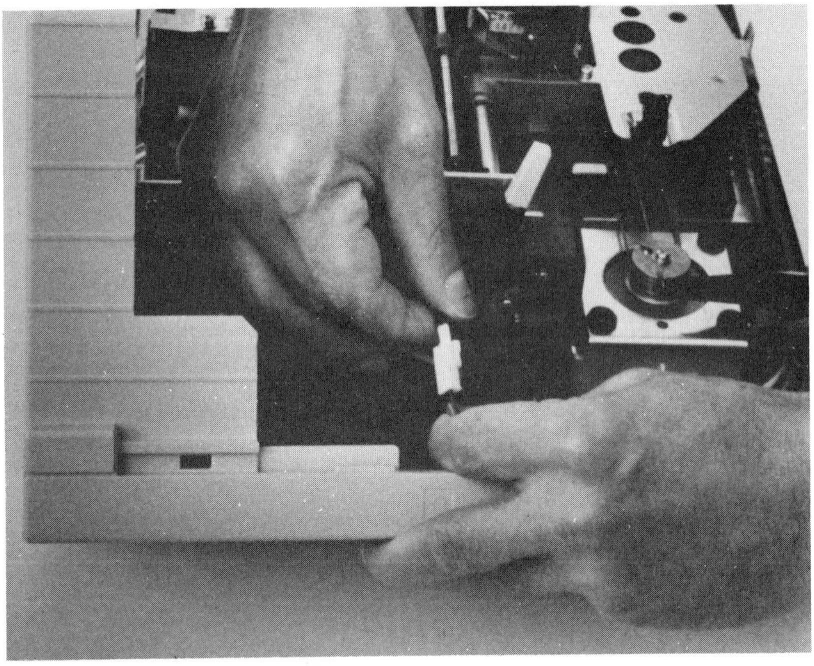

Figure 9-7 Disconnect the carrier-cover switch.

Figure 9-8 Some Imagewriter cabinets are marred by packing-tape residue.

Not only does the packing-tape residue look bad, but it makes working on the printer very unpleasant. Everything you touch sticks to your fingers. It's maddening. Unless you clean it all up, you'll never get anything fixed.

Normally, the tape residue is very difficult to remove. The printer is heavy, and you have to be careful to keep cleaning solvents off the platen and the drive gears. Now that the cabinet top has been removed, the job is much easier. Peel as much of the tape away as possible. Soak the rest with kerosene-based solvent. After a few minutes, wipe away the dissolved residue and finish up with household spray cleaner.

Weather permitting, you can take the cabinet top outdoors, scrub it with a floor brush, and rinse it with a garden hose. Use the same treatment on the carrier cover, the paper cover, and the platen knob. By the time you're done, your hands will be clean, the covers will be clean, and, once they sun dry, they'll look better than ever.

Clear plastic lids can be restored with plastic-windshield cleaner. This cleaner is normally used on boat windshields and plexiglass windowpanes. Apply it according to the manufacturer's directions and minor scratches will completely disappear. Even the deepest scratches become much less noticeable. The difference is amazing. Plastic-windshield cleaner is sold in auto-parts stores and marine departments.

Blow Out the Mechanism More often than not, the printer mechanism is covered with paper dust and pollen, generous amounts of human hair, and, sometimes, large amounts of pet fur. All of that buildup has to go. The best way to remove it is with an air compressor.

Alternately, you can reverse the hose of a vacuum cleaner and remove it with the vacuum-cleaner exhaust. It's best to do this outside. Blowing out the mechanism makes a sizeable dust cloud.

Platen Removal and Restoration

As shown in Figure 9-9, the platen rotates on plastic bushings which are secured to the printer frame by metal platen-shaft holders.

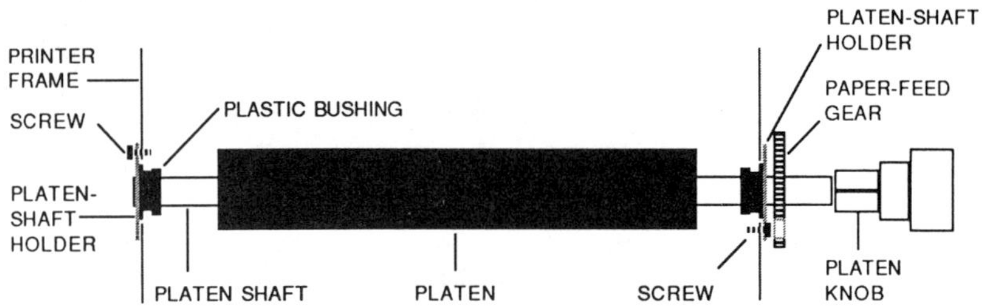

Figure 9-9 The platen rotates on plastic bushings which are secured to the printer frame by metal platen-shaft holders.

Each platen-shaft holder is held by a single screw. To remove the platen, all you have to do is unscrew the holders. Here's the complete procedure:

1. Pull back the roller shaft (as though you were going to insert paper).
2. Unscrew the left-side platen-shaft holder using a #1 Phillips-head screwdriver. Note that the screw tip is pointed. The cabinet-top screws removed previously are exactly the same size and color, except they have flat tips.
3. The platen-shaft holder may stick to the printer frame. If so, hook a finger inside the frame, and push out to pop it free.
4. The right-side platen-shaft holder is underneath the paper-feed gear. Rotate the paper-feed gear until the access hole (in the paper-feed gear) lines up with the screw head. Unscrew the platen-shaft holder using a #1 Phillips-head screwdriver. Note that the screw tip is pointed.

5. If the right-side platen-shaft holder sticks to the chassis, hook a finger inside the frame, and push out to pop it free, as explained in Step 3.
6. Hook your thumbs on both ends of the platen shaft and pull straight up. Don't pull at a 45° angle. Pull straight up. The metal paper guide behind the platen will bow a little, but provided you pull straight up (not at an angle), the entire platen assembly will pop right out. The idea here is to release both sides (of the platen assembly) simultaneously.
7. The platen assembly is now completely removed. Lift it away and put it aside.

When removing the platen-shaft holders, it's best to use a top-quality #1 Phillips-head screwdriver, something with a precision-ground, chrome-vanadium tip. The platen-shaft holder screws tend to be tight (very tight). If the screwdriver tip is soft, or the least bit chewed, all you're going to do is mangle the screw heads. Use a cheap tool, and you may regret it! Use a quality tool and the screws will come right out.

Sticky Residue Removal Remove sticky residue from the metal paper-guide parts with a kerosene-based spray solvent. Liquid kerosene also works. Let the solvent soak for a few minutes, and then wipe off the dissolved residue. With the platen out of the way, you'll have the metal parts sparkling clean in no time at all.

Be sure to clean under the paper-error detector (paper-end switch). If necessary, the paper-error detector can be loosened as shown in Figure 9-10.

Figure 9-11 shows the realignment details. This procedure comes after (assumes that) the platen is reinstalled. When correctly aligned, the detector arm should be parallel to the paper. In Figure 9-11, the top position is too tight—there's barely enough room for one sheet of paper. The middle position is too loose—look at the angle on the detector arm! The bottom position is just right; the detector arm is parallel to the paper, there's exactly enough room for four sheets of paper.

Burr Removal Occasionally, you may encounter metal paper-guide parts that are deeply scratched and burred. Scratches and metal splinters result from scraping at stuck labels with sharp objects (letter openers, nail files, pocketknives, etc.). Scraping at stuck labels almost never works. Not only is it much harder and more time-consuming than *unscrewing* the platen, the inevitable metal burrs which result tend to snag the advancing paper the same way a broken fingernail catches on your clothes.

Figure 9-10 If necessary, the paper-error detector can be loosened.

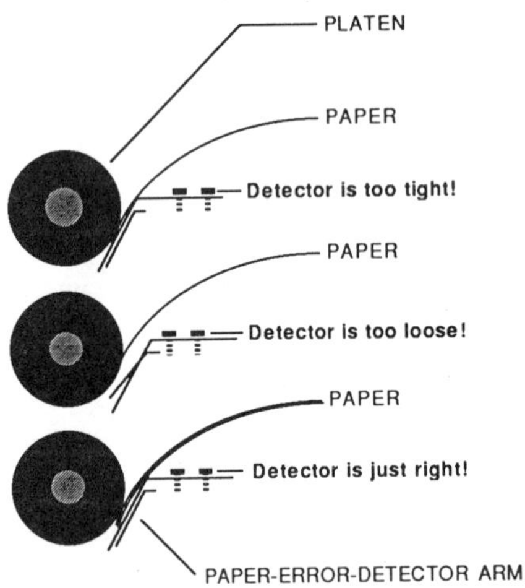

Figure 9-11 Paper realignment details.

When you encounter burred and splintered paper guides, they should be smoothed with #650 ultrafine abrasive paper. With a small piece of #650 paper, you can remove the burrs in seconds, without damaging the paper guide and faster than you can file a fingernail. Buy a single sheet of #650 paper at a hardware store, or remove whatever burrs you find using the smooth side of an emery board.

Platen Restoration To clean the printer platen, use typewriter-platen restorer, or tape-recorder rubber cleaner. The same rubber cleaner used on typewriter platens and tape-recorder pinch rollers works wonders on printer platens.

Apply a liberal amount with a paper towel and let it soak for a few minutes. Allowing the cleaning agent to soak into the rubber is very important. When it starts to evaporate, rub the platen vigorously (with the paper towel). The soaking action will have softened the rubber, and years of dried-up (dead-rubber) glaze will rub off right into the rag. In cases of severe neglect, you may have to repeat the application two or three times to fully restore the platen. When you're done, the platen will be dull, not shiny.

It's best to do this outside. Most rubber cleaners smell like maximum-strength moth flakes. The chemical treatment works great on rubber, but if you breathe the fumes, you may get a headache.

Try to buy typewriter-platen restorer and/or tape-recorder rubber cleaner locally. If it's not available, check Appendix B for vendors.

Gear Lubrication

Before putting the printer back together, it's worth a few minutes to lubricate the transfer gear. Rather than squirting the gear with oil, it's best to remove it, wipe the shaft clean, and apply fresh lubricant. It only takes a minute. Here's the complete procedure:

1. As shown in Figure 9-12, locate the transfer gear and spread its C-ring with an ⅛-inch slotted screwdriver. Cover the general area with your opposite hand to prevent the C-ring from flying into parts unknown. Use a screwdriver with a short (2-inch) shaft for maximum control.
2. As shown in Figure 9-13, slip the gear off its axle.
3. With a straightened paper clip, poke a tissue through the gear bearing (the hole in the center of the gear). This step removes the old lubricant. Old lubricant is generally contaminated with paper dust (sticky). Dust is the enemy of all mechanical devices. You have to remove it, or it'll just contaminate the new lubricant.
4. Wipe the gear shaft with a paper towel.
5. Apply a drop of sewing-machine (or tape-recorder) oil to the clean gear shaft. It's not necessary to lubricate the gear bearing. One drop on the shaft is plenty. Resist the temptation to overlubricate.
6. Slide the transfer gear back onto the shaft.
7. Reattach the C-ring.

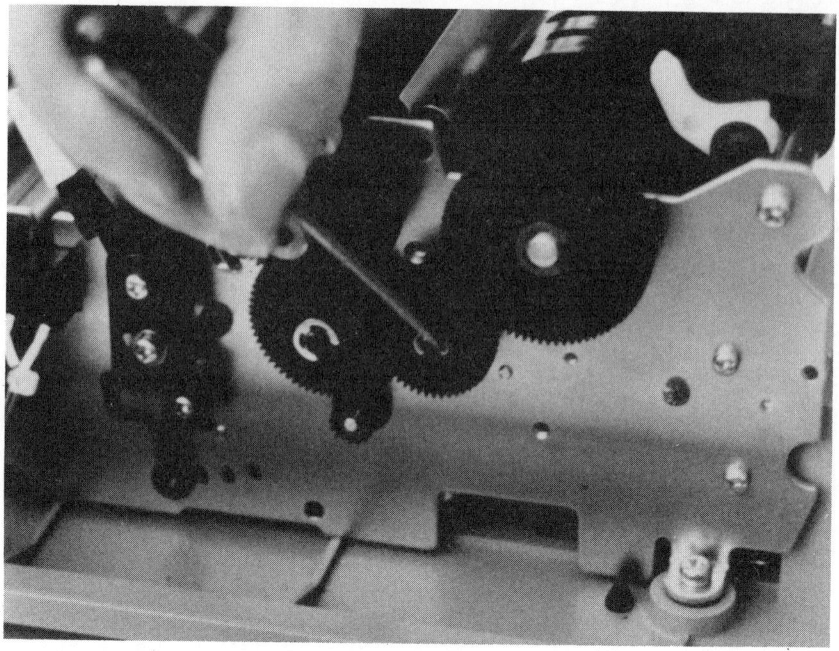

Figure 9-12 C-ring removal.

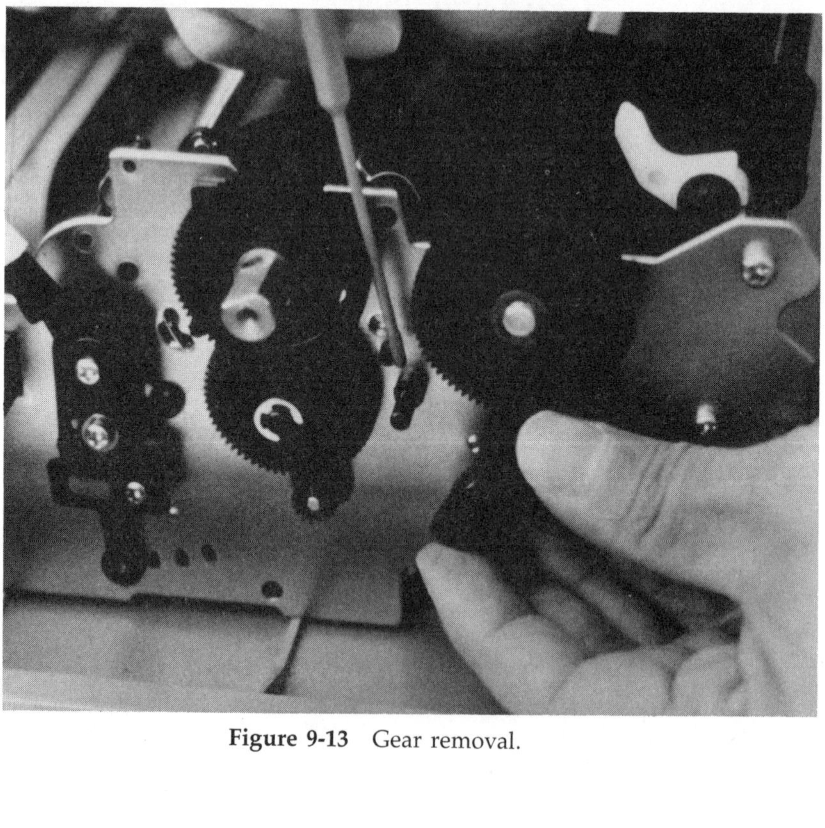

Figure 9-13 Gear removal.

Roller-Shaft Lubrication

The roller shaft is lubricated exactly the same way. As shown in Figure 9-14, the roller shaft is under light spring tension. Note the orientation of the spring coils. Be sure to point them the same way when you reinstall them.

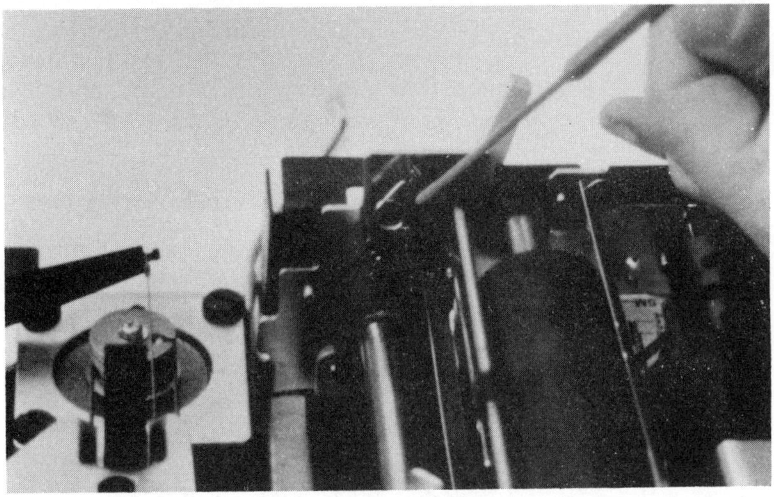

Figure 9-14 Roller-shaft spring-coil orientation.

With the correct, spring-coil orientation in mind, here's the complete roller-shaft lubrication procedure:

1. Set up a plastic container, suitable for holding small parts.
2. Squeeze the base of the springs to remove them; put them in the container.
3. Use a short-shaft ⅛-inch slotted screwdriver to remove the C-rings at both ends of the roller shaft. Put each C-ring in the container as soon as you remove it.
4. Slip the roller shaft out of its holders.
5. Remove the C-rings adjacent to the rollers and put them in the parts container.
6. Wipe the roller shaft clean.
7. With a straightened paper clip, poke a tissue through each of the roller bearings (holes in the centers of the rollers). The purpose of this step is to remove the old-lubricant residue. Generally, old lubricant is contaminated with paper dust (sticky). Unless you remove the dust, it will immediately contaminate the new lubricant.

8. Reverse Steps 2 through 5, applying a tiny drop of fresh sewing-machine or tape-recorder oil to each roller bearing. Resist the temptation to overlubricate.

When flicked with a finger, the freshly lubed rollers should spin through several revolutions like a top. Instead of buckling the paper as it advances, they'll now offer minimum resistance to the advance, which is just what the designers intended.

It's a good idea to lubricate the roller shaft now, before reinstalling the platen. The procedure is oily. The platen is rubber; oil and platen rubber generally don't mix.

Imagewriter (Standard and Wide) Reassembly Procedure

Reverse Steps 1 through 7 of the platen-removal procedure, if necessary, to reinstall the platen. Remember, the platen retaining screws have pointed tips; the cabinet-top screws (used below) have flat tips.

With the roller shaft, the gears, and the platen reinstalled, it's time to reassemble the cabinet. Here's the complete reassembly procedure:

1. As shown in Figure 8-9, push the release lever into the pin-feed position.
2. Check the left rear corner of the printer. Make sure the wires leading to and from the Fujiken noise filter, marked part number NF-25030PL8, are tucked neatly alongside the filter. When the wires crisscross the filter, it's very difficult to get the cabinet top back on.
3. As shown in Figure 9-7, stand the cabinet top on its left side, and reconnect the safety switch.
4. With the safety switch connected, reach through the opening in the cabinet top, and hook one hand around the tractor bar. Lift the printer by the tractor bar. Rotate the cabinet and concentrate on reconnecting the rear plastic hinges. You've got to rehinge the back of the cabinet top before seating the front. Remember to pull up on the tractor bar. It's not possible to reconnect the cabinet-top hinges unless the printer is elevated.
5. With the rear hinges caught and the front of the cabinet top approximately 3 inches up from the table, tuck the control-cluster harness out of the way.
6. Pull out on the front grill in order to clear the front carrier bar and, simultaneously, push the cabinet top all the way down.
7. Check the rear hinges. If they're not connected, remove the cabinet top and try again.

8. With the cabinet top properly hinged and seated, lift up slightly on the front grill and reinstall the release-lever trim piece, as shown in Figure 9-6.
9. Reinstall the two hidden cabinet-top screws as shown in Figures 9-1 and 9-5.
10. The platen shaft has a flat spot. Check for the matching flat spot on the platen knob, and press it home.
11. Reconnect the control-cluster harness. Snap the control cluster into place.
12. Reinstall the paper and carrier covers.
13. Reattach the Mac to Imagewriter cable to the DB-25S connector at the back of the printer.
14. Reconnect the AC power cord to the printer.
15. Reconnect the AC power cord to the wall outlet.

The printer is now completely reassembled and ready to go. Up to this point, from the time we started the take-apart procedure, but not counting the time it takes to wash down the cabinet parts, we've invested about 20 minutes, certainly no more than a half hour. The first time (learning how) always takes longer, but when you think about it, all we removed was just four screws. The only tool we used was a #1 Phillips-head screwdriver. So how much is this exercise worth?

The going rate for stuck-label repairs is $65.00. At 20 minutes per repair (less time than it takes most people to *drive* to the repair shop), the value of this exercise works out to $195.00 per hour, which is a very nice return from a $35.00 computer book.

Missing Dots in the Printout

The two main causes of missing dots in the printout are corroded contacts on the type head, and distended striker wires. Corroded contacts are easily repaired by removing the type head and rubbing them with a pencil eraser. Here's the complete procedure:

1. Disconnect the AC power cord from the printer.
2. Refer to Figure 9-1. Remove the carrier cover. Put it aside.
3. Remove the ribbon cassette. Put the ribbon cassette aside.
4. As shown in Figure 9-15, rotate the type-head lock plates approximately 180°. Note that the lock plates rotate in opposite directions.
5. As shown in Figure 9-16, lift the roller shaft out of the way, grip the type head, and pull straight up.

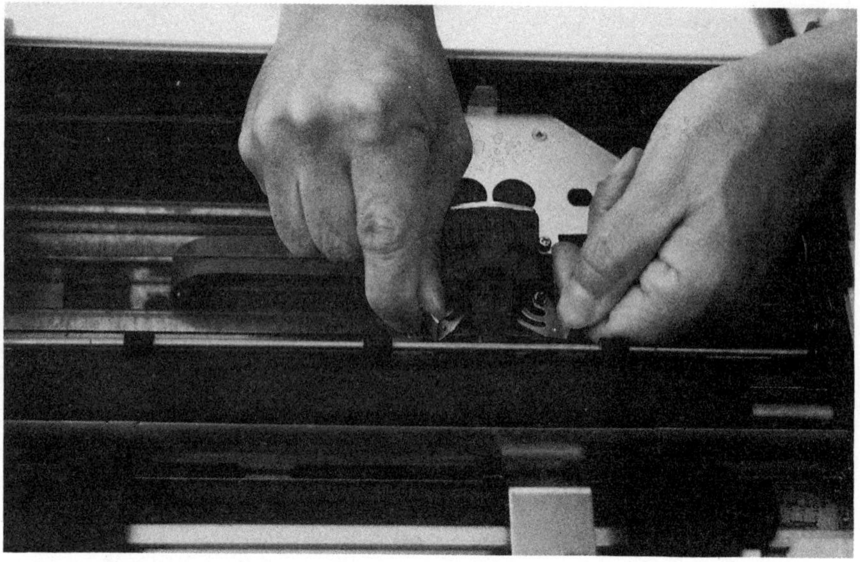

Figure 9-15 With the ribbon cassette removed, rotate the type-head lock plates approximately 180°.

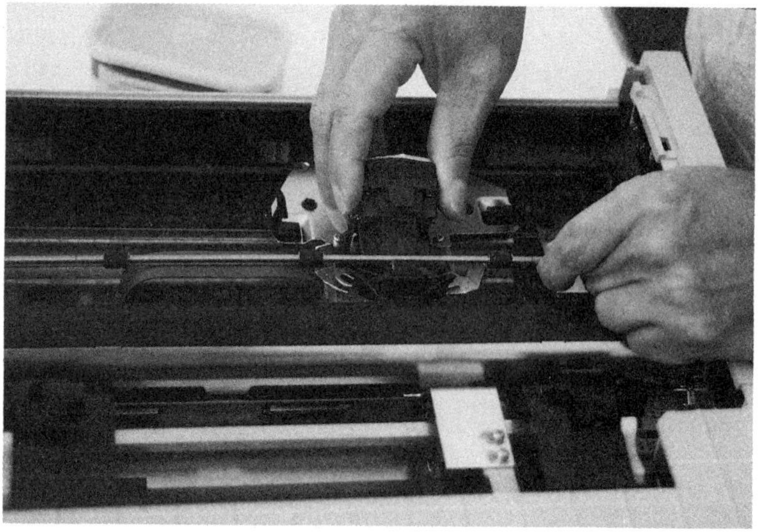

Figure 9-16 With the lock plates fully rotated, lift the roller shaft out of the way, grip the type head, and pull straight up.

Type heads which have never been removed may offer considerable resistance. Continue pulling until the type head lifts away as shown in Figure 9-17.

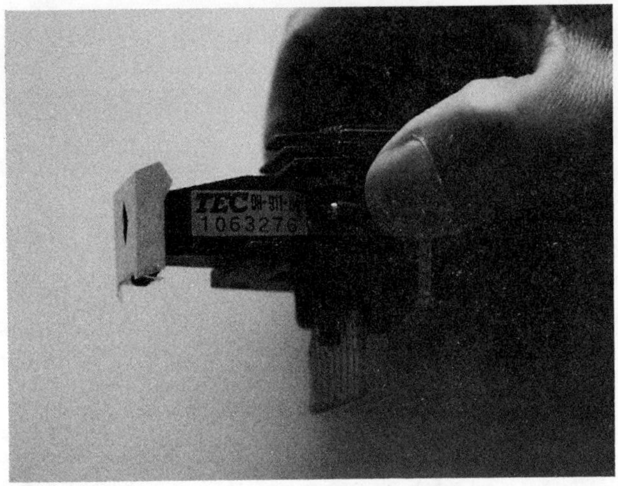

Figure 9-17 Imagewriter (Standard and Wide) type head.

6. Type-head contacts are shown in Figure 9-18. Rub both sides of the board gently with a soft pencil eraser to remove corrosion.

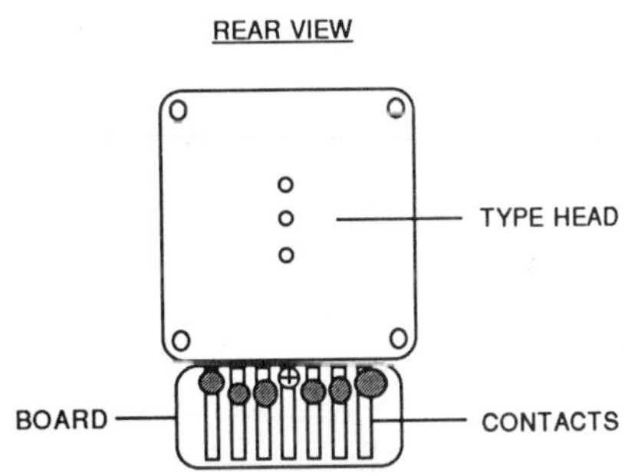

Figure 9-18 Rub both sides of the board gently with a soft pencil eraser to remove corrosion.

7. Lubricate the carrier shaft as described below, if necessary.
8. Reverse Steps 1 through 6 to reinstall the type head.

Carrier-Shaft Lubrication

As shown in Figure 9-19, the carrier-shaft lubrication ring is located under the type head. To access the ring, the ribbon cassette and the type head have to be removed as explained above.

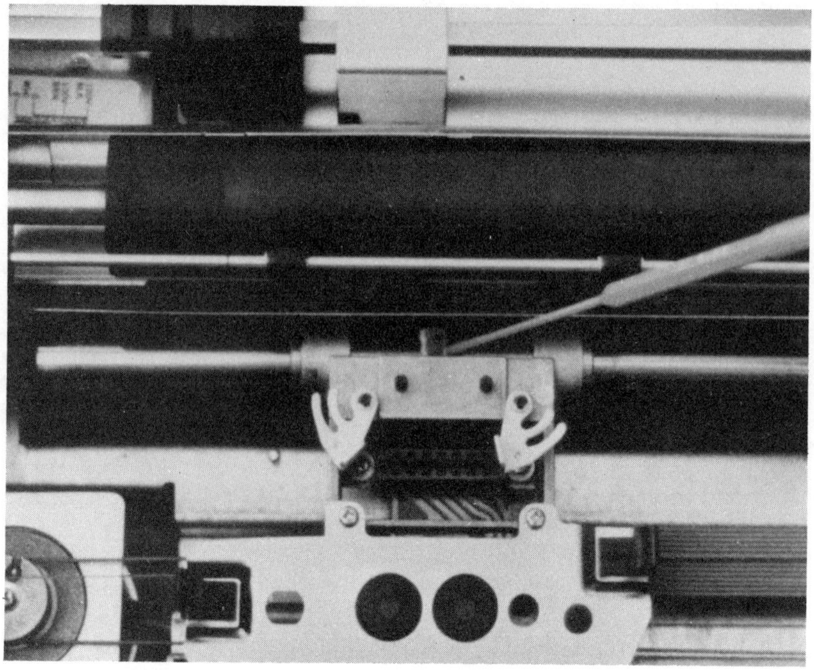

Figure 9-19 Imagewriter (Standard and Wide) carrier-shaft lubrication ring.

The felt ring is designed to hold a few drops of oil. As the carrier moves back and forth, the oil wipes off on the carrier shaft, which keeps it lubricated. Over time, the oil dissipates and has to be replenished.

Due to the wiping action of the mechanism, accumulated dust tends to build up at the ends of the carrier shaft. Carefully remove the dust, and then refill the lubrication ring with 2 or 3 drops of sewing-machine (or tape-recorder) oil. Resist the temptation to overlubricate. The lubrication ring should be moist, but not dripping. Move the carrier from side to side to spread the fresh oil evenly across the shaft, and then reinstall the type head and the ribbon cassette.

Page 29 of the *Apple Imagewriter User's Manual, Part I: Reference* warns against using electric-motor oil or any oil that contains rust inhibitors. Vendors of high-quality electronic-servicing oils that meet this criteria are listed in Appendix B.

Distended Striker Wires

When rubbing the type-head contacts with a pencil eraser fails to restore missing dots in the printout, the most likely cause is a distended striker wire. Check for distended striker wires by examining the type head. If one or more striker wires protrude further than the others, as shown in Figure 9-20, you'll have to replace the type head (or send it out for repair), and replace the ribbon cassette.

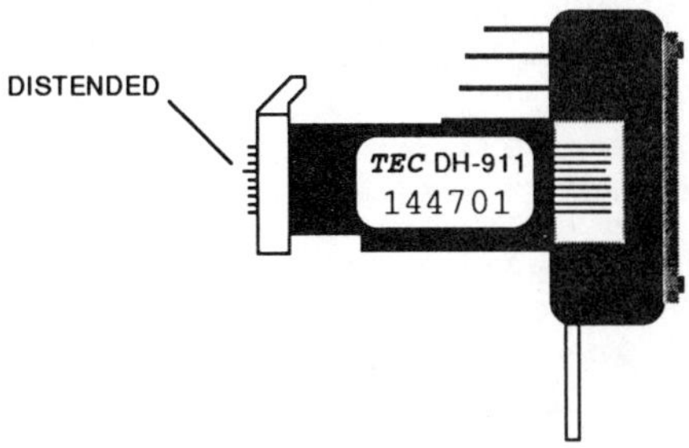

Figure 9-20 Imagewriter (Standard and Wide) type head. Distended striker wire protrudes further than the others.

In fact, it's poorly designed ribbon cassettes that usually cause this problem. When built-in character sets are selected on-the-fly in high-speed draft mode, the printer changes speeds very quickly. Some ribbon cassettes can't shift that fast; either an extra length of ribbon spills out, or they momentarily jam. When that happens, the momentarily stalled ribbon fabric is pulverized. If the cassette mechanism doesn't recover quickly enough, one or more striker wires puncture the ribbon fabric. If the striker wires are still inside the fabric when the cassette recovers, the sudden lateral movement can twist them out of alignment. Once they're out of alignment (bent out of shape), they don't return. If they don't return, they don't fire. Even when the wires do return, the ribbon fabric tears, which leads to further snagging.

The symptom of this problem is an unexplained dropout in the printout. When running TCG's CPI - Character Sets test, watch for it when shifting from ultracondensed, 17-cpi type to Pica 10 cpi. Typical symptoms are simulated in Figure 9-21.

It's no coincidence that ultracondensed 17 is the slowest typeface and Pica 10 is the fastest. That merely proves the point. *Poorly designed ribbon cassettes are the number one cause of type-head failure.* Bear in mind that we're not talking about individual ribbons. Certain brands fail this test nearly 100% of the time. Other brands almost never fail. Furthermore, ribbon-cassette testing will prove that quality is generally *not* related to price. You can pay a lot of money for junk, while great ribbon cassettes are sometimes quite inexpensive.

```
CONTROL SECTION - DP (DATA PROCESSING)
PICA (10 CPI) abcdefghijklmnopqrstuvwxyz-123456789
EXTENDED (9 CPI) abcdefghijklmnopqrstuvwxyz-123456789
ELITE (12 CPI) abcdefghijklmnopqrstuvwxyz-123456789
SEMICONDENSED (13.4 CPI) abcdefghijklmnopqrstuvwxyz-123456789
CONDENSED (15 CPI) abcdefghijklmnopqrstuvwxyz-123456789
ULTRA CONDENSED (17 CPI) abcdefghijklmnopqrstuvwxyz-123456789

TEST SECTION - NLQ (NEAR LETTER QUALITY)
PICA (10 CPI) abcdefghijklmnopqrstuvwxyz-123456789
EXTENDED (9 CPI) abcdefghijklmnopqrstuvwxyz-123456789
ELITE (12 CPI) abcdefghijklmnopqrstuvwxyz-123456789
SEMICONDENSED (13.4 CPI) abcdefghijklmnopqrstuvwxyz-123456789
CONDENSED (15 CPI) abcdefghijklmnopqrstuvwxyz-123456789
ULTRA CONDENSED (17 CPI) abcdefghijklmnopqrstuvwxyz-123456789
```

Figure 9-21 This kind of dropout suggests a poorly designed ribbon cassette.

Use Test Character Generator to precheck individual ribbons and/or to separate good designs from the bad designs. If you find any of the latter designs, don't use them. It's senseless to destroy an expensive type head over a $2.00 ribbon.

Wavy, Uneven Printing

A common problem with all dot-matrix printers (not just Imagewriters) is wavy, uneven printout. Over time, the carrier-wire loosens, hammer-fire timing drifts, and character linearity distorts, just like wavy reflections in a fun-house mirror. Officially, it's called character deviation. The deviation is most noticeable when printing bidirectionally in Best or High quality. You can't stop character deviation from happening, but with Test Character Generator, you can easily correct it. Figure 9-22 shows TCG's Bidirectional Alignment test.

In theory, test printout from a properly aligned printer should look just like a window screen. In practice, characters at the edges of the printout almost always deviate, because of ricochet from the carriage return. In other words, we can get the middle of the page just about perfect, but there'll always be a *little* wave at the edges. Format your documents with 1-inch left and right margins and you'll never see it.

With reasonable expectations in mind, here's the complete bidirectional alignment procedure:

1. As shown in Figure 9-23, remove the carrier cover. Note the hidden magnet.

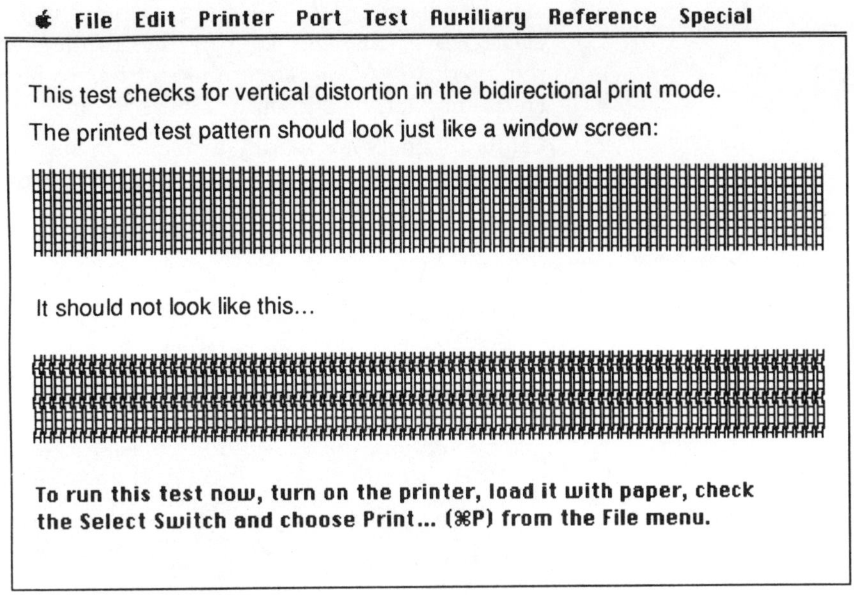

Figure 9-22 Test Character Generator Bidirectional Alignment test.

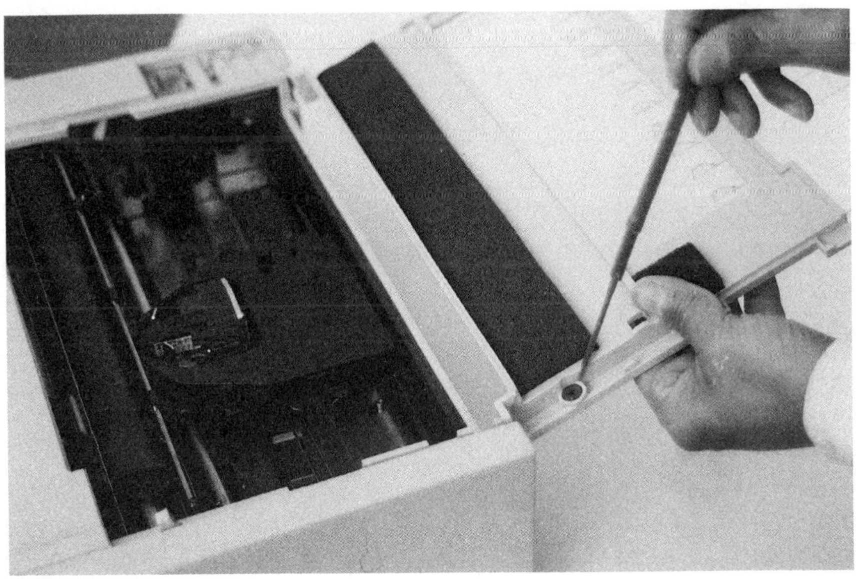

Figure 9-23 Imagewriter (Standard and Wide) carrier-cover magnet.

2. As shown in Figure 9-24, the carrier-cover magnet activates the carrier-cover switch. To run the printer with the carrier-cover removed, the carrier cover magnet has to be replaced with a small crafts magnet, as shown in Figure 9-25.

Crafts magnets are readily available in sewing and notions departments. The magnet shown in Figure 9-25 measures $\frac{5}{16}$-inch wide, $\frac{17}{16}$-inch long and $\frac{5}{32}$-inch thick (approximately $\frac{1}{4} \times 1 \times \frac{1}{8}$ inch).

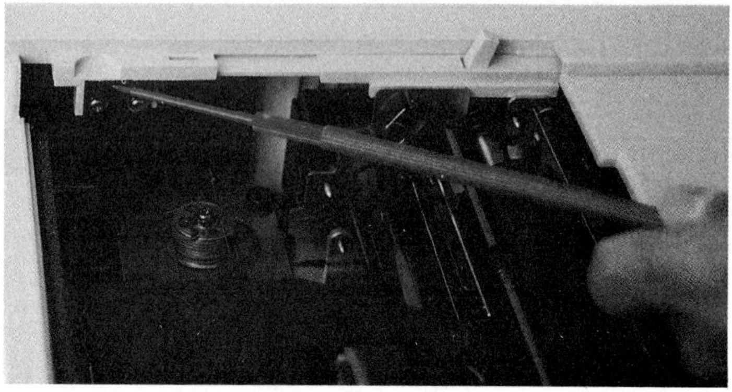

Figure 9-24 Imagewriter (Standard and Wide) carrier-cover switch.

Figure 9-25 To run the printer with the carrier-cover removed, the carrier-cover magnet has to be replaced with a small crafts magnet.

3. Load paper, and switch on the printer.
4. Press the SELECT switch. If the green LED (light-emitting diode) blinks out as soon as you release the SELECT switch, turn the magnet around and try again. Repeat, as necessary, until you get the green LED to stay lit.
5. Run TCG's Bidirectional Alignment test. After 10 lines, TCG stops and asks whether to "Repeat this test?", as shown in Figure 9-26.

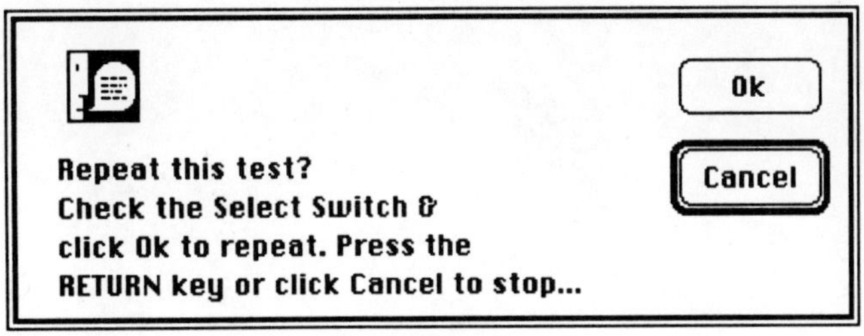

Figure 9-26 Test Character Generator "Repeat this test?" dialog box.

6. Examine the printout, and then locate VR1, the Imagewriter's character-deviation potentiometer. As shown in Figure 9-27, VR1 is under the drive cabling next to the DIP switches. Tweak the character-deviation pot (VR1) just a hair, one way or the other, and then click the OK button to repeat the test.

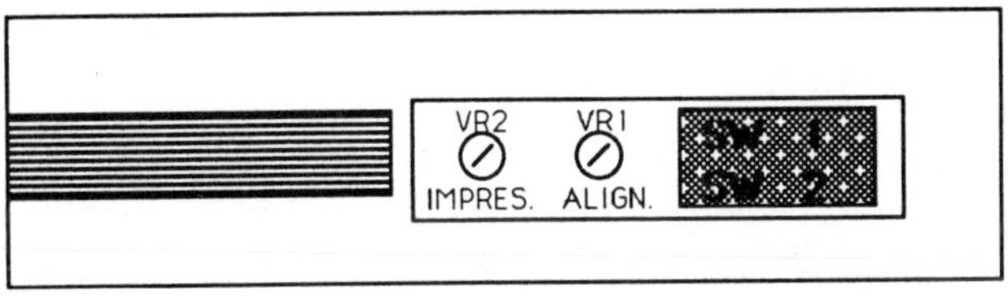

Figure 9-27 Imagewriter (Standard and Wide). The character-deviation potentiometer, VR1, is under the drive cabling next to the DIP switches.

7. Repeat Step 6, as necessary, for best results. Tap the Return key, or click the Cancel button to discontinue testing.
8. If the printed test pattern is still unsatisfactory, the carrier-wire tension arm will have to be adjusted. Remove the cabinet as explained in Steps 1 through 15 of the Imagewriter take-apart procedure.
9. As shown in Figure 9-28, locate the carrier-wire tension arm. Turn the screw just a little to tighten the wire.
10. Jumper the carrier-cover switch connector with an alligator clip.
11. Reconnect the control cluster and the AC power cord.
12. Repeat Steps 5 through 7, adjusting both the character-deviation pot (VR1) and the carrier-wire tension arm until the printout is satisfactory. Concentrate on the center of the test pattern. When you get the center aligned properly, character deviation at the edges should be 0.3 mm or less.
13. Disconnect the alligator clip from the carrier-cover switch connector.

Figure 9-28 Imagewriter (Standard and Wide) carrier-wire tension arm.

14. Follow Steps 1 through 15 of the Imagewriter reassembly procedure to reassemble the top cabinet.

If neither adjustment seems to improve the printout, one or more of the striker wires in the type head may be out of alignment. Remove the type head and examine the striker wires under a magnifying glass. All nine wires should be in a straight line. If one or more of the wires is clearly out of line, you'll never align the printout until you replace the type head.

For type-head ordering information, see the replacement parts subheading at the end of this chapter.

When making these adjustments, bear in mind that all you need to do is compensate for normal wear and tear. A little tweak, one way or the other, is all it's going to take. Turn the screws carefully. A little trim generally goes a long way!

Dead Sets

When an Imagewriter (or any printer, for that matter) fails to print, most people immediately assume the worst. Let a single screw loosen up, and they assume that the printer is "totally blown." They assume, or they're told, that they're going to need a "whole new logic board," and that repairs will cost "hundreds of dollars." In fact, most dead-set failures have nothing to do with the logic board. They're peripheral related, and fairly easy to spot. This section shows you how. We'll use a process of elimination involving five logical steps:

1. Check the usual (software, cables, etc.). If that passes....
2. Run the printer's built-in self-test. If that passes....
3. Check the printer's serial interface. If that passes....
4. Check the computer's serial interface. If that passes....
5. Repeat Step 1—try new System software, try a new cable.

Dead sets fall into two categories: control cluster lit, control cluster not lit. First, we'll look at control cluster lit.

Dead Sets—Control Cluster Lit

If the control cluster is lit, but absolutely nothing happens when you try to print, it's usually due to one of the following:

1. Printer resource (driver) is not installed. See Chapter 3.
2. Printer resource (driver) is not selected. Use the Choose-Printer or Chooser DA to select the printer. See Chapter 3.
3. Printer is out of paper, or printer is off-line. Load paper and press the Select button. See Chapter 8.
4. Cable is disconnected or incorrect. See Chapter 8.
5. DIP switches are set incorrectly. See Chapter 8.

When you're absolutely sure that none of the above is responsible, the next thing to do is to determine whether the problem is in the printer or the computer. We can clear the printer with two quick tests.

Built-in Self-Test The Imagewriter (Standard and Wide) is equipped with a built-in self-test. This test checks the carrier motor, the line feed motor, the type head, the carriage return switch, and the out-of-paper switch—everything but the printer's serial-communications interface. To run the printer's self-test:

1. Switch off the printer (if it's on).
2. Load the printer with maximum-size paper. Use 8½ × 11, or 8½ × 12-inch paper on a standard-size Imagewriter. Use 14 × 11 or 14 × 12-inch paper on a wide-carriage Imagewriter. If you fail to load maximum-size paper, the self-test will print right across the platen. That's not good for the platen and it's not good for the type head.

3. Hold down the FORM FEED button, and, while keeping it held down, press the ON/OFF button.

As shown in Figure 9-29, the built-in self-test prints a repeating alphanumeric test pattern. To suspend the test pattern, press the LINE FEED button. To resume the test pattern, press the SELECT button. To stop the test pattern, turn the printer off.

Nine times out of ten, the test pattern prints fine. If it doesn't, see component-level repairs at the end of this chapter.

```
OPQRSTUVWXYZ[\]^_`abcdefghijklmnopqrstuvwxyz{|}~ !"#$%&'()*+,-./0123456789:;<=>?@ABCDEFGHIJKLMNO
PQRSTUVWXYZ[\]^_`abcdefghijklmnopqrstuvwxyz{|}~ !"#$%&'()*+,-./0123456789:;<=>?@ABCDEFGHIJKLMNOP
QRSTUVWXYZ[\]^_`abcdefghijklmnopqrstuvwxyz{|}~ !"#$%&'()*+,-./0123456789:;<=>?@ABCDEFGHIJKLMNOPQ
RSTUVWXYZ[\]^_`abcdefghijklmnopqrstuvwxyz{|}~ !"#$%&'()*+,-./0123456789:;<=>?@ABCDEFGHIJKLMNOPQR
STUVWXYZ[\]^_`abcdefghijklmnopqrstuvwxyz{|}~ !"#$%&'()*+,-./0123456789:;<=>?@ABCDEFGHIJKLMNOPQRS
TUVWXYZ[\]^_`abcdefghijklmnopqrstuvwxyz{|}~ !"#$%&'()*+,-./0123456789:;<=>?@ABCDEFGHIJKLMNOPQRST
UVWXYZ[\]^_`abcdefghijklmnopqrstuvwxyz{|}~ !"#$%&'()*+,-./0123456789:;<=>?@ABCDEFGHIJKLMNOPQRSTU
VWXYZ[\]^_`abcdefghijklmnopqrstuvwxyz{|}~ !"#$%&'()*+,-./0123456789:;<=>?@ABCDEFGHIJKLMNOPQRSTUV
WXYZ[\]^_`abcdefghijklmnopqrstuvwxyz{|}~ !"#$%&'()*+,-./0123456789:;<=>?@ABCDEFGHIJKLMNOPQRSTUVW
XYZ[\]^_`abcdefghijklmnopqrstuvwxyz{|}~ !"#$%&'()*+,-./0123456789:;<=>?@ABCDEFGHIJKLMNOPQRSTUVWX
YZ[\]^_`abcdefghijklmnopqrstuvwxyz{|}~ !"#$%&'()*+,-./0123456789:;<=>?@ABCDEFGHIJKLMNOPQRSTUVWXY
Z[\]^_`abcdefghijklmnopqrstuvwxyz{|}~ !"#$%&'()*+,-./0123456789:;<=>?@ABCDEFGHIJKLMNOPQRSTUVWXYZ
[\]^_`abcdefghijklmnopqrstuvwxyz{|}~ !"#$%&'()*+,-./0123456789:;<=>?@ABCDEFGHIJKLMNOPQRSTUVWXYZ[
\]^_`abcdefghijklmnopqrstuvwxyz{|}~ !"#$%&'()*+,-./0123456789:;<=>?@ABCDEFGHIJKLMNOPQRSTUVWXYZ[\
]^_`abcdefghijklmnopqrstuvwxyz{|}~ !"#$%&'()*+,-./0123456789:;<=>?@ABCDEFGHIJKLMNOPQRSTUVWXYZ[\]
^_`abcdefghijklmnopqrstuvwxyz{|}~ !"#$%&'()*+,-./0123456789:;<=>?@ABCDEFGHIJKLMNOPQRSTUVWXYZ[\]^
_`abcdefghijklmnopqrstuvwxyz{|}~ !"#$%&'()*+,-./0123456789:;<=>?@ABCDEFGHIJKLMNOPQRSTUVWXYZ[\]^_
`abcdefghijklmnopqrstuvwxyz{|}~ !"#$%&'()*+,-./0123456789:;<=>?@ABCDEFGHIJKLMNOPQRSTUVWXYZ[\]^_`
abcdefghijklmnopqrstuvwxyz{|}~ !"#$%&'()*+,-./0123456789:;<=>?@ABCDEFGHIJKLMNOPQRSTUVWXYZ[\]^_`a
bcdefghijklmnopqrstuvwxyz{|}~ !"#$%&'()*+,-./0123456789:;<=>?@ABCDEFGHIJKLMNOPQRSTUVWXYZ[\]^_`ab
```

Figure 9-29 Imagewriter (Standard and Wide) built-in self-test prints a repeating alphanumeric test pattern.

Serial-Interface Test When the self-test passes, it proves that the printer mechanism is working, but it doesn't indicate whether or not the printer is able to communicate with a computer. If the printer can't communicate, it can't hear the computer's instructions. If it can't hear the computer's instructions, it doesn't print, even though it's able to.

The communications part of the printer is called the serial interface. To test it, we use an inexpensive RS-232 mini-tester, as shown in Figure 9-30.

Inexpensive RS-232 mini-testers typically have seven dual-color LEDs (light-emitting diodes). These LEDs monitor the printer's TD, RTS, DSR, CD, RD, CTS, and DTR lines. The LED color indicates the line's current logic level. Table 9-1 explains the RS-232C serial-interface notation. Table 9-2 shows how to read the LEDs.

Figure 9-30 RS-232 mini-tester.

Table 9-1. RS-232C Serial-Interface Signals

Notation	Signal	DB-25 pin
FG	Frame ground	1
TD	Transmit data	2
RD	Receive data	3
RTS	Request to send	4
CTS	Clear to send	
DSR	Data set ready	
SG	Signal ground	7
CD	Carrier detect	
DTR	Data terminal ready	20

Table 9-2. RS-232 Mini-Tester LED Indications

LED Color	Logic Level	DC Voltage Level
Bright Red	High/True/0	+6 V to +25 V
Dim Red	High/True/0	+3 V to +6 V
Clear	Off	+3 V to −3 V
Dim Green	Low/False/1	−3 V to −6 V
Bright Green	Low/False/1	−6 V to −25 V

In Chapter 1, we talked about how 1s and 0s are sent back and forth between the computer and the printer. In practice, 1s and 0s are represented by regularly spaced, DC voltage pulses. As shown in Table 9-2, voltage levels are indicated by the color of the LEDs.

To test the Imagewriter's serial interface, unscrew the Mac-to-Imagewriter cable from the DB-25S connector at the back of the printer, insert the mini-tester, and load the paper. What happens next depends on the position of DIP switch SW2-3 when you turn the printer on.

If DIP switch SW2-3 is OPEN (set up for data-terminal-ready hardware handshaking), TD goes green and stays green; RTS and DTR momentarily light green, then go red, and stay red. The other four lights remain unlit.

TD, RTS, and DTR go green when you turn the printer on to indicate that the lines have come up but are not ready. RTS and DTR go red (send ready data) as soon as the printer's SELECT (on-line) light goes green. You should be able to toggle the status of RTS and DTR (from red to green) by pushing the SELECT button.

If DIP switch SW2-3 is CLOSED (set up for X-ON/X-OFF software handshaking) when you turn the printer on, TD goes green and stays green; RTS and DTR momentarily light green, then go red, and stay red. The other four lights remain unlit.

TD, RTS, and DTR go green when you turn the printer on to indicate that the lines have come up but are not ready. RTS and DTR go red (send ready data) as soon as the printer's SELECT (on-line) light goes green. You should be able to toggle the status of the RTS LED, but not the DTR LED, by pushing the SELECT button. The fact that DTR cannot be toggled (stays red) when SW2-3 is closed indicates that DTR signaling has been switched off.

Normal RS-232 mini-tester results are summarized in Tables 9-3 and 9-4. Any other results indicate that there is something wrong with the interface; see component-level repairs at the end of the chapter.

Table 9-3. RS-232 Mini-Tester Results—SW2-3 OPEN

Signal	Initial	SELECT ON	SELECT OFF
TD	green	green	green
RTS	green	red	green
DSR	off	off	off
CD	off	off	off
RD	off	off	off
CTS	off	off	off
DTR	green	red	green

Table 9-4. RS-232 Mini-Tester Results—SW2-3 CLOSED

Signal	Initial	SELECT ON	SELECT OFF
TD	green	green	green
RTS	green	red	green
DSR	off	off	off
CD	off	off	off
RD	off	off	off
CTS	off	off	off
DTR	green	red	red

Loopback Test When the printer's serial-interface and self-tests both pass but you still can't print, and you're absolutely sure it's not the cable, the DIP-switch settings, or the printer resource, the problem may be in the computer's serial interface. We can verify whether or not the problem is in the computer's serial interface with TCG's loopback test. To run TCG's loopback test, choose Test Serial Port from the Aux. menu. As explained in Figure 9-31, this test requires a properly constructed loopback plug. Details are given in Figure 9-32.

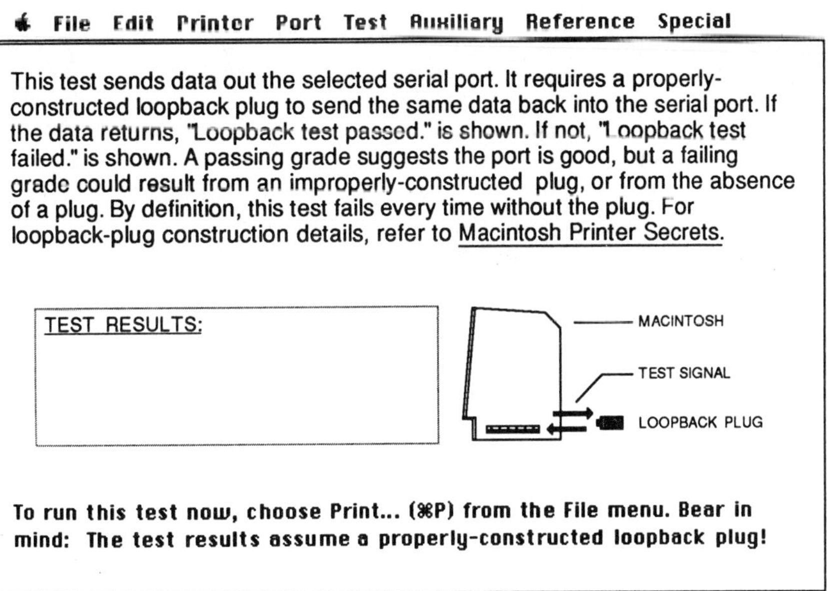

Figure 9-31 Test Character Generator loopback test.

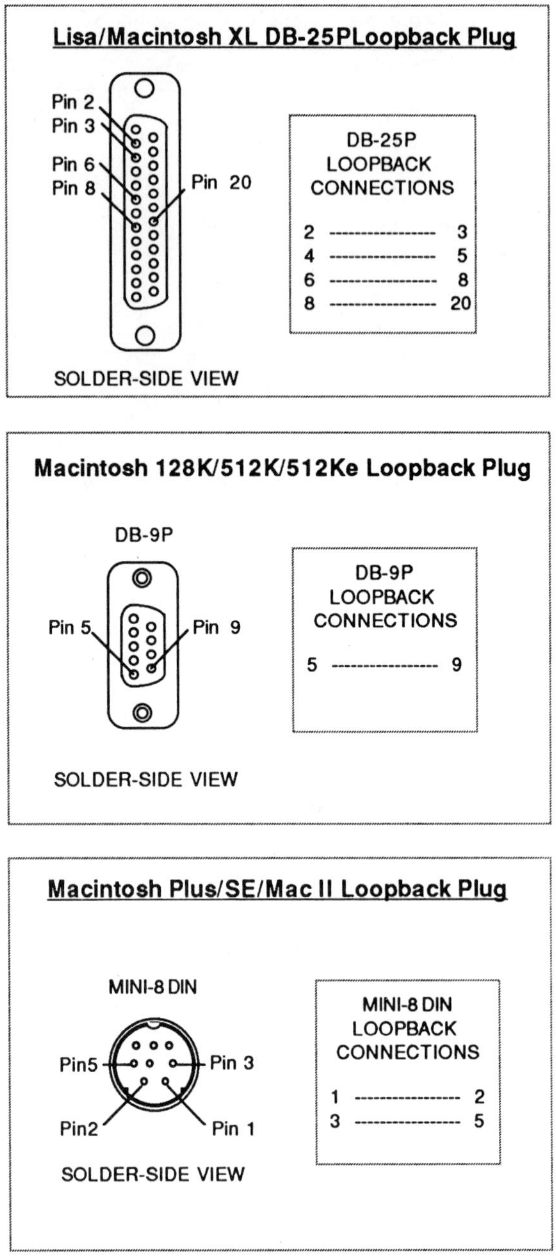

Figure 9-32 Loopback plug wiring details.

If you've made a loopback plug, inserted it into the printer port and the test fails, double-check TCG's Port menu. Make sure the check mark is beside the Printer Port menu item. If not, select the Printer Port menu item and try again. Alternately, if you're testing the modem port, make sure the Modem Port menu item is check marked (and try again).

If the test still fails, verify that the loopback plug is inserted into the correct port. On all Macs from the 128K to the Macintosh II, the printer and modem ports are identified by icons. On Lisas and Mac XLs, the printer and modem ports are marked with uppercase letters. The Lisa/XL modem port is identified by an uppercase A; the Lisa/XL printer port is identified by an uppercase B.

If the loopback test still fails, and you're testing a 128K, a 512K, or a 512K Enhanced, the computer's RFI shield may be shorted to the logic board. In that case, all you generally need to do is insulate the shield. Complete take-apart and repair details are covered in Chapter 1 of *Macintosh Repair & Upgrade Secrets*, published by Sams.

Dead Sets—Control Cluster Not Lit

A surprising number of completely dead printers have nothing wrong with them other than a bad fuse. The reason for the failure appears to be fuse fatigue. Over time, the fuse element fails. There's generally no evidence of circuit failure. When you replace the fuse, the printer operates just as it always did. Table 9-5 gives replacement-part information.

Table 9-5. Imagewriter (Standard and Wide) Fuse Information

Board Reference	Electrical Size	Physical Size	Action
F1	2 A, 250-V AC	1 ¼ × ¼ inch	fast-acting
FU1	3 A, 125-V AC	5 × 20 mm	slow-blow
FU2	3 A, 125-V AC	5 × 20 mm	slow-blow
FU3	5 A, 125-V AC	5 × 20 mm	slow-blow

F1 is the line fuse at the back of the printer. Fuses FU1, FU2, and FU3 are on the logic board, as shown in Figure 9-33.

Most other sources state that the Imagewriter doesn't have internal fuses. Figure 9-33 is provided so that you can look at the board and decide for yourself.

Here's how to get at the nonexistent fuses:

1. Disconnect the AC power cord from the wall outlet.
2. Disconnect the AC power cord from the printer.
3. Unscrew the Mac-to-Imagewriter cable from the DB-25S connector at the back of the printer.
4. Set up a container suitable for holding small parts.

Figure 9-33 Imagewriter (Standard and Wide). Fuses FU1, FU2, and FU3 are on the logic board.

5. Unscrew the logic-board cover with a 7-mm (or 9/32-inch) nutdriver. If you misplace the nuts, or if any are missing, the correct thread size is 3-0.5 mm.
6. Unscrew the logic-board studs with a 7-mm (or 9/32-inch) nutdriver. Note that the rounded area of the stud nuts points toward the board (not toward the cover).
7. The logic board is attached to the printer by various cables. The fuses are at the left-rear corner of the board; you can generally remove them just by lifting the board, without having to disconnect anything. Remove the fuses.

Examine the fuse filaments for breaks. Because fuse fatigue is nonviolent (no evidence of burning), the filaments may appear to be fine, but still be open. Check the filaments with a continuity tester or a multimeter. Replace any fuses that you find open, reverse Steps 1 through 7, and the problem may be fixed.

If replacement fails to restore full operation, or if the fuse failure does appear to be violent, check for metallic foreign objects inside the printer. When people remove the paper cover, coins and paper clips tend to fall inside. These can do real damage.

Component-Level Repairs Component-level troubleshooting of the Imagewriter logic board requires a Sams COMPUTERFACTS folder, product number CP8/08941. Sams COMPUTERFACTS are industry-standard service folders designed for working technicians. Besides a full set of schematics (with clearly marked reference voltages), they provide oscilloscope waveforms, truth tables, semiconductor cross-reference data, and miscellaneous adjustment information.

To benefit from the information in this folder, you need at least a logic probe, a logic pulser, a digital multimeter, and minimal soldering/desoldering equipment. For a solid introduction to component-level troubleshooting, including instructions on how to use the necessary test equipment, I recommend Howard W. Sams & Company's *Microcomputer Troubleshooting & Repair*, ISBN 0-672-22629-4, written by John G. Stephenson and Bob Cahill.

Replacement Parts Most people think that Apple Computer Corporation designed and built the original Imagewriter completely within the United States. In fact, Tokyo Electric Company (TEC) of Japan was the OEM (original equipment manufacturer). The printers were imported by C.Itoh, and then resold to Apple.

Other TEC printers that are built on the same frame as the Imagewriter include the C.Itoh M-8510a and the NEC PC-8023A-N. Comparing these TEC-printer models is like comparing General Motors products. When you compare Chevrolets to Pontiacs and Oldsmobiles, you find that the bodies (cabinet parts) are different, but many mechanical parts are interchangeable.

With that in mind, Table 9-6 provides an interchangeable parts cross-reference guide. For a complete list of interchangeable OEM parts, compare Sams COMPUTERFACTS folders CP8 (Apple Imagewriter) to CP10 (NEC PC-8023A-N) and CP12 (C.Itoh M-8510a).

Table 9-6. Interchangeable-Parts Cross-Reference

Imagewriter	C.Itoh M-8510a	NEC PC-8023A-N
Type head	CLABK-13001	CLABK-13001
Paper-feed motor	CLAAK-10301	CLAAK-10301
Carriage-return motor	CLAAK-10402	CLA45-14601
Paper clamp (L)	CLA35-13301	CLA35-20901
Paper clamp (R)	CLA35-13401	CLA35-21001

Before ordering parts, note that naturally occurring line-feed problems are usually related to IC4 (7406) on the logic board. When there's no SELECT light and no line feed, the problem is usually with FU3 (5A @ 125-V AC) and/or IC10 (8085A) on the logic board. Experience shows that the paper-feed motor and/or the platen drive gears are almost never the cause of a line-feed problem.

That's it for the Imagewriter (Standard and Wide). Next we'll look at the ImageWriter II.

CHAPTER 10

ImageWriter II Setup Secrets

This chapter provides a Macintosh-specific ImageWriter II owner's guide. The ImageWriter II is a 9-pin, color printer with a 10- inch carriage. Early models tend to have plain white cabinets bearing model number A9M0310. As shown in Figure 10-1, early models of the ImageWriter II (white cabinets) are not identified by name.

Figure 10-1 ImageWriter II model number A9M0310.

Later models tend to have platinum-color cabinets bearing model number A9M0320. These units (platinum-color cabinets) are easily identified by "ImageWriter II," which is printed near the Apple logo. The two printers are electrically and mechanically different, but other than the cabinet color change, both models are cosmetically identical.

Cabinet Parts and Setup Controls

Figure 10-2 identifies the ImageWriter II's major cabinet parts and Figure 10-3 the major setup controls.

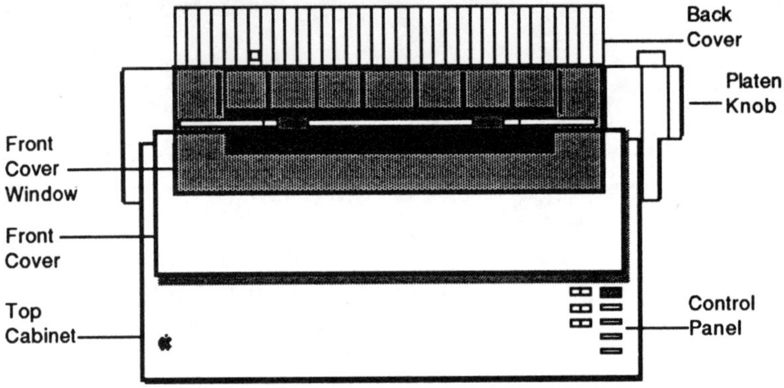

Figure 10-2 ImageWriter II cabinet parts.

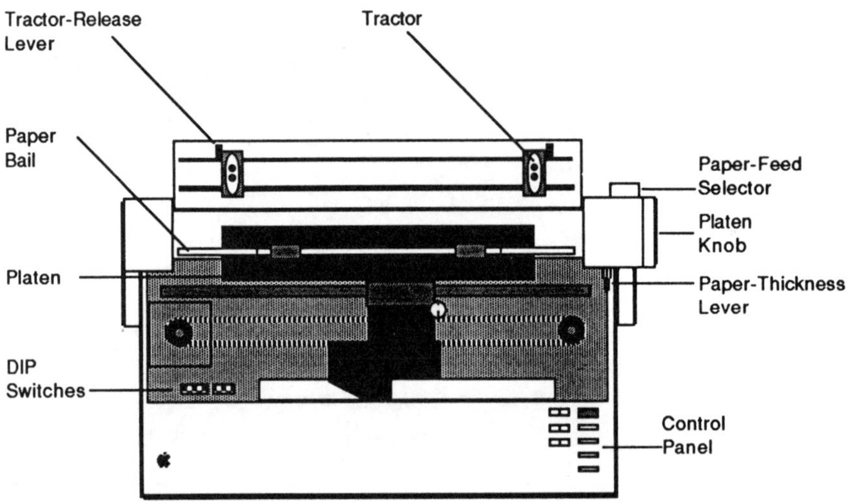

Figure 10-3 ImageWriter II setup controls.

The cabinet parts and setup controls shown in Figures 10-2 and 10-3 are labeled (and spelled) exactly as they are in the *Apple ImageWriter II Owner's Guide*. Unfortunately, these same parts are labeled and spelled differently from Imagewriter model to ImageWriter model. They are also labeled and spelled differently from printer manufacturer to printer manufacturer.

To minimize confusion, Table 10-1 provides an ImageWriter II cabinet part and setup-guide control cross reference guide.

Table 10-1. ImageWriter II Cabinet-Part and Setup-Control Cross-Reference Guide

Imagewriter Std	ImageWriter II	ImageWriter LQ
Carrier Bar	Carrier Rod	Carrier Rod
Carrier Cover	Front cover	Front cover
Clear Plastic Lid	Front cover window	Clear plastic window
Control Cluster	Control panel	Control panel
N/A	Minicircular plug	Minicircular plug
N/A	Minicircular socket	Minicircular socket
Paper Cover	Back cover	Rear cover
Paper Cover Slot	Unnamed	Single-sheet guide
Release Lever	Paper-feed selector	Paper-feed lever
Ribbon Cassette	Ribbon cartridge	Ribbon cartridge
Ribbon Deck	Ribbon cartridge deck	N/A
Roller Shaft	Paper bail	Paper bail
Sprocket	Tractor	Tractor
Type Head	Print head	Print head

If you ever asked a printer-related question and thought that no one knew what they were talking about, study Table 10-1 and you'll begin to understand why. Intelligent conversation is very difficult when you can't agree on the language.

Cabinet Parts

As shown in Figure 10-2, the ImageWriter II is equipped with two top covers. The **front cover** is mounted over the ribbon cartridge deck. The **front cover window** is a piece of smoke-colored plastic that extends the front cover to the back of the platen assembly.

To release the front cover, press in at the spot pointed to in Figure 10-4.

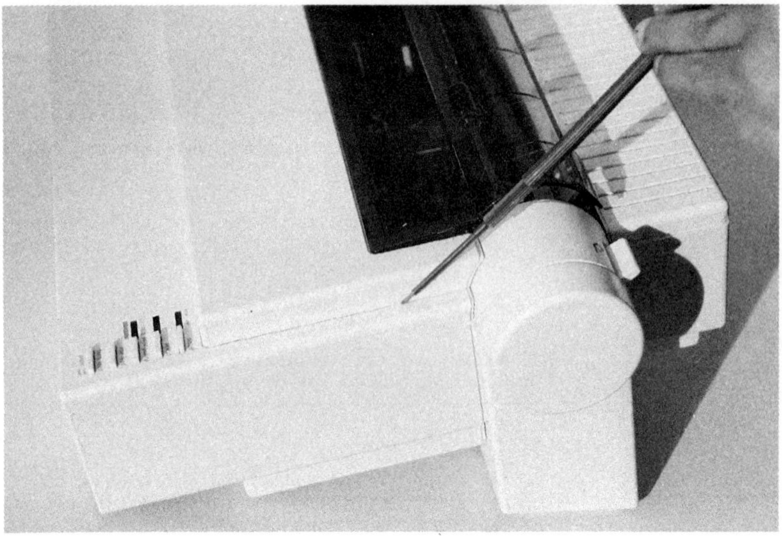

Figure 10-4 ImageWriter II front cover release location.

The two release spots are suggested by arrow-shaped icons etched onto the top cabinet, but the icons are the same color as the cabinet, so they're easily overlooked. To make them noticeable, trace the icons with a red fine-point marker as shown in Figure 10-5.

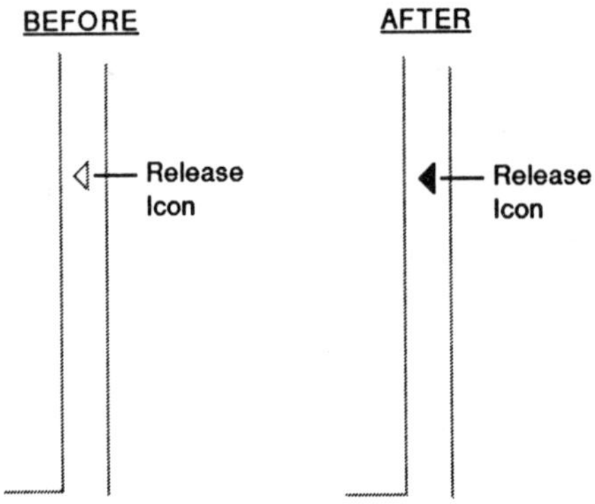

Figure 10-5 Trace the icons with a red fine-point marker to make them more noticeable.

To release the front cover window, remove the front cover and press in at the spot pointed to in Figure 10-6.

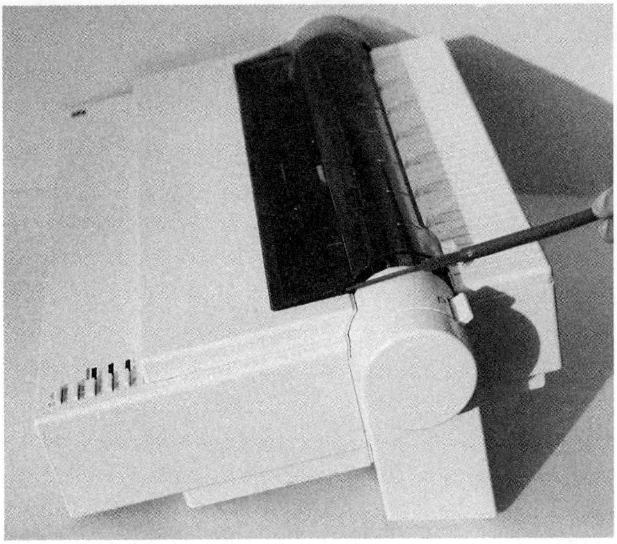

Figure 10-6 ImageWriter II front cover window release location.

In hot weather, the front cover window can be propped open as shown to increase ventilation and lower the printer's operating temperature. This helps to keep the print head cool, and extends lubricant life. Resist the temptation to remove the front cover window altogether. It's there for safety reasons. Without a physical barrier covering the ribbon cartridge deck, curious users might stick their fingers into the printer and suffer serious physical injury.

The window also keeps coins, paper clips, and staples out of the printer. Unless they are removed immediately, loose metallic objects invariably short out the circuit boards.

The **back cover** covers the pin-feed paper stock. Made of smooth plastic, it reduces friction, and helps to keep pin-feed stock from interfering with the printed pages. Some people remove the back cover (when they're loading paper) and never replace it. That's a mistake. The back cover should be kept in place at all times, *and* it should be cleaned from time to time. Figure 10-7 shows the paper exit path. A slippery back cover reduces exit friction and minimizes jamming.

Setup Controls

The **platen knob** extends from the right side of the printer. It's attached to a steel shaft which runs lengthwise through the black-rubber drive **platen**. When loading single sheets of paper, you turn the platen knob to advance the paper by hand, the same as on a typewriter.

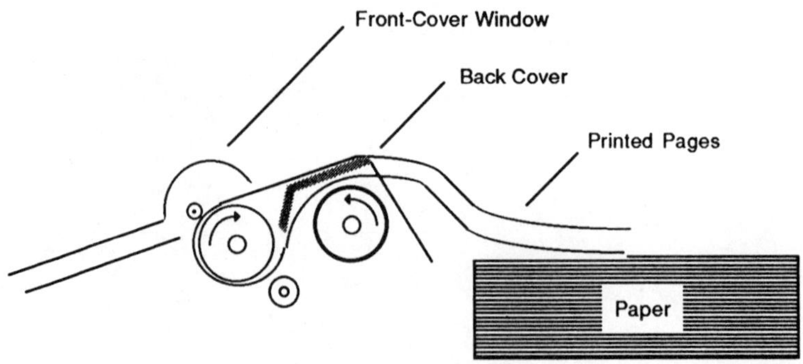

Figure 10-7 ImageWriter II paper exit path.

Two plastic **bail rollers** are attached to a metal **paper bail**. The paper bail setting is adjustable. In the normal (lower) position, the rollers press against the drive platen for printing on paper stock. In the upper position, the rollers pull away from the platen for printing card stock and envelopes.

As their names imply, the rollers are supposed to *rotate* on the paper bail. When new, you can spin the rollers like a top. Over a period of time, the roller bearings get clogged with paper dust. Clogged rollers can barely make a single revolution. The increased roller-bearing friction resists the initial line feed and eventually it becomes so great that the first few millimeters of paper buckle. The same thing happens if you forget to lift the paper bail out of the way when printing envelopes. Instead of slipping beneath the rollers, the stock actually has to lift the paper bail up and out of the way. In the meantime, the stock fails to advance and the printout squashes.

Squashed lines at the top of the page, due to dry roller bearings is a common problem with all push-tractor printers, not just ImageWriter IIs. Maintaining the bearings, is, or at least it should be, part of routine maintenance. The complete procedure is described in Chapter 11.

Paper-Feed Selector The **paper-feed selector** controls a second set of rollers underneath the platen. These are called **friction rollers**. When the paper-feed selector is pulled up, as shown in Figure 10-8, the friction rollers are released and, subsequently, the **friction drive** is disengaged.

As shown in Chapter 8 (Figures 8-10 and 8-11), this clears the way for single sheets of paper to feed manually, and also clears the path for pin-feed paper to feed automatically. The lower roller shaft functions as a clutch. The paper-feed selector functions as a clutch pedal. Letting up releases the clutch, pushing down engages the clutch, exactly the opposite of the way it works on a standard-shift automobile.

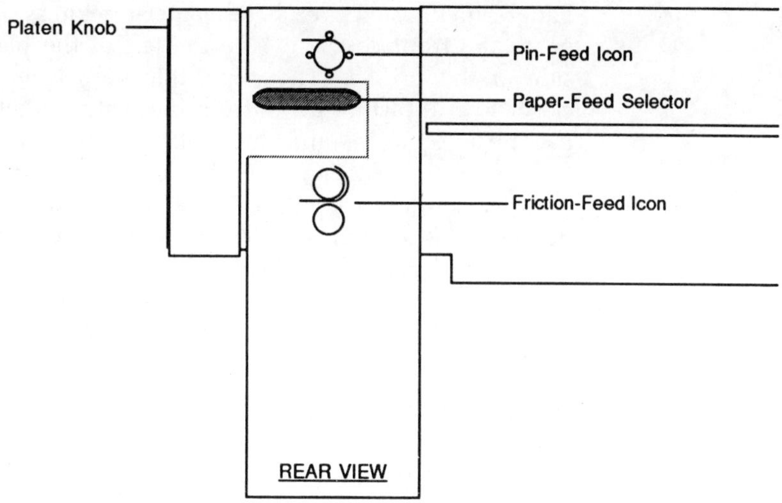

Figure 10-8 ImageWriter II paper-feed selector.

When the clutch pedal is down (friction rollers holding close or clutching), the paper is *directly advanced* by friction between the lower rollers and the platen. When the clutch pedal is up (friction rollers pulled away, not clutching), the paper is *indirectly advanced* by the tractor drive, which directly advances the pin-feeder stubs that are loosely connected to the paper.

A problem occurs when you try to run pin-feed paper using the friction drive: when the paper-feed selector is down (into the friction-drive position), the tractor drive is *completely disengaged*. With the tractor-drive disengaged, the tractors act like cogwheels (rather than drive wheels), and the paper stubs act like drive belts. Instead of having the tractor push the paper, the paper has to pull the tractor.

Pulling (towing) works for a while, but for the same reason you can't push a tow rope backwards, the first rollback buckles the pin-feeder stubs (the rope), which tears the perforations, which invariably results in a paper jam.

To avoid paper jams, pull the paper-feed selector up for pin-feed paper, and push it down for cut-sheet paper. The correct positions are suggested by icons etched onto the cabinet next to the release lever.

Note: The correct positions are different on the Imagewriter (Standard and Wide). If you switch back and forth from an Imagewriter (Standard and Wide) to an ImageWriter II, try to remember that the Imagewriter (Standard and Wide) works the same as a car; the ImageWriter II works the opposite of a car. Don't rely on a mechanical response. Unless you *mindfully* consider this relationship every time you switch printers, there's only a 50/50 chance that your mechanical response will be correct.

Paper-Thickness Lever The **paper-thickness lever** is located underneath the front cover, just to the left of the platen knob, on the right side of the printer. The paper-thickness lever moves the carrier rod closer to and farther away from the platen to allow clearance for multipart business forms and thicker-than-average paper.

As shown in Figure 10-9, model number A9M0310 printers have four paper-thickness positions (detents on the mechanism), while model number A9M0320 printers have six. Almost every other source (including OEM) assumes four paper-thickness positions regardless of model, but that's incorrect. To verify the actual number of positions on your printer, remove the front cover, examine the mechanism, and count detents for yourself.

Each of the detents corresponds to a specific paper thickness:

1. When the paper-thickness lever is pulled all the way toward the back of the printer (in the upper detent), the print head is positioned correctly for 1 sheet of paper.
2. When the paper-thickness lever is pushed one click away from the back of the printer into the second detent (counting from top to bottom), the print head is positioned correctly for 2 sheets of paper (2-part business forms and most mailing labels).
3. When the paper-thickness lever is pushed two clicks away from the back of the printer into the third detent (counting from top to bottom), the print head is positioned correctly for 3 sheets of paper (3-part business forms).
4. When the paper-thickness lever is pushed three clicks away from the back of the printer into the fourth detent (counting from top to bottom), the print head is positioned correctly for 4 sheets of paper (4-part business forms).
5. When the paper-thickness lever is pushed four clicks away from the back of the printer into the fifth detent (counting from top to bottom), the print head is positioned correctly for thin envelopes. Complete envelope printing instructions for model number A9M0320 are given at the end of this chapter.
6. When the paper-thickness lever is pushed five clicks away from the back of the printer into the sixth detent (counting from top to bottom), the print head is positioned correctly for thick envelopes and post-card stock.

Hiding the paper-thickness lever has caused countless problems. The lever's location is not obvious; consequently, many ImageWriter II owners are not aware of its existence.

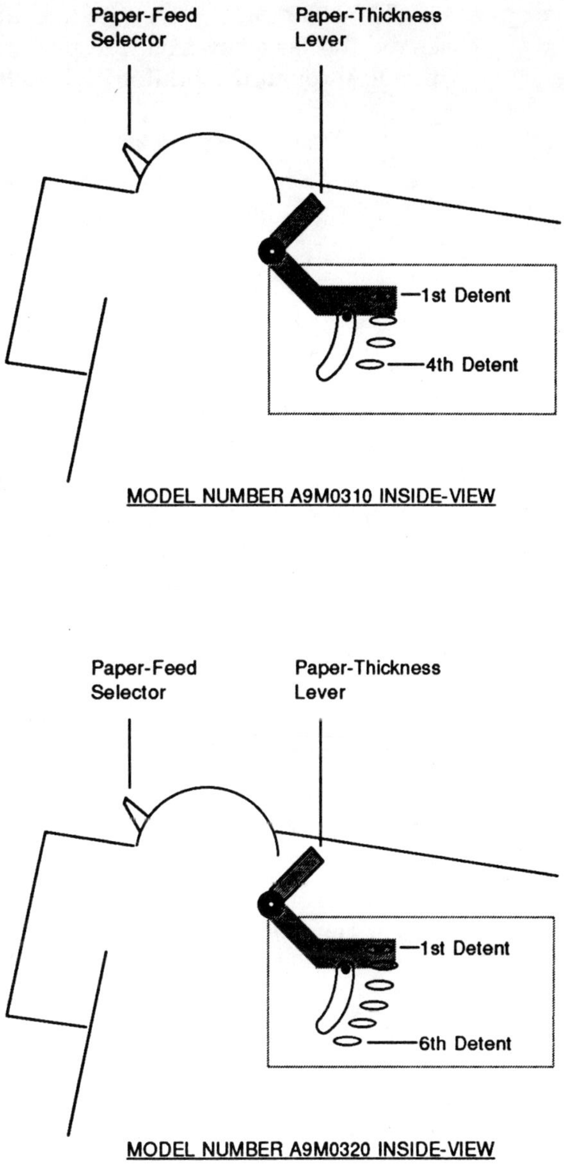

Figure 10-9 ImageWriter II paper-thickness lever.

Understating the number of detents in the mechanism has caused even more problems. When the paper-thickness lever is not set correctly, mailing labels, business forms, and envelopes jam and single sheets print much lighter than normal.

The symptoms of a paper-thickness lever that's too far down (carrier rod too far away from the platen) are regularly spaced white lines running through the printout. This effect is shown in Figure 10-10.

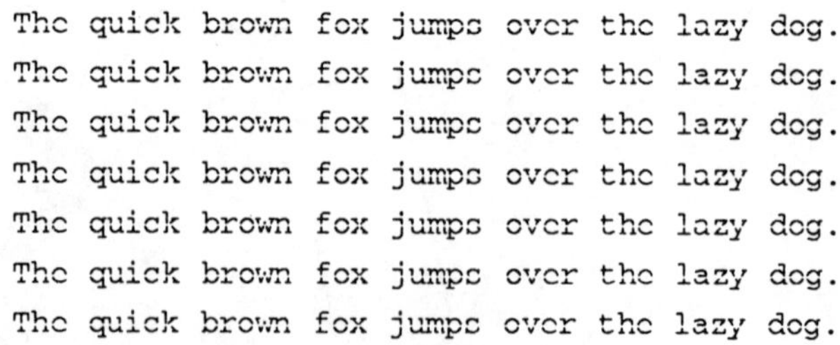

Figure 10-10 Regularly spaced white lines running through the printout indicate that the paper-thickness lever is too far down.

The symptoms of a paper-thickness lever that's too far up (carrier rod too close to the platen) are squashed lines running through the printout. This effect is shown in Figure 10-11.

Figure 10-11 Squashed lines running through the printout indicate that the paper-thickness lever is too far up.

The majority of ImageWriter II complaints are directly related to incorrectly positioned paper-feed selectors (see above), incorrectly positioned paper guides (see Chapter 11), and incorrectly positioned paper-thickness levers. To remind you to check the paper-thickness lever, mark the front cover with a red, fine-point marker as shown in Figure 10-12. Red naturally suggests "stop," which draws attention to the lever.

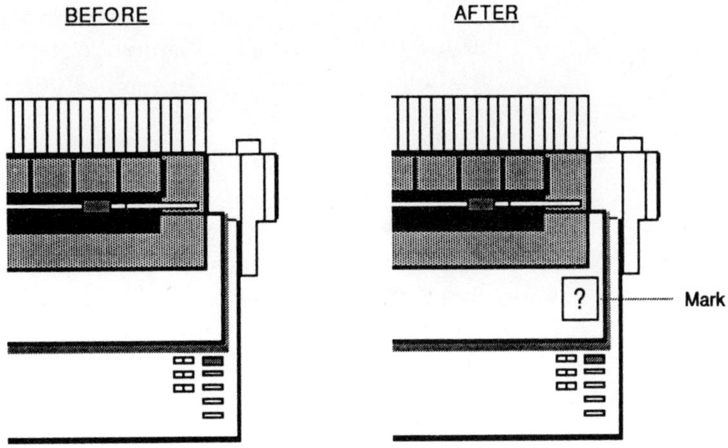

Figure 10-12 Paper-thickness lever. Mark the front cover with a red, fine-point marker.

Envelope Printing While envelope printing on the Imagewriter (Standard and Wide) is intuitive (exactly the same as on a typewriter), envelope printing on the ImageWriter II (A9M0320) requires further explanation:

1. The paper bail has to be raised, away from the platen. If the paper bail is down, pressed against the platen, envelopes don't feed cleanly and the printout squashes. The fact that the paper bail raises into a secondary position above the platen is not obvious. The fact that it should be in that position when printing envelopes is often overlooked.
2. Thick and thin are relative terms, so unless you've already proved otherwise, it's best to set the paper-thickness lever on the sixth detent (all the way down). Otherwise, the envelope may jam, and the printout may squash.
3. Likewise, the front cover window has to be propped open as shown in Figure 10-6. If the front cover window is closed, envelopes don't eject cleanly, and the printout at the bottom of the envelope squashes.
4. Envelopes should always be autoloaded to the print line on the paper holder (not wound in by hand). To autoload the envelope, clear any pin-feed or cut-sheet paper from under the platen, set the paper-feed selector to the friction-feed position, press the *form feed* button, and then press the *select* button.

5. The correct Page Setup... is very important. Open the envelope document, choose Page Setup... from the File menu, and confirm the following selections:

   Paper: Custom Size
   Paper Width: 9.5 inches (not 8.5 × 11)
   Paper Height: 5 inches (not 4.125)
   Special Effects: No Gaps Between Pages
   Left Margin: 0.0 inches
   Right Margin: 0.0 inches
   Top Margin: 1.0 inch (not 0.0 inches)
   Bottom Margin: 0.0 inches

6. The correct document format is also important. As shown in Figure 10-13, your return address should start on the first line of the document. Type everything exactly the same as if you were filling out an envelope on a typewriter.

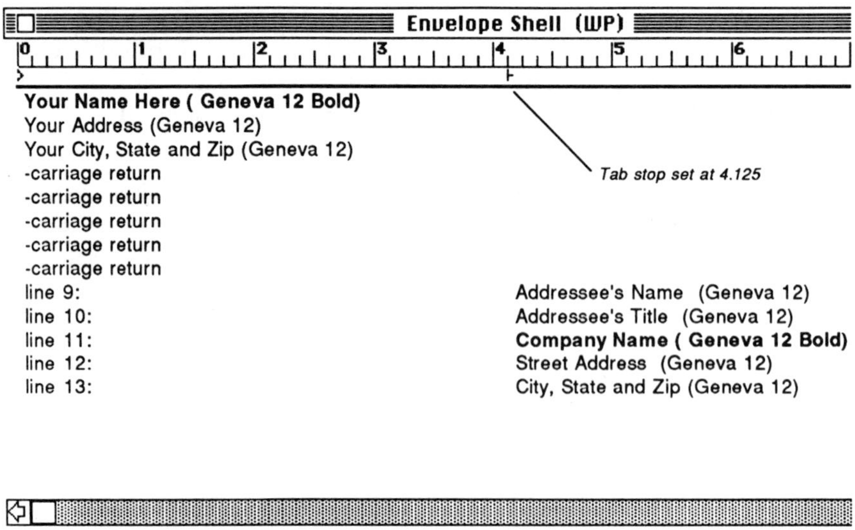

Figure 10-13 Recommended document format for printing envelopes on an ImageWriter II.

7. When all the above has been confirmed, choose Print... from the File menu. Confirm the following selections:

   Quality: Best or Faster (not Draft)
   Page Range: All
   Copies: 1 (or as many as you want)
   Paper Feed: Automatic (not Hand Feed)

8. When you're sure that Automatic, not Hand Feed, is selected, click the OK button.

If you observe each of the above steps, the envelope should print perfectly, and eject cleanly. If you get regularly spaced white lines running through the printout, it means the paper-thickness lever is too far down for the current envelope thickness. Move it to the fifth detent and try again.

Squashed lines in the printout mean the paper-thickness lever is too high. Move it to the sixth detent and try again. If the printout still squashes and/or the paper-thickness lever is already in the sixth detent, it means the plastic paper guide (card holder) is too close to the paper bail. Readjustment details are given in Chapter 11.

Control Panel As shown in Figure 10-14, the **control panel** contains the *on/off, select, print quality, line feed, form feed,* and *paper load/eject* buttons. The *on/off button* applies AC power. The *select* button selects on-line status and off-line status. When the printer is on-line, as evidenced by a green light, it's under computer control. When it's off-line, as evidenced by no light, it's under manual control.

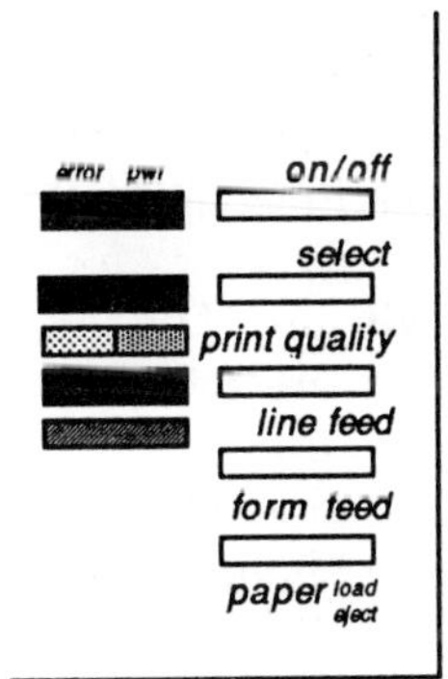

Figure 10-14 ImageWriter II control panel.

The printer has to be under manual control (off-line) in order to work the *line feed* button. The *line feed* button always advances the paper ⅙ inch. As far as the *line feed* button is concerned, all lines are ⅙-inch high. Even when you choose a 36-point font (approximately ½-inch line height), taking the printer off-line and pressing the *line feed* button only advances the paper by ⅙ inch. In other words, the *line feed* button does not consider bitmapped font heights.

The only way to use the *line feed* button effectively is to set up your programs for 6 lines-per-inch spacing. If a program doesn't support 6 lines-per-inch spacing, choose either the Courier 10 or the Monaco 12 font. Both fonts automatically give 6 lines-per-inch spacing, as explained in Chapter 5.

Likewise, the printer has to be under manual control (off-line) to work the *form feed* button. The distance fed varies, depending on the current page length and the current print-head position. Here's how the distance is calculated: whenever you turn the printer on, wherever the top of the paper happens to be, is recorded as the **top of form** position.

Initially, the *form feed* button advances the paper by 11 inches or 12 inches, measured from the current top of form position, minus however many line feeds have been executed, depending on the setting of DIP switch 1-4.

Once you print a document, however, the setting of DIP switch 1-4 is overridden by the length value entered in the document's Page Setup... dialog box. If the last page printed was a 9½ × 7-inch business form, pressing the form feed button will advance the stock by exactly 7 inches to accommodate that form. The same is true for 210-mm × 297-mm A4 letter paper and 8½-inch × 14-inch US legal paper. In other words, the ImageWriter II's *form feed* button registers custom page sizes on-the-fly. Print one page, and the *form feed* button is updated with the current page length.

For use with the ImageWriter II sheet feeder, the *form feed* button also serves as a *paper-load/eject* button. This feature is explained in context, when we look at the sheet feeder and other ImageWriter II upgrades in Chapter 12.

DIP Switches DIP is an acronym for dual in-line package. Dual means that there are two rows of pins on the switch. In-line means that both rows are straight.

The ImageWriter II's DIP switches are marked SW1 and SW2. As shown in Figure 10-15, these switches are located under the front cover, just above the Apple logo. Tables 10-2 through 10-6 contain DIP switch function details. Figure 10-16 shows the recommended US-Macintosh settings.

Table 10-2. ImageWriter II DIP Switch 1 Functions

Switch	Function	CLOSED	OPEN	US-Mac Setting
1-1	Alphabet	See Table 10-4	Open	
1-2	Alphabet	See Table 10-4		Open
1-3	Alphabet	See Table 10-4		Open
1-4	Paper length	12 inch	11 inch	Open
1-5	Perforation	Skip	Don't skip	Open
1-6	CPI	See Table 10-5		Open
1-7	CPI	See Table 10-5		Open
1-8	CR code	CR + LF	CR	Open

Figure 10-15 ImageWriter II. The DIP switches are located under the front cover, just above the Apple logo.

Table 10-3. ImageWriter II DIP Switch 2 Functions

Switch	Function	CLOSED	OPEN	US-Mac Setting
2-1	Baud rate	See Table 10-6		Closed
2-2	Baud rate	See Table 10-6		Closed
2-3	Handshaking	X-ON/X-OFF	DTR	Open
2-4	Option card	Enabled	Disabled	Open
2-5	Hammer timing	Varies	Varies	Varies*
2-6	Hammer timing	Varies	Varies	Varies*

* SW 2-5 and SW 2-6 control bidirectional alignment. Optimum settings vary from printer to printer.

Table 10-4. ImageWriter II DIP Switches 1-1 through 1-3 (Alphabet- Selection) Settings

SW 1-1	SW 1-2	SW 1-3	Alphabet Selection
Open	Open	Open	American English
Closed	Closed	Open	European English
Open	Open	Closed	German

(continued)

Table 10-4. *(continued)*

SW 1-1	SW 1-2	SW 1-3	Alphabet Selection
Open	Closed	Closed	French
Closed	Open	Closed	Swedish
Closed	Open	Open	Italian
Closed	Closed	Closed	Spanish
Open	Closed	Open	Danish

Table 10-5. ImageWriter II DIP Switches 1-6 and 1-7 (Character Set) Settings

SW 1-6	SW 1-7	Character Set/CPI
Open	Open	Pica 10 CPI (characters per inch)
Closed	Open	Elite 12 CPI (characters per inch)
Open	Closed	Ultracondensed 17 CPI (characters per inch)
Closed	Closed	Elite Proportional 160 DPI (dots per inch)

Table 10-6. ImageWriter II DIP Switches 2-1 and 2-2 (Baud-Rate) Settings

SW 2-1	SW 2-2	Baud Rate
Open	Open	300 baud
Closed	Open	1200 baud
Open	Closed	2400 baud
Closed	Closed	9600 baud

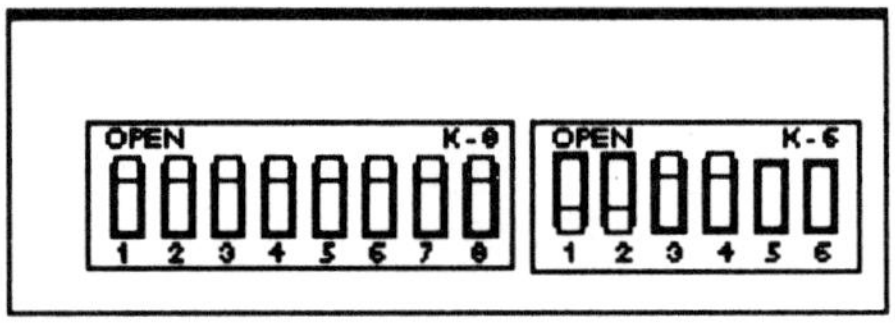

Figure 10-16 Recommended ImageWriter II DIP switch settings.

The recommendations shown in Figure 10-16 differ slightly from those given in other sources. Most sources recommend the Elite 12 font. Elite 12 almost never works with business forms. Elite 12 is also incorrect for WYSIWYG PC-compatible use. If you want the printer to work properly with forms (as well as stationery), on all computers (not just Macintosh), set the switches according to Figure 10-16.

Paper-Handling Secrets

The ImageWriter II has a **pin-feed alignment icon** located on the back panel of the printer and an **alignment notch** directly above it. Most sources state that you should adjust the ImageWriter II's left tractor so the left perforation of the paper stock aligns the icon's vertical mark with the notch. If you follow this practice, your left margin will always be 1/16-inch short. To determine exactly where the left margin starts, run TCG's Tractor - TOF Alignment test as explained in Chapter 7.

Bidirectional Printing

In Faster quality, the ImageWriter II will print *even faster,* with only a slight difference in print quality, if you select bidirectional printing. To finish big pin-feed form jobs in approximately half the time (Faster quality only):

1. Turn on the computer and the printer.
2. Open a document.
3. Choose Print... from the File menu.
4. Enter the From-To range and the number of copies required.
5. Click the Faster button.
6. Engage the Caps Lock key.
7. Hold down the Shift and Option keys while clicking OK.

Bidirectional Faster-quality printing stays in effect until you reverse it. It's not necessary to repeat the procedure every time you print. To reverse the procedure:

1. Turn on the computer and the printer.
2. Open a document.
3. Choose Print... from the File menu.
4. Enter the From-To range and the number of copies required.
5. Click the Faster button.
6. Hold down the Command key while clicking OK.

These procedures work only on the ImageWriter II. They do not work on the Imagewriter (Standard and Wide). They also have no effect on the ImageWriter driver's Draft and Best print qualities.

If the bidirectional Faster-quality printout doesn't line up properly, the carrier belt may need a tension adjustment. Complete details are in Chapter 11.

Cable Requirements

Tables 10-7 and 10-8 show DB-9S and 8-pin minicircular socket Mac-to-ImageWriter II connector functions.

Table 10-7. 128K/512K/512K Enhanced (RS-422) DB-9S Functions

Pin	Function	Description	Direction
1	FG	Frame ground	
2	+5 V DC	Positive five volts	
3	SG	Signal ground	
4	TxD+	Transmitted data +	Output to printer
5	TxD−	Transmitted data −	Output to printer
6	+12 V DC	Positive twelve volts	
7	HSKi	Handshake input	Input from printer
8	RxD+	Received data +	Input from printer
9	RxD−	Received data −	Input from printer

Table 10-8. Mac Plus/SE/II 8-pin Mini-Circular Socket Functions

Pin	Function	Description	Direction
1	DTR	Data terminal ready	Output to printer
2	DSR	Data set ready	Input from printer
3	TxD−	Transmitted data −	Output to printer
4	SG	Signal ground	
5	RxD−	Received data −	Input from printer
6	TxD+	Transmitted data +	Output to printer
7	NC	Not connected	
8	RxD+	Received data +	Input from printer

Figures 10-17 through 10-19 are wiring diagrams for various Macintosh to ImageWriter II cables. Dotted lines between pin numbers indicate a connection. NC between pin numbers indicates no connection.

PC-Compatible Cable Requirements

Ask the typical Macintosh dealer how to connect an ImageWriter II printer to a PC-compatible computer and, more than likely, the answer will be "It can't be done." The truth is it *can* be done, very easily. This section shows you how.

Figure 10-20 shows the wiring diagram for an ImageWriter II to PC/XT-compatible computer cable.

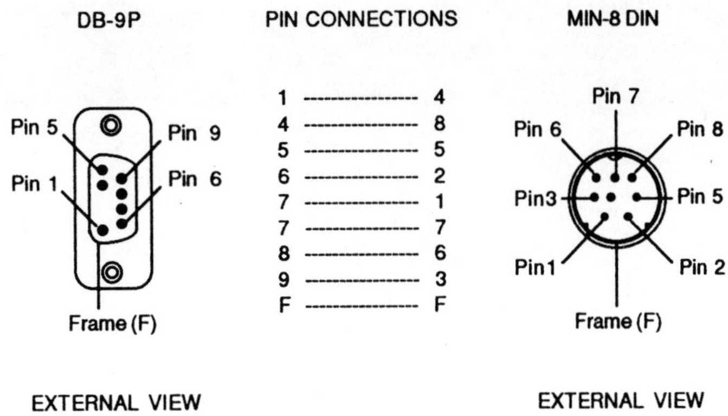

Figure 10-17 Wiring diagram for OEM part number 590-0551-A, Mac (128K/512K/512K Enhanced) to ImageWriter II/LQ cable.

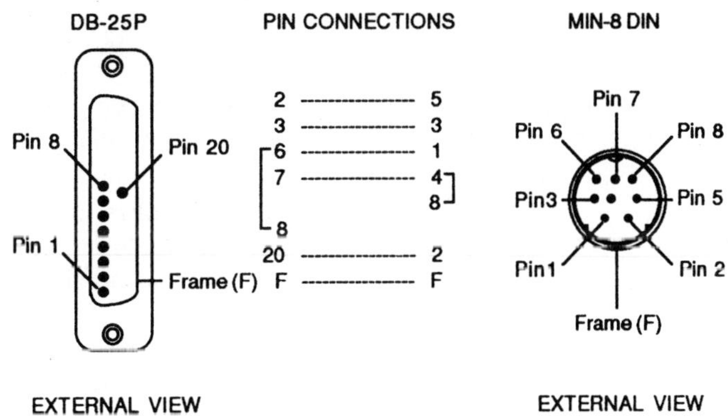

Figure 10-18 Wiring diagram for OEM part number 590-0031, Lisa/Mac XL to ImageWriter II/LQ cable.

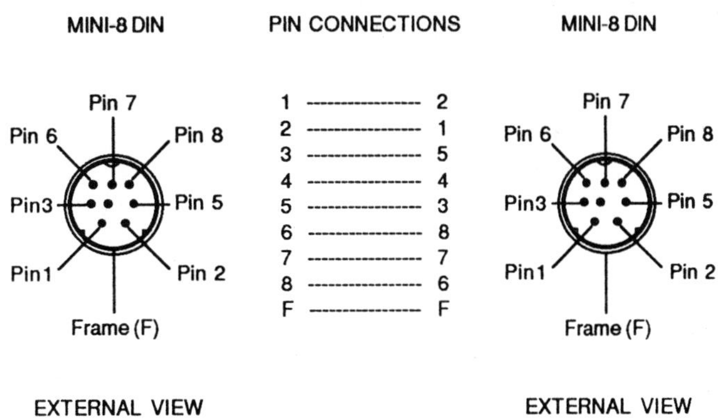

Figure 10-19 Wiring diagram for OEM part number 590-0552-A, Mac Plus/SE/II to ImageWriter II/LQ cable.

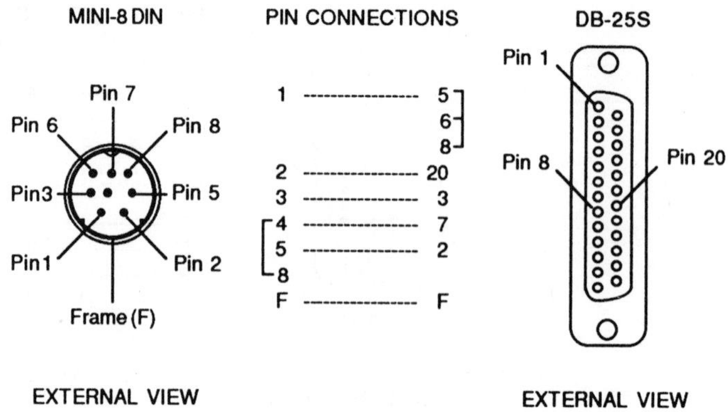

Figure 10-20 Wiring diagram for ImageWriter II/LQ to PC/XT-compatible computer cable.

This diagram assumes a standard PC/XT (eXtra Technology) class of computer fitted with a DB-25P (P for plug) serial connector. Some PC/XT-class computers have DB-25S (S for socket) serial connectors. In that case, you can make the same cable with a DB-25P connector, or you could use the specified cable together with a gender changer.

Gender changers come in plug-to-plug (male-to-male), which converts female connections to male connections, and socket-to-socket (female-to-female), which converts male connections to female connections. The required gender changer should have two DB-25P (plug) connectors in order to change the female connection to a male connection.

AT-class (Advanced Technology) computers generally have DB-9P connectors. In that case, you also need a DB-9S to DB-25P (AT to XT) adapter in order to change the 9-pin male AT serial port into a 25-pin-male XT serial port.

Prewired gender changers and prewired AT-to-XT serial adapters are both inexpensive and readily available. Check Appendix B for vendors.

PC-Compatible DIP Switch Settings PC-compatible computers do not support X-ON/X-OFF (software) handshaking so the ImageWriter II has to be configured for DTR (hardware) handshaking. In other words, DIP switch SW 2-3 has to be open. If DIP switch 2-3 is closed for X-ON/X-OFF handshaking, there'll be garbage and/or missing characters in the printout after just a few pages (unless the communications rate is stepped down to 1200 baud as explained below).

In order for the printout to match the computer display, DIP switches SW 1-6 and SW 1-7 have to be open. These positions enable the Pica 10 character set, which prints 80 characters per line.

To use readily available Mac Plus/SE/II to Imagewriter (Standard and Wide) cables, DIP switch SW 2-1 has to be closed, and DIP switch SW 2-2 has to be open. These positions select the 1200-baud communications rate, which compensates for a missing handshaking line (Mini-8 DIN pin 1 to DB-25P pins 5, 6, and 8) in the readily available cable.

The fact that stepping down the communications rate (to 1200 baud) compensates for the missing handshaking line is further proof that OEM CPS ratings are invalid. In Chapter 5, under the heading "Effects of Baud Rate on Printer Speed," we stated that "None of the ImageWriters released to date have carrier mechanisms that can work any faster than 1200 baud," and promised to explain the math, in context, right here in this chapter. Here's the explanation:

1. 8 data bits + 1 start bit + 1 stop bit = 10 bits per character.
2. 1200 baud = 1200 bits per second
3. 1200 bits per second ÷ 10 bits per character = 120 cps
4. 2400 baud = 2400 bits per second
5. 2400 bits per second ÷ 10 bits per character = 240 cps

The ImageWriter II is rated at 250 cps, so logically, it should be able to keep up with the computer at 2400 baud (240 cps), without handshaking. Try it, and there'll be garbage and/or missing characters in the printout after just a few pages. In other words, not only is the computer faster than the printer, but it's so much faster that it completely overruns the printer's built-in 2K buffer. If the printer's optional 32K buffer is installed, it takes a little longer for the computer to overrun the printer (because 32K is 1600% larger than 2K), but it still happens. Not even the optional 32K buffer allows the ImageWriter II to keep pace at 2400 baud!

Step the communications rate down to 1200 baud (120 cps) however, and the ImageWriter II keeps pace just fine, without slowing down a bit! That's the important thing. It doesn't take any longer to print the file at 1200 baud than it does at 2400 or 9600 baud. All higher communications rates do is release the computer a little sooner.

Reset to 9600 baud, plug in an RS-232 mini-tester and you'll see that most of the time (assuming the handshaking line is there) DSR lights green, indicating that the printer is full and the computer is simply marking time.

> If you want it to work, build the correct cable yourself, or use a Mac Plus to Imagewriter cable and set the communications rate to 1200 baud. If you'd rather prove that it can't be done, leave the communications rate at 9600 baud, and circulate the garbage printout as evidence.

PC-Compatible MS-DOS MODE Commands Once the cables and the DIP switches are correct, you need to enter two MS-DOS MODE commands on the PC-compatible computer. At the DOS prompt, type:

```
MODE COM1: 9600,N,8,1,P
MODE LPT1: = COM1:
```

The first MODE command configures the specified COM<n>: port (COM1: or COM2:) for 9600 baud, no parity, 8 data bits, and 1 stop bit. These terms were explained in Chapter 1. The P (at the end of the command) indicates that the device is a serial printer.

If the ImageWriter II is plugged into COM2:, specify COM2: instead of COM1:. If the baud rate is stepped down to 1200 (because you don't have the right cable), specify 1200 instead of 9600.

The second MODE command redirects LPT1: (the usually designated line printer) to the specified COM<n>: port. With this command in place, output from any program expecting a parallel printer on the parallel port (LPT1:) is automatically redirected to the ImageWriter II.

To avoid having to enter these commands every time you switch on the PC-compatible computer, you can create a batch file. At the PC-compatible drive prompt, type:

```
COPY CON IW.BAT
ECHO OFF
MODE COM1: 9600,N,8,1,P
MODE LPT1: = COM1:
ECHO COM1: is now set for the Apple ImageWriter II
ECHO ON
```

Type the instructions exactly as shown. Don't edit the instructions, add spaces, or change the punctuation. When you're finished, hold down the Control key, and, while keeping it down, type a Z. Let up the Control key and press the Return key. "1 File(s) copied" will appear on the display, followed by the usual drive prompt (A>).

From now on, whenever you want to set up for ImageWriter II printing, all you'll have to do is type IW at the drive prompt (A>) and press the Return key.

PC-Compatible ImageWriter II Printer Drivers Text printing from MS-DOS is automatic. Text printing from an application requires a TTY (teletypewriter) print driver. Graphics printing from an application requires a C.ITOH 8510a driver. The C.ITOH 8510a printer is 95% code-compatible with ImageWriter II printers. To use the C.ITOH 8510a on a Mac, all you need is an ImageWriter II driver. Conversely, to use an ImageWriter II on a PC-compatible computer, all you need is a C.ITOH 8510a driver.

With the 8510a driver selected, the ImageWriter II will print mixed text and graphics exactly the same as when it's connected to a Macintosh. Under Microsoft Windows, Microsoft Windows Write works pretty much like MacWrite. Microsoft Windows Paint works a lot like MacPaint. As far as the ImageWriter II is concerned, there's no difference.

Apple II Cable Requirements

Table 10-9 shows the Apple IIc's DIN-5 connector functions. Figure 10-21 shows the wiring diagram for an ImageWriter II to Apple IIc-compatible computer cable.

Table 10-9. Apple IIc DIN-5 Connector Functions

Pin	Function	Description	Direction
1	DTR	Data terminal ready	Output to printer
2	TxD	Transmit data	Output to printer
3	SG	Signal Ground	
4	RxD	Receive data	Input from printer
5	DSR	Data set ready	Input from printer

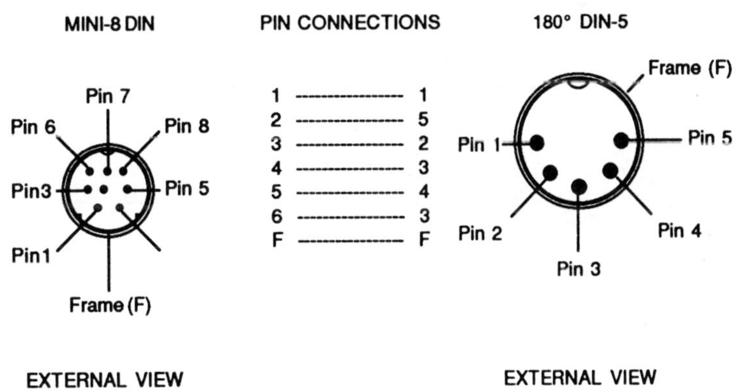

Figure 10-21 Wiring diagram for ImageWriter II/LQ to Apple IIc-compatible computer cable.

The ImageWriter II can also be used with an Apple II, Apple II+, or Apple IIe, provided the computer is fitted with an optional Super-Serial Card (OEM #661-91067 or equivalent). Connection is made using the cable shown in Figure 10-22, and the modem/terminal jumper block on the Super-Serial Card has to be rotated toward terminal (away from modem).

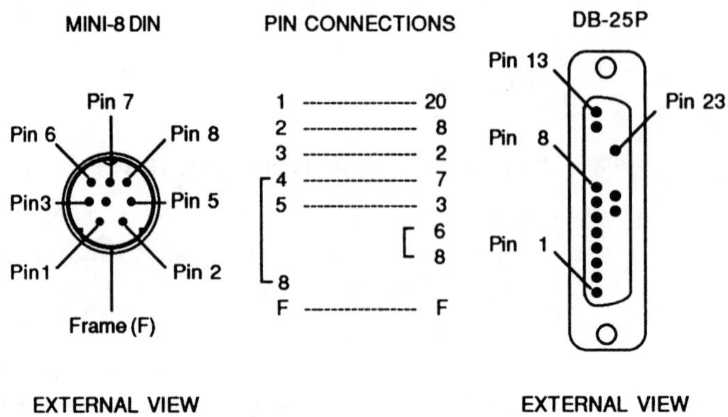

Figure 10-22 Wiring diagram for ImageWriter II/LQ to Apple II/II+/IIe-compatible computer cable.

Tables 10-10 through 10-13 contain Apple II Super-Serial Card DIP-switch function details. Figure 10-23 shows the recommended settings for use with an ImageWriter II. The same settings are also correct for use with an Imagewriter (Standard and Wide).

Table 10-10. Apple II Super-Serial Card DIP Switch 1 Functions

Switch	Function	CLOSED	OPEN	US-Mac Setting
1-1	Baud rate	See Table 10-12		Open
1-2	Baud rate	See Table 10-12		Open
1-3	Baud rate	See Table 10-12		Open
1-4	Baud rate	See Table 10-12		Open
1-5	Communications mode	Modem	Printer	Open
1-6	Communications mode	On	Off	Open
1-7	CTS	Normal		Closed

Table 10-11. Apple II Super-Serial Card DIP Switch 2 Functions

Switch	Function	CLOSED	OPEN	IW-II Setting
2-1	Stop bits	1	2	Closed
2-2	Delay	On	Off	Open
2-3	Line width	See Table 10-13		Open
2-4	Line width	See Table 10-13		Closed
2-5	CR code	CR + LF	CR	Closed
2-6	Interrupts	On	Off	Open
2-7	CTS		Normal	Open

Table 10-12. Apple II Super-Serial Card DIP Switches 1-1 through 1-4 (Baud Rate) Settings

SW 1-1	SW 1-2	SW 1-3	SW 1-4	Baud Rate
Closed	Closed	Closed	Open	50 baud
Closed	Closed	Open	Closed	75 baud
Closed	Closed	Open	Open	110 baud
Closed	Open	Closed	Closed	135 baud
Closed	Open	Closed	Open	150 baud
Closed	Open	Open	Closed	300 baud
Closed	Open	Open	Open	600 baud
Open	Closed	Closed	Closed	1200 baud
Open	Closed	Closed	Open	1800 baud
Open	Closed	Open	Closed	2400 baud
Open	Closed	Open	Open	3600 baud
Open	Open	Closed	Closed	4800 baud
Open	Open	Closed	Open	7200 baud
Closed	Closed	Closed	Open	9600 baud
Open	Open	Open	Open	19,200 baud

Table 10-13. Apple II Super-Serial Card DIP-Switch 2-3 and 2-4 (Line Width) Settings

SW 2-3	SW 2-4	Line-Width
Closed	Closed	40 characters
Closed	Open	70 characters
Open	Closed	80 characters
Open	Open	132 characters

Figure 10-23 shows the recommended Apple II Super-Serial Card DIP-switch settings for use with an ImageWriter II, an ImageWriter LQ, or an Imagewriter (Standard and Wide). "On" indicates closed.

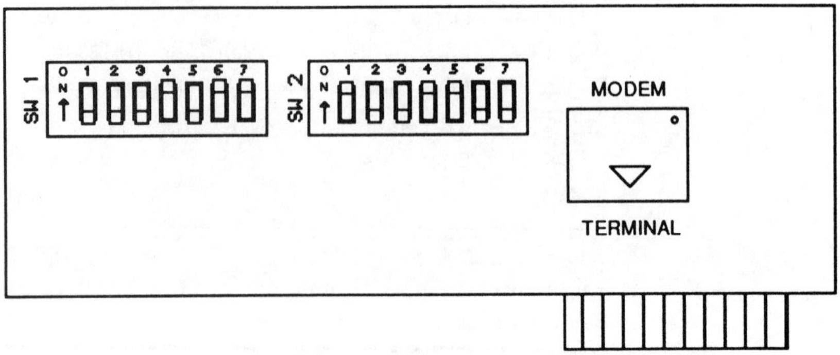

Figure 10-23 Apple II Super-Serial Card DIP-switch settings.

That's it for ImageWriter II setup secrets. Next, we'll look at repairs and maintenance.

CHAPTER

11

ImageWriter II Repair Secrets

This chapter covers ImageWriter II repair and maintenance. Primarily concerned with mechanical repairs, it shows how to remove stuck mailing labels, tells what to do about missing dots in the printout, shows how to spot bad ribbons, tells how to correct deviated (uneven) printout, shows how to align color-ribbon cams, and tells how to deal with completely dead sets.

Stuck Mailing Labels—Routine Maintenance

There's an old saying: "If it ain't broke, don't fix it." As a result, most people neglect their printers until there's a work-stopping mechanical problem. By far and away, the most common work-stopping mechanical problem is a stuck mailing label.

This section shows how to remove the label. In the process, we'll clean and lubricate the various mechanical parts, and generally restore the platen mechanism to like-new condition.

ImageWriter II Take-Apart Procedure

For safety, always start the ImageWriter II take-apart procedure by disconnecting the AC power cord. Disconnect means to physically separate it from the printer. Simply switching off the power is not enough. As long as the power cord is connected, every component between the power socket and the power switch is still alive. Taking the printer apart is hard enough as it is, without having to worry about live electrical connections. Be smart. Play it safe. Disconnect the power cord before beginning!

With electrical safety foremost in mind, here's the complete ImageWriter II take-apart procedure:

1. Disconnect the AC power cord from the wall outlet.
2. Disconnect the AC power cord from the printer.
3. Disconnect the Mac-to-ImageWriter II cable from the printer.
4. Lift off the front and back covers. Put the covers aside.
5. Remove the ribbon cartridge and put it aside.
6. As indicated by the wand in Figure 11-1, the print head is held by a barbed, plastic latch. Pry back the latch with the index finger of your right hand, and pull the print head straight up (not at an angle) using your left hand. Print heads which have never been removed may offer considerable resistance. Pull straight up until the contacts release, and then lift the print head away as shown in Figure 11-2.

Figure 11-1 ImageWriter II print-head latch.

Figure 11-2 ImageWriter II print-head removal.

In Figure 11-2, the already released print head is tilted to show contact details. When removing the print head, remember to pull straight up, not at an angle as shown, otherwise you may snap the contact board.

7. Set up a container for holding small parts.
8. As shown in Figure 11-3, remove the paper-guide screws using a #0 Phillips-head screwdriver. Put the paper-guide screws inside the parts container. Remove the paper-guide and put it aside.

In Figure 11-3, both the print head and the ribbon cartridge are shown installed. Although it is possible to squeak the paper guide past them, it's much easier to remove the paper guide *after* removing the ribbon cartridge and the print head, especially when there's a label stuck to the guide.

9. As shown in Figure 11-4, the cabinet top is fastened by two permanently attached #1 Phillips-head screws. Loosen (but don't remove) the screws using a #1 Phillips-head screwdriver. The screws will be fully loosened when you feel them hit the end stops.

Figure 11-3 ImageWriter II paper-guide screws.

Figure 11-4 ImageWriter II take-apart procedure.

10. Slide the ribbon cartridge deck all the way to the left, as shown in Figure 11-5.

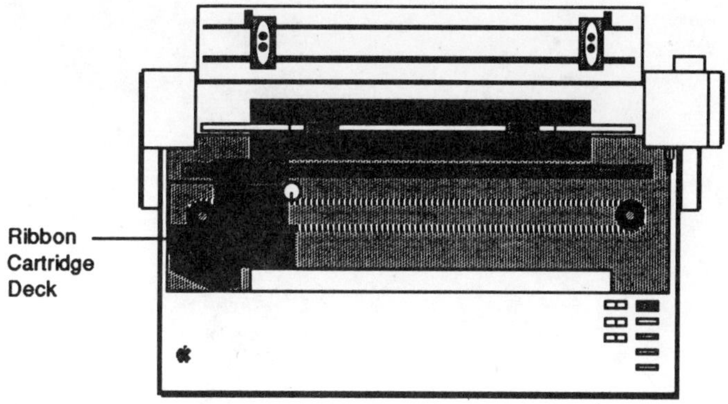

Figure 11-5 ImageWriter II ribbon cartridge deck.

11. With the ribbon cartridge deck all the way to the left, rotate the cabinet-top forward, as shown in Figure 11-6. If one or both sides catch, loosen the cabinet-top screws a little more.

Figure 11-6 ImageWriter II cabinet top.

12. Make absolutely sure that the AC power cord is disconnected from the printer, and then, as shown in Figure 11-7, reach inside the cabinet top and disconnect the control-panel wiring harness. Put the cabinet top aside.

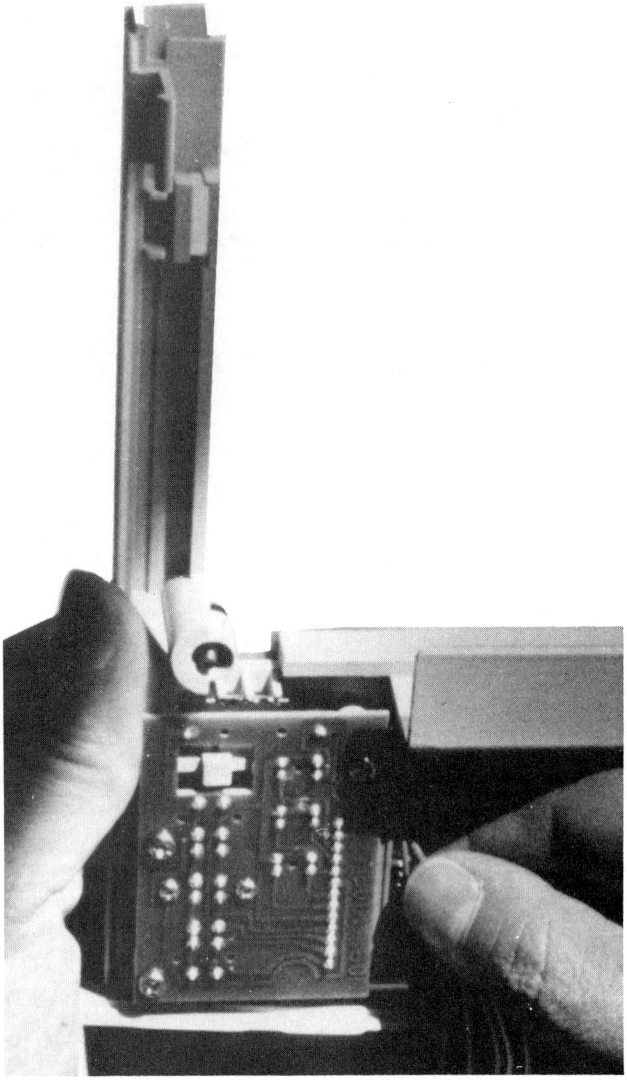

Figure 11-7 ImageWriter II control-panel wiring harness.

13. As shown in Figure 11-8, pull off the platen knob and put it aside.
14. Pull off the paper-feed selector knob (Figure 11-9) and put it aside.
15. The cabinet legs are each fastened by a *single,* permanently attached, #1 Phillips-head screw as shown in Figure 11-10. Loosen (but don't remove) both leg screws using a #1 Phillips-head screwdriver. The leg screws will be fully loosened when you feel them

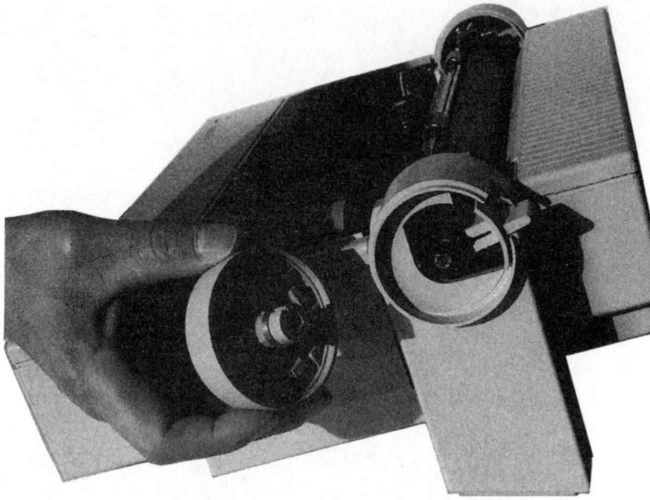

Figure 11-8 ImageWriter II platen knob.

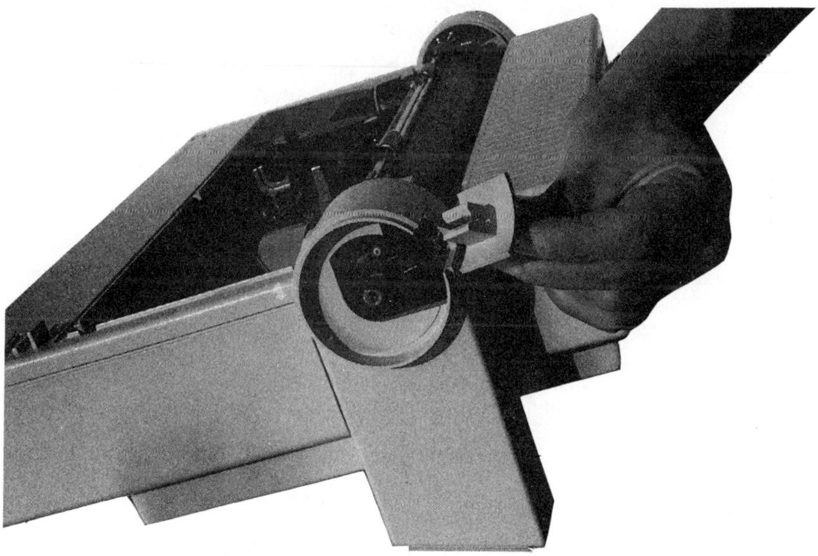

Figure 11-9 ImageWriter II paper-feed selector knob.

hit the end stops. The remaining four screws shown in Figure 11-10 hold the bottom cover. They *do not* have to be loosened.

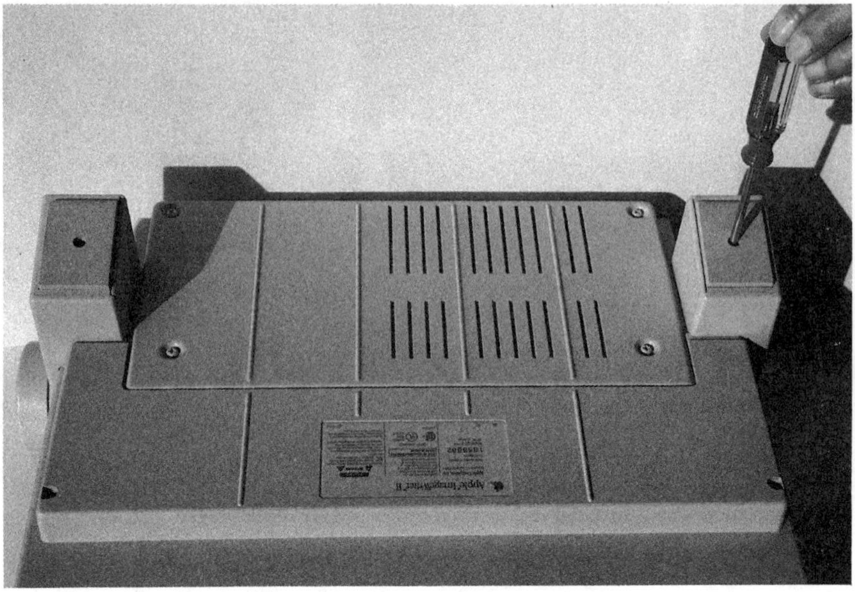

Figure 11-10 ImageWriter II cabinet leg screws.

16. Lift the loosened platen knob leg (shown on the left in Figure 11-11) straight up to release the two leg mounting tabs, and then pull gently at a 90° left angle. In the process, slip the AC power socket out of its holder. Assuming the printer is oriented exactly as shown in Figures 11-10 and 11-11, the removal action is *straight* up and then *sharp* left. Resist the temptation to rotate the leg, or you may snap the tabs.

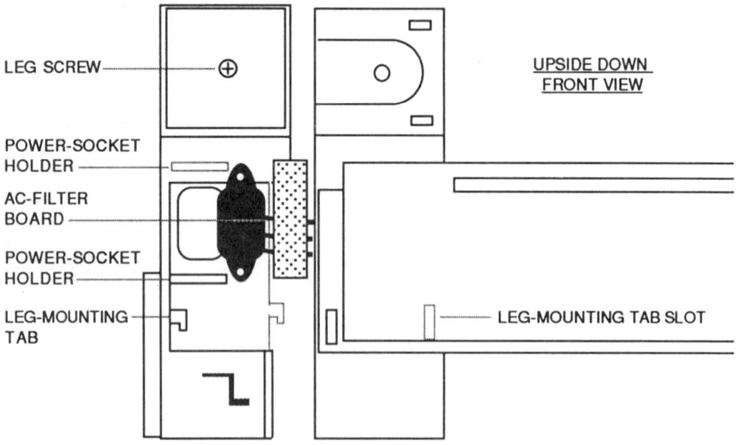

Figure 11-11 ImageWriter II platen knob leg.

17. Lift the loosened minicircular socket leg (shown on the right in Figure 11-12) straight up to release the two leg mounting tabs, and then pull gently at a 90° right angle. In the process, slip the minicircular socket board out of its holder. Assuming the printer is oriented exactly as shown in Figures 11-10 and 11-12, the removal action is *straight* up and then *sharp* right. Resist the temptation to rotate the leg, or you may snap the tabs.

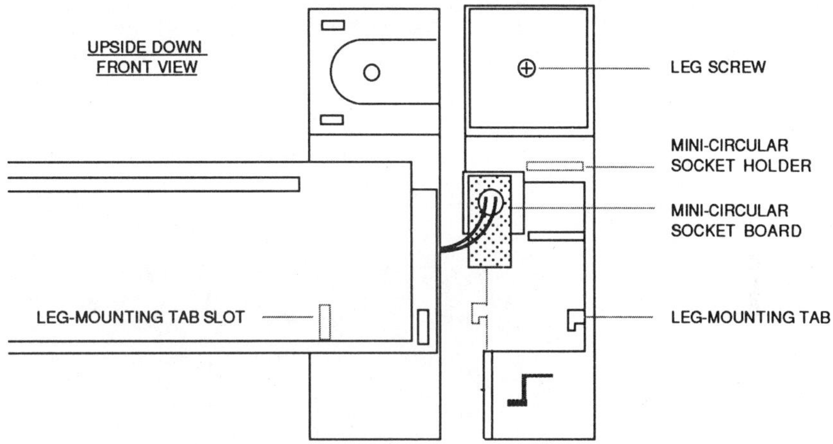

Figure 11-12 ImageWriter II minicircular socket leg.

18. With both legs removed, turn the printer right side up.

More often than not, the printer mechanism will be covered with paper dust and pollen, generous amounts of human hair, and, sometimes, large amounts of pet fur. If so, all of that has to go, *before* removing the platen. The easiest way to remove it is with an air compressor.

You can also remove it with a vacuum-cleaner exhaust. Either way, it's best to do this outside. Blowing out the mechanism can make a sizeable dust cloud.

Platen Removal Procedure

As shown in Figure 11-13, the platen rotates on plastic bushings which are secured to the printer frame by metal holders called platen-bush plates.

To remove the platen, all you have to do is unscrew the plates. Here's the complete procedure:

1. As shown in Figure 11-14, unscrew the ground wire, leading from the mechanical paper-empty sensor to the left-side platen-bush plate, using a #1 Phillips-head screwdriver. If there is no ground

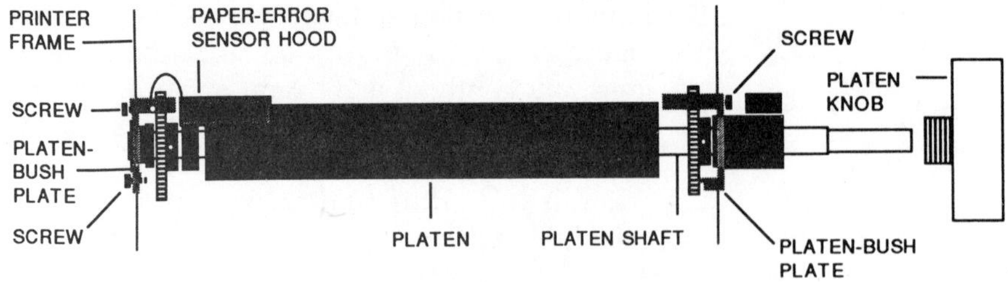

Figure 11-13 The ImageWriter II platen rotates on plastic bushings which are secured to the printer frame by metal holders called platen-bush plates.

wire, it means you have a photoelectric paper-empty sensor; you can skip this step.

Figure 11-14 ImageWriter II mechanical paper-empty sensor ground wire removal.

2. The left-side platen-bush plate is secured to the printer frame by two Phillips-head screws. Note that the front screw is smaller (#0). As shown in Figure 11-15, unscrew the left-side platen-bush plate, using #1 and #0 Phillips-head screwdrivers.

3. The right-side platen-bush plate is secured to the printer frame by one screw. Pull the paper-feed selector forward (into the pin-feed position). Unscrew the platen-bush plate using a #1 Phillips-head screwdriver, as shown in Figure 11-16. Note that the screw tip is pointed.

Figure 11-15 ImageWriter II left-side platen-bush plate removal.

When removing the platen-bush holders, it's best to use a top-quality #1 Phillips-head screwdriver, something with a precision-ground, chrome-vanadium tip. The platen bush holder screws tend to be tight (very tight). If the screwdriver tip is soft, or the least bit chewed, all you're going to do is mangle the screw heads; then, you'll need vise-locking pliers to get the screws out!

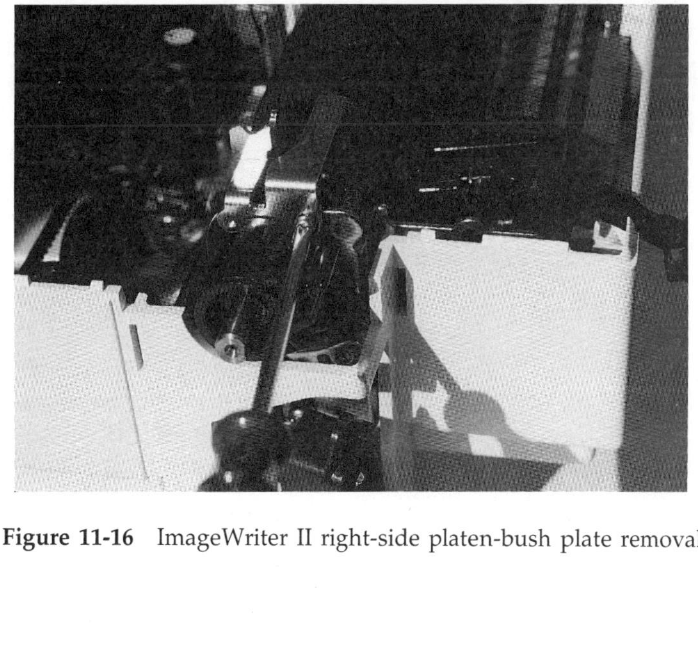

Figure 11-16 ImageWriter II right-side platen-bush plate removal.

4. Release and remove the two paper-bail springs (one on each side of the paper-bail), as shown in Figure 11-17. Carefully place the springs into the parts container.

Figure 11-17 ImageWriter II paper-bail springs.

Be alert when you handle the springs. It's a proven fact that tiny springs have minds of their own. Take your eyes off them for just for a second, and they'll bounce away, never to be seen again.

5. Move the paper bail out of the way. It rotates 180° backwards.
6. Push the paper-thickness lever all the way down (into the sixth detent).
7. Remove the platen. The left side lifts straight up. The right side slips out towards the left. It's not necessary to remove the paper-feed selector.
8. The platen assembly is now completely disconnected. Lift it away and put it aside. The metal paper-guide parts beneath the platen are now completely exposed.
9. As shown in Figures 11-18 and 11-19, the paper-empty sensor hood is fastened to the platen shaft with a roll pin. If there's a label stuck under the hood, drive out the roll pin using a ball-peen hammer and a 1/16-inch punch. Be careful. Plastic gears are easily broken.

Figure 11-18 The ImageWriter II paper-empty sensor hood is fastened to the platen shaft with a roll pin.

Figure 11-19 ImageWriter II paper-empty sensor hood disassembly details.

Pin punches are usually sold in kits. If you need to buy one, check for a kit with 3/32-inch size, as well. A 3/32-inch punch will be needed to reinstall the pin.

Sticky Residue Removal—Plastic Paper-Guide Parts The plastic paper guide (removed earlier in Step 8) is shown in Figure 11-20. Since the print head gets very hot, any label residue stuck here will have become actually baked-on. Remove it very carefully, with nonabrasive soap and water, as best you can.

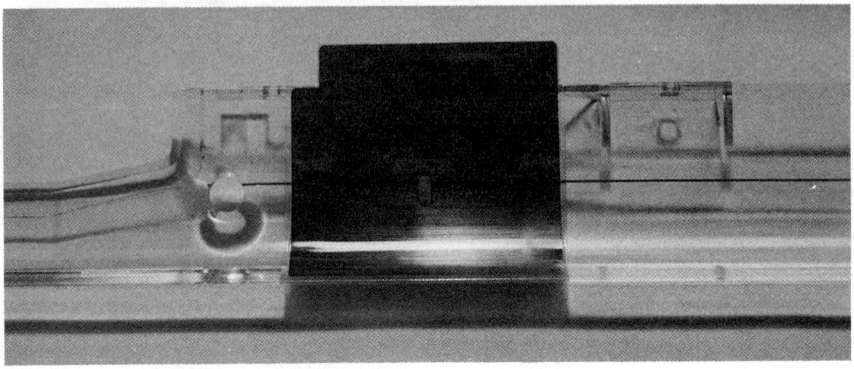

Figure 11-20 ImageWriter II paper guide.

Crusty, dark-brown material around the striker-wire opening is generally melted plastic. Any melted plastic that protrudes towards the platen should be carefully trimmed away with a small razor knife. Otherwise, the melted material will snag the paper, which makes a scraping noise, distorts the printout, and encourages further jamming.

Sticky Residue Removal—Metal Paper-Guide Parts Remove sticky residue from the exposed, metal paper-guide parts with a kerosene-based spray solvent. Liquid kerosene also works. Let the solvent soak for a few minutes, and then wipe off the dissolved residue. With the platen out of the way, you'll have the metal parts sparkling clean in no time at all.

The paper-empty sensor is shown in Figure 11-21. Generally, the stuck label will have mangled at least one of the two contacts. Remove the label residue from the plastic parts around the sensor, clean the contacts carefully, and return them to the shape indicated in Figure 11-21.

Platen Restoration—Rubber Parts To clean the printer platen, use typewriter-platen restorer or tape-recorder rubber cleaner. The same rubber cleaner used on typewriter platens and tape-recorder pinch rollers works wonders on printer platens.

Apply a liberal amount with a paper towel and let it soak for a few minutes. Allowing the cleaning agent to soak into the rubber is very important. When it starts to evaporate, rub the platen vigorously. The soaking action will have softened the rubber, and years of dried-up

Figure 11-21 ImageWriter II paper-empty sensor.

(dead rubber) glaze will rub off right into the towel. In cases of severe neglect, you may have to repeat the application two or three times to fully restore the platen. When you're done, the platen will be dull, not shiny.

It's best to do this job outside. Most rubber cleaners smell like maximum-strength moth flakes. The chemical treatment works great on rubber, but if you breathe the fumes, you may get a headache.

Roller-Bearing Maintenance Plastic shields keep the ImageWriter II paper-bail rollers cleaner than usual. If necessary, however, the paper bail can be removed and disassembled as shown in Figure 11-22.

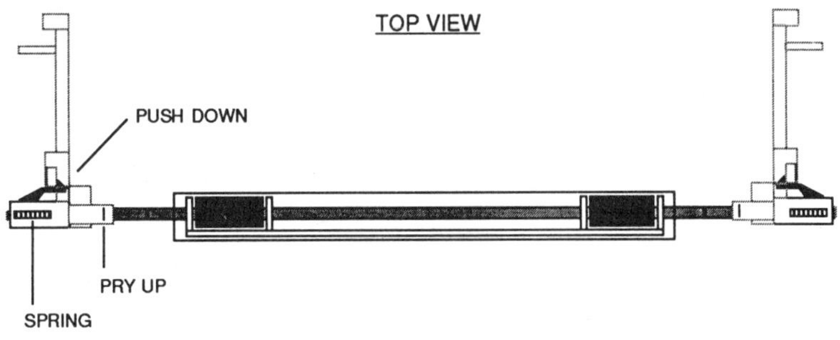

Figure 11-22 ImageWriter II paper-bail disassembly details.

Here's how to tell whether the rollers need cleaning: When flicked with a finger, clean rollers will spin through several revolutions like a top. Clogged rollers barely make it through a single revolution. If the rollers don't roll, the paper has to lift them out of the way, which results in squashed printout. Disassemble and clean the roller shaft now, if necessary, before reinstalling the platen. It's generally not necessary to oil the roller bearings. They're designed to run dry; once you get the grit out, they generally spin fine.

ImageWriter II Reassembly Procedure

Before putting the printer back together, it's best to wipe the platen-shaft clean. Old lubricant is generally contaminated with paper dust (sticky). If you don't remove it, it will just contaminate the new lubricant. With that in mind, here's the complete ImageWriter II reassembly procedure:

1. If appropriate, reposition the paper-empty sensor hood on the platen shaft, and replace the roll pin using a ball-peen hammer and a 3⁄32-inch punch.
2. Wipe the ends of the platen shaft with a clean paper towel.
3. Apply a drop of sewing-machine (or tape-recorder) oil to each end of the clean platen shaft. One drop on each end is plenty. Resist the temptation to overlubricate.
4. Refer to Figure 11-18. Slide the platen gear and the leftside bushing back onto the platen shaft.
5. As shown in Figure 11-23, make sure the paper-feed selector gear is centered.

Figure 11-23 ImageWriter II paper-feed gear.

6. When the paper-feed selector gear is centered, slide the right side of the platen shaft into the paper-feed selector; when the bushing mounted on the opposite side (of the platen shaft) is correctly positioned over the frame, snap it into place.
7. Check the action of the paper-feed selector. If it's not working properly, repeat Steps 5 and 6.
8. Move the paper bail back into position. It rotates forwards.
9. Refer to Figures 11-17 and 11-22. Reattach the two paper bail springs (one on each side of the paper bail).
10. Refer to Figure 11-16. The right-side platen-bush plate is secured to the printer frame by one Phillips-head screw. The screw has a pointed tip. Pull the paper-feed selector forward (into the pin-feed position); reattach the platen-bush plate using a #1 Phillips-head screwdriver.
11. Refer to Figure 11-15. The left-side platen-bush plate is secured to the printer frame by two Phillips-head screws. The screws have pointed tips. Reattach the left-side platen-bush plate using a #1 Phillips-head screwdriver.
12. Refer to Figure 11-14. Reattach the ground wire leading from the mechanical paper-empty sensor to the left-side platen-bush plate, using a #1 Phillips-head screwdriver. (If there is no ground wire, it means you have a photoelectric paper-empty sensor; you can skip this step.)
13. Turn the printer upside down.
14. Refer to Figure 11-12. Slip the minicircular socket back into its holder (as far as it'll go) and then reattach the left leg. Assuming the printer is oriented exactly as shown in Figures 11-10 and 11-12, the replacement action is *straight* in and then *straight* down. Resist the temptation to rotate the leg, or you may break the plastic tabs.
15. Refer to Figure 11-11. Slip the AC power socket back into its holder (as far as it will go) then reattach the right leg. Assuming the printer is oriented exactly as shown in Figures 11- 10 and 11-11, the replacement action is *straight* in and then *straight* down. Resist the temptation to rotate the leg, or you may break the plastic tabs.
16. Refer to Figure 11-10. The cabinet legs are each fastened by a *single,* permanently attached, #1 Phillips-head screw. Retighten the screws using a #1 Phillips-head screwdriver.
17. Refer to Figure 11-9. Replace the paper-feed selector knob.
18. Refer to Figure 11-8. Note that the platen shaft has a flat spot. Check for the matching flat spot on the platen knob, and press it home.

19. Refer to Figure 11-7. Make absolutely sure that the AC power cord is disconnected from the printer, and then reconnect the control-panel wiring harness.
20. Refer to Figure 11-5. Slide the ribbon cartridge deck all the way to the left.
21. Refer to Figure 11-4. Reattach the two cabinet-top screws using a #1 Phillips-head screwdriver.
22. Refer to Figure 11-3. Reinstall the paper guide and start (but don't tighten) the paper-guide screws using a #0 Phillips-head screwdriver. Skip to "Readjusting the Paper Guide" immediately following this section.
23. Refer to Figures 11-2 and 11-1. With the paper guide readjusted and tightened, reinstall the print head.
24. Reinstall the ribbon cartridge.
25. Replace the front cover.
26. Replace the back cover.
27. Reconnect the Mac-to-ImageWriter II cable to the minicircular connector.
28. Reconnect the AC power cord to the printer.
29. Reconnect the AC power cord to the wall outlet.

The printer is now completely reassembled and ready to go. Up to this point, from the time we started the take-apart procedure, we've invested 30 to 45 minutes, certainly no more than an hour. The first time (learning how) always takes longer (closer to an hour), but even then, the going rate for stuck-label repairs is typically $65.00. At 30 to 45 minutes per repair (less time than it takes most people to *drive* back-and-forth to the repair shop), the value of this information works out to over $100.00 per hour, which is a very nice return from a $35.00 computer book.

Readjusting the Paper Guide

If you can't get envelopes or multipart business forms through the printer, and you're sure the paper-thickness lever is set properly, the paper guide may be out of adjustment. That could have happened if someone removed the guide (most likely, to clear a stuck label) and reinstalled it without regard to adjustment. Here's the complete procedure:

1. As shown in Figure 11-3, loosen (but don't remove) the paper-guide screws.

2. Pull the paper-feed selector up, into the pin-feed position.
3. Push the paper-thickness lever down, into the fourth detent.
4. Simulate a 4-part business form by making a sandwich out of four sheets of paper. Load the 4-sheet thickness into the printer.
5. Push the paper-feed selector down into the cut-sheet position.
6. With four sheets of paper under the paper bail, the paper guide should fit like comfortable clothing—not too tight, not too loose. Unless you've never used a printer or a typewriter before, the correct setting is obvious. Turn the platen knob with one hand, while using the thumb and index finger of your other hand to adjust the guide. When the paper feeds normally (not too tight, not too loose), stop turning the platen knob and tighten the two screws.

Follow this adjustment/reinstallation procedure whenever you remove the paper guide to clear a stuck label.

Missing Dots in the Printout

The two main causes of missing dots in the printout are corroded contacts on the print head and distended striker wires. Corroded contacts are easily repaired by removing the print head and rubbing them with a pencil eraser. Here's the complete procedure:

1. Disconnect the AC power cord from the printer.
2. Remove the front cover. Put the front cover aside.
3. Remove the ribbon cartridge. Put the ribbon cartridge aside.
4. As shown in Figures 11-1 and 11-2, pry back the print-head latch and remove the print head. Bear in mind that print heads which have never been removed may offer considerable resistance.
5. Print-head contacts are shown in Figure 11-24. Rub both sides of the board gently with a soft pencil eraser to remove corrosion.

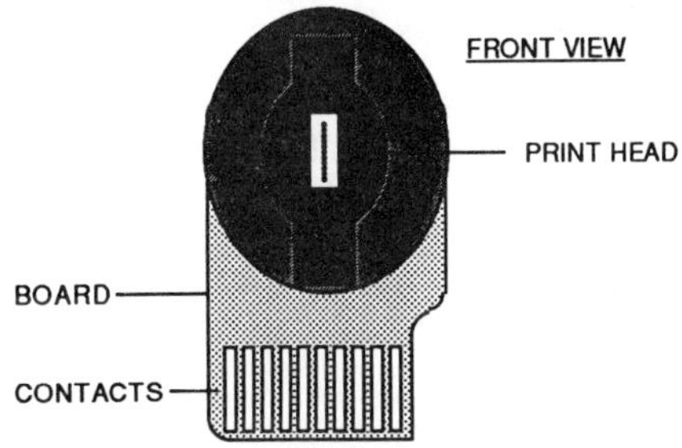

Figure 11-24 ImageWriter II print-head contact details. Rub both sides of the board gently with a soft pencil eraser to remove corrosion.

6. Reverse Steps 1 through 5 to reinstall the print head.

Distended Striker Wires

When rubbing the print-head contacts with a pencil eraser fails to restore missing dots in the printout, the most likely cause is a distended striker wire. Check for distended striker wires by examining the print head. If one or more striker wires protrudes further than the others, as shown in Figure 11-25, you'll have to replace the print head (or send it out for repair), and replace the ribbon cartridge.

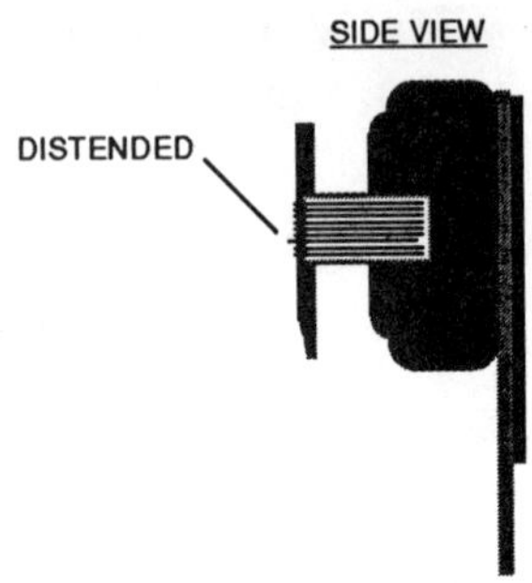

Figure 11-25 ImageWriter II print head. Distended striker wire protrudes further than the others.

In fact, it's poorly designed ribbon cartridges that usually cause this problem. When built-in character sets are selected on-the-fly in high-speed draft mode, the printer changes speeds very quickly. Some ribbon cartridges can't shift that fast; either an extra length of ribbon spills out, or they momentarily jam. When that happens, the momentarily stalled ribbon fabric is pulverized. If the cartridge mechanism doesn't recover quickly enough, one or more striker wires punctures the ribbon fabric. If the striker wires are still inside the fabric when the cartridge recovers, the sudden lateral movement can twist them out of alignment. Once they're out of alignment (bent out of shape), they don't return. If they don't return, they don't fire. Even when the wires do return, the ribbon fabric tears, which leads to further snagging.

The symptom of this problem is an unexplained dropout in the printout. When running TCG's CPI - Character Sets test, watch for it when shifting from ultracondensed, 17-cpi type to Pica 10 cpi. Typical symptoms are illustrated in Figure 11-26.

It's no coincidence that ultracondensed 17 is the slowest typeface and Pica 10 is the fastest. That merely proves the point. *Poorly designed ribbon cartridges are the number one cause of print-head failure.* Bear in mind that we're not talking about individual ribbons. Certain brands fail this test nearly 100% of the time. Other brands almost never fail. Further-

CONTROL SECTION - DP (DATA PROCESSING)
PICA (10 CPI) abcdefghijklmnopqrstuvwxyz-123456789
EXTENDED (9 CPI) abcdefghijklmnopqrstuvwxyz-123456789
ELITE (12 CPI) abcdefghijklmnopqrstuvwxyz-123456789
SEMICONDENSED (13.4 CPI) abcdefghijklmnopqrstuvwxyz-123456789
CONDENSED (15 CPI) abcdefghijklmnopqrstuvwxyz-123456789
ULTRA CONDENSED (17 CPI) abcdefghijklmnopqrstuvwxyz-123456789

TEST SECTION - NLQ (NEAR LETTER QUALITY)
PICA (10 CPI) abcdefghijklmnopqrstuvwxyz-123456789
EXTENDED (9 CPI) abcdefghijklmnopqrstuvwxyz-123456789
ELITE (12 CPI) abcdefghijklmnopqrstuvwxyz-123456789
SEMICONDENSED (13.4 CPI) abcdefghijklmnopqrstuvwxyz-123456789
CONDENSED (15 CPI) abcdefghijklmnopqrstuvwxyz-123456789
ULTRA CONDENSED (17 CPI) abcdefghijklmnopqrstuvwxyz-123456789

Figure 11-26 ImageWriter II. This kind of dropout suggests a poorly designed ribbon cartridge.

more, ribbon cartridge testing will prove that quality is generally *not* related to price. You can pay a lot of money for junk, while great ribbon cartridges are sometimes quite inexpensive.

Use Test Character Generator to precheck individual ribbon cartridges and/or to separate good ribbon cartridge designs from the bad designs. If you find any of the latter, don't use them. It's senseless to destroy an expensive print head over a $2.00 item.

Wavy, Uneven Printing

A common problem with all dot-matrix printers (not just ImageWriter II printers) is wavy, uneven printout. Over time, the carrier belt stretches, hammer-fire timing drifts, and character linearity distorts. Officially, it's called character deviation. The deviation is most noticeable when printing bidirectionally, in Best or High quality.

You can't stop character deviation from happening, but with Test Character Generator, you can easily correct it. Figure 11-27 shows TCG's Bidirectional Alignment test.

In theory, test printout from a properly aligned printer should look just like a window screen. In practice, characters at the edges of the printout almost always deviate, because of ricochet from the carriage return. In other words, we can get the middle of the page just about perfect, but there'll always be a *little* wave at the edges. Format your documents with 1-inch left and right margins and you'll never see it.

With reasonable expectations in mind, here's the complete bidirectional alignment procedure:

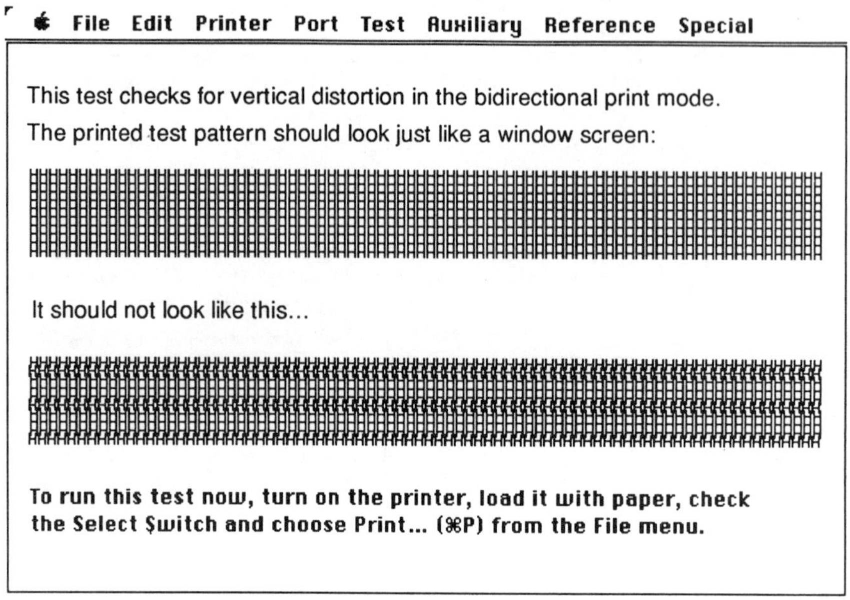

Figure 11-27 Test Character Generator Bidirectional Alignment test.

1. Remove the front cover. Note the hidden magnet shown in Figure 11-28.

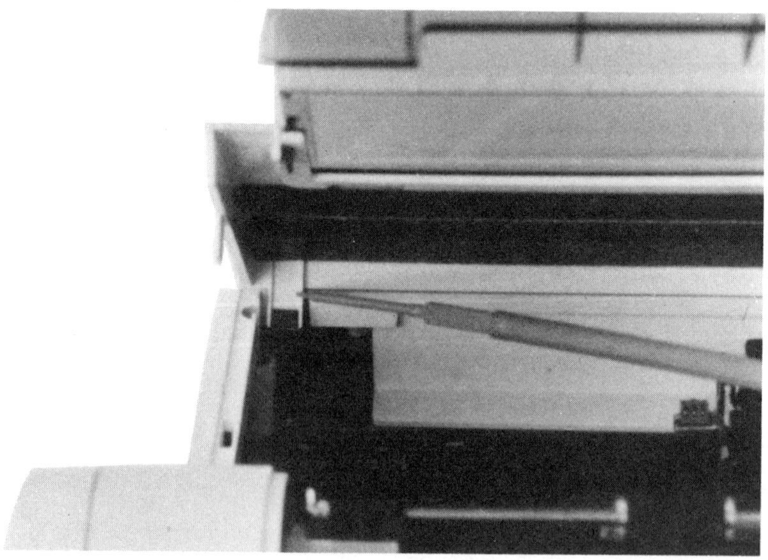

Figure 11-28 ImageWriter II front-cover magnet.

2. As shown in Figure 11-29, the front-cover magnet activates a reed switch in the control panel. To run the printer with the front cover removed, the front-cover magnet has to be replaced with a small crafts magnets as shown in Figure 11-30.

Crafts magnets are readily available in sewing and notions departments. The magnet shown in Figure 11-30 measures $\frac{5}{16}$-inch wide, $\frac{17}{16}$-inch long and $\frac{5}{32}$-inch thick (approximately $\frac{1}{4} \times 1 \times \frac{1}{8}$-inch).

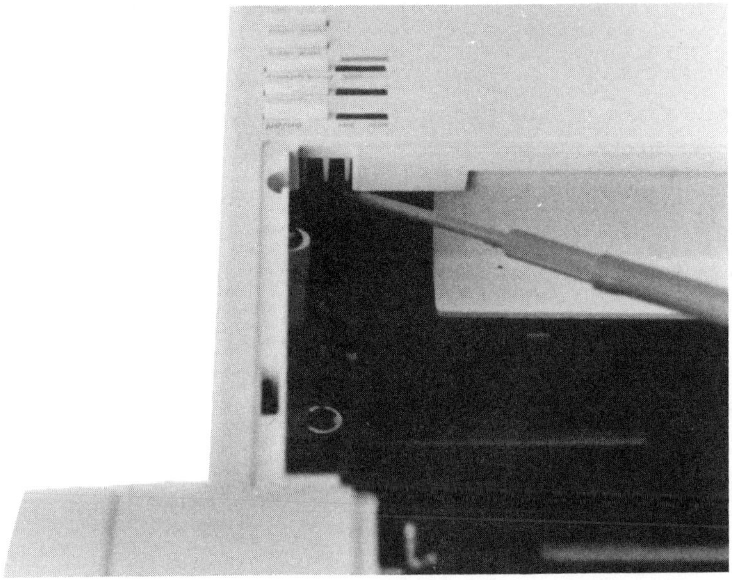

Figure 11-29 ImageWriter II control-panel reed switch.

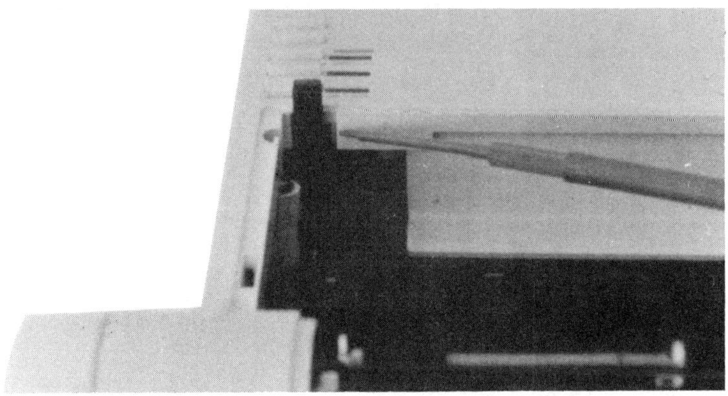

Figure 11-30 ImageWriter II. To run the printer with the front cover removed, the front-cover magnet has to be replaced with a small crafts magnet.

3. Load paper, and switch on the printer.
4. Press the Select switch. If the green LED (light-emitting diode) blinks out as soon as you release the Select switch, turn the magnet around and try again. Repeat, as necessary, until you get the green LED to stay lit.
5. Run TCG's Bidirectional Alignment test. After 10 lines, TCG stops and asks whether to "Repeat this test?", as shown in Figure 11-31.

Examine the printout, and then locate DIP switches SW2-5 and SW2-6, the ImageWriter II's character-deviation adjustment. As shown in Figure 11-32, DIP switches SW2-5 and SW2-6 are located under the front cover, just above the Apple logo.

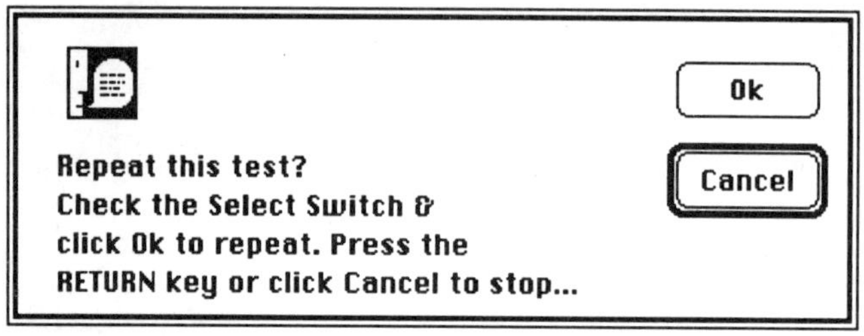

Figure 11-31 Test Character Generator "Repeat this test?" dialog box.

Figure 11-32 ImageWriter II DIP switches SW2-5 and SW2-6 are located under the front cover, just above the Apple logo.

6. Note the initial positions of each switch (On or Off). Try resetting one switch or the other, and click the Ok button to repeat the test.
7. Repeat Step 6, as necessary, for best results. Tap the Return key, or click the Cancel button to discontinue testing.
8. If the printed test pattern is still unsatisfactory, the carrier belt is probably stretched and the carrier-belt tension lever will have to be adjusted. As shown in Figure 11-33, the carrier-belt tension lever is on the right side of the printer, just in front of the paper- thickness switch.

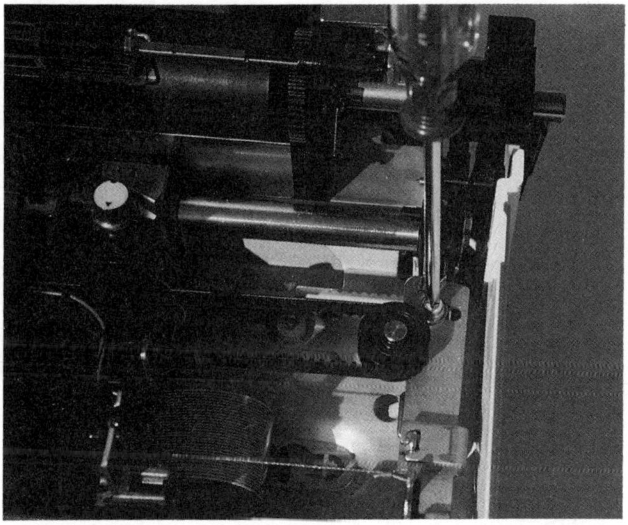

Figure 11-33 ImageWriter II. Carrier-belt tension lever.

The lever is designed to be self-adjusting. Correct tension is determined by a spring. Loosen the screw, snap the lever to shake up the spring, and very carefully retighten the screw. Try not to overtighten or undertighten. If you overtighten, the screw head will twist the tension lever, applying even more tension. The belt will be too tight. If you undertighten (or if the screw loosens up), the spring will act like a shock absorber. Belt tension will vary and bidirectional alignment will be impossible.

9. Repeat Step 8, as necessary, until the printout is satisfactory. Concentrate on the center of the test pattern. When you get the center aligned properly, character deviation at the edges should be 0.3 mm or less.
10. When the printout is satisfactory, remove the magnet and replace the top cover.

Overlapping Colors

When color printout overlaps slightly on character descenders and underlines, it means the color (ribbon-shift) cam is out of alignment. The realignment procedure varies, depending on which version of the ImageWriter II **ribbon-adjustment assembly** is installed in the printer. Figure 11-34 shows an early ribbon-adjustment assembly. Figures 11-33 and 11-42 show a subsequent style.

Figure 11-34 ImageWriter II (A9M0310) ribbon-adjustment assembly.

With TCG's Color Ribbon Alignment test, you can easily realign either style (if necessary), although the procedures are slightly different. Here's the procedure for the early style:

1. Locate the knurled nut in the middle of the ribbon-adjustment assembly. While holding the knurled nut with small pliers, loosen (but don't remove) the 9/32-inch lock nut at the top of the assembly with a 9/32-inch nut driver.
2. Examine the test printout. If color lines overlap at the bottom, turn the knurled adjustment nut ½ turn clockwise. If color lines overlap at the top, turn the knurled adjustment nut ½ turn counterclockwise.
3. While holding the knurled nut with small pliers, tighten the 9/32-inch lock nut at the top of the assembly with a 9/32-inch nut driver.
4. Repeat TCG's Color Ribbon Alignment test.
5. Repeat Steps 1 through 4, as necessary, turning the adjustment nut a little more or a little less, until the color alignment is satisfactory.

Subsequent ribbon-adjustment assemblies don't use a metal locknut. Instead, they use a plastic lock knob. In place of a metal knurled nut, they use a plastic adjustment ring. All-plastic assemblies are very *fragile*, but they can easily be adjusted without using tools. Here's the procedure:

1. Disregard the lock knob at the top of the assembly. It does not generally need to be turned. Instead, locate the spring-loaded, red plastic adjustment ring immediately below the lock knob. Examine its position relative to the lock knob. Ideally, it should be centered on the lock knob.
2. Examine the test printout. If colors overlap at the bottom of lines, grip the adjustment ring between your thumb and index finger, push down to free the ring-locking teeth, and turn the red ring 90° (¼-turn) clockwise. If colors overlap at the top of lines, push down and turn the adjustment ring 90° counterclockwise.

> Never attempt to turn the red plastic ring more than ½ turn (180°) in either direction. The ring plastic is very thin. Force the adjustment and you'll surely break the plastic.

3. Repeat TCG's Color Ribbon Alignment test.
4. Repeat Steps 1 through 3, as necessary, turning the adjustment ring a little more or a little less, until the color alignment is satisfactory.

Both procedures can also be used to align monochrome ribbons. If the tops of characters are cut off, the ribbon-cam position is too low. To correct it, turn the adjustment counterclockwise. If the bottoms of characters are cut off, the ribbon-cam position is too high. To correct that, turn the adjustment clockwise.

If color ribbons don't work at all, the color-ribbon sensor may be broken, or disconnected. As shown in Figure 11-35, the color-ribbon sensor is normally open (up) when a monochrome ribbon is installed, and closed (depressed) when a color ribbon is installed.

Dead Sets

When an ImageWriter II (or any printer, for that matter) fails to print, most people immediately assume the worst. Let a single screw loosen up, and they assume that the printer is "totally blown." They assume, or they're told, that they're going to need a "whole new circuit board,"

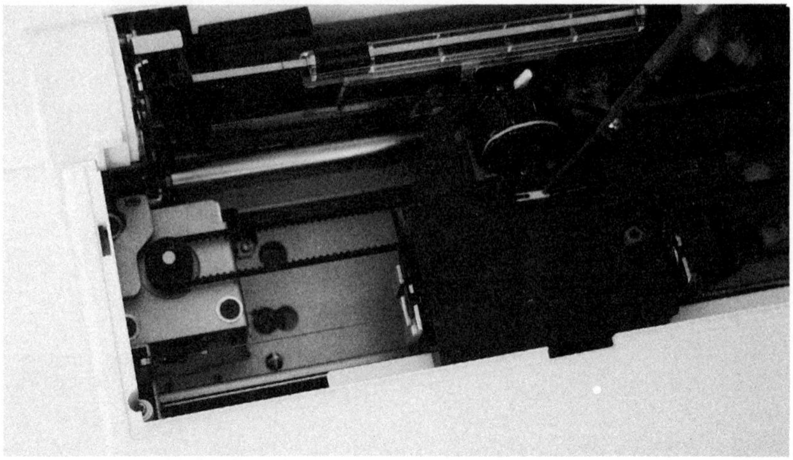

Figure 11-35 ImageWriter II color-ribbon sensor.

and that repairs will cost "hundreds of dollars." In fact, most dead-set failures have nothing to do with the circuit boards. They're peripheral related, and fairly easy to spot. This section shows you how. We'll use a process of elimination involving five logical steps:

1. Check the usual (software, cables, etc.). If that passes....
2. Run the printer's built-in self-test. If that passes....
3. Check the printer's serial interface. If that passes....
4. Check the computer's serial interface. If that passes....
5. Repeat Step 1—try new System software, try a new cable.

Dead sets fall into two categories: control panel lit, control panel not lit. First we'll look at control panel lit.

Dead Sets—Control Panel Lit

If the control panel is lit, but absolutely nothing happens when you try to print, it's usually due to one of the following:

1. Printer resource (driver) is not installed. See Chapter 3.
2. Printer resource (driver) is not selected. Use the Choose-Printer or Chooser DA to select the printer. See Chapter 3.
3. Printer is out of paper, or printer is off-line. Load paper and press the *select* button. See Chapter 10.
4. Cable is disconnected or incorrect. See Chapter 10.
5. DIP switches are set incorrectly. See Chapter 10.

When you're absolutely sure that none of the above is responsible, the next thing to do is to determine whether the problem is in the printer or the computer. To facilitate the process of elimination, the ImageWriter II is equipped with three built-in tests.

Built-In Carrier-Motor Test The first built-in self-test checks the carriage assembly, the carrier belt, and the carrier motor. To run the test:

1. Switch off the printer (if it's on).
2. Make sure the top cover is in place, or use a crafts magnet to close the reed switch, as shown in Figures 11-28 through 11-30.
3. Hold down the *line feed* button, and, while keeping it held down, press the *on/off* button.

If the top cover (or the magnet) is in place, and the carrier motor is working, the ribbon cartridge deck will move back and forth without firing and without executing any line feeds. To suspend the test, press the *line feed* button. To resume the test, press the *select* button. To stop the test altogether, turn the printer off.

For 99 times out of 100, the carrier-motor test passes. If it doesn't, locate the ribbon cartridge winder knob shown in Figure 11-36. Turn the winder knob clockwise. The knob should turn freely. If it binds, try another ribbon cartridge. If it doesn't bind, try sliding the ribbon cartridge deck back and forth by hand. If the ribbon cartridge and the ribbon cartridge deck both check out, fuse FU1 on the power-supply/driver board may be open. See Dead Sets—Control Panel Not Lit at the end of this chapter.

Figure 11-36 ImageWriter II ribbon cartridge winder knob.

Built-In Self-Test The second built-in self-test checks the carrier motor, the line-feed motor, the ribbon-drive motor, and the print head. To run the test:

1. Switch off the printer (if it's on).
2. Load the printer with 8½ × 11, or 8½ × 12-inch (maximum-width) paper. If you fail to load maximum-width paper, the self-test will print right across the platen. That's bad for the print head and the platen.
3. Hold down the *form feed* button, and, while keeping it held down, press the *on/off* button.

This test prints the ROM (read-only memory) version number, shows the current DIP-switch settings, reports on the current option card status (RAM= 0 KB or RAM= 32 KB; AT=ON or AT=OFF), and then it prints a repeating, alphanumeric test pattern. If a 4-color ribbon is installed, the test pattern prints alternating black, yellow, magenta, cyan, orange, green, and purple lines. If a monochrome (1-color) ribbon is installed, the test pattern prints every line the same. Even with a 4-color ribbon, the initial ROM, DIP switch, and option-card information always print black.

To suspend the alphanumeric test pattern, press the *line feed* button. To change the print quality, press the *print quality* button. To resume the test pattern, press the *select* button. To stop the test pattern, press the *on/off* button.

Nine times out of ten, the test pattern prints fine. If it doesn't, see component-level repairs at the end of this chapter.

Built-in Loopback Test When the self-test passes, it proves that the printer mechanism is working, but it doesn't indicate whether or not the printer is able to communicate with a computer. If the printer can't communicate, it can't hear the computer's instructions. If it can't hear the computer's instructions, it doesn't print, even though it's able to.

The communications part of the printer is called the serial interface. To test it, we need a loopback plug. Wiring details for a loopback plug are shown in Figure 11-37.

Unless you have a properly constructed loopback plug, the built-in loopback test fails (by definition) every time. With that in mind, here's the procedure:

1. Switch off the printer (if it's on).
2. Disconnect the Mac-to-ImageWriter II cable from the back of the printer. Replace it with a properly constructed minicircular loopback plug.

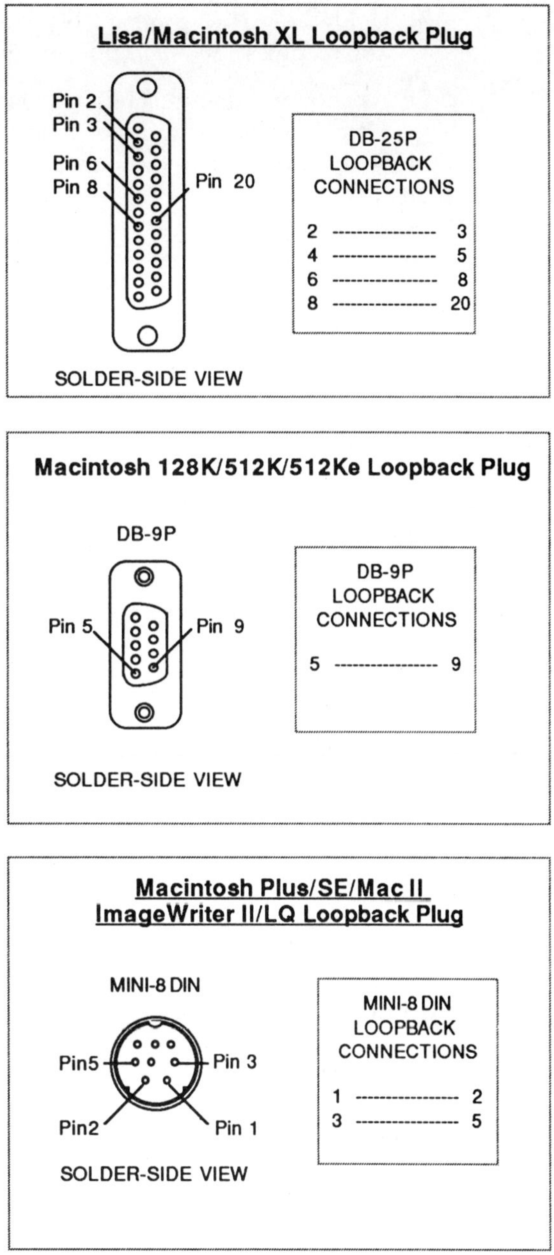

Figure 11-37 Loopback plug wiring details.

3. Load the printer with 8½ × 11, or 8½ × 12-inch (maximum-width) paper. If you fail to load maximum-width paper, the loopback test will print right across the platen.

4. Hold down the *print quality* button, and, while keeping it held down, press the *on/off* button.

As shown in Figure 11-38, the loopback test prints the ROM (read-only memory) version number, shows the current DIP-switch settings, reports on the current option-card status, and then it either prints a repeating, alphanumeric test pattern (just like the self-test) indicating that the loopback test passed, or it prints "LOOPBACK TEST FAILS," stops testing, and flashes the red error light on the control panel.

```
LOOP TEST

ROMREV(05)

DIPSW1(00000100) DIPSW2(1100),'1=ON,0=OFF'

RAM= 0 KB  AT=OFF




LOOP BACK TEST FAILS
```

Figure 11-38 ImageWriter II built-in loopback test printout.

To suspend the alphanumeric test pattern, press the *line feed* button. To change the print quality, press the *print quality* button. To resume the test pattern, press the *select* button. To stop the test pattern, press the *on/off* button.

Nine times out of ten, the test pattern prints fine. If it doesn't, see Component-Level Repairs at the end of this chapter.

Macintosh Loopback Test When all three of the printer's built-in tests pass but you still can't print, and you're absolutely sure it's not the cable, the DIP-switch settings, or the printer resource, the problem may be in the computer's serial interface. We can verify whether or not the problem is in the computer's serial interface with TCG's Loopback test.

As explained in Figure 11-39, this test requires a properly constructed loopback plug. Wiring details were given in Figure 11-37. To run TCG's Loopback test, choose Test Serial Port from the Aux. menu.

Assuming you insert a properly constructed loopback plug into the computer's printer port and the test fails, double-check TCG's Port menu. Make sure the check mark is beside the Printer port menu item. If not, select the Printer Port menu item and try again. Alternately, if

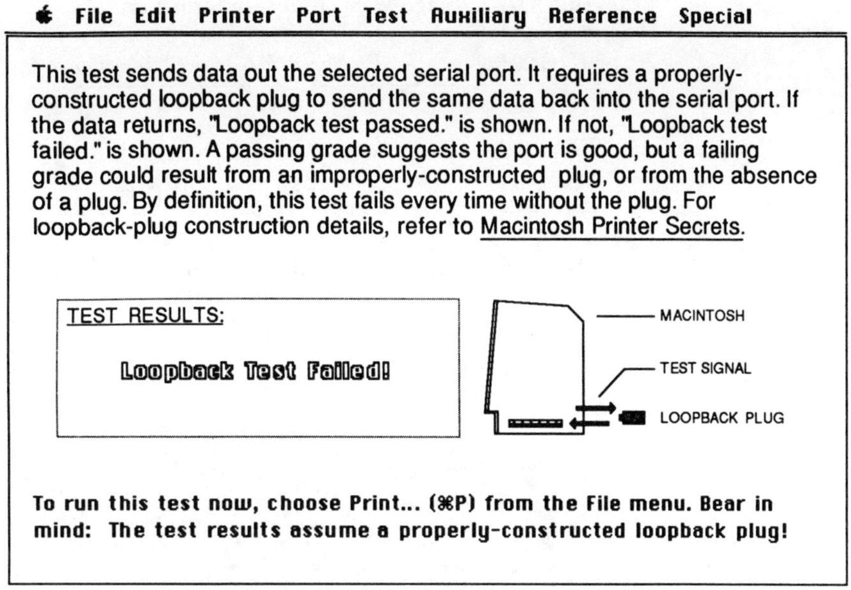

Figure 11-39 Test Character Generator Loopback test.

you're testing the modem port, make sure the Modem Port menu item is check marked (and try again).

If the test still fails, verify that the loopback plug is inserted into the correct port. On all Macs from the 128K to the Macintosh II, the printer and modem ports are identified by icons. On Lisas and Mac XLs, the printer and modem ports are marked with uppercase letters. The Lisa/XL modem port is identified by an uppercase A; the Lisa/XL printer port is identified by an uppercase B.

If the loopback test still fails, and you're testing a 128K, a 512K, or a 512K Enhanced, the computer's RFI shield may be shorted to the logic board. In that case, all you generally need to do is insulate the shield. Complete take-apart and repair details are covered in Chapter 1 of *Macintosh Repair & Upgrade Secrets*, ISBN 0-672-48452-8, published by SAMS.

Dead Sets—Control Panel Not Lit

A surprising number of completely dead printers have nothing wrong with them other than a bad fuse. The reason for the failure appears to be fuse fatigue. Over time, the fuse element fails. There's generally no evidence of circuit failure. When you replace the fuse, the printer operates just as it always did. Table 11-1 gives replacement-part information.

Table 11-1. ImageWriter II Fuse Information

Board Reference	Electrical Size	Physical Size	Action
FU	2 A, 250-V AC	1¼ × ¼-inch	fast-acting
FU1	1 A, 125-V AC	5 × 20 mm	slow-blow
FU2	5 A, 125-V AC	5 × 20 mm	slow-blow

The line fuse (FU) is hidden inside the platen-knob leg. Fuses FU1 and FU2 are on the power, supply/driver board, as shown in Figure 11-40.

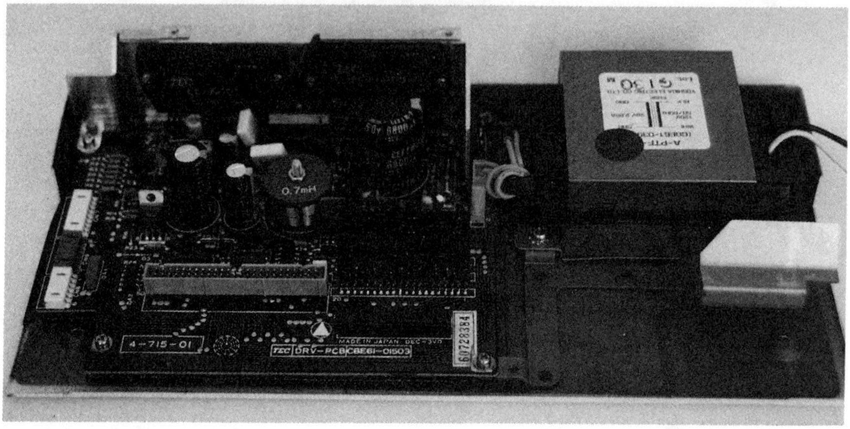

Figure 11-40 ImageWriter II fuses FU1 and FU2 are on the power-supply/driver board.

Most other sources state that the ImageWriter II doesn't have internal fuses. Figure 11-40 is provided so that you can look at the board and decide for yourself.

Here's how to get at the nonexistent fuses on the power-supply/driver board:

1. Disconnect the AC power cord from the wall outlet.
2. Disconnect the AC power cord from the printer.
3. Disconnect the Mac-to-ImageWriter II cable from the minicircular connector at the back of the printer.
4. Set up a container suitable for holding small parts.
5. As shown in Figure 11-41, there are two screws directly behind the tractor (not platen) assembly. These screws hold the power-supply/driver board from the top. Remove both screws (not the three screws behind the platen) using a #1 Phillips-head screw-driver.

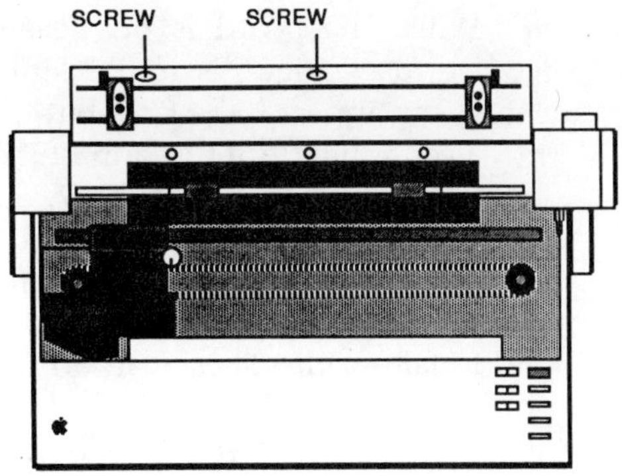

Figure 11-41 ImageWriter II power-supply/driver board screws.

6. As shown in Figure 11-42, the bottom cover is held by four screws. Turn the printer upside down and remove all four screws with a #1 Phillips-head screwdriver.

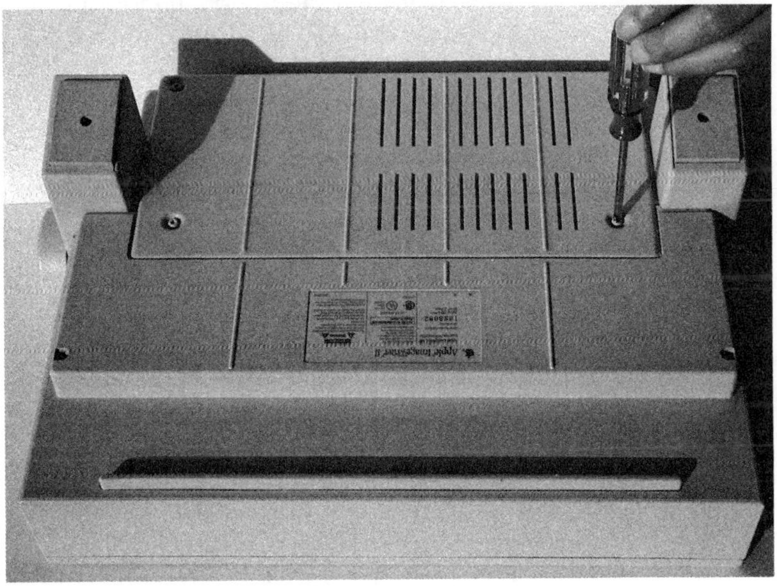

Figure 11-42 ImageWriter II bottom-cover screws.

7. The power-supply/driver board is attached to the bottom cover by additional screws (as shown in Figure 11-41) and to the printer by various cables. Carefully lift the bottom cover and disconnect the cables, one at a time. The angle works against you, and the power transformer is heavy. Start at the back and gradually tilt the cover forward as you disconnect the cables.

When the board is out, examine the fuse filaments for breaks. Because fuse fatigue is nonviolent (no evidence of burning), the filaments may appear to be fine, but may still be open. Check the filaments with a continuity tester or a multimeter. Replace any fuses that you find open, reverse Steps 1 through 7, and the problem may be fixed.

If replacement fails to restore full operation, or if the fuse failure does appear to be violent, check for metallic foreign objects inside the printer. When people remove the paper cover, coins and paper clips tend to fall inside. These can do real damage.

Component-Level Repairs Component-level troubleshooting of the ImageWriter II (A9M0310) circuit boards requires a Sams COMPUTERFACTS folder, product number CP27. Sams COMPUTERFACTS are industry-standard service folders designed for working technicians. Besides a full set of schematics (with clearly marked reference voltages), they provide oscilloscope waveforms, truth tables, semiconductor cross-reference data, and miscellaneous adjustment information.

To benefit from the information in this folder, you need at least a logic probe, a logic pulser, a digital multimeter, and minimal soldering/desoldering equipment. For a solid introduction to component-level troubleshooting, including instructions on how to use the necessary test equipment, I recommend Howard W. Sams & Company's *Microcomputer Troubleshooting & Repair*, ISBN 0-672-22629-4, written by John G. Stephenson and Bob Cahill.

Replacement Parts Many people think that Apple Computer Corporation builds ImageWriter II printers completely within the United States. In fact, the ImageWriter II is manufactured by Tokyo Electric Company (TEC) of Japan. It's merely imported by Apple Computer.

Other TEC printers that are built on similar frames include the C.Itoh C310R and the C.Itoh C315R. Comparing brand-name TEC printer models is like comparing General Motors products. When you compare Chevrolets to Pontiacs and Oldsmobiles (all built by General Motors), you find that the bodies (cabinet parts) are different, but major mechanical parts are interchangeable.

With that in mind, Table 11-2 provides an interchangeable parts cross-reference guide. For a complete list of interchangeable OEM parts, compare Sams COMPUTERFACTS folder CP27 (Apple ImageWriter II) to CP33 (C.Itoh C310).

Before ordering parts, note that naturally occurring line-feed problems are usually related to ZD3 (ECG 5082A) and C11 (2200 μF, 35 V) on the power-supply/driver board, and/or IC8 (7406) on the logic board. When there's no *select* light and no line feed, the problem is usually with IC9 (EC-A056) on the logic board. Experience shows that the

Table 11-2. Interchangeable Parts Cross-Reference Guide

ImageWriter II	C.Itoh C310
Print head	CBABK-12902
Paper guide (card holder)	CQAAK-10501
Paper-feed motor	CBA45-01202
Carrier motor	CBA45-01101

paper-feed motor and/or the platen-drive gears are almost never the cause of a line-feed problem.

That's it for ImageWriter II repair and maintenance. Next we'll look at the ImageWriter II upgrades.

CHAPTER 12

ImageWriter II Upgrades

This chapter provides do-it-yourself installation information for various ImageWriter II upgrades. Products covered include:

1. ImageWriter II Sheet Feeder, Model Number A9G0432.
2. ImageWriter II 32K Memory Option Card, Model Number A9B0312.
3. ImageWriter II AppleTalk Option Card, Model Number A9B0311.

We also look at AppleTalk option card alternatives.

ImageWriter II Sheet Feeder

The ImageWriter II Sheet Feeder, model number A9G0432, is shown mounted on an ImageWriter II printer in Figure 12-1. As shown in Figure 12-2, the main parts of the sheet feeder are the input tray and the output tray.

Appropriately named, the *feeder* mechanism works something like a mouth. The input tray is like an upper jaw. When the input tray is mounted over the tractor mechanism, it does not move. The output tray is like a lower jaw. You can open and close it, as necessary, to get inside the printer.

Sheet-Feeder Installation

Cosmetically, the input tray replaces the back cover; the output tray replaces the front cover window. Once you understand how the sheet feeder fits on the printer (in place of the back cover and the front cover

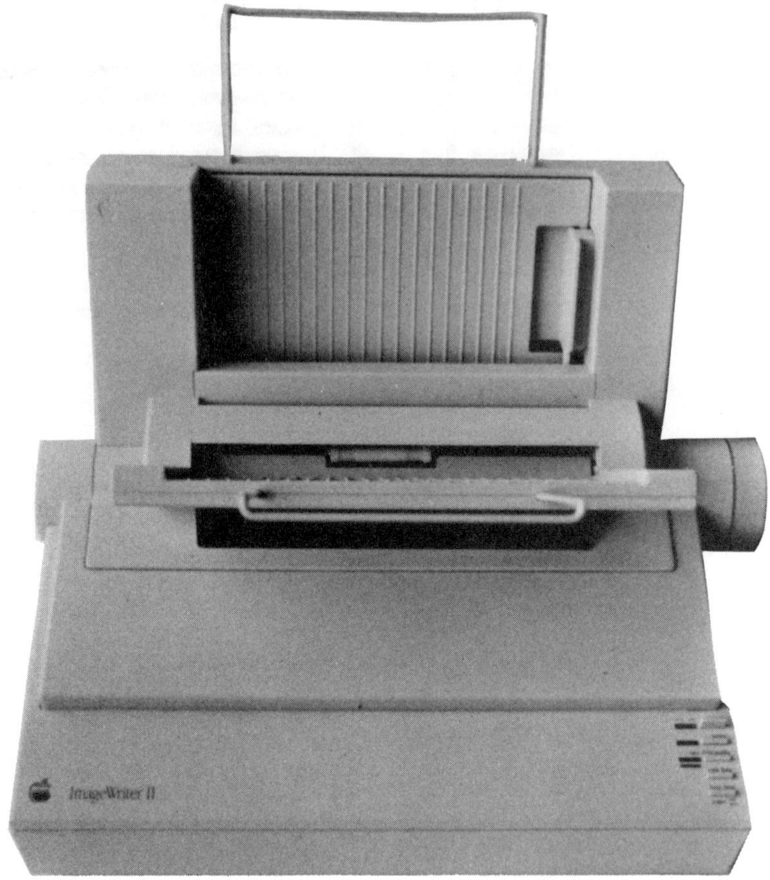

Figure 12-1 ImageWriter II Sheet Feeder, model number A9G0432.

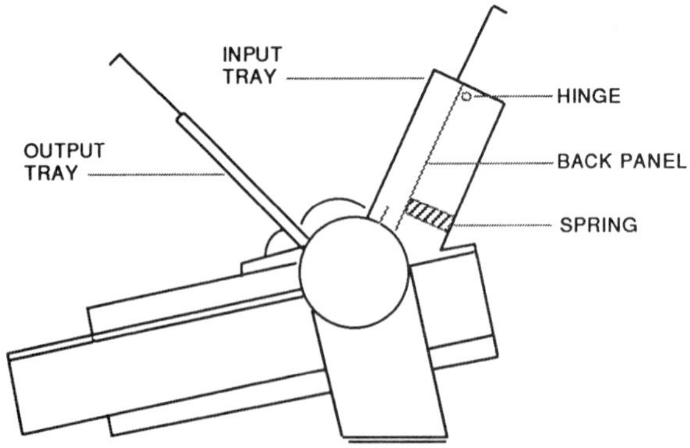

Figure 12-2 ImageWriter II Sheet Feeder (side view).

window), installation or removal takes about 30 seconds. Here's the complete procedure:

1. Disconnect the AC power cord from the back of the printer.
2. Lift off the front cover and remove the front cover window. Refer to Chapter 10, Figures 10-4 and 10-6, for details, if necessary. Put the front cover window aside.
3. Replace the front cover (but not the front cover window).
4. Remove the back cover. Put the back cover aside.
5. If necessary, remove pin-feed paper; close the paper clamps.
6. If necessary, push the paper-feed lever down (into the friction-feed position).
7. If necessary, open the output tray. Grip the sheet feeder with both hands, and hold it above the printer.
8. Line up the blue socket just behind the ImageWriter II's left-rear tractor with the matching 10-pin plug underneath the sheet feeder. Gently lower the sheet feeder over the socket. As the sheet-feeder plug fits into the printer socket, line up the rear edge of the sheet feeder with the rear edge of the printer cabinet. When the rear edges align, gently rock the sheet feeder forward until the sheet-feeder sides are flush with the printer legs.
9. When the sheet-feeder sides are flush with the printer legs, gently close (lower) the output tray.
10. Reconnect the AC power cord.

Sheet-Feeder Operation

The sheet feeder is designed *exclusively* for use with standard width (8½-inch or 210-millimeter wide) letterhead paper. It does not work with other widths, like 7-inch business forms, or 9½-inch wide #10 envelopes.

As shown in Figure 12-2, the top of the input tray's back panel is hinged. The bottom of the input tray's back panel is spring loaded. The input tray springs have to be compressed to load paper, and expanded to feed paper. When expanded, they hold the remaining stock firmly between the back panel and the feeder rollers, and automatically compensate for paper consumption.

Before loading fresh paper, you have to push the back panel backward to compress the springs. Here's the complete paper-loading procedure:

1. Push the bottom of the input tray backward to compress the springs.

2. If necessary, slide the paper guide to the right.
3. Fan the stock to be loaded. Maximum capacity is 100 sheets of 16- to 24-pound paper.
4. As shown in Figure 12-3, insert the stock behind the brass-color clips at the bottom of the input tray. It's very important to load the stock *behind* the clips. If even a single sheet is loaded in front of the clips, the feeder will jam.

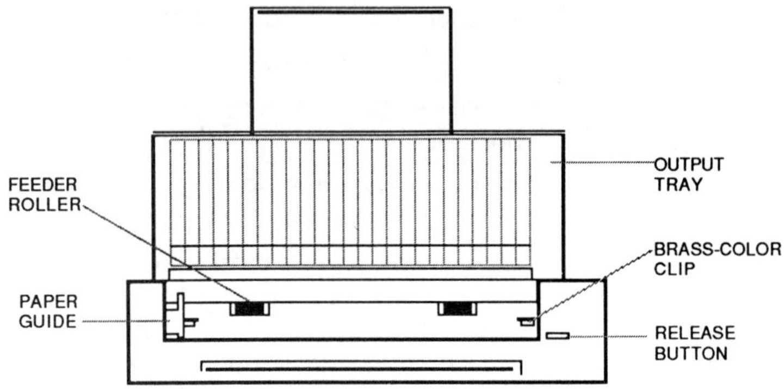

Figure 12-3 ImageWriter II Sheet Feeder (top view).

5. Press the back-panel release button to expand the springs.

At this point, many sources (including OEM) state that you have to press the *select* button (to take the printer off-line), then press the *form feed* button to load the first sheet of paper, and then press the *select* button again to bring the printer back on-line. *That procedure is completely unnecessary.* In fact, it's counterproductive.

The sheet-feeder operation is fully automatic. The ImageWriter driver loads (and ejects) paper as necessary. There's absolutely no reason to preload the first sheet of paper.

In addition, preloaded paper has to be used right away; otherwise, it begins to curl just like hair under a curling iron. Left for an hour or so, the curl is so tight that the preloaded sheet is no longer capable of advancing. Instead, it wraps around and around the platen the moment you try to print, which invariably results in a printer jam.

Print... Dialog Box Settings Contrary to what the Print... dialog box might lead you to believe, and despite the fact that the sheet feeder uses cut sheet, not continuous paper, the correct paper-feed selection is Continuous (or Automatic), *not* Cut Sheet (or Hand Feed)! In other words, the implied instructions are backwards. If you select Cut Sheet (or Hand Feed), even though the feeder does use cut-sheet paper, you'll get the nuisance dialog box shown in Figure 12-4 between each and every page. That means you'll have to babysit the print job, which is not necessary.

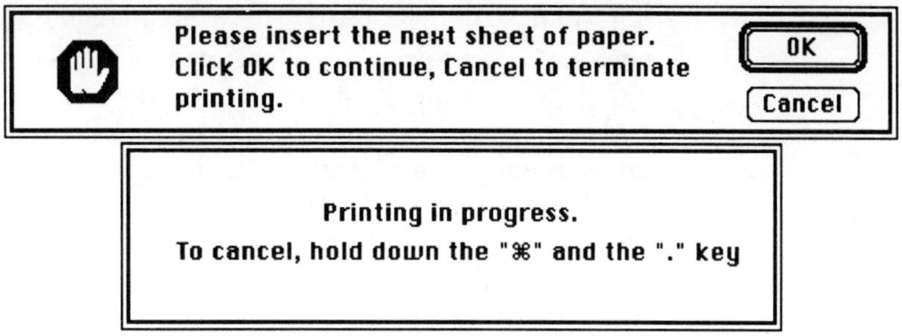

Figure 12-4 If you select Cut Sheet (or Hand Feed), you'll get this dialog box between each and every page.

Margin Settings Running TCG's Tractor - Top of Form Alignment test reveals that the sheet feeder's fixed (hardware) margins are off (relative to ImageWriter driver v2.7), by the following amounts:

1. The top margin is 3/32-inch long.
2. The bottom margin is 3/32-inch short.
3. The left margin is 1/16-inch short.
4. The right margin is 1/16-inch long.

There's no way to correct the hardware margins. The only way to compensate is to reformat every document. For 1-inch margins all around:

1. The top margin should be set to 0.9 inches.
2. The bottom margin should be set to 1.1 inches.
3. The left margin should be set to 1.1 inches.
4. The right margin should be set to 0.9 inches.

Although it's only a 1/10-inch adjustment, the total shift (2 × 1/10 inch, or 1/5 inch) is quite noticeable. The margins are still imperfect, but the page is not obviously lopsided. The difference is so small, most people won't notice.

Sheet-Feeder Advantages When used with Adobe Type Manager, the sheet feeder turns an ImageWriter II into a credible office printer. ATM, discussed in Chapter 3, provides near letter quality (160 × 144-dpi) ImageWriter II output using industry standard Laser fonts (Courier, Helvetica, Symbol, and Times). Without ATM, ImageWriter documents look cute, unprofessional, distinctly Macish. With ATM, the same documents appear to have been professionally typed.

The sheet feeder also provides deluxe paper handling. Instead of shooting printed pages out behind the printer (generally onto the floor), pages are collated and neatly stacked within arm's reach. Having the output tray deliver the ready-to-mail pages right into your hand (no need to separate pages or tear off the pin-feed stubs) is a pleasure that has to be experienced to be appreciated. It's *very* nice.

Sheet-Feeder Compatibility Contrary to other sources, the ImageWriter II Sheet Feeder is 100% compatible with the ImageWriter II 32K Memory option and the ImageWriter II AppleTalk option described below. Installing the sheet feeder does not preclude installing either card. Installing either card does not preclude installing the sheet feeder. In general, option cards and sheet feeders have nothing to do with each other.

ImageWriter II 32K Memory Option Card

The stock communications buffer on an ImageWriter II is 2K, barely enough to hold a single page of text. With the 32K Memory option card, that capacity is increased to 16 pages.

To realize the benefits of a 32K communications buffer, the computer has to be capable of uploading entire files, all at once. Apple-compatible computers and PC-compatible computers can do that, but the Macintosh tends to upload files page by page, regardless of how much printer memory is installed. In other words, the 32K Memory option is of limited use with present versions of the Macintosh.

Once the card is installed, provided the printer is connected to an Apple-compatible or a PC-compatible computer, it only takes about 45 seconds to upload a 16-page file. After that, the computer comes back, you can continue working, even switch applications, with no decrease in performance. Spoolers operate in similar fashion, except they generally slow down the computer.

Once the file is uploaded, the job is entirely under printer control. As far as the computer is concerned, it's already printed. The only way to cancel the print job at that point (if necessary) is to switch off the printer.

ImageWriter II Option Card Installation

To install any ImageWriter II option card, follow this procedure:

1. Disconnect the AC power cord from the wall outlet.
2. Disconnect the AC power cord from the printer.

3. Disconnect the Mac-to-ImageWriter II cable from the printer.
4. Lift off the front and back covers. Put the covers aside.
5. Remove the ribbon cartridge and put it aside.
6. As shown in Chapter 11, Figure 11-4, the front-edge cover (previously known as the cabinet top) is fastened by two permanently attached #1 Phillips-head screws. Loosen (but don't remove) the screws using a #1 Phillips-head screwdriver. The screws will be fully loosened when you feel them hit the end stops.
7. Slide the ribbon cartridge deck all the way to the left, as shown in Chapter 11, Figure 11-5.
8. As shown in Figure 12-5, the front-edge cover is hinged. With the ribbon cartridge deck all the way to the left, rotate the front-edge cover until it locks open at a 90° angle.

Figure 12-5 ImageWriter II front-edge cover hinge location.

Alternately, the front-edge cover can be removed as shown in Chapter 11, Figure 11-7.

> In Figure 12-5, the ribbon cartridge is reinstalled for clarity. In practice, the ribbon cartridge has to be removed before you can rotate the front-edge cover.

9. Ground yourself. If it's cold and dry, if you can't walk across the carpet and pet the cat without getting a static shock, put on a wrist-strap as shown in Figure 12-6.

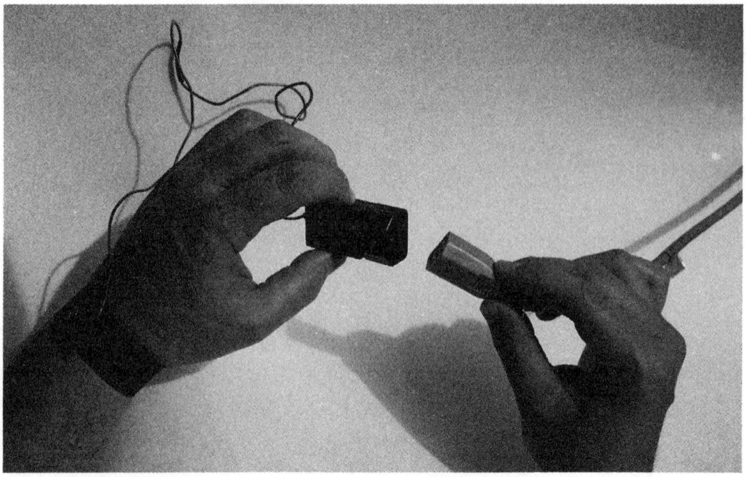

Figure 12-6 Wrist-strap grounding details.

10. As shown in Figure 12-7, insert the option-card support posts (stand offs) into the ImageWriter II logic board. Just as in building construction, the wide part of the support post faces down (toward the logic board).

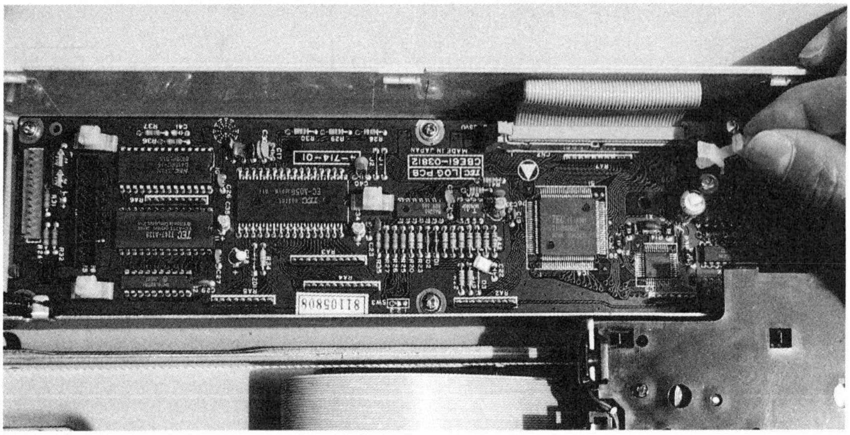

Figure 12-7 ImageWriter II option-card support post installation.

It's very important to get the posts all the way through the logic board. Unless all four posts snap into place, the option-card connector may not seat properly.

11. As shown in Figure 12-8, the option card is mounted on top of the support posts. Hold the option card over the logic board, line up

the post holes with the post tops, and press down until the posts pop through the card.

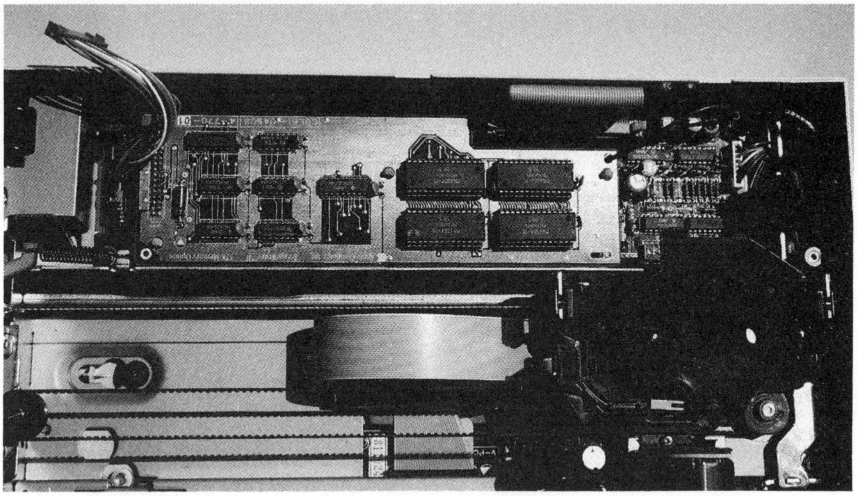

Figure 12-8 The option card is mounted on top of the support posts.

> In Figure 12-8, the front-edge cover has been removed for clarity. In practice, the front-edge cover doesn't need to be removed. It can be hinged as shown in Figure 12-5.

12. As shown in Figure 12-9, connect the option card's green ground wire to the logic board.

Figure 12-9 The option card's green ground wire goes to the logic board.

13. Slide the ribbon cartridge deck to the right and set DIP switch SW2-4 (Figure 12-10) to the closed position.

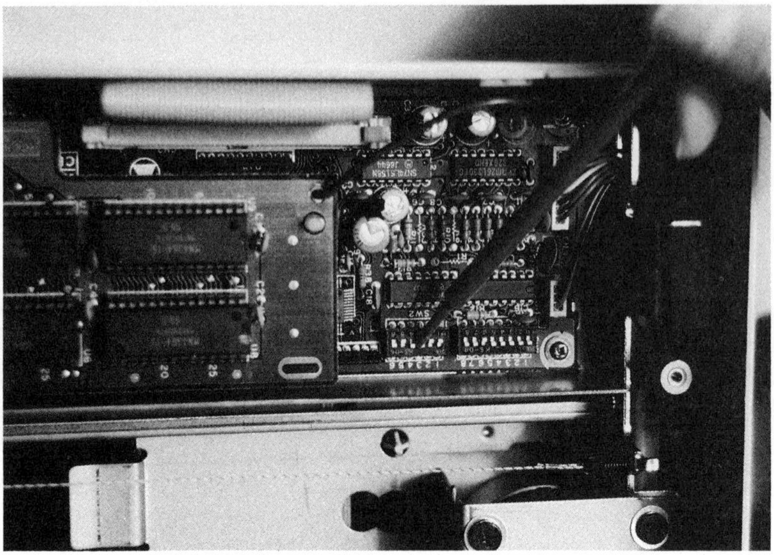

Figure 12-10 ImageWriter II DIP switch SW2-4 location.

14. If you're installing an AppleTalk option card, verify that DIP switch SW2-3 is open. If necessary, open DIP switch SW2-3. Open is the DTR (data terminal ready), or hardware handshaking position. Closed is the X-ON/X-OFF (transmission on/transmission off), or software handshaking position. AppleTalk does not support X-ON/X-OFF software handshaking.
15. Slide the ribbon cartridge deck back to the left, unhinge the front-edge cover, and lower it into place.
16. Reinstall the ribbon cartridge.
17. Retighten the front-edge cover screws.
18. Replace the front cover and the back cover.
19. Reconnect the Mac-to-ImageWriter II cable.
20. Reconnect the AC power cable to the printer.
21. Reconnect the AC power cable to the wall outlet.

To temporarily disable (turn off) an option card, open DIP switch SW2-4. This feature allows you to run time trials and judge the effectiveness of a memory option card without having to physically remove the card between trials. It also allows you to transport an AppleTalk ImageWriter II to another location, hook it up it via a direct-connect cable, and use it on a nonAppleTalk system simply by throwing a switch.

To restore the printer to AppleTalk service, close DIP switch SW2-4 *before* reconnecting it to the network. If DIP switch SW2-4 is open when you reconnect it, the whole network may stop working.

The ImageWriter II logic board is provided with only one option-card connector. Since there's no matching piggyback connector on the option card, only one card fits in the printer at a time.

ImageWriter II AppleTalk Option Card

AppleTalk refers to the networking protocol built into every Macintosh. AppleTalk is not built into the ImageWriter II. That's the reason for the ImageWriter II AppleTalk option card. It adds the circuitry necessary to make the printer AppleTalk compatible.

LocalTalk generally refers to the cables and connectors that make the AppleTalk network functional. As shown in Figure 12-11, typical LocalTalk-compatible connector kits consist of 3 items: a 2-meter shielded cable, a cable extender (coupler), and a system connector (node). Generally, you get one of each, with each and every kit.

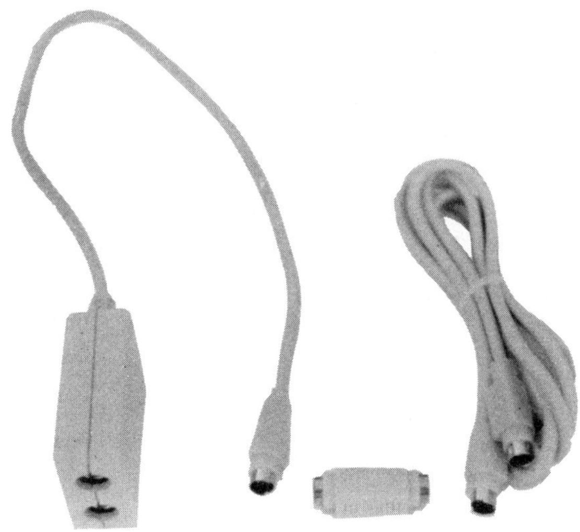

Figure 12-11 Typical LocalTalk-compatible connector kits consist of 3 items: a 2-meter shielded cable, a cable extender (coupler), and a system connector (node).

Unlike a direct connection (where one cable connects two devices), each device on the AppleTalk network requires its own system connector. To connect a single ImageWriter II (equipped with an AppleTalk option card) to two Macs, you need three LocalTalk-compatible connector kits. These wire together as shown in Figure 12-12.

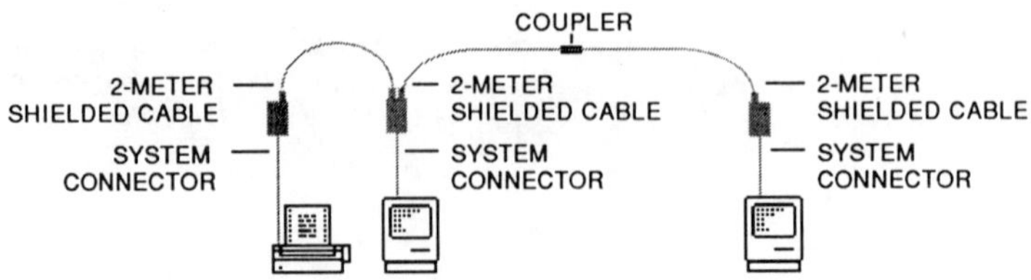

Figure 12-12 To connect a single ImageWriter II (equipped with an AppleTalk option card) to two Macs, you need three (not two) LocalTalk-compatible connector kits.

With the exception of laser printers, especially when only two computers are involved, this makes the network prohibitively expensive. By the time you add up the cost of the AppleTalk option card and the three LocalTalk connector kits, you may as well buy a second printer.

AppleTalk Alternatives

In most cases, all you need to connect two Macs to a single ImageWriter is a mini DIN-8 switchbox, a straight-through mini DIN-8 cable, and two Apple-compatible system/peripheral-8 cables. These wire together as shown in Figure 12-13.

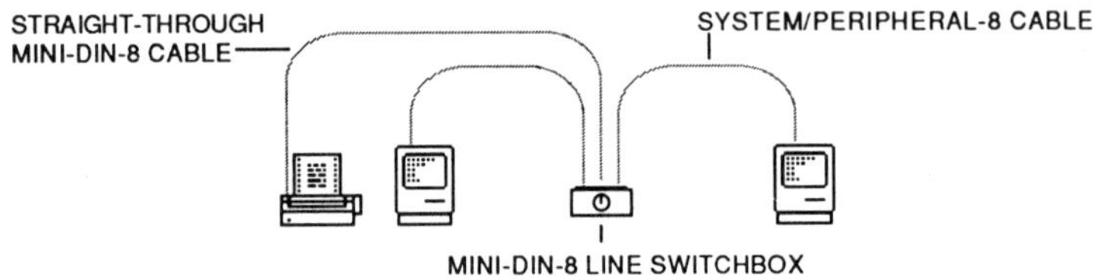

Figure 12-13 In most cases, all you need to connect two Macs to a single ImageWriter is a mini DIN-8 line switchbox, a straight-through mini DIN-8 cable and two Apple-compatible system/peripheral-8 cables.

Figure 12-13 shows a two-way switchbox. Three-way switchboxes can handle three Macs. Four-way switchboxes can handle four Macs, and so on.

Alternately, line switchboxes (also known as data switches) can be used to connect more than one printer to a single computer. With DB-25 connections, you can even share Imagewriter (Standard and Wide) and Imagewriter-compatible printers.

Switchboxes are relatively inexpensive. A three-way setup complete with all necessary cables generally costs less than a single LocalTalk connector kit!

Switchbox quality varies. Some have tight minicircular fittings; some have very loose minicircular fittings. If the fitting is loose, the cables may fall out every time you knock a knee against the desk.

If possible, shop for switchboxes in person; bring along an ImageWriter II cable and test the fittings thoroughly. Inexpensive or not, a switchbox is worthless if it doesn't work properly. If the cable falls out when you turn the box upside down, try another brand.

That's it for ImageWriter II upgrades. In Chapter 13, we'll look at the ImageWriter LQ.

CHAPTER

13

ImageWriter LQ Setup Secrets

When the ImageWriter LQ was introduced in the fall of 1987, it was given glowing (red hot) reviews in all of the Macintosh computer magazines. Paying customers weren't so generous. Most people found the printer's noise level unacceptable. Many complained of registration problems in the upper and lower areas of the page. Certain applications missed the top of the paper and started printing across the platen, or on previous pages. There were serious problems with Microsoft Word version 3.01. There were problems with version 1.0 of the LQ ImageWriter driver.

On March 10, 1989 (a little over one year later) version 2.0 of the LQ ImageWriter driver was released and an enhanced ImageWriter LQ was announced—coincidentally with an optional exchange policy for original ImageWriter LQ printers. The exchange was free. All exchanged printers were covered by a renewed 90-day warranty.

The exchange didn't help very much. By year end, the same magazines which had originally loved the ImageWriter LQ were now calling it: "The printer from hell."

In truth, the enhanced version of ImageWriter LQ is not *that* bad; neither was the original. The real problem is that its outrageously high price tag raised people's expectations to way beyond what they should have been in the first place. A second problem has to do with absolutely horrendous documentation.

With that out of the way, this chapter looks at the ImageWriter LQ through the eyes of an ImageWriter II owner. If the "printer from hell" should ever cross your path, the information contained here will help you to deal with the devil.

Cabinet Parts and Setup Controls

As shown in Figure 13-1, the ImageWriter LQ, model number A9M0340, is a 27-pin (not 24-pin) color printer with a 15-inch wide carriage.

Figure 13-1 ImageWriter LQ, model number A9M0340.

Figure 13-2 identifies the ImageWriter LQ's major cabinet parts and Figure 13-3, the major setup controls.

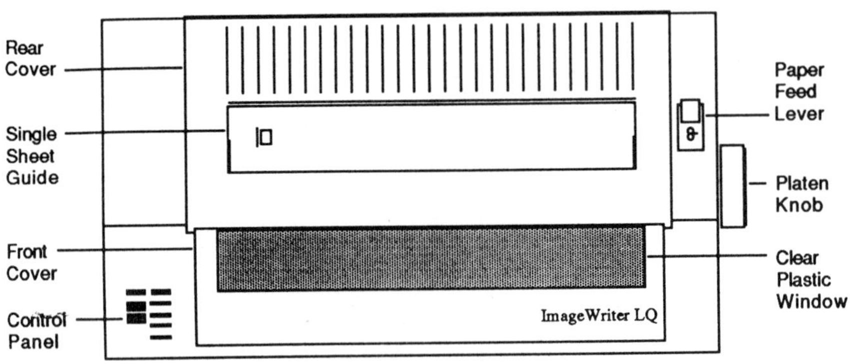

Figure 13-2 ImageWriter LQ cabinet parts.

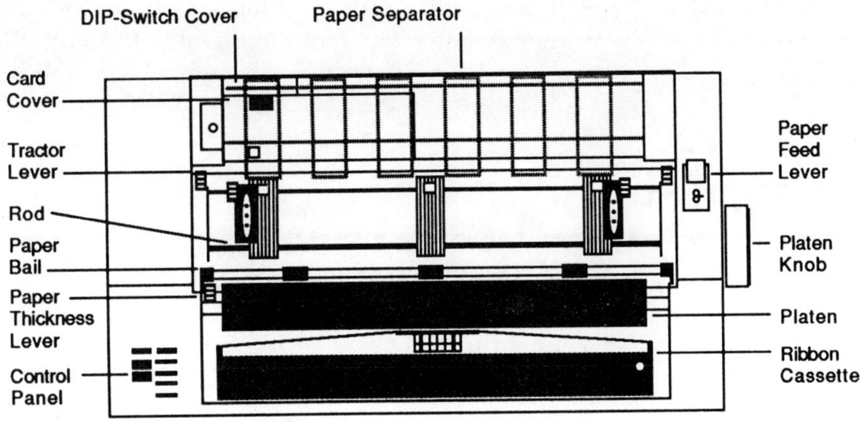

Figure 13-3 ImageWriter LQ setup controls.

The cabinet parts and setup controls shown in Figures 13-2 and 13-3 are labeled (and spelled) exactly as they are in the *ImageWriter LQ Owner's Guide* and/or the *Using Your ImageWriter LQ* HyperCard stack. Unfortunately, these same parts are labeled and spelled differently from Imagewriter model to ImageWriter model.

To minimize confusion, Table 13-1 provides an ImageWriter LQ cabinet-part and setup-control cross-reference guide.

Table 13-1. ImageWriter LQ Cabinet-Part and Setup-Control Cross Reference Guide

Imagewriter Std	ImageWriter II	ImageWriter LQ
Carrier Bar	Carrier Rod	Carrier Rod
Carrier Cover	Front cover	Front cover
Clear Plastic Lid	Front cover window	Clear plastic window
Control Cluster	Control panel	Control panel
N/A	Mini-circular plug	Minicircular plug
N/A	Mini-circular socket	Minicircular socket
Paper Cover	Back cover	Rear cover
Paper Cover Slot	Unnamed	Single-sheet guide
Release Lever	Paper-feed selector	Paper-feed lever
Ribbon Cassette	Ribbon cartridge	Ribbon cartridge
Ribbon Deck	Ribbon cartridge deck	N/A
Roller Shaft	Paper bail	Paper bail
Sprocket	Tractor	Tractor
Type Head	Print head	Print head or printhead

If you ever asked a printer-related question and thought that no one knew what they were talking about, study Table 13-1 and you'll begin to understand why. Intelligent conversation is very difficult when you can't agree on the language.

DIP Switches

Another problem has to do with the OEM ImageWriter LQ DIP switch settings. Unless SW2-8 is set to the closed position as shown in Figure 13-4, the printer does not work properly with a Macintosh.

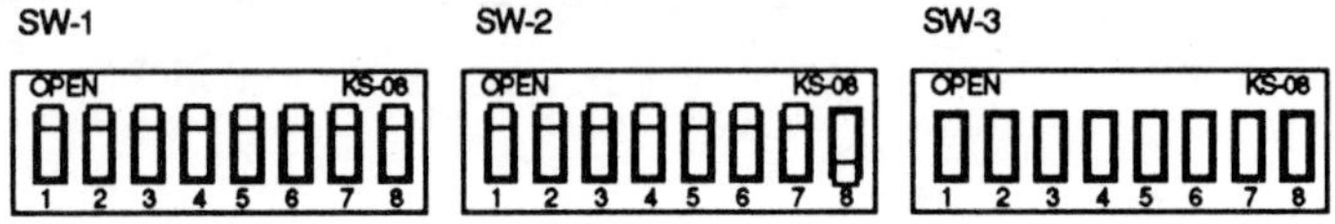

Figure 13-4 ImageWriter LQ recommended DIP switch settings for use with a Macintosh.

Checking the switches is somewhat of a job. As shown in Figure 13-5, the switches are located in a special covered compartment beneath a metal paper separator, which is normally wrapped in one to two layers of paper. All of this lies beneath the rear cover, which is, in turn, held down by the front cover.

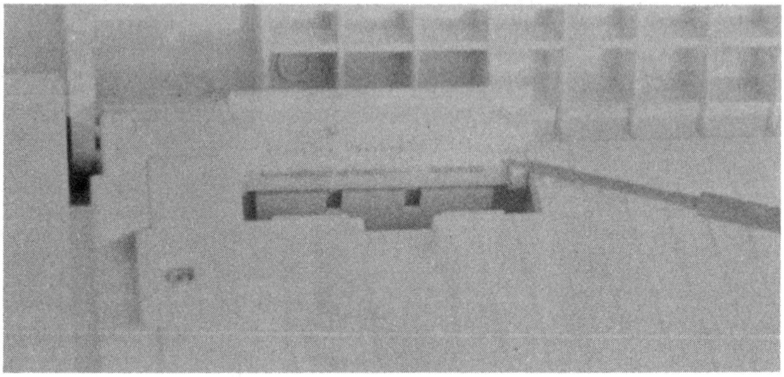

Figure 13-5 ImageWriter LQ DIP switch compartment location.

To get at the switches, you have to open both covers, unload the paper, and remove the metal paper separator. The DIP switches are at the bottom of a well—3-inches deep.

Depending on lighting conditions, you may need a high-intensity flashlight to see how the switches are set. Tables 13-2 through 13-7 contain DIP switch function details. If any need to be reset, use a 3/32- to 1/8-inch flat-head screwdriver with at least a 4-inch-long shaft. Otherwise, you'll have a hard time reaching the switches.

Table 13-2. ImageWriter LQ DIP Switch 1 Functions

Switch	Function	CLOSED	OPEN	US-Mac Setting
1-1	Alphabet	See Table 13-5		Open
1-2	Alphabet	See Table 13-5		Open
1-3	Alphabet	See Table 13-5		Open
1-4	Paper length	12 inch	11 inch	Open
1-5	Perforation	Skip	Don't skip	Open
1-6	CPI	See Table 13-6		Open
1-7	CPI	See Table 13-6		Open
1-8	CR code	CR + LF	CR	Open

Table 13-3. ImageWriter LQ DIP Switch 2 Functions

Switch	Function	CLOSED	OPEN	US-Mac Setting
2-1	Baud rate	See Table 13-7		Open*
2-2	Baud rate	See Table 13-7		Open*
2-3	Handshaking	X-ON/X-OFF	DTR	Open
2-4	Option card	Enabled	Disabled	Open
2-5	CSF select	See Table 13-8		Open
2-6	CSF select	See Table 13-8		Open
2-7	CSF select	See Table 13-8		Open
2-8	Auto Load	To paper bail	To ribbon	Closed

* Assumes LQ ImageWriter driver version 1.0 or later. When used with ImageWriter (without the LQ prefix) driver version 2.3 or later, DIP switches SW 2-1 and SW 2-2 should both be closed.

Table 13-4. ImageWriter LQ DIP Switch 3 Functions

Switch	Function	CLOSED	OPEN	US-Mac Setting
3-1	Hammer timing	Varies	Varies	Varies*
3-2	Hammer timing	Varies	Varies	Varies*
3-3	Hammer timing	Varies	Varies	Varies*
3-4	Hammer timing	Varies	Varies	Varies*
3-5	Hammer timing	Varies	Varies	Varies*
3-6	Hammer timing	Varies	Varies	Varies*

(continued)

Table 13-4. *(continued)*

Switch	Function	CLOSED	OPEN	US-Mac Setting
3-7	Hammer timing	Varies	Varies	Varies*
3-8	Hammer timing	Varies	Varies	Varies*

* SW 3-1 through SW 3-8 control bidirectional alignment. Optimum settings vary from printer to printer. See ImageWriter LQ self-tests given later.

Table 13-5. ImageWriter LQ DIP Switches 1-1 Through 1-3 (Alphabet Selection) Settings

SW 1-1	SW 1-2	SW 1-3	Alphabet Selection
Open	Open	Open	American English
Closed	Closed	Open	European English
Open	Open	Closed	German
Open	Closed	Closed	French
Closed	Open	Closed	Swedish
Closed	Open	Open	Italian
Closed	Closed	Closed	Spanish
Open	Closed	Open	Danish

Table 13-6. ImageWriter LQ DIP Switches 1-6 and 1-7 (Character Set) Settings

SW 1-6	SW 1-7	Character Set/CPI
Open	Open	Pica 10 CPI (characters per inch)
Closed	Open	Elite 12 CPI (characters per inch)
Open	Closed	Ultracondensed 17 CPI (characters per inch)
Closed	Closed	Elite Proportional 160 DPI (dots per inch and/or Pica Proportional 216 DPI)

Table 13-7. ImageWriter LQ DIP Switches 2-1 and 2-2 (Baud Rate) Settings

SW 2-1	SW 2-2	Baud Rate
Open	Open	19,200 baud
Closed	Open	1200 baud
Open	Closed	2400 baud
Closed	Closed	9600 baud

Table 13-8. ImageWriter LQ DIP Switches 2-5 Through 2-7 (Cut-Sheet Feeder) Settings

SW 2-5	SW 2-6	SW 2-7	CSF Selection
Open	Open	Open	Bin 1 plus envelope
Closed	Open	Open	Bin 2 plus envelope
Open	Closed	Open	Bin 3 plus envelope
Closed	Closed	Open	Bin 3 plus envelope
Open	Open	Closed	Bin 1
Closed	Open	Closed	Bin 2
Open	Closed	Closed	Bin 3
Closed	Closed	Closed	Bin 3

Additional confusion stems from the fact that the enhanced printer's self-test marks open DIP switches with a 0, indicating off, and closed DIP switches with a 1, indicating on.

On the compartment lid, open (off) is also indicated as up, which actually means towards-the-back of the printer. Closed (on) is indicated as down, which actually means towards-the-front of the printer.

Fortunately, it's not necessary to make sense out of this. Just set the switches according to Figure 13-4, follow the pin-feed paper-loading secrets revealed next, and the printer will work fine.

> Do not use this printer on a Macintosh without verifying that DIP switch SW 2-8 is set to the closed position. Missing the paper can ruin the print head. Repairs to a 27-pin print head can be very costly!

Paper-Handling Secrets

The ImageWriter LQ can be set for pull-tractor duty like the Seikosha SP-1000AP (described in Chapter 14) or push-tractor duty like the ImageWriter II (described in Chapter 10). For use with pin-feed paper, the preferred setup is push-tractor duty.

To determine which position the tractors are in now, check the orientation of the tractor assembly. In the almost horizontal (across or flat) position, the ImageWriter LQ tractor assembly is set up for pull-tractor duty. The pull-tractor setup is preferred for use with heavy-duty forms and mailing labels.

In the almost vertical (up-and-down) position, the ImageWriter LQ tractor assembly is set up for push-tractor duty. Push-tractor duty is preferred for light-duty forms and 16- to 24-pound bond paper. Push-tractor duty is what we want now.

If necessary, unload the paper and reset the tractors for push-tractor duty according to the following procedure:

1. Refer to Figure 13-3. The tractor levers are the large blue levers at the ends of the tractor assembly. Open the left and right tractor levers.
2. Note that the tractors slide on two connecting rods. The aft rod is round. The forward rod is square. Using both hands, grip the ends (not the middle) of the square tractor-connecting rod, push it back and up slightly, and, then, allow it to slip down. The push-tractor position (almost vertical) is approximately 30° from true perpendicular.
3. Close the left and right tractor levers.

Provided the tractors are in the almost vertical position for push-tractor duty and provided the DIP switches are set correctly, the next hurdle is figuring out how to load pin-feed paper. The correct procedure is not obvious!

As shown in Figure 13-6, the metal paper separator has a back separator and a top separator.

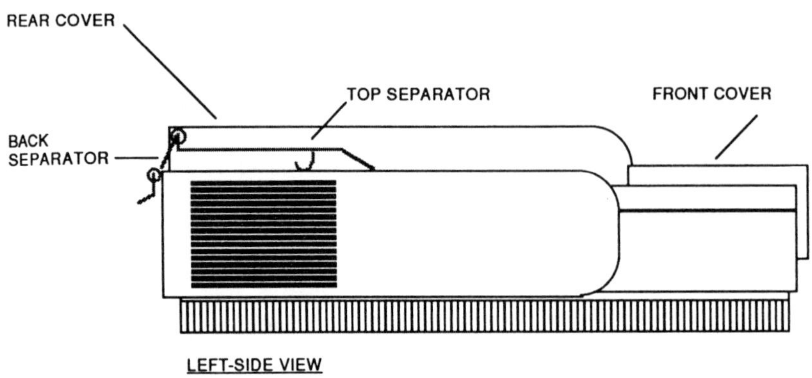

Figure 13-6 ImageWriter LQ paper separator.

The back separator hangs over the back of the printer, and the top separator lays on top of the printer. Rear-feed paper *always* goes over the back separator, and either over or under the front separator, depending on whether the tractors are set for push-tractor duty or pull-tractor duty. For pull-tractor duty, the paper goes under the front separator; for push-tractor duty (which is what we want right now), the paper goes over the front separator. Table 13-9 summarizes the paper-separator path information.

Table 13-9. Paper-Separator Path Information

Tractors	Back Separator	Front Separator
Pull	Paper goes over	Paper goes under
Push	Paper goes over	Paper goes over

With that understanding, follow this procedure to load pin-feed paper:

1. Switch off the printer, if necessary.
2. Open the front and rear covers.
3. Thread the pin-feed paper *over* the back separator, *under* the rear cover, and *over* the front separator.
4. As shown in Figure 13-7, align the left edge of the pin-feeder stub (not the perforation between the stub and the paper) with the stripe to the left of the pin-feed alignment icon on the printer case.

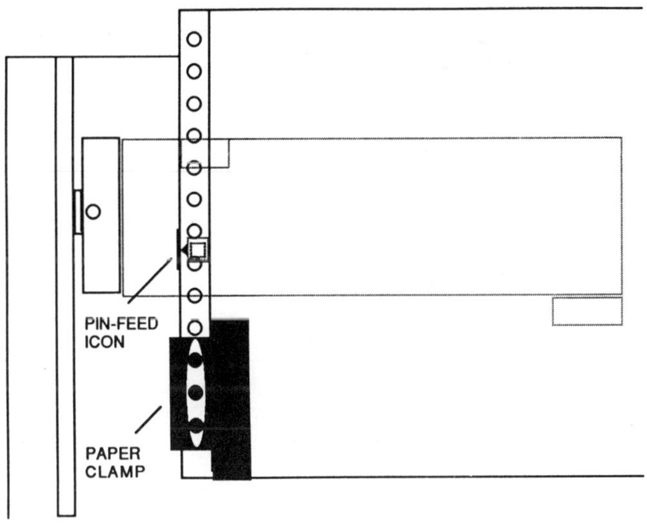

Figure 13-7 ImageWriter LQ pin-feed alignment icon.

Alignment to the icon sets the left margin to within 1⁄16-inch of where it should be. To determine exactly where the left-margin starts, run TCG's Tractor - TOF Alignment test (when convenient), as explained in Chapter 7.

5. Unlock the tractors, line them up with the paper, and clamp the stubs. When the stubs are clamped, lock the tractors.

6. Wind the paper forward with the platen knob and center the first three pin holes in the tractor-clamp opening as shown in Figure 13-8. Don't advance the paper any further!

Figure 13-8 Center the first three pin holes in the tractor-clamp opening. Don't advance the paper any further.

7. Refer to Figure 13-3. Check the paper-thickness lever. If necessary, move the paper-thickness lever into position number 1.
8. Check the paper-feed lever. If necessary, pull it forward.
9. Close the rear cover and the front cover.
10. Switch on the printer.

Figure 13-9 shows the ImageWriter LQ control panel. As soon as you switch on the printer, the print head will jog and the red error lamp should light. The green select lamp should not be lit.

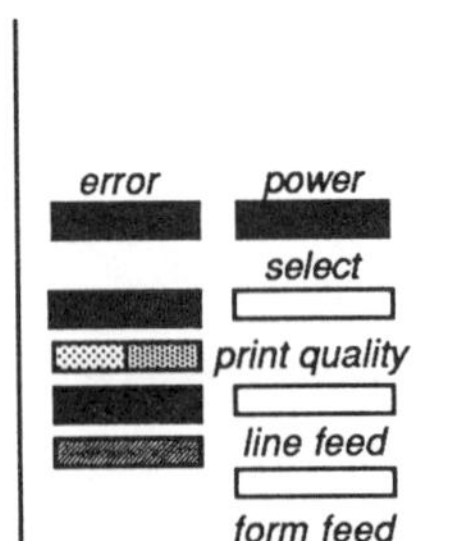

Figure 13-9 ImageWriter LQ control panel.

Assuming the DIP switches, the metal paper guide, the paper itself, the tractors, and the paper clamps have all been set correctly, and assuming the control-panel status is exactly as described, press the form-feed button to autoload the paper. When the paper reaches a position under the paper bail, the red error lamp should go out. Now, press the select button. The green select lamp should light indicating that the printer is on-line and ready to print.

> One of the biggest problems with the ImageWriter LQ has to do with the fact that once the rear cover is closed, you can't see anything. The clear plastic window in the front cover is inadequate. No matter how you bend your body, and no matter how you twist your neck, you still can't see the paper bail. The platen knob is right there, and you can wind the stock forward all you want, but there's no way to see when to stop. As a result, it's impossible to load pin-feed paper accurately by hand. Either both covers (front and rear) have to be wide open in order to load pin-feed paper, or you have to know the secret (inobvious) autoloading procedure described above.

Printer-Driver Requirements

Figures 13-10 and 13-11 show the Page Setup... and Print... dialog boxes from LQ ImageWriter driver version 2.0. Figure 13-12 shows the Print... Help dialog box, and Figures 13-13 and 13-14 show the Print... Options and Print... Options Help dialog boxes.

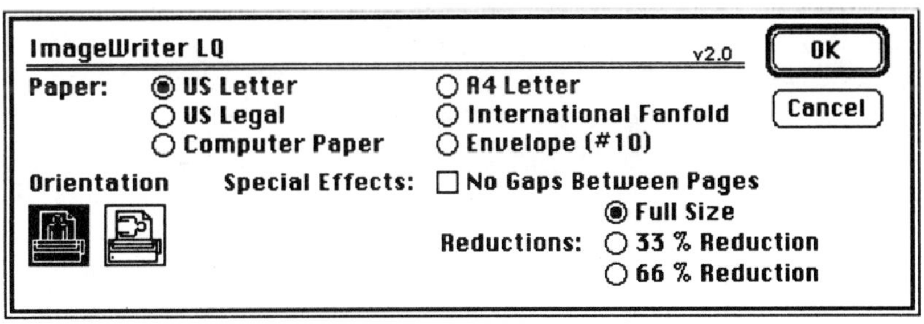

Figure 13-10 Page Setup... dialog box from LQ ImageWriter driver, version 2.0.

As supplied, the driver is designed to work *primarily* with 3× bit-mapped fonts. Courier, Helvetica, Symbol, and Times are included on two disks in 9, 10, 12, 14, 18, 24, 27, 30, 36, 42, 54, and 72 point. All 48 fonts have to be moved into the System File with Font/DA Mover version 3.8 (or later), as explained in Chapter 2. Font/DA Mover version

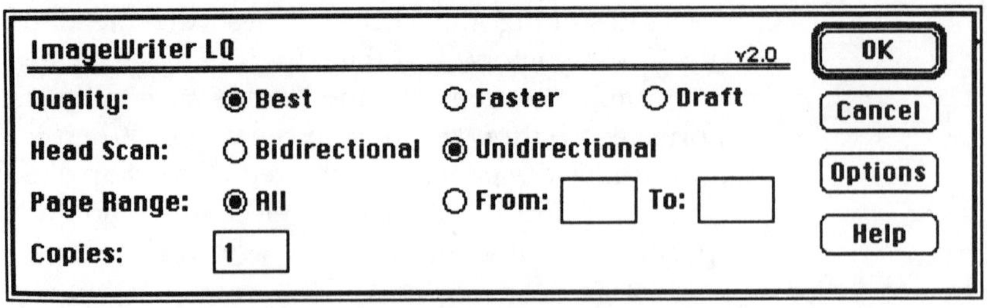

Figure 13-11 Print... dialog box from LQ ImageWriter driver, version 2.0.

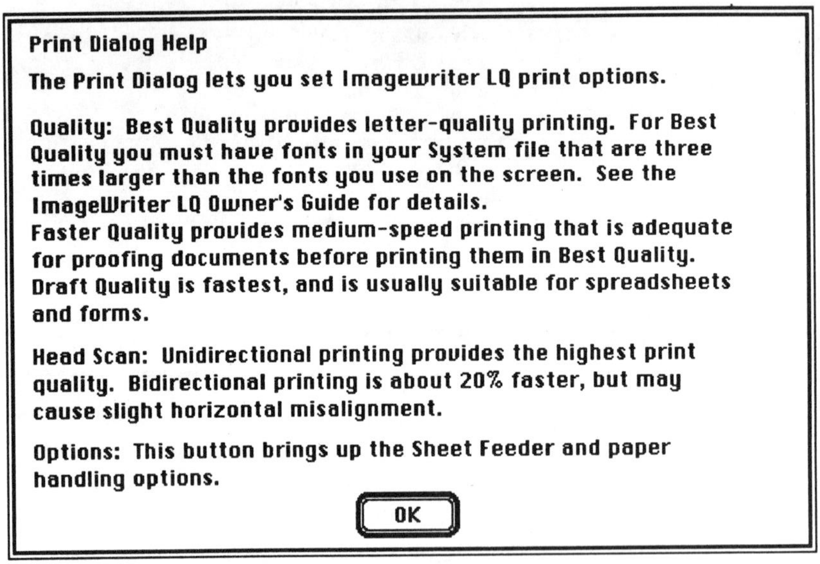

Figure 13-12 Print... Help dialog box from LQ ImageWriter driver, version 2.0.

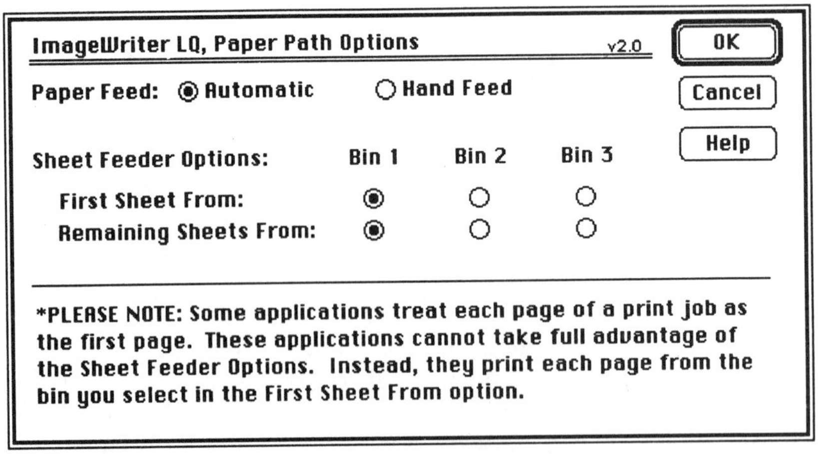

Figure 13-13 Print... Options dialog box from LQ ImageWriter driver, version 2.0.

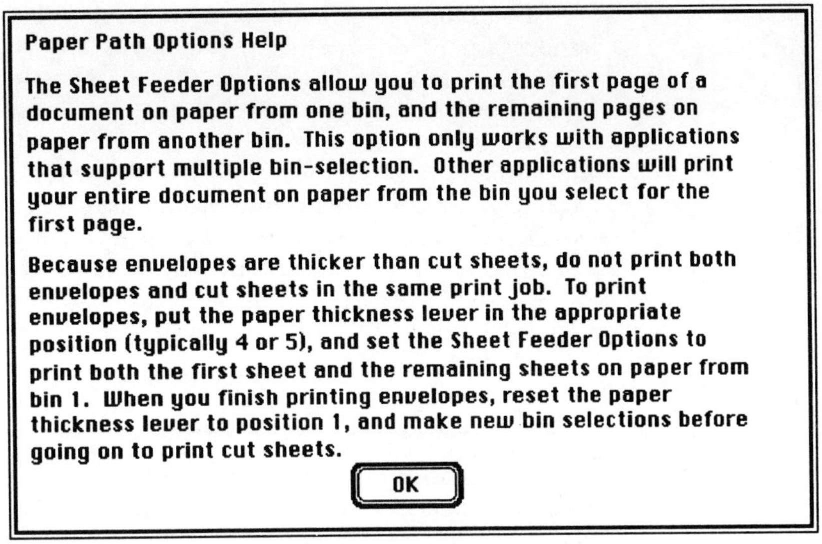

Figure 13-14 Print... Options Help dialog box from LQ ImageWriter driver, version 2.0.

3.8 is also included. Provided a 3× printer font is in the System file, Best quality printing results in 216-dpi resolution. Table 13-10 shows which sizes are supported at maximum resolution.

Table 13-10. Effects of Screen Font on ImageWriter LQ Resolution

1× Screen Font	3× Printer Font	216-DPI Resolution
9 point	27 point	yes
10 point	30 point	yes
12 point	36 point	yes
14 point	42 point	yes
18 point	54 point	yes
24 point	76 point	yes
27 point	none	no
30 point	none	no
36 point	none	no
42 point	none	no
54 point	none	no
72 point	none	no

Unless a 3× printer font is in the System file, Best quality printing *does not* result in best-quality output.

The full set of 48 fonts occupies 815 kilobytes of disk space. Besides a hard drive, other requirements are System software version 4.1 or later, Chooser DA version 3.1 or later, and Finder software version 5.5 or later.

To use the ImageWriter LQ with older, 400K, floppy-drive Macs, and earlier System software, close DIP switches SW 2-1 and SW 2-2 (9600 baud) and run the printer from ImageWriter (without the LQ prefix) driver version 2.3, or later. In Faster quality, the ImageWriter LQ will work just like an ImageWriter II. Best quality output is not as good, not even when 3× printer fonts are installed in the System file.

Self-Tests

The ImageWriter LQ is equipped with four built-in self-tests. The first built-in test checks the carriage assembly, the carrier belt, and the carrier motor. To run the test:

1. Switch off the printer (if it's on).
2. Remove any installed paper. Installed paper invariably snags the print head, which could damage it. Do not proceed without removing the paper!
3. Hold down the *line feed* button, and, while keeping it held down, switch on the printer.

Assuming the covers are down and the carrier motor is working, the ribbon-cartridge deck will move back and forth without firing and without executing any line feeds. To suspend the test, press the *line feed* button. To resume the test, press the *select* button. To stop the test altogether, turn the printer off.

Comprehensive Self-Test

The second built-in self-test checks the carrier motor, the line-feed motor, the ribbon-drive motor, and the print head. This test can be run with 8½-inch-wide paper or with 14-inch-wide paper. To run the test with 8½-inch-wide paper:

1. Switch off the printer (if it's on).
2. Load the printer with 8½ × 11-inch, or 8½ × 12-inch paper.
3. Hold down the *form feed* button, and, while keeping it held down, switch on the printer.

To run the same test with 14-inch wide paper:

1. Switch off the printer (if it's on).

2. Load the printer with 14 × 11-inch paper.
3. Hold down the *form feed* and *line feed* buttons and, while keeping them down, switch on the printer.

This test prints the ROM (read-only memory) version number, reports on the current option-card status, shows the current DIP switch settings, and then it prints a repeating, alphanumeric test pattern. If a 4-color ribbon is installed, the test pattern prints alternating black, yellow, magenta, cyan, orange, green, and purple lines. If a monochrome (1-color) ribbon is installed, the test pattern prints every line the same. Even with a 4-color ribbon, the initial ROM, option card, and DIP switch, and information always print black.

To suspend the alphanumeric test pattern, press the *line feed* button. To change the print quality, press the *print quality* button. To resume the test pattern, press the *select* button. To stop the test pattern, switch off the printer.

Built-in Loopback Test

The third built-in self-test checks the printer's serial interface. To run the test:

1. Switch off the printer (if it's on).
2. Disconnect the Mac-to-ImageWriter LQ cable from the back of the printer. Replace it with a properly constructed 8-pin minicircular loopback plug. Wiring details for the plug are shown in Chapter 11, Figure 11-37.
3. Load the printer with 8½ × 14-inch (maximum-width) paper. If you fail to load maximum-width paper, the loopback test will print right across the platen. That might damage the print head.
4. Hold down the *print quality* button and, while keeping it held down, switch on the printer.
5. Release the button when the print head begins to move.

As shown in Chapter 11, Figure 11-39, the loopback test prints the ROM (read-only memory) version number, shows the current DIP switch settings, reports on the current option-card status, and prints a repeating, alphanumeric test pattern (just like the self-test), indicating that the loopback test passed; or, it prints "LOOP BACK FAILS," stops testing, and flashes the red error light on the control panel.

The only substantial difference between ImageWriter II loopback test results and ImageWriter LQ loopback test results is that the latter requires 14-inch-wide paper.

To suspend the alphanumeric loopback test pattern, press the *line feed* button. To change the print quality, press the *print quality* button. To resume the test pattern, press the *select* button. To stop the loopback test pattern, switch off the printer, and remove the loopback plug.

> Unless a properly constructed loopback plug is inserted into the 8-pin minicircular socket at the back of the printer, the built-in loopback test fails (by definition) every time. This does not mean there's anything wrong with the printer!

Bidirectional Alignment Test

The fourth built-in self-test checks the printer's bidirectional alignment. To run the test:

1. Switch off the printer (if it's on).
2. Remove the loopback plug (if necessary).
3. Load the printer with 8½ × 11-inch or 8½ × 12-inch paper.
4. Hold down the *select, form feed,* and *line feed* buttons, and, while keeping them held down, switch on the printer.
5. Release the buttons when the print head begins to move.

As shown in Figure 13-15, this test prints a series of vertical-bar test patterns, each of which is identified by a binary number between 000 and 111.

The most-significant digit in the number corresponds to the setting of DIP switch SW 3-6. The middle digit corresponds to the setting of DIP switch SW 3-7. The least-significant digit in the number corresponds to the setting of DIP switch SW 3-8.

While the test is running, the actual DIP switch settings are overridden. The purpose of the test is to demonstrate what the output would be like if the switches were permanently set to the positions indicated by the binary number.

As indicated by the asterisk in Figure 13-15, all three switches are currently open, which is also the best setting for this particular printer, at this particular time.

Option-Card Setup

The ImageWriter LQ accepts the same 32K memory and AppleTalk option cards as the ImageWriter II. To install either card in an ImageWriter LQ, follow this procedure:

1. Disconnect the AC power cord from the wall outlet.
2. Disconnect the AC power cord from the printer.
3. Disconnect the Mac-to-ImageWriter LQ cable from the printer.
4. Open the front and rear covers.

Figure 13-15 ImageWriter LQ bidirectional alignment test.

5. Lift off the rear cover and remove the metal paper separator from the printer.
6. As shown in Figure 13-16, the option-card compartment is located at the left-rear corner of the printer. The card cover is fastened by a Phillips-head screw. Remove the screw with a #1 Phillips-head screwdriver and put the cover aside.

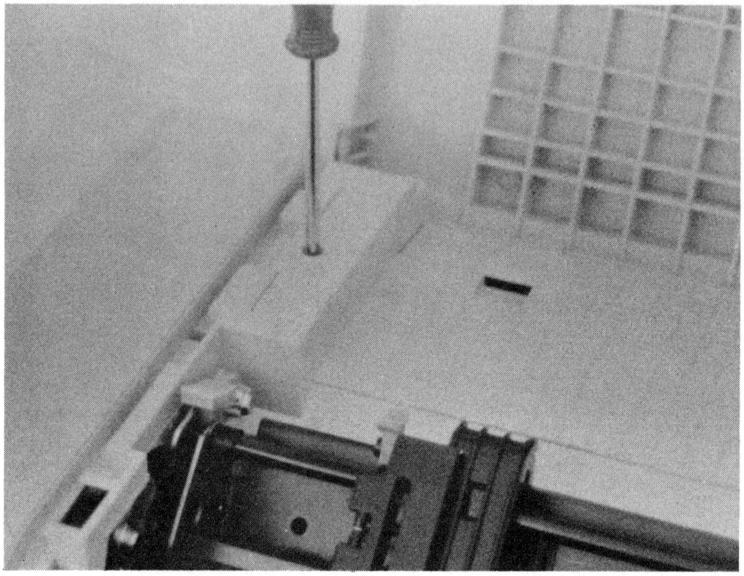

Figure 13-16 The ImageWriter LQ option-card cover is held by a #1 Phillips-head screw.

7. Ground yourself. If it's cold and dry, if you can't walk across the carpet and pet the cat without getting a static shock, put on a wrist-strap as shown in Chapter 12, Figure 12-6.
8. Connect the option card's green ground wire to a metal lug on the logic board as shown in Figure 13-17.
9. Plug the option card into a socket at the left end of the logic board, as indicated in Figure 13-18.
10. As shown in Figure 13-19, press down until the support post on the logic board pops through the post hole in the card.
11. When the option card appears as shown in Figure 13-20, the installation is complete. Replace the card cover.
12. As shown in Figure 13-5, open the DIP switch compartment cover.

Figure 13-17 The option card's green ground wire connects to a metal lug on the logic board.

Figure 13-18 The option card itself plugs into a socket at the left end of the logic board.

Figure 13-19 Press down until the support post on the logic board pops through the post hole in the card.

Figure 13-20 The option-card installation is complete.

13. Refer to Figure 13-4. Unless a card was previously installed, DIP switch SW 2-4 should be open. As indicated in Table 13-3, an open SW 2-4 tells the ImageWriter LQ to ignore option cards; a closed SW 2-4 tells the ImageWriter LQ to recognize option cards. If necessary, close DIP switch SW 2-4. Use a 3⁄32- to 1⁄8-inch flat-head screwdriver with a 4-inch shaft.

14. If you're installing an AppleTalk option card, verify that DIP switch SW 2-3 is open. Open is the DTR (data-terminal-ready) or hardware-handshaking position. Closed is the X-ON/X-OFF (transmission-on/transmission off) or software-handshaking position. AppleTalk does not support X-ON/X-OFF software handshaking. If necessary, open DIP switch SW 2-3. Use a 3/32- to 1/8-inch flat-head screwdriver with a 4-inch shaft.
15. Close the DIP switch compartment cover.
16. Replace the metal paper guide.
17. Replace the paper.
18. Replace the rear cover.
19. Close the front cover.
20. Reconnect the Mac-to-ImageWriter LQ cable.
21. Reconnect the AC power cable to the printer.
22. Reconnect the AC power cable to the wall outlet.

Working with ImageWriter LQ Option Cards

As shown in Figures 13-18 through 13-20, the ImageWriter LQ logic board is provided with only one option-card connector. Since there's no matching piggyback connector on the option card, only one card fits in the printer at a time.

To temporarily disable (turn off) an option card, open DIP switch SW 2-4. This feature allows you to run time trials and judge the effectiveness of a memory option card without having to physically remove the card between trials. It also allows you to transport an AppleTalk ImageWriter LQ to another location, hook it up it via a direct-connect cable, and use it on a nonAppleTalk system, simply by throwing a switch.

To restore the printer to AppleTalk service, close DIP switch SW 2-4 *before* reconnecting it to the network. If DIP switch SW 2-4 is open when you reconnect it, the whole network may stop working.

That completes our discussion of the ImageWriter LQ setup secrets. Next we'll look at ImageWriter alternatives.

CHAPTER

14

Apple-Compatible Alternatives

Up to now we've looked at Apple-brand ImageWriter printers originally manufactured in Japan by Tokyo Electric Company. In this chapter, we'll look at Apple-compatible printers manufactured in Japan by Seikosha Company Limited and Nakajima All Precision Company Limited.

Apple Compatibility Defined

Under the American Standard Code for Information Interchange (ASCII, pronounced ASK-ee), every character, every command, and every number that you type on a keyboard is represented by a numerical code. As explained in Chapter 1, the code ranges from 0 to 255. Code numbers 0 to 31 represent unprintable standard control instructions, such as line feed (10) and carriage return (13); code numbers 32 to 127 represent printable standard characters, such as lowercase a (97) and lowercase z (122); and code numbers 128 to 255 represent printable special characters, which often include Greek letters and scientific symbols.

Brand compatibility generally has to do with nonstandard control codes. As listed in Appendixes C to F, control codes instruct the printer to switch character sets, change type styles, increase resolution, reset itself, etc.

Compatibility with a particular brand is like the ability to understand a particular language. Just as any language can be spoken to any person, any control code can be sent to any printer. If the printer understands (is compatible with) the code, the desired result is achieved. If the printer doesn't understand (is not compatible with) the code, either nothing happens (the printer stands mute), or the results are quite different from what you expected.

When a person learns a foreign language, that knowledge is stored in the human brain. When a printer learns a set of control codes, that knowledge is stored in a ROM (read-only memory) chip. Since ROM chips are generally plugged into sockets (not soldered), all that's generally needed to make a printer Apple-compatible is to replace its existing Epson-compatible ROM with an Apple-compatible ROM.

Even then, Apple-compatible (just like PC-compatible) does not necessarily mean 100% Apple-compatible. Certain control codes are going to be missed. The implementation of those codes that are not missed is going to be different. There are two reasons for that.

First, the printer mechanisms are different. Different printer mechanisms invariably means different margin handling.

Second, the circuitry is different. Some printers don't allocate any buffer space for download characters. That makes them incompatible with certain Macintosh print spoolers and text editors.

Legality of Apple-Compatible Printers

A lot of people think that it's illegal, immoral, and/or unethical to build, buy, or use an Apple-compatible printer. That's not so. If you scan Appendixes C to E, you'll see that the codes used to control Apple-brand printers consist of ordinary alphanumeric characters. The codes are simple on/off switches. The type styles and printer features they switch on and off have been with us since the days of Gutenberg. In the United States, everyone has an equal right to use them. It's protected by the First Amendment:

> "Congress shall make no law respecting an establishment of religion, or prohibiting the free exercise thereof; or abridging the freedom of speech, or of the press; or the right of the people peaceably to assemble, and to petition the government for a redress of grievances."

So, as long as the electromechanical implementation of those features is original, there's nothing illegal about building, buying, or using an Apple-compatible printer.

Seikosha SP-1000AP

Seikosha Company Limited is an OEM (original equipment manufacturer) located in Tokyo, Japan. They have a clock division that makes Seiko wristwatches, and an OEM printer division that makes Tandy-brand printers for Radio Shack. The Seikosha SP-1000AP is similar to many low-end Tandy-brand printers (ribbon cartridges and most other parts are compatible with the DMP 130 series), except that it has an Apple-compatible ROM and an RS-232C serial interface. Since the Imagewriter (Standard and Wide) also has an RS-232C serial interface, that means you can connect an SP-1000AP to any Macintosh, using an ordinary Mac-to-ImageWriter (Standard and Wide) cable, and you can drive it with an ordinary ImageWriter driver.

This section looks at the Seikosha SP-1000AP from the point of view of an Imagewriter (Standard and Wide) owner. It's not an owner's guide, just a list of what's different. If you've never worked with an Imagewriter (or an ImageWriter II) before, it might be helpful to review Chapters 8 and 10 before proceeding.

SP-1000AP Specifications

As shown in Figure 14-1, the Seikosha SP-1000AP is an inexpensive 9-pin, dot-matrix printer with a 10-inch-wide carriage. The SP-1000AP can print Macintosh text and graphics at a maximum resolution of 160 × 144 dots per inch (dpi), exactly the same as the Imagewriter (Standard and Wide). It's slower than the Apple printers (75 cps vs. 120 cps) but output is generally straighter. The SP-1000AP has much better paper handling. It's also quieter.

In addition, the SP-1000AP has built-in NLQ character sets. These are not code compatible with *any* Apple printer. To access them, you have to take the printer off line and press the NLQ button on the SP-1000AP's control panel before printing.

Although it's a monochrome printer, inexpensive solid-red, solid-green, and solid-blue ribbon cassettes are readily available at Radio Shack. They also sell solid-black ribbon cassettes. Any ribbons marked Tandy DMP 130 work equally well in the SP-1000AP.

Figure 14-1 Seikosha SP-1000AP. *(Courtesy Seikosha America Inc.)*

SP-1000AP Paper Handling

In the Imagewriter (Standard and Wide), continuous paper is pushed around the platen. The **sprockets** are underneath. If the paper is too thick, or if the rollers have not been maintained, the first sheet buckles momentarily under the roller shaft; the top line is squashed and distorted. This effect was illustrated in Chapter 8, Figure 8-8.

In the Seikosha SP-1000AP, continuous paper is pulled around the platen. As shown in Figure 14-2, its heavy-duty **pull tractors** are mounted on top. Regardless of how thick the stock may be, the first sheet of paper never buckles; the first line always prints perfectly.

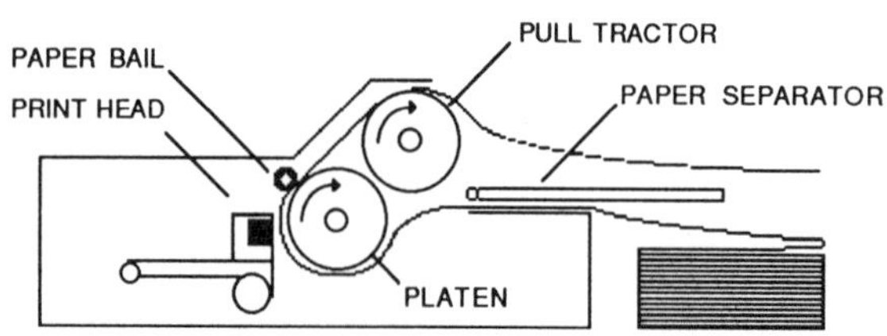

Figure 14-2 In the Seikosha SP-1000AP, continuous paper is pulled around the platen.

Pull tractors may be preferable for long print jobs, but they have two built-in disadvantages. For the same reason that you can't push a rope backwards, reverse line feeds don't work. That makes the SP-1000AP incompatible with certain Macintosh graphics programs.

By design, pull tractors also waste paper. The first sheet has to be wound past the paper bail. The perforation between the first and second sheets is aligned to the top of the ribbon. Printing always starts on the second sheet. The last page always has to be form fed past the tractor before it can be torn off. There's no way around it; with pull tractors, there's always a blank page at the beginning of every print job, and another blank page at the end of every print job.

Cut-Sheet Printing For use with letterhead stationery, the pull-tractor mechanism can be removed. The **paper rack** (nothing similar on the Imagewriter) props open at a 45° angle. Insert a sheet, touch the **paper-loading lever** (release lever), and the paper is automatically pulled around the platen and locked under the paper bail! The SP-1000AP works like a front-loading VCR. Pull the lever so slightly to suggest that you want the tape (paper) in the machine, and the mechanism does the rest.

The autoloading design also makes it impossible to run continuous paper in the wrong mode. With an Imagewriter (Standard and Wide), it's very easy to forget the release lever when switching from cut sheets to pin-feed paper. If you try to print pin-feed paper in the wrong mode, some lines on the first and second pages will be squashed. By the third or fourth page, the feeder stubs derail. By the fifth or sixth page, the stock jams. If by chance you've left the Imagewriter unattended, it keeps on printing and completely mangles the paper. None of this is possible on the Seikosha. The design simply does not allow it.

Envelope Printing Envelope printing on the SP-1000AP is almost exactly the same as on a typewriter, provided you have very thin envelopes. In general, thick envelopes don't work. With that in mind, here's the procedure:

1. Thick and thin are relative terms, so unless you've already proved otherwise, it's best to set the **head-position adjustment** (paper-thickness lever) on the fourth detent (half-way down). Otherwise, the envelope may jam, and the printout may squash. The SP-1000AP only works with very thin envelopes.
2. To autoload the envelope, open the envelope flap, prop up the printer's paper rack, adjust the paper guides, insert the envelope (flap first), and pull the paper-loading lever forward.
3. Press the Select button to bring the printer on line.

4. The correct Page Setup... is very important. Open the envelope document, choose Page Setup... from the File menu, and confirm the following selections:

   Paper: Custom Size

   Paper Width: 9.5 inches (not 8.5)

   Paper Height: 5 inches (not 4.125)

   Special Effects: None (not No Gaps Between Pages)

   Left Margin: 0.0 inches

   Right Margin: 0.0 inches

   Top Margin: 0.0 inches (not 1.0 inches)

   Bottom Margin: 0.0 inches

5. The correct document format is also important. As shown in Figure 14-3, your return address should start on the third line (not the first line) of the document. Other than that, type everything exactly the same as if you were filling out an envelope on a typewriter.

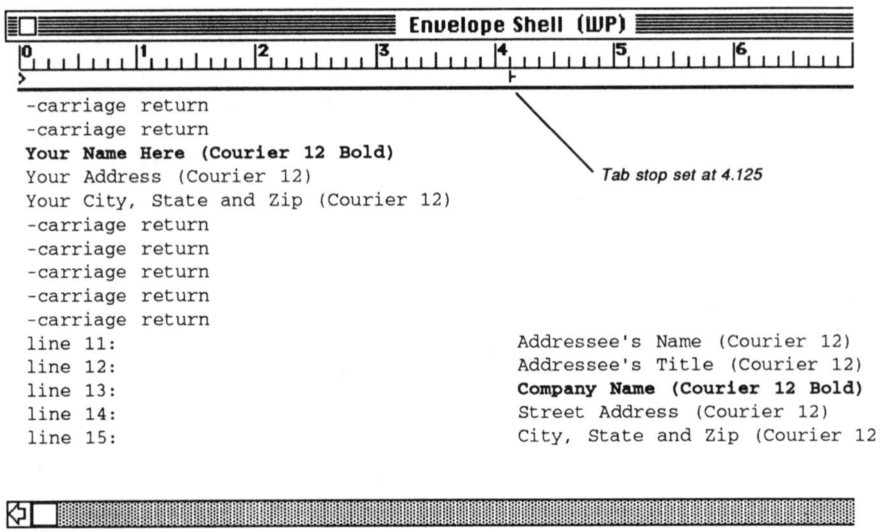

Figure 14-3 Recommended document format for printing envelopes on the Seikosha SP-1000AP.

6. Choose Print... from the File menu. Confirm the following selections:

   Quality: Best or Faster or Draft

   Page Range: All

Copies: 1 (or as many as you want)
Paper Feed: Automatic (not Hand Feed)

7. Click the OK button.

If you observe each of the preceding steps, very thin envelopes should print perfectly, and eject cleanly. If the envelope snags on the bail rollers, it may help to flex the flap, prior to inserting the envelope, to smooth out the crease.

If your return address prints fine, but the send-to address squashes, the envelope is simply too thick. Don't waste any time with it. Buy the cheapest, thinnest envelopes you can find, and try again.

SP-1000AP Margin Handling

The SP-1000AP cannot print on the first or last inch of a page while in the autoloading mode. WYSIWYG printing on 8½ × 11-inch letterhead stationery requires that you set up a 9-inch custom-page size with 0.0-inch top and bottom software margins (11-inch long paper − 2 inches of hardware margins = 9-inch custom-page size). Otherwise, printing starts way too low and the page breaks you see on the screen are not what you get on paper! In effect, the first and last inches are default margins set by the hardware. You have to compensate for it by shrinking the page size via the Page Setup... dialog box. If the program doesn't support custom-page sizes, there's going to be a problem. For example, you can't print an 8 × 10-inch (full-sized) MacPaint 1.5 graphic in the cut-sheet mode. An 8 × 9-inch graphic is the limit.

In tractor mode, everything works as expected. MacDraw, MacPaint, and MacWrite all work fine. Printed margins are exactly the same as you see on the screen, even when using early versions that don't support custom-page sizes.

SP-1000AP DIP Switches

The SP-1000AP's DIP switches are located under an opaque-plastic dust cap at the back of the printer. Tables 14-1 through 14-3 contain DIP switch function details. Figure 14-4 shows the recommended US-Macintosh settings.

Table 14-1. Seikosha SP-1000AP DIP Switch 1 Functions

Switch	Function	On	Off	US-Mac Setting
1-1	Alphabet	See Table 14-4		Off
1-2	Alphabet	See Table 14-4		Off

(continued)

Table 14-1. *(continued)*

Switch	Function	On	Off	US-Mac Setting
1-3	Alphabet	See Table 14-4		Off
1-4	Paper length	12 inch	11 inch	Off
1-5	Data bits	7	8	Off
1-6	CR code	CR + LF	CR	Off
1-7	Autoeject	Enabled	Disabled	On
1-8	Baud rate	1200 baud	9600 baud	Off

Table 14-2. Seikosha SP-1000AP DIP Switch 2 Functions

Switch	Function	On	Off	US-Mac Setting
2-1	SheetFeeder	Installed	Removed	Off
2-2	Character Set	Pica	Elite	On
2-3	Handshaking	X-ON/X-OFF	DTR	Off
2-4	Not used			Off

Table 14-3. Seikosha SP-1000AP DIP Switches 1-1 through 1-3 (Alphabet Selection) Settings

SW 1-1	SW 1-2	SW 1-3	Alphabet Selection
Off	Off	Off	American English
On	On	Off	European English
Off	Off	On	German
Off	On	On	French
On	Off	On	Swedish
On	Off	Off	Italian
On	On	On	Spanish
Off	On	Off	Danish

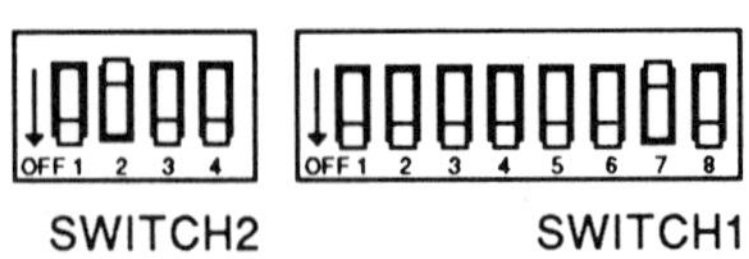

Figure 14-4 Seikosha SP-1000AP recommended DIP switch settings.

The recommendations in Figure 14-4 differ slightly from those of the factory. The factory setting for DIP switch 1-5 is on. But to work with PC-compatible computers as well as Macs, DIP switch 1-5 should be off (8 data bits). The factory setting (7 bits) is only for the Apple IIe.

The factory setting for DIP switch 1-7 is off. But, if you're using letterhead stationery and you want each sheet of paper to autoeject from the printer as soon as it's finished, DIP switch 1-7 has to be on. Otherwise, the bottom margin will remain under the paper bail and you'll have to eject the sheet manually. That leads to all kinds of trouble.

Having finished with the first sheet, the printer believes it's at the top of the second. By advancing the mechanism one inch (to remove the paper) the printer will now assume you want a 2-inch top margin and it will only place eight inches of text on the next sheet, instead of nine. To print the last inch, you have to insert still another sheet! The fix is to set DIP switch 1-7 to on. In some cases, you also have to turn the printer off and on after every page to reset the mechanism.

The factory setting for DIP switch 2-2 is off (Elite font). Elite 12 almost never works with business forms. Elite 12 is also incorrect for WYSIWYG PC-compatible use. If you want the printer to work properly with forms (as well as stationery) on PC-compatible computers (as well as Macintosh), set the switches according to Figure 14-4.

SP-1000AP Cable Requirements

Table 14-4 shows the SP-1000AP's DB-25S serial-interface connector functions. Chapter 8, Figures 8-18 through 8-20, are wiring diagrams for various Macintosh-to-Imagewriter (Standard and Wide) cables. These cables work equally well with the Seikosha SP-1000AP.

Table 14-4. Seikosha SP-1000AP DB-25S Connector Functions

Pin	Function	Description	Direction
1	FG	Frame ground	
2	TxD	Transmitted data	Output to computer
3	RxD	Received data	Input from computer
4	NC	Not connected	
5	NC	Not connected	
6	NC	Not connected	
7	SG	Signal ground	
8	NC	Not connected	
9	NC	Not connected	
10	NC	Not connected	

(continued)

Table 14-4. *(continued)*

Pin	Function	Description	Direction
11	RTS	Request to Send	Output to computer*
12	NC	Not connected	
13	NC	Not connected	
14	NC	Not connected	
15	NC	Not connected	
16	NC	Not connected	
17	NC	Not connected	
18	NC	Not connected	
19	NC	Not connected	
20	DTR	Data terminal ready	Output to computer
21	NC	Not connected	
22	NC	Not connected	
23	NC	Not connected	
24	NC	Not connected	
25	NC	Not connected	

* *Valid only if Jumper J3 (on the logic board) is closed. J3 is open when shipped from the factory.*

SP-1000AP Self-Tests

The Seikosha SP-1000AP is equipped with two built-in self-tests and a hexadecimal-dump mode. The first built-in self-test checks the carrier motor, the line-feed motor, the ribbon-drive motor, the print head, and both character sets. To run the test:

1. Switch off the printer (if it's on).
2. Hold down the LINE FEED button and, while keeping it held down, switch on the power.

If everything is all right, the SP-1000AP will begin a repeating alphanumeric test pattern. The first five lines print using the standard character set. The next five lines print using the NLQ character set. Every five lines, it switches character sets, until the paper runs out or until you stop the test. To stop the test, press the ON LINE button, or turn the printer off.

SP-1000AP NLQ Test The second built-in self-test checks everything the first test does, except for the standard character set. To run the test:

1. Switch off the printer (if it's on).

2. Hold down the NLQ button and, while keeping it held down, switch on the power.

If everything is all right, the SP-1000AP will print a repeating alphanumeric test pattern, without switching back and forth between character sets. To stop the NLQ test, press the ON LINE button or turn the printer off.

SP-1000AP Hexadecimal-Dump Mode To engage the SP-1000AP's built-in debugging mode, also known as the hex-dump mode:

1. Switch off the printer (if it's on).
2. Hold down the FORM FEED button and, while keeping it held down, switch on the power.

As shown in Chapter 5, Figure 5-3, the hex-dump printout consists entirely of hexadecimal numbers. These numbers represent printable text, as well as nonprinting control codes. TCG has a calculator that converts these numbers to ASCII codes. By looking up the codes in Appendix C, you can determine which (if any) control codes are not supported by the SP-1000AP's Apple-compatible ROM. For complete hex-dump instructions, refer to Chapter 5.

The hex-dump mode stays in effect until you turn the printer off. If necessary, turn the printer off, and then on again, to resume the normal mode.

SP-1000AP Upgrades

The SP-1000AP logic board is designed to hold extra RAM. Simply by plugging an *inexpensive* 8K 6264-LP15 RAM chip into the provided socket, you can increase the stock 1.28K buffer size to 9.28K.

With the usual static-electricity precautions in mind, here's the complete procedure:

1. Remove the paper cover, the paper rack, and, if necessary, the tractors. Put all three aside.
2. The cabinet top is held by five clearly visible Phillips-head screws. Loosen them with a #1 Phillips-head screwdriver.
3. Lift the cabinet top straight up, and put it aside.
4. The 6264 socket is clearly visible, but it's too close to the platen for easy installation. Loosen the four screws holding the platen with a #2 Phillips-head screwdriver. Move the platen out of the way.
5. Ground yourself. If it's cold and dry, if you can't walk across the carpet and pet the cat without getting a static shock, put on a wrist-strap, as described in Chapter 12, Figure 12-6.

6. Locate the notch on the 6264 RAM chip. Point it in the same direction as other chips on the board, and plug in the chip.
7. If appropriate, when the chip is firmly seated, take off the wriststrap.
8. Reposition the platen. Refasten the platen-holder screws with a #2 Phillips-head screwdriver.
9. Reposition the cabinet top. Refasten the cabinet-top screws with a #1 Phillips-head screwdriver.
10. Replace the paper cover, the paper rack, and, if necessary, the tractors.

   Allow about 15 minutes to complete the job.

Olympia NP 30 APL

Nakajima All Precision Company Limited is an OEM (original equipment manufacturer) located in Tokyo, Japan. They make private-label typewriters, and Epson-compatible and Apple-compatible printers, which are sold by Fortis, Laser, and Olympia USA.

Nakajima's Apple-compatible printers all have an RS-232C serial port. Just like the Seikosha SP-1000AP, they can be connected to any Macintosh via a Mac-to-ImageWriter (Standard and Wide) cable, and driven from an ordinary ImageWriter driver.

This section looks at the Olympia NP 30 APL, which is similar to the Fortis 1310A and the Laser 190A, from the point of view of an Imagewriter (Standard and Wide) owner. It's not a comprehensive owner's guide, just a list of what's different. If you've never worked with an Imagewriter (or an ImageWriter II) before, it might be helpful to review Chapters 8 and 10 before proceeding.

NP 30 APL Specifications

The Olympia NP 30 APL is an inexpensive 9-pin, dot-matrix printer with a 10-inch-wide carriage. It can print Macintosh text and graphics at a maximum resolution of 160 × 144 dots per inch (dpi), which is comparable to the Imagewriter (Standard and Wide). It's rated a little faster than the Apple printers (130 cps vs. 120 cps) and, at the same time, it's much quieter.

In addition, the NP 30 APL has built-in NLQ character sets. These are code compatible with the Apple Scribe printer. They are not compatible with programs written strictly for ImageWriter II. To access them, you generally have to take the printer off line and press the NLQ button on the control panel before printing.

Although it's a monochrome printer, inexpensive solid-red, solid-green, and solid-blue ribbon cassettes are readily available from various mail-order sources. Ribbons marked Epson LX-80/90 work equally well in the Olympia NP 30 APL.

NP 30 APL Paper Handling

Unlike the Imagewriter (Standard and Wide), the built-in push tractor *cannot* be adjusted for use with narrow business forms and/or mailing labels. Most forms and mailing labels require an optional pull tractor.

The built-in mechanism is strictly for use with 9½- to 10-inch-wide pin-feed stock. To position the built-in tractor for use with 9½-inch-wide (U.S. letter size) pin-feed paper:

1. Switch off the printer, if necessary.
2. Slide the tractors as close to the center of the printer as they will go.
3. Set the pin-feed stubs into the sprockets by hand.
4. When the stub holes are centered on the sprockets, pull back the paper bail and wind the stock forward, using the platen knob.
5. When the paper is high enough to clear the bail rollers, push the paper bail against the platen.
6. Switch on the printer.

Since there are no paper clamps over the NP 30 APL's sprockets, mastering this procedure may take some practice.

Cut-Sheet Printing When pin-feed stock is left under the platen (especially in hot humid weather), the top edge of the first sheet of paper begins to curl, and that curl sometimes causes the stock to feed back into the printer and jam. ImageWriters (all models) are notorious for this problem. Paper left under the NP 30's platen also curls, but an adjustable, anti-jamming **paper separator** (nothing like it on an Imagewriter) absolutely prevents the stock from jamming. This feature works so well, it's almost impossible to load single sheets manually, unless you remove the separator, or at least slide it out of the way. Whenever you encounter difficulty inserting envelopes or cut-sheet stationery, check to see whether the paper separator is installed, and, if it is, simply remove it or slide it out of the way.

For use with letterhead stationery, the hinged **noise cover** (equivalent to the Imagewriter's clear plastic lid) props open at a 60° angle. In the upright position, the noise cover serves as a paper rack, which supports the paper, making it easier to load single sheets. This feature is not obvious, especially since the Imagewriter's clear plastic lid opens in the opposite direction and always gets in the way.

Semi-automatic loading is standard. Once you insert the paper, just pull the loading lever, and away it goes. If you've never used an ImageWriter II, you might not think to try this feature. With the Imagewriter (Standard and Wide), single sheets have to be wound in by hand.

Envelope Printing While envelope printing on the Imagewriter (Standard and Wide) is intuitive (exactly the same as on a typewriter), envelope printing on the Olympia NP 30 APL requires further explanation:

1. Remove the NP 30's paper separator and its hinged noise cover.
2. Set the **manifold lever** (paper-thickness lever) all the way towards the front of the printer.
3. Move the paper-release lever to the friction (rear) position.
4. Pull back the paper-bail lever. Open the envelope and insert it sideways into the printer.
5. Wind the envelope forward using the platen knob until the envelope's left edge just catches under the paper bail. This position is shown in Figure 14-5.

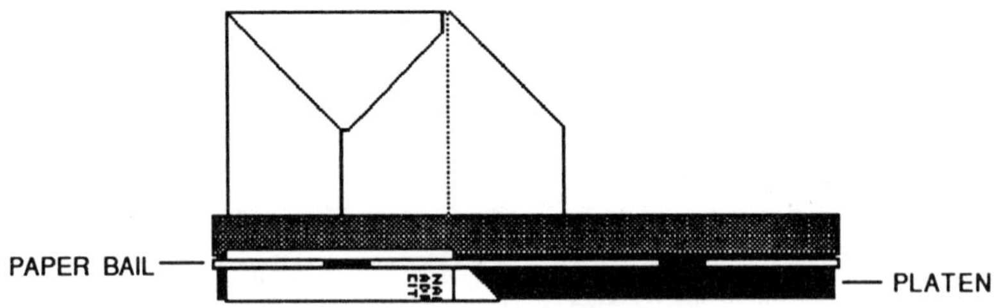

Figure 14-5 Olympia NP 30 APL. Wind the envelope forward using the platen knob until the envelope's left edge just catches under the paper bail.

6. Push the paper-bail lever forward. If necessary, bring the printer on line.
7. Open the envelope document, choose Page Setup... from the File menu, and confirm the following selections:

   Paper: Custom Size
   Orientation: Landscape (sideways)
   Special Effects: None
   Paper Width: 4 inches (not 8.5)
   Paper Height: 9.5 inches (not 11)
   Left Margin: 0.0 inches
   Right Margin: 0.0 inches

Top Margin: 0.5 inches (not 1.0 inches)

Bottom Margin: 0.0 inches

8. Format the envelope document exactly the same as if you were filling out an envelope on a typewriter. Unlike Figure 14-3, your return address should start on the first line, not the third line.
9. Choose Print... from the File menu. Confirm the following selections:

   Quality: Best or Faster or Draft

   Page Range: All

   Copies: 1 (or as many as you want)

   Paper Feed: Automatic (not Hand Feed)

10. When Steps 1 through 9 have been confirmed, click the OK button.

If you observe each of the preceding steps, even relatively thick envelopes should print perfectly, and eject cleanly. The manifold (paper-thickness lever) and pressure system on the NP 30 APL works much better than the Imagewriter's. The Imagewriter can also print envelopes, but they have to be real thin; otherwise, they jam and don't feed properly.

NP 30 APL Margin Handling

Relative to the Imagewriter (Standard and Wide), and the ImageWriter II, the NP 30's top margin is approximately 2 lines lower. When using an ImageWriter driver, you can compensate by choosing Page Setup... from the File menu and changing the usual 1-inch top margin to 0.67 inch (4 lines) and the usual 1-inch bottom margin to 1.33 inches (8 lines). By setting the top margin to 0.67 inch and the bottom margin to 1.33 inches, documents printed on the NP 30 APL will always have 1-inch margins—top and bottom.

NP 30 APL Cable Requirements

The NP 30 APL comes with two cable connectors and can accommodate three completely different printer cables:

1. Mac-to-modem cables attach to the upper cable connector and require that front-panel DIP switch number 8 be set to the *on* position. In addition, all of the odd-numbered positions on internal DIP switches 852 and 851 must be switched *on;* all of the even-numbered positions on internal DIP switches 852 and 851 must be switched *off.*

2. Mac-to-ImageWriter (Standard and Wide) cables also attach to the upper cable connector and also require that front-panel DIP switch 8 be set to the *on* position. In addition, all of the odd-numbered positions on internal DIP switches 852 and 851 must be switched *off*; all of the even-numbered positions on internal DIP switches 852 and 851 must be switched *on*. Wiring diagrams for Macintosh-to-Imagewriter (Standard and Wide) cables are shown in Chapter 8, Figures 8-18 through 8-20.
3. Centronics-parallel cables attach to the lower cable connector and require that front-panel DIP switch number 8 be set to the *off* position. This configuration is normally used with PC-compatible computers. The settings of internal DIP switches 852 and 851 are irrelevant.

Provided you set the switches according to the preceding list, Mac-to-modem and Mac-to-ImageWriter (Standard and Wide) cables work equally well on the Olympia NP 30 APL.

NP 30 APL Printer-Driver Requirements

The NP 30 APL is 100% compatible with the Apple ImageWriter driver in Faster and Best quality modes. Provided that there is an ImageWriter driver in the System folder (a standard Macintosh requirement), printing to the NP 30 APL in Faster and Best quality is exactly the same as printing to an ImageWriter.

Draft and NLQ printing is somewhat different. In Draft and NLQ, the NP 30 APL is screen-font specific. Screen-font specific means that the chosen screen font has to match the NP 30 APL's built-in character sets, exactly. If you choose a screen font that doesn't match, or if you use multiple fonts, sizes, and styles, the results will be unpredictable.

To print reliably in Draft and NLQ using the NP 30's built-in Elite 12 character set:

1. Limit formatting to normal, bold, and underline. Italic, outline, shadow, superscript, and subscript aren't supported in draft and NLQ (not even on the Imagewriter II).
2. When ready, save your work, and select the entire document.
3. Choose Monaco 10 from the Font and Style menus. As shown in Chapter 5, Figure 5-5, the Monaco-10 screen font looks unattractive, but provides perfectly spaced, draft-quality printout.
4. To print in data-processing quality, go directly to Step 5. To print in near-letter quality, take the printer off-line, and push the NLQ button. The green light will come on. Put the printer back on-line.
5. Choose Print... from the File menu and click the Draft radio button in the Print... dialog box. If the NP 30's NLQ button was pushed,

you should get excellent near-letter-quality results. Otherwise, you'll get draft-quality results. Either way, the NP 30's NLQ light will normally be off or it may flicker during printing.

6. After printing, to restore the screen display, reselect your entire document, and switch back to the original font and size.

The NP 30 APL is also compatible (Draft and NLQ only) with Microsoft Word's Serial-Printer driver (included with Microsoft Word version 3.0, 3.1, and 3.2) and with GDT-Softworks' Mac-Daisy Link driver. Both drivers yield excellent results and offer multiple-printer choices. Choose typewriter emulation for use with the NP 30 APL. Use the Chooser desk accessory to switch back and forth between these drivers and the ImageWriter driver as needed.

NP 30 APL Upgrades

Unlike the Imagewriter (Standard and Wide), where what you bought was what you got, the Olympia NP 30 APL can be upgraded, just like an ImageWriter II. This section looks at the optional pull tractor, sheet feeder, and buffer upgrades.

Push Tractor The NP 30 APL comes with a built-in semiadjustable push tractor made to handle letter size (9½- to 10-inch wide), pin-feed stock. If you need to print 3½- × 1-inch mailing labels (4½ × 1 with the pin-feed stubs) and/or 7-inch-wide business forms, Olympia offers an optional, fully adjustable pull-tractor unit. The pull-tractor unit can handle pin-feed stock from 4- to 10-inches wide. It can be removed and installed in seconds and it comes with an effective, smoke-colored noise cover. You can't see through it very well, but it does keep the noise down.

Sheet Feeder For use with letterhead stationery, Olympia carries an automatic sheet feeder for the NP 30 APL. The sheet feeder is made by BDT in Germany; while it works fine, the color is definitely lighter than that of the NP 30 APL. Paper capacity is 100 sheets. Once you get past the initial somewhat vague BDT directions, removal and installation takes seconds. You can switch from the sheet feeder, to the pull tractors, to the push tractors, with no trouble at all.

RAM Upgrade The NP 30 APL logic board is designed to hold extra RAM. Simply by plugging an inexpensive 8K D4168C-20 RAM chip into the provided socket, you can increase the stock 4K buffer to 12K.

With the usual static-electricity precautions in mind, here's the complete procedure:

1. Remove the hinged paper cover, the carrier cover and, if necessary, the pull tractors and/or the sheet feeder. Put all three aside.

2. Remove the platen knob.
3. Remove two clearly visible Phillips-head screws at the back of the printer with a #1 Phillips-head screwdriver.
4. Turn the printer upside down. The cabinet top is fastened to the cabinet bottom with four heavy-duty plastic snaps. These snaps are visible through access holes, one in each corner of the printer. Pry back the snaps (one at a time) by sticking a large flat-head screwdriver into the access holes. Considerable force is required. A long-handled screwdriver works best.
5. Remove the cabinet top; turn the printer rightside up.
6. Locate the 4168C-20 socket in the left-rear corner of the printer.
7. Ground yourself. If it's cold and dry, if you can't walk across the carpet and pet the cat without getting a static shock, put on a wrist-strap, as described in Chapter 12, Figure 12-6.
8. Locate the notch on the 4168C-20 RAM chip. Point it in the same direction as other chips on the board, and plug in the chip.
9. When the chip is firmly seated, take off the wrist-strap.
10. Reposition the cabinet top. Snap it into place.
11. Replace the two screws at the back of the printer.
12. Replace the platen knob.
13. Replace the hinged paper cover, the carrier cover, and, if necessary, the pull tractors and/or the sheet feeder.

Separating the cabinet (at least the first time) is quite a challenge. You need a *very* big screwdriver and confidence in your mechanical ability. Other than that, there's really nothing to it.

In the next chapter, we'll learn how to use Epson-compatible printers on a Mac.

CHAPTER

15

Epson-Compatible Alternatives

This chapter explains how to connect Epson-compatible printers to a Macintosh. It's not a complete owner's guide for every Epson-compatible printer ever made, just a list of how to connect them and what to expect. The instructions assume a general familiarity with the material presented in Chapter 1, and prior experience with dot-matrix printers. If it's been some time since you read Chapter 1, or if you've never worked with a dot-matrix printer before, please review Chapters 1, 8, and 10 before proceeding.

Epson Compatibility Defined

Epson-compatible printers differ from Apple-compatible printers in two important ways:

1. Epson-compatible ROM (read-only memory) chips do not understand the Apple-compatible control codes given in Appendixes C to E. Since they *only* understand the Epson-compatible control codes given in Appendix F, they require an Epson-compatible printer driver.
2. Epson-compatible printer interfaces may be different. Some Epson-compatible printers have RS-232C serial ports, just like an Imagewriter (Standard and Wide). Others have Centronics-compatible parallel ports, just like an IBM printer. To work on a Mac, these printers also require a serial-to-parallel interface converter, and a Centronics-compatible parallel cable.

The following sections discuss both differences in detail. First we'll look at Epson-compatible printer drivers.

Epson-Compatible Printer Drivers

Since Epson-compatible printers do not respond properly to Apple-compatible (ImageWriter) control codes, many people assume that Epson-compatible printers are completely incompatible with the Macintosh. In truth, Epson-compatible printers are merely incompatible with the ImageWriter *driver.* PostScript-compatible laser printers do not respond properly to ImageWriter control codes, either. Yet, everyone knows PostScript printers are compatible with the Macintosh!

To use a PostScript-compatible laser printer on a Macintosh, you need a PostScript-compatible laser-printer driver. To use an Epson-compatible printer on a Macintosh, you need an Epson-compatible printer driver. Conceptually, the requirements are exactly the same.

Just as there are 9-pin ImageWriter drivers and 27-pin LQ ImageWriter drivers, Epson-compatible printer drivers can either be 9-pin Epson-FX compatible or 24-pin Epson-LQ compatible. The Page Setup... and Print... dialog boxes from compatible drivers developed by GDT Softworks are shown in Figures 15-1 through 15-4. Both drivers are so similar to their ImageWriter and LQ ImageWriter counterparts that little or no explanation of how to use them is generally necessary.

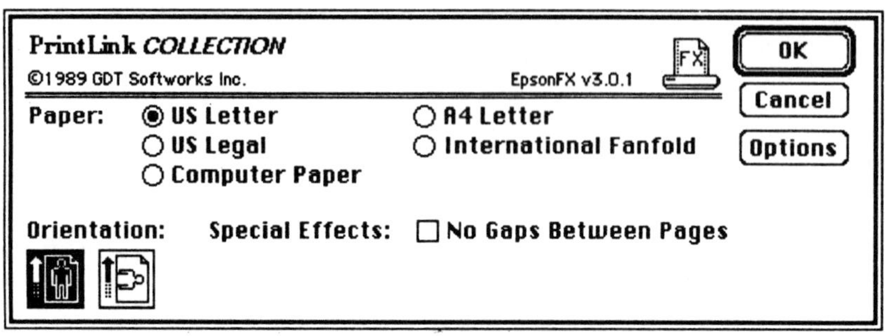

Figure 15-1 Page Setup... dialog box from GDT Softworks' Epson-FX-compatible printer driver, version 3.0.1.

Supported Printers

GDT Softworks' Epson-compatible printer drivers are supplied with a set of Kodak-Diconix 150/300 drivers, and one other printer driver, as part of the company's PrintLink Collection. Table 15-1 provides a partial list of printers supported by GDT's PrintLink-driver software.

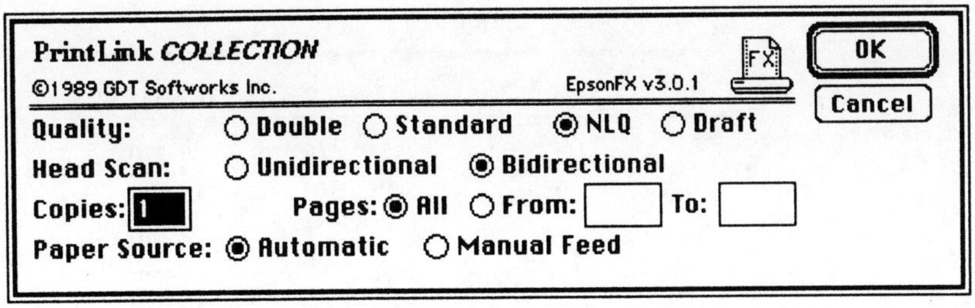

Figure 15-2 Print... dialog box from GDT Softworks' Epson-FX-compatible printer driver, version 3.0.1.

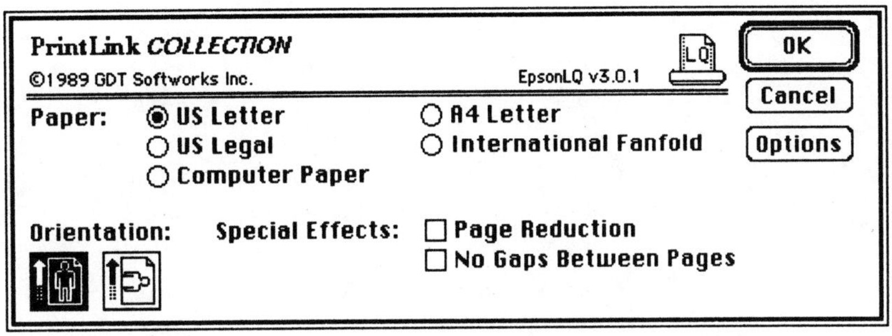

Figure 15-3 Page Setup... dialog box from GDT Softworks' Epson-LQ-compatible printer driver, version 3.0.1.

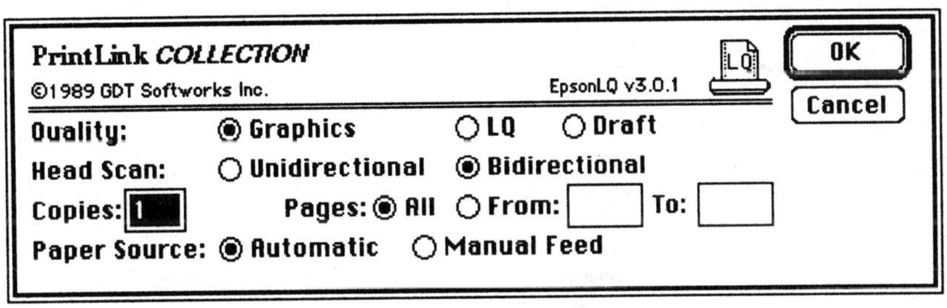

Figure 15-4 Print... dialog box from GDT Softworks' Epson-LQ-compatible printer driver, version 3.0.1.

Table 15-1. Partial List of Printers Supported by GDT's PrintLink Driver Software

Brand	Model No.	Print Head	Compatibility
Alps	Allegro 24	24-pin	LQ
Alps	ASP 1000	9-pin	FX
Alps	ALQ 200	24-pin	LQ
Alps	ALQ 218	18-pin	JX/FX

continued

Table 15-1. *continued*

Brand	Model No.	Print Head	Compatibility
Alps	ALQ 224	24-pin	LQ/JX
Alps	ALQ 318	18-pin	JX/FX
Alps	ALQ 324	24-pin	LQ/JX
Alps	P2100	18-pin	FX
Alps	P2400 C	24-pin	LQ
Alps	ALQ P2418	18-pin	JX/FX
Alps	P2424 C	24-pin	JX/LQ
Alps	ALQ 3001	24-pin	FX
AMT ACCEL	500	24-pin	LQ/JX/FX
Brother	M 1509	9-pin	FX
Brother	M 1709	9-pin	FX
Brother	M 1724 L	24-pin	LQ
Citizen	MSP 40	9-pin	FX
Citizen	MSP 55	9-pin	FX
Copal Writehand	5900	18-pin	FX
Copal Writehand	5930	18-pin	FX
Copal Writehand	6700	24-pin	FX
Copal Writehand	6730	24-pin	LQ
DataProducts	9044	24-pin	LQ
DataProducts	SI 480	Inkjet	LQ
DataProducts	6298	Inkjet	FX
Diconix	150	Inkjet	Diconix 150
Diconix	300/300W	Inkjet	Diconix 300
Dynax (Fortis)	DH 45	9-pin	FX
Dynax (Fortis)	DM 1310	9-pin	FX
Epson	EX 800	9-pin	FX
Epson	EX 1000	9-pin	FX
Epson	FX 80/85	9-pin	FX
Epson	FX 86E	9-pin	FX
Epson	FX 286E	9-pin	FX
Epson	FX 850	9-pin	FX
Epson	FX 1050	9-pin	FX
Epson	LQ 500	24-pin	LQ
Epson	LQ 800	24-pin	LQ
Epson	LQ 850	24-pin	LQ
Epson	LQ 950	24-pin	LQ
Epson	LQ 1000	24-pin	LQ
Epson	LQ 2500	24-pin	LQ
Epson	LQ 2550	24-pin	LQ

Table 15-1. *(continued)*

Brand	Model No.	Print Head	Compatibility
Epson	LX 800	9-pin	FX
Facit	B3350	18-pin	JX/FX
Facit	C 7400	18-pin	FX
Facit	C 7500	18-pin	JX/FX
Fujitsu	DX 2300	9-pin	FX
Fujitsu	DX 2400	9-pin	FX
Fujitsu	DL 2400	24-pin	FX (9-pin)
Fujitsu	DL 2600	24-pin	FX
Fujitsu	DL 3300	24-pin	JX
Fujitsu	DL 3400	24-pin	JX (optional)
Fujitsu	DL 5600	24-pin	FX/JX (optional)
Genicom	240	24-pin	FX
Genicom	1020	18-pin	JX/FX
Genicom	1025	18-pin	JX/FX
Genicom	1030	24-pin	LQ
Honeywell Bull	462	18-pin	JX
Honeywell Bull	466	18-pin	FX
Hewlett-Packard	DeskJet	Inkjet	FX (optional)
Juki	7100	24-pin	JX
Juki	7200	24-pin	JX
Mannesman Tally	87	9-pin	FX
Mannesman Tally	MT 490	18-pin	FX
Mannesman Tally	222	24-pin	LQ
Mannesman Tally	230	24-pin	LQ
Mannesman Tally	330	24-pin	LQ
Mannesman Tally	340	18-pin	FX
Nissho	NP 2405	24-pin	LQ
Nissho	NP 2410	24-pin	LQ
Okidata	390/391	24-pin	LQ
Okidata	392/393	24-pin	LQ
Olympia	NP 30	9-pin	FX
Olympia	NP 80	9-pin	FX
Olympia	NP 136	9-pin	FX
Panasonic	KX-P1091i	9-pin	FX
Panasonic	KX-P1092i	9-pin	FX
Panasonic	KX-P1124	24-pin	LQ
Panasonic	KX-P1524	24-pin	LQ
Panasonic	KX-P1592	9-pin	FX
Relisys	RP 1814	9-pin	FX

continued

Table 15-1. *(continued)*

Brand	Model No.	Print Head	Compatibility
Relisys	RP 2410	9-pin	FX
Sanyo	PR 241	24-pin	LQ
Seikosha	MP 1200	9-pin	FX
Seikosha	MP 1300	9-pin	FX
Seikosha	MP 3000	9-pin	FX
Seikosha	MP 5300	9-pin	FX

These aren't the only printers supported by GDT's driver software. The complete list includes hundreds of printers.

Screen-Font Requirements

When printing from the Epson-FX-compatible driver in draft and NLQ, best results are obtained when characters are formatted using the simulated Monaco 10-point font. For details on this procedure, refer to Chapter 5.

When printing from the LQ driver in draft and LQ, results vary according to the screen-font selections given in Table 15-2.

Table 15-2. Mac Screen Font-to-Epson Character Set Cross-Reference

Quality	Screen Font/Points	Character Set/Pitch
LQ	Courier 9-point	Roman 15-cpi
Draft	Courier 9-point	Draft 15-cpi
LQ	Courier 10-point	Roman 12-cpi
Draft	Courier 10-point	Draft 12-cpi
LQ	Courier 12-point	Roman 10-cpi
Draft	Courier 12-point	Draft 10-cpi
LQ	Monaco 9-point	Roman 15-cpi
Draft	Monaco 9-point	Draft 15-cpi
LQ	Monaco 12-point	Roman 10-cpi
Draft	Monaco 12-point	Draft 10-cpi

Epson-Compatible DIP Switch Settings

For the printer driver to work properly, the printer's DIP switches must be set correctly. If even a single switch is out of position, the first character of every word may be missed, the printer may print gibberish, or it might not work at all.

For use with Epson-compatible printers, the standard PrintLink communications protocol is 9600 baud, no parity, 8 data bits, 2 stop bits, and X-ON/X-OFF (a.k.a. DC1/DC3 or ready/busy) software handshaking.

The printer's carriage-return DIP switch should be set to CR = CR (carriage return only), *not* CR = CR + LF (carriage return equals carriage return plus line feed).

If the printer has a Centronics parallel port, the DIP switch controlling the interface selection should be set to RS-232C serial (not parallel).

If the printer is capable of emulating an IBM Proprinter, the emulation DIP switch should be set to Epson or Standard (not IBM).

IBM character-set selection should be switched off. The printer's download character function (if available) should be switched on.

Troubleshooting DIP Switch Settings DIP switch problems can easily be identified by comparing the errant printout to the following list of symptoms.

1. If the baud rate is incorrect, the printer will tend to beep incessantly, overprint characters, and/or issue successive form feeds.
2. If the data length (a.k.a. word length) is incorrect, the printer will tend to overprint lines in two ragged columns separated by a large white space.
3. If parity is incorrect, the printer will tend to print gibberish peppered with @ (ASCII 64) and # (ASCII 35) characters.
4. If handshaking is incorrect, the printer will proceed normally halfway down the page, and then generally malfunction. In draft mode, random characters will be missed. Otherwise, the printout may appear normal. In graphics mode, the printout will tend to fracture, as shown in Chapter 1, Figure 1-10, followed by gibberish liberally sprinkled with x (ASCII 120), @ (ASCII 64), and ` (ASCII 96) characters.
5. If the printer is inadvertently set for IBM emulation, the first character of each and every word will be missed when printing in draft, NLQ, or LQ mode. Carriage returns may not be interpreted correctly.
6. If the download character function is disabled (turned off), printing from a program that uses download characters will result in beeps, line feeds, form feeds, and generally staggered printout. So will running TCG's High {128 - 255} ASCII test.

Experiencing any of the preceding symptoms tends to make people very nervous. It shouldn't. Printer-interface malfunctions are completely predictable. Once you identify the errant DIP switch, and throw it in the opposite direction, everything will be fine.

A good computer-science exercise involves forcing the above symptoms (one at a time, not all at once), by deliberately setting a DIP switch incorrectly. Once you see for yourself that interface malfunctions *do* occur predictably, you'll be able to approach future setup problems with confidence (not anxiety). That confidence will allow you to solve interface problems in no time at all, just like a crossword puzzle you might read on a place mat, while waiting for a pizza.

Epson-Compatible Cable Requirements

Some Epson-compatible printers come with RS-232C serial-interface connectors, just like the Imagewriter (Standard and Wide). Some come with Centronics-parallel interface connectors, just like the IBM Proprinter. These will be dealt with in the next section. Others come with both serial *and* parallel interface connectors.

Figures 15-5 through 15-7 give the wiring diagrams for general-purpose Mac-to-Epson-compatible RS-232C serial-printer cables. Dotted lines between pin numbers indicate a connection.

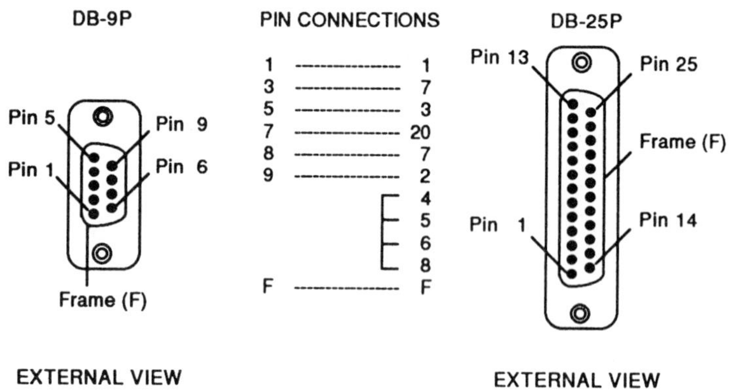

Figure 15-5 Wiring diagram for 128K/512K/512K E Mac-to-serial-printer cable.

All three cables work equally well as direct-connect Mac-to-Imagewriter (Standard and Wide) cables, but the converse is not necessarily true. As noted throughout the book, some Mac-to-ImageWriter cables have missing wires. For that reason, Mac-to-Imagewriter (Standard and Wide) cables *do not* always work as Mac-to-serial-printer cables.

A properly wired serial-printer cable and an Epson-compatible printer driver are generally all that's needed to run Epson-compatible

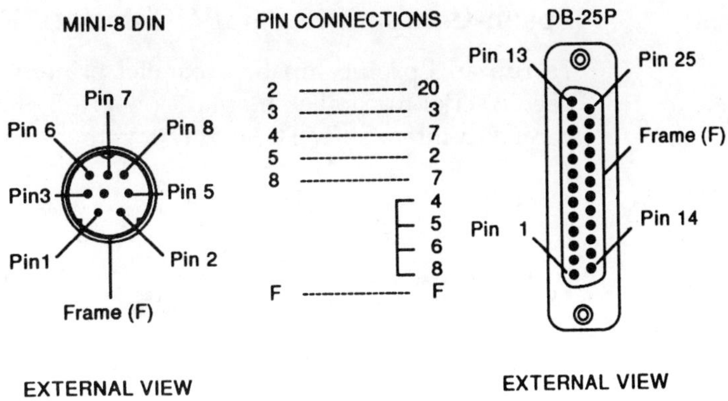

Figure 15-6 Wiring diagram for Mac Plus/SE/II-to-serial-printer cable.

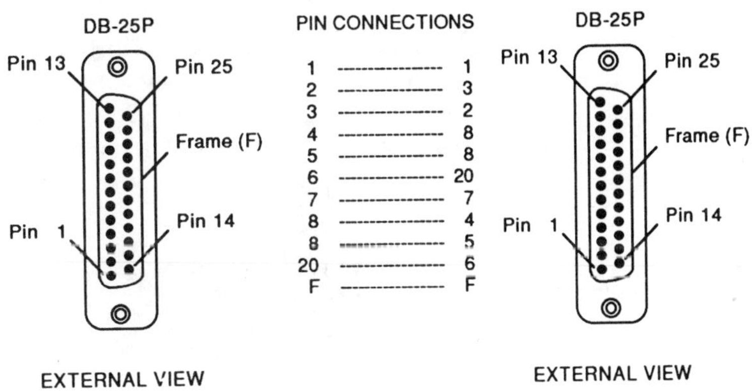

Figure 15-7 Wiring diagram for Lisa/Mac XL-to-serial-printer cable.

RS-232C serial printers on a Macintosh. Both requirements are no different than needing an ImageWriter cable and an ImageWriter driver to run an ImageWriter printer on a Macintosh. Once you install the Epson-compatible driver in the System folder, and select it with the Chooser DA (desk accessory), it works pretty much like any other Macintosh printer driver.

For use with floppy-drive Macs (Macs without a hard drive), the Epson-compatible printer driver has to be installed on each and every startup disk. Unless the Mac is also connected to an ImageWriter printer, the ever-present ImageWriter driver (along with any unnecessary AppleTalk-ImageWriter drivers, LQ ImageWriter drivers, LaserWriter drivers, etc.) can be dragged to the trash can (deleted) to save room.

Epson-Compatible Parallel-Interface Requirements

To run an Epson-compatible parallel printer on a Macintosh, you also need a serial-to-parallel interface converter, and a Centronics-compatible parallel printer cable. These wire together as shown in Figure 15-8.

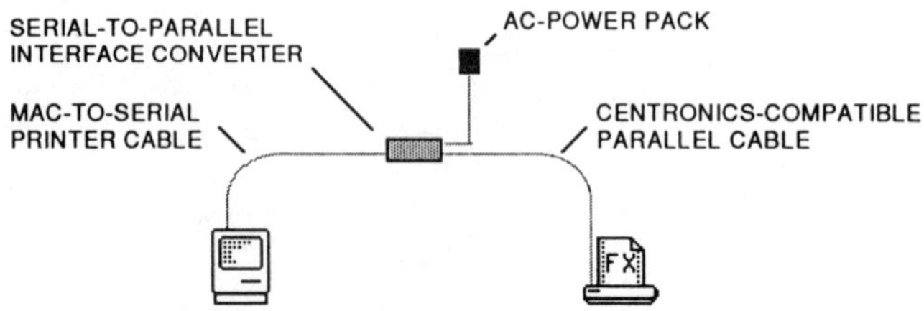

Figure 15-8 To run an Epson-compatible parallel printer on a Macintosh, you also need a serial-to-parallel interface converter and a Centronics-compatible parallel-printer cable.

Centronics-compatible parallel printer cables can easily be identified by their connectors. For use with serial-to-parallel interface converters, both ends should have 36-pin Centronics-compatible plugs (male connectors), as shown in Figure 15-9.

Figure 15-9 A 36-pin Centronics-compatible plug.

As shown in Figure 15-10, the parallel printer cable plugs into a 36-pin Centronics-compatible socket (female connector) located on the parallel side of the converter. Figure 15-11 shows how the serial printer cable plugs into a 25-pin DB-25S socket located on the serial side of the converter.

Interface conversion is always defined from the computer's perspective (not from the printer's perspective). **Serial-to-parallel interface converters** are used to connect computers with serial ports to printers with parallel interfaces. Since all Macs have serial ports, these generally work fine on a Macintosh.

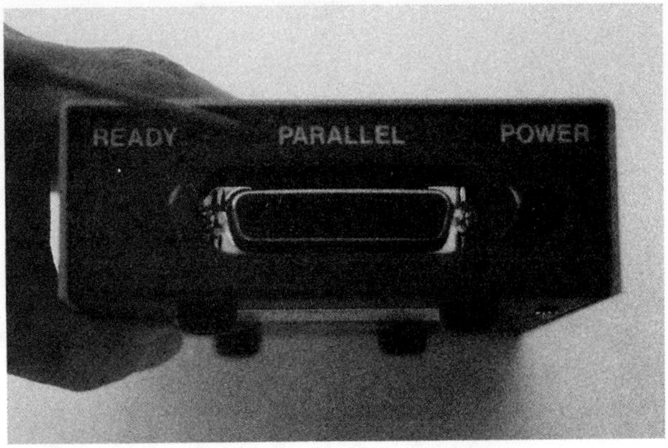

Figure 15-10 A 36-pin Centronics-compatible socket.

Figure 15-11 A 25-pin DB-25S socket.

Parallel-to-serial interface converters are used to connect computers with parallel ports to printers with serial interfaces. With the exception of Lisas and XLs (which have both serial and parallel ports), these don't work at all on a Macintosh.

Universal-interface converters (UICs), like the popular J.F.D. 2000 shown in Figure 15-12, can handle either conversion, but only one at a time. Signal direction (as defined from the computer's perspective) is selected with a slide switch. For use with a Macintosh, make sure the UIC's slide switch is set for SERIAL TO PARALLEL, as shown in Figure 15-12.

Communications settings are generally selected with removable 2-pin shorting blocks (jumpers). As shown in Figure 15-13, removable shorting blocks on the J.F.D 2000 are located just behind the DB-25S socket.

Figure 15-12 J.F.D. 2000. For a use on a Macintosh, make sure the UIC's slide switch is set for SERIAL TO PARALLEL.

Figure 15-13 J.F.D. 2000. Shorting blocks are located just behind the DB-25S socket.

Table 15-3 summarizes the critical Mac-specific jumper information for the J.F.D. 2000 UIC. Note that jumper numbers 0 to 7 refer to two-pin (communications) jumpers; jumper numbers 20 to 2 refer to 3-pin (configuration) jumpers. All numbers in this table should be cross-referenced from left to right, just the way they're printed on the UIC's circuit board.

Table 15-3. Mac-Specific Jumper Information for J.F.D. 2000 UIC

Jumper	Shorting Block	Meaning	Function
0	Out	Not jumpered	9600 baud
1	In	Jumpered	9600 baud
2	In	Jumpered	9600 baud
3	In	Jumpered	9600 baud
4	Out	Not jumpered	No parity
5	Out	Not jumpered	If 4, odd parity
6	In	Jumpered	8-bit data
7	Out	Not jumpered	Self-test disabled
20	In low	Lower pins jumpered	Connect DTR line
19	Out	No pins jumpered	
11	Out	No pins jumpered	
8	Out	No pins jumpered	
6	Out	No pins jumpered	
5	Out	No pins jumpered	
4	Out	No pins jumpered	
3	In low	Lower pins jumpered	Connect TXD line
2	In high	Upper pins jumpered	Connect RXD line

Table 15-4 summarizes baud-rate jumper information for the J.F.D. 2000 UIC.

Table 15-4. Baud-Rate Jumper Information for J.F.D. 2000 UIC

Jumper 0	Jumper 1	Jumper 2	Jumper 3	Baud Rate
Out	Out	Out	Out	50 baud
In	Out	Out	Out	75 baud
Out	In	Out	Out	110 baud
In	In	Out	Out	134.5 baud
Out	Out	In	Out	150 baud
In	Out	In	Out	300 baud
Out	In	In	Out	600 baud

(continued)

Table 15-4. *(continued)*

Jumper 0	Jumper 1	Jumper 2	Jumper 3	Baud Rate
In	In	In	Out	1200 baud
Out	Out	Out	In	1800 baud
In	Out	Out	In	2000 baud
Out	In	Out	In	2400 baud
In	In	Out	In	3600 baud
Out	Out	In	In	4800 baud
In	Out	In	In	7200 baud
Out	In	In	In	9600 baud
In	In	In	In	19,200 baud

The factory setting is 9600 baud, which is pretty much the industry standard. Presumably, you can pick up a little data-transfer speed by changing both the UIC and the GDT printer driver to 19,200 baud. How much speed depends on the size of the printer's communications buffer.

As explained in Chapters 5 and 10, increasing the baud rate does not make a print head fire any faster. It does not make the ribbon-cartridge deck move back and forth any faster. It'll still take just as long for pages to come out of the printer, but provided the printer's communications buffer is large enough, the computer should be able to upload the data faster, and return to service sooner. In other words, with a high baud rate, and a big communications buffer, the computer is not tied up as long during big print jobs.

Upgrading the printer buffer varies from printer to printer. Some printers are designed to accept memory-option cards. Others are socketed for extra RAM chips. Others are designed to accept memory-upgrade cartridges. Typical upgrades are discussed in Chapters 12, 13, 14, and 16.

To raise the baud rate of the UIC from 9600 to 19,200, place a 2-pin shorting block over jumper number 0. To raise the baud rate of the GTD driver, choose Page Setup... from the File menu, click the Options button, then click on 9600 (or whatever the current rate is) and hold the mouse button down. As shown in Figure 15-14, clicking on the current rate results in a drop-down list.

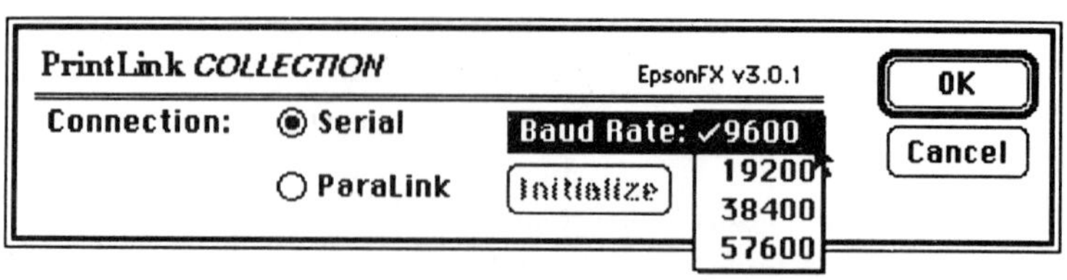

Figure 15-14 Options dialog box from GDT Softworks' Epson-FX-compatible printer driver, version 3.0.1.

The currently selected baud rate has a check mark beside it. To change the rate to 19,200, drag the mouse pointer over 19,200 and then release the mouse button.

Remember that the UIC and the printer driver are designed to communicate at the *same* baud rate. If you increase one to 19,200 baud, be sure to increase the other, or it's not going to work!

> Regardless of baud rate, the UIC's ready light always flashes when data is being transferred. The flashing light indicates normal ready/busy handshaking. It does not indicate a malfunction!

Testing the UIC The J.F.D. 2000 UIC is equipped with a built-in self-test. This test checks the converter's built-in RAM, and verifies that everything on the output side, including the Centronics cable and the parallel printer, is working properly. To run the test:

1. Four screws along the sides of the UIC hold the top cover. Remove the screws with a #0 Phillips-head screwdriver.
2. Connect the UIC to the parallel printer using a 36-pin Centronics-compatible parallel-printer cable.
3. Load the printer with paper and turn it on. Make sure the on-line (or select) light is lit.
4. Plug the UIC's power-pack cable into the UIC.
5. Plug the UIC's power pack into an AC outlet.
6. When the UIC's ready light glows red, install a 2-pin shorting block over jumper number 7.

If everything is all right, the converter capacity (in K) will be printed, followed by a repeating set of ASCII test characters, as shown in Figure 15-15. If not, an error message will be printed.

```
** UNIVERSAL INTERFACE CONVERTER **
SELF TEST IN PROGRESS, PLEASE WAIT.

Converter Capacity: .25K

ASCII Character Set:
 !"#$%&'()*+,-./0123456789:;<=>?@ABCDEFGHIJKLMN
OPQRSTUVWXYZ[\]^_`abcdefghijklmnopqrstuvwxyz{|}~
 !"#$%&'()*+,-./0123456789:;<=>?@ABCDEFGHIJKLMN
OPQRSTUVWXYZ[\]^_`abcdefghijklmnopqrstuvwxyz{|}~
 !"#$%&'()*+,-./0123456789:;<=>?@ABCDEFGHIJKLMN
OPQRSTUVWXYZ[\]^_`abcdefghijklmnopqrstuvwxyz{|}~
 !"#$%&'()*+,-./0123456789:;<=>?@ABCDEFGHIJKLMN
OPQRSTUVWXYZ[\]^_`abcdefghijklmnopqrstuvwxyz{|}~
 !"#$%&'()*+,-./0123456789:;<=>?@ABCDEFGHIJKLMN
OPQRSTUVWXYZ[\]^_`abcdefghijklmnopqrstuvwxyz{|}~
 !"#$%&'()*+,-./0123456789:;<=>?@ABCDEFGHIJKLMN
OPQRSTUVWXYZ[\]^_`abcdefghijklmnopqrstuvwxyz{|}~
```

Figure 15-15 J.F.D. 2000 self-test results.

To stop the test, switch off the printer, unplug the UIC's power pack, and remove the 2-pin shorting block over communications jumper number 7.

Assuming the test passes, whatever printing difficulty you might be experiencing would have to be on the input side. The jumpers behind the DB-25S serial connector may be shorted (jumpered) incorrectly, or the Mac-to-serial printer cable may be wired incorrectly. Refer to Figure 15-13 and Tables 15-3 and 15-4 for jumper information. Refer to Figures 15-5, 15-6, and 15-7 for cable-wiring details.

Testing Epson-Compatible Printers

Provided the cable, interface, and DIP switch requirements are met, TCG works just as well with Epson-compatible printers as it does with Apple-compatible printers. To set up for Epson-compatible printers with 10-inch (standard-width) carriages, select Epson-FX Std from the Printer menu. To set up for Epson-compatible printers with 15-inch (wide) carriages, select Epson-FX Wide from the Printer menu.

Selecting one of the two Epson emulations is very important. If you attempt to test Epson-compatible printers under Imagewriter emulation, the printer will misunderstand every instruction issued by the program, and the test results will be completely invalid. The same thing happens when you attempt to test ImageWriter printers under Epson emulation.

Other than that, all tests work exactly the same, with two minor exceptions:

1. The CPI - Character Sets test makes only two passes (not three) as shown in Figure 15-16. NLQ/LQ switching is automatic. Epson-FX-compatible printers are tested for NLQ. Epson-LQ-compatible printers are tested for LQ.
2. If download characters are disabled on the printer, or if they are not supported by the printer driver, printing TCG's High {128 - 255} ASCII test (in Draft, NLQ, or LQ) may show that all characters from 129 through 255 are undefined, or it may cause the printer to beep, execute form feeds, and print strange staggered characters.

TCG's High {128 - 255} ASCII test is shown in Chapter 1, Figure 1-9. If the test results show that all characters are undefined, it means that the printer driver is blocking the high-ASCII codes.

If the printer beeps, executes form feeds, and prints strange staggered characters, it means the codes are getting through, and the printer is doing exactly what it's being instructed to do.

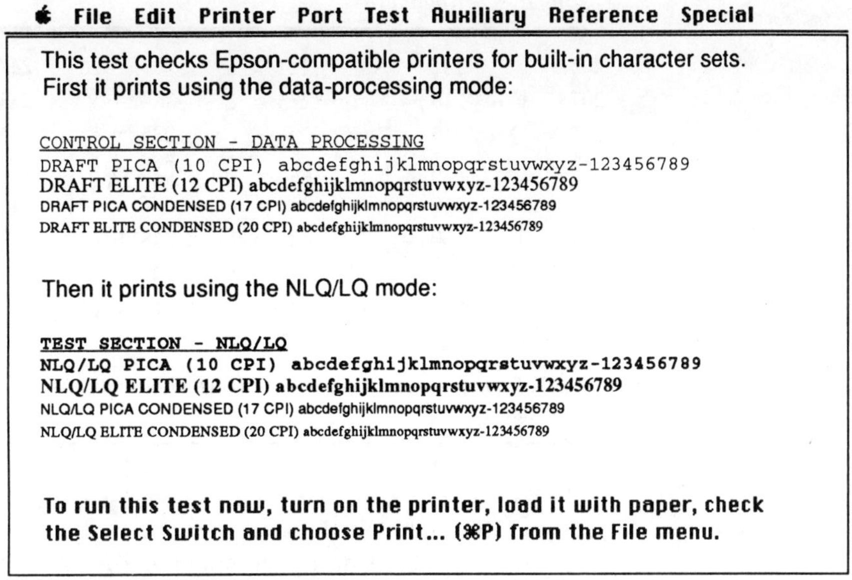

Figure 15-16 Test Character Generator CPI - Character Sets test for Epson-compatible printers.

As shown in Table 15-5, ASCII 128 through 133 is undefined under the standard code, but ASCII 134 is a beep, 135 is a backspace, 136 is a horizontal tab, 137 is a line feed, 138 is a vertical tab, 139 is a form feed, and so on. When all this happens in sequence, the printer appears to be going haywire.

Table 15-5. Standard High (8-bit) ASCII

128 =	141 = SO	154 = ESC	167 = (	180 = 5	193 = B
129 =	142 = SI	155 =	168 =)	181 = 6	194 = C
130 =	143 =	156 = GS	169 = *	182 = 7	195 = D
131 =	144 = DC1	157 =	170 = +	183 = 8	196 = E
132 =	145 = DC2	158 =	171 = ,	184 = 9	197 = F
133 =	146 = DC3	159 = SP	172 = -	185 = :	198 = G
134 = BEL	147 = DC4	160 = !	173 = .	186 = ;	199 = H
135 = BS	148 =	161 = "	174 = /	187 = <	200 = I
136 = HT	149 =	162 = #	175 = 0	188 = =	201 = J
137 = LF	150 =	163 = $	176 = 1	189 = >	202 = K
138 = VT	151 = CAN	164 = %	177 = 2	190 = ?	203 = L
139 = FF	152 = EM	165 = &	178 = 3	191 = @	204 = M
140 = CR	153 =	166 = '	179 = 4	192 = A	205 = N

continued

Table 15-5. *(conitnued)*

206 = O	215 = X	224 = a	233 = j	242 = s	251 = |
207 = P	216 = Y	225 = b	234 = k	243 = t	252 = }
208 = Q	217 = Z	226 = c	235 = l	244 = u	253 = ~
209 = R	218 = [	227 = d	236 = m	245 = v	254 = DEL
210 = S	219 = \	228 = e	237 = n	246 = w	255 =
211 = T	200 =]	229 = f	238 = o	247 = x	
212 = U	211 = ^	230 = g	239 = p	248 = y	
213 = V	222 = _	231 = h	240 = q	249 = z	
214 = W	223 = `	232 = i	241 = r	250 = {	

NOTE: Blank spaces after an equals sign indicates that the code number is undefined.

To prevent that, early GDT Epson-FX-compatible printer drivers stripped the high-ASCII codes. That made them incompatible with certain desk accessories and print spoolers (like miniWRITER MockPrinter, and MockWrite).

Version 3.0.1 of the GTD Epson-FX driver (included in the Print-Link collection) now supports these programs, and even downloads an *Apple-compatible* high-ASCII character set of its own. These characters replace the standard high-ASCII code assignments given in Table 15-5. Provided the printer's DIP switches are set for download characters and standard (not IBM) emulation, version 3.01 of the GTD Epson-FX driver actually makes them *more* Apple-compatible than the Nakajima printers (lacking download-character support) discussed in Chapter 14.

So much for the commonly held belief that "Epson printers aren't compatible with the Macintosh." Next, we'll look at Mac-compatible printers from Hewlett-Packard, Kodak, and Toshiba.

CHAPTER 16

Macintosh-Compatible Alternatives

A Macintosh-compatible printer is defined as any printer that's neither Apple-compatible nor Epson-compatible but, nevertheless, is perfectly compatible with the Macintosh. Models covered here which fit that definition include:

1. The Kodak Diconix M150 Plus.
2. The Hewlett-Packard DeskWriter.
3. The Toshiba P321SLC.

The Kodak Diconix M150 Plus and the Hewlett-Packard DeskWriter are ink-jet printers. The Toshiba P321SLC is a 24-pin, color, dot-matrix printer, with features similar to an ImageWriter LQ.

This chapter looks at all three printers, *and at their PC-compatible counterparts* through the eyes of an Imagewriter owner. It's not an owner's guide, just a list of how the printers connect and what to expect.

Kodak Diconix M150 Plus

As shown in Figure 16-1, the Kodak Diconix M150 Plus is a 3½-pound, portable, ink-jet printer with an 9-inch-wide carriage.

Figure 16-1 Kodak Diconix M150 Plus. *(Courtesy Eastman Kodak Company.)*

Portable means that the printer runs on rechargeable C cells or AC line voltage. A 120-V AC, 60-Hz, wall-mount transformer is standard equipment. International 220-V AC, 50-Hz, and 240-V AC, 50-Hz, wall-mount transformers are optional. The printer's size and weight are comparable to two copies of *Macintosh Printer Secrets*, stacked one on top of the other.

Ink-jet describes the print head. Ink-jets draw liquid ink from a well and *shoot* it onto the paper. The ink-jets are like tiny water pistols. They're virtually silent. All you hear is the low-pitched hum of the carrier mechanism as it moves the print head back and forth. Ink-jet printers make less noise than a cooling fan or a hard drive. So much less that *you can easily carry on a telephone conversation while the printer is working*. ImageWriter owners may find that hard to believe. Nevertheless, it's true.

Kodak Diconix M150 Plus Printer-Driver Requirements

Figures 16-2 and 16-3 show the Page Setup... and Print... dialog boxes from the factory bundled Kodak Diconix M150 Plus printer driver. Factory bundled means that the driver is packed in the same box as the printer. You don't need to buy it separately.

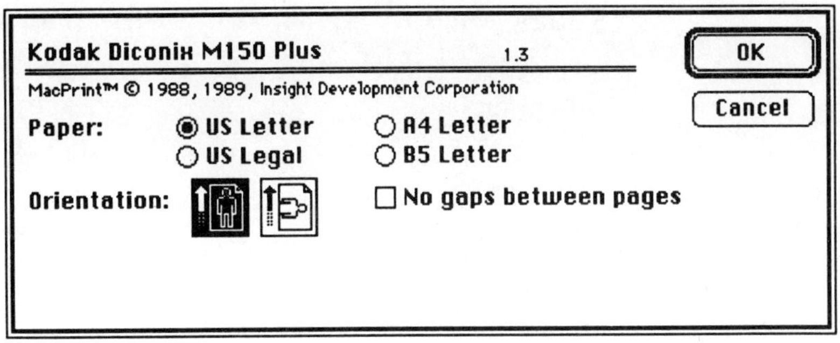

Figure 16-2 Page Setup... dialog box from the Kodak Diconix M150 Plus printer driver.

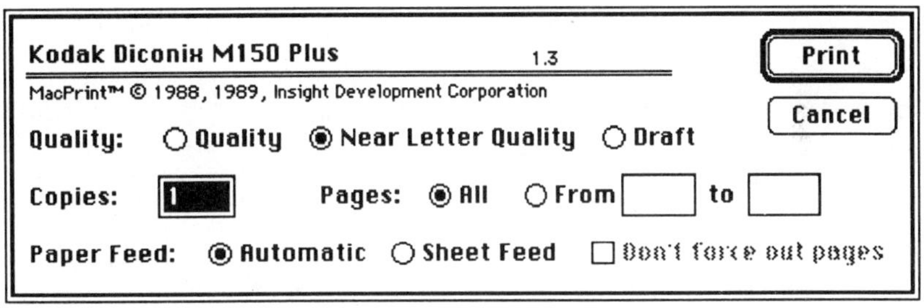

Figure 16-3 Print... dialog box from the Kodak Diconix M150 Plus printer driver.

The bundled driver is designed to work *primarily* with outline fonts. Adobe Type Manager software and 13 Adobe Type 1 outline fonts (Helvetica, Helvetica Italic, Helvetica Bold, Helvetica-Bold Italic, Times Roman, Times-Roman Italic, Times-Roman Bold, Times-Roman Bold Italic, Courier, Courier Italic, Courier Bold, Courier-Bold Italic, and Symbol) are also bundled. Provided Adobe Type 1 fonts are in the System folder and provided the matching Adobe screen fonts are in the System file, output is reasonably crisp at 192 × 192 dpi. In other words, when ATM is installed and working, what you see is essentially what you get.

Bitmapped fonts (Chicago, Geneva, Monaco) take a very long time to print, and output is not as good.

> Bitmapped fonts, outline fonts, and Adobe Type Manager are the subject of Chapter 3.

Kodak Diconix M150 Plus Print-Head Requirements

Besides the outline-font requirement, two other factors affect the M150 Plus printout:

1. The ink-jet print head must be primed properly.
2. The paper stock must be carefully matched to the ink formula contained in the print head.

As shown in Figure 16-4, specially formulated inks (one for regular paper, one for clay-coated ink-jet paper) are supplied inside small rubber bladders, which are protected by clear plastic housings. The entire print-head assembly weighs less than $\frac{1}{2}$ ounce. Other than the ink formula, both print heads are the same. They are also the same as the print heads designed for the Hewlett-Packard Think Jet, Hewlett-Packard Quiet Jet, and Hewlett-Packard Quiet Jet Plus printers.

Figure 16-4 Kodak Diconix M150 Plus print head.

To prevent the ink supply from leaking out while in storage, the print head's twelve $\frac{1}{96}$-inch, diameter ink jets are sealed prior to shipment. Just like a fountain pen, the jets have to be primed before use. The procedure involves pushing a straightened paper clip through a hole in the plastic housing. The tip of the paper clip compresses the bladder. The pressure forces the ink through the seals.

Some seals break easily, as evidenced by a small blot of ink at the business end of the print head. Some seals are more difficult to break. Once the ink blot spreads, it's hard to tell which seals are broken, and which aren't. Unless you break all of the upper seals, all the way, printout quality suffers.

In general, new users tend not to prime hard enough. This results in a light output and white lines running through the printout. If the printout is not as good as you expected, prime the print head a little harder and try again.

> Of the twelve 1/96-inch-diameter jets in the print head, only jets 4 through 11 are significant. Jets 0 through 3 are not used.

Kodak Diconix M150 Plus Paper Requirements

Although the M150 Plus is capable of reasonably good 196 × 196-dpi output, the paper selection is critical. Some papers absorb ink faster than it can dry. That kind of paper acts like a blotter. Other papers don't absorb ink fast enough. That kind of paper tends to smear. These are the same paper problems that fountain-pen users face.

In theory, consistently good results are assured only when special clay-coated ink-jet paper is used, together with specially formulated clay-paper inks. In practice, smooth-white paper often gives equally good results when it's used with clay-paper inks. For some reason, smooth-white paper doesn't seem to work as well when it's used with inks designed for regular paper! Glossy paper and coarse, yellow-tinted paper tend to give poor results with either ink. Glossy paper tends to smear. Coarse paper is too absorbant.

Kodak Diconix M150 Plus Self-Tests

The M150 Plus is equipped with a self-test designed primarily to check paper absorbency and the print-head condition. To engage the self-test:

1. Turn the printer off, if necessary.
2. Load paper, if necessary.
3. Hold down the Form-Feed button and, while keeping it down, turn the printer on.

Typical results using the factory bundled clay-coated paper and the factory bundled ink-jet cartridge are shown in Figure 16-5.

Kodak Diconix M150 Plus

Portable Printing for the Apple Macintosh™

Figure 16-5 Kodak Diconix M150 Plus self-test results.

The self-test can be run at any time. It's not necessary for the printer to be connected to a computer or plugged into a wall outlet in order to run the test. With a set of fully charged nickel-cadmium C cells, you can take the printer with you into a stationery store and run your own tests to see which papers give the best results.

Kodak Diconix M150 Plus Nicad-Battery Requirements

The M150 Plus is factory bundled with a plug-in power supply rated for 120-V AC, 60-Hz, 16-W input to 9-V DC, 1-A output, wired negative to the pin, positive to the shell. The same supply doubles as a battery charger. The printer platen is hollow. The battery consists of five 1.2-amp-hour, nickel-cadmium, C cells that fit inside the platen.

Believe it or not, all nicad cells have a memory. When fully discharged and fully recharged, the M150 Plus battery lasts about 12 hours standing by and 50 minutes in service. This is long enough to print 50 to 60 pages. If you recharge the battery before it's fully discharged, a proportionally shorter life cycle is introduced. Instead of 50 minutes in service, the battery might only last 25 minutes.

To maintain the specified in-service life, it's best to run the battery all the way down before charging it. If necessary, let the printer stand by until the Battery Low light flashes, then press and hold the On Line, Form Feed, and Line Feed buttons until the Recharging light comes on. When the battery is fully charged, recharging stops automatically, and the Power light comes on. A full recharge takes 10 to 14 hours.

During that time, the printer is not out of service. If you need to print a file, just print it normally; the printer will temporarily suspend charging and pull itself on-line, and then go right back to charging as soon the file is printed.

Just like any other cell, nicad-cell quality varies *tremendously* from manufacturer to manufacturer. The strongest cells are generally not sold in department stores. Best results are obtained by breaking up military weapons batteries, which generally have to be mail-ordered from a surplus vendor.

Kodak Diconix M150 Plus Interface Requirements

The M150 Plus is factory bundled with a DB-25P to mini DIN 8 cable wired exactly the same as the Mac Plus/SE/II-to-ImageWriter (Standard and Wide) cable shown in Chapter 8, Figure 8-20. The Mac-to-serial-printer cables given in Chapter 15, Figures 15-5 through 15-7, also work. Other requirements are a 128K ROM, 1 Mb RAM, two 800K drives (or one 800K drive and a hard drive), and System 6.0.2 (or later).

The printer has three banks of DIP switches. DIP switch SW 1 is on the logic board, hidden by a strip of tape, inside the carriage opening, just in front of the Power and Add Paper lights. The other two DIP switches are to the left of the print head, right behind the DB-25S interface connector. All three switch banks are accessible from inside the carriage opening. The factory recommended settings are shown in Figure 16-6. The DIP switch function details for the two banks behind the DB-25S interface connector are given later in Tables 16-3 through 16-6.

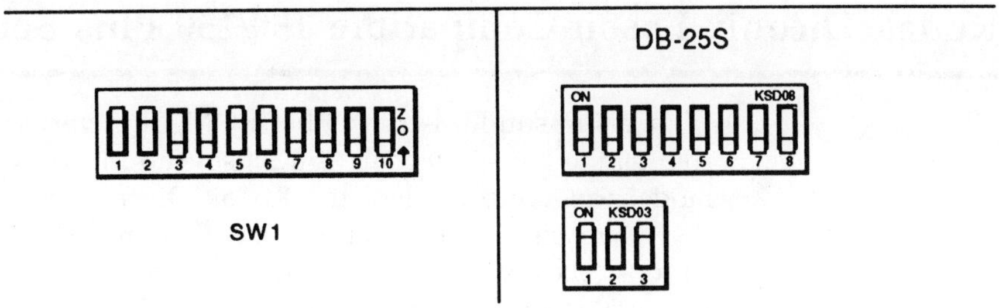

Figure 16-6 Kodak Diconix M150 Plus DIP Switch Settings.

Kodak Diconix M150 Plus Setup Secrets

The M150 Plus has semi-adjustable built-in push tractors designed strictly for use with 9½- to 10-inch-wide pin-feed stock. They can't be adjusted for use with narrow stock, like 3½ × 1-inch 1-up mailing labels. The printable area is a full inch shorter than the ImageWriter II (7.1 inches as opposed to 8 inches). Anything outside of that area is simply not printed. Otherwise, what you see is exactly what you get. All margins set up perfectly. The aspect ratio is exactly 1 to 1.

To install paper, you simply pull back the paper bail, insert the stock, and push the paper bail forward. What could be simpler? The only thing that's not obvious about paper loading is where to position the right-hand bail roller. Since it takes a few seconds for the ink to dry, it's very important that the roller be pushed as far to the right as possible. If the roller runs over wet ink, it acts like a house-painter's roller and the ink is spread over the document as shown in Figure 16-7.

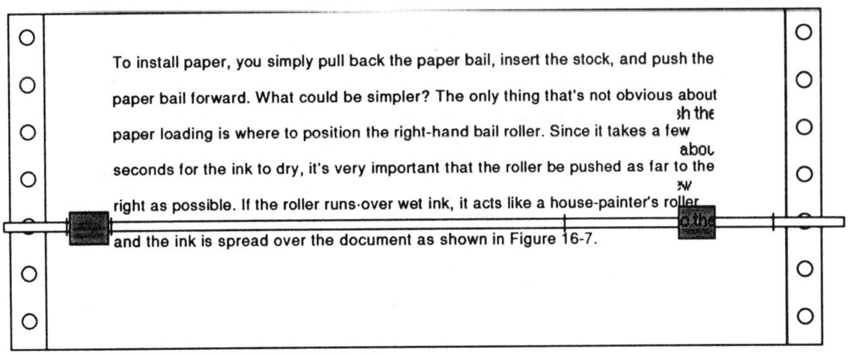

Figure 16-7 This kind of printout means the right-hand bail roller is too far left.

In that case, cancel the print job, clean the roller (with soap and water if necessary), and move it all the way to the right, so that it falls outside of the printable area.

Kodak Diconix Epson-Compatible 150/150 Plus Serial Printers

With an Epson/IBM-compatible ROM, this very same serial printer is sold as the Kodak Diconix 150 Plus/S (no M, for Macintosh). An earlier model was simply called the Kodak Diconix 150/S (no Plus). Since an ever-increasing number of Mac owners are investing in PC-compatible laptops (because the software is just as easy to use and the hardware is *so much* cheaper), this section shows how to connect other Kodak Diconix printers to a Macintosh.

Diconix 150 Printer-Driver Requirements

Familiar-looking Page Setup... and Print... dialog boxes from a Diconix 150-compatible printer driver developed by GDT Softworks are shown in Figures 16-8 and 16-9.

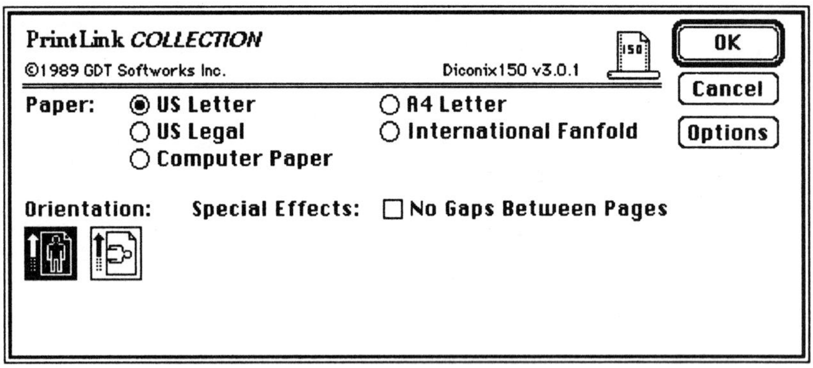

Figure 16-8 Page Setup... dialog box from GDT Softworks' Diconix 150 Macintosh printer driver, version 3.0.1.

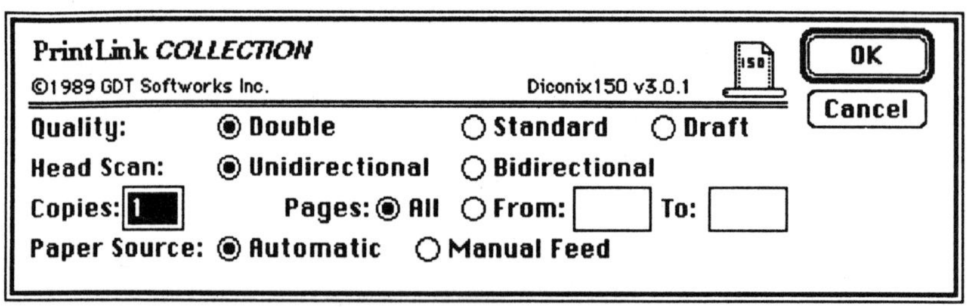

Figure 16-9 Print... dialog box from GDT Softworks' Diconix 150 Macintosh printer driver, version 3.0.1.

Version 3.0.1 of GDT's Diconix driver uses a pop-up menu which requires enhanced (Mac Plus or better) ROMs and System 6.02 or later. Earlier versions of the GDT driver (which don't use pop-up menus) work equally well with original ROMs, 512K Macs, and System 2.0.

Diconix 150 Self-Tests

The Diconix 150 is equipped with a comprehensive built-in self-test designed to check built-in character sets as well as mechanical operation. To run the self-test:

1. Turn the printer off, if necessary.
2. Load paper, if necessary.
3. Hold down the form-feed button and, while keeping it down, turn the printer on.

Typical results are shown in Figure 16-10.

Remember, the self-test can be run at any time. It's not necessary for the printer to be connected to a computer (or plugged into a wall outlet) in order to run the test. With a set of fully charged batteries, you can take the printer with you into a stationery store and run your own tests to see which papers give the best results.

Diconix 150 Interface Requirements

All Diconix 150/S serial printers are compatible with the Mac-to-serial-printer cables shown in Chapter 15, Figures 15-5 through 15-7. Diconix 150/P parallel printers require a serial-to-parallel converter as well.

Tables 16-1 through 16-4 contain DIP switch function details for the Diconix 150 printer and show the correct settings for use with GDT Softworks' Diconix 150 Macintosh driver. These settings differ from the Kodak Diconix M150 Plus settings shown in Figure 16-6. To run the M150 Plus printer, you absolutely need the bundled Kodak driver. To run the 150/S, you need the optional GDT driver or some other third-party equivalent. *Neither driver is capable of running the other printer.*

Table 16-1. Diconix 150/S DIP Switch SW1 Function Details

Switch	Function	On/Up	Off/Down	US-Mac/GDT-Driver Setting
1-1	CR code	CR + LF	CR	Off
1-2	LF code	LF	CR + LF	Off
1-3	Perforation	1-inch skip	No skip	Off
1-4	Paper length	12 inch	11 inch	Off
1-5	Font Selection	NLQ	Draft	Off
1-6	Emulation	IBM	Epson	Off
1-7	Alphabet	See Table 16-2		Off
1-8	Alphabet	See Table 16-2		Off
1-9	Alphabet	See Table 16-2		Off
1-10	not used			Off

```
*****************************************************************
    INK JET PRINTER      DICONIX      A KODAK COMPANY
*****************************************************************
```

```
 !"#$%&'()*+,-./0123456789:;<=>?@ABCDEFGHIJKLMNOPQRSTUVWXYZ[\]^ `abcdefghijklmnop
qrstuvwxyz{¦}~àèùòì˚£¡¿Ññ¤₧Ååç§ßÆæØø¨ÄÖÜäöüÉé¥ !"#$%&'()*+,-./0123456789:;<=>?@AB
CDEFGHIJKLMNOPQRSTUVWXYZ[\]^ `abcdefghijklmnopqrstuvwxyz{¦}~ !"#$%&'()*+,-./01234
56789:;<=>?@ABCDEFGHIJKLMNOPQRSTUVWXYZ[\]^ `abcdefghijklmnopqrstuvwxyz{¦}~àèùòì˚£
¡¿Ññ¤₧Ååç§ßÆæØø¨ÄÖÜäöüÉé¥ !"#$%&'()*+,-./0123456789:;<=>?@ABCDEFGHIJKLMNOPQRSTUVW
XYZ[\]^ `abcdefghijklmnopqrstuvwxyz{¦}~
```

```
 !"#$%&'()*+,-./0123456789:;<=>?@ABCDEFGHIJKLMNOPQRSTUVWXYZ[\]^ `abcdefghijklmnop
qrstuvwxyz{¦}~àèùòì˚£¡¿Ññ¤₧Ååç§ßÆæØø¨ÄÖÜäöüÉé¥ !"#$%&'()*+,-./0123456789:;<=>?@AB
CDEFGHIJKLMNOPQRSTUVWXYZ[\]^ `abcdefghijklmnopqrstuvwxyz{¦}~ !"#$%&'()*+,-./01234
56789:;<=>?@ABCDEFGHIJKLMNOPQRSTUVWXYZ[\]^ `abcdefghijklmnopqrstuvwxyz{¦}~àèùòì˚£
¡¿Ññ¤₧Ååç§ßÆæØø¨ÄÖÜäöüÉé¥ !"#$%&'()*+,-./0123456789:;<=>?@ABCDEFGHIJKLMNOPQRSTUVW
XYZ[\]^ `abcdefghijklmnopqrstuvwxyz{¦}~
```

```
 !"#$%&'()*+,-./0123456789:;<=>?@ABCDEFGHIJKLMNOPQRSTUVWXYZ[\]^ 'abcdefghijklmnop
qrstuvwxyz{¦}~àèùòì˚£¡¿Ññ¤₧Ååç§ßÆæØø¨ÄÖÜäöüÉé¥ !"#$%&'()*+,-./0123456789:;<=>?@AB
CDEFGHIJKLMNOPQRSTUVWXYZ[\]^ 'abcdefghijklmnopqrstuvwxyz{¦}~ !"#$%&'()*+,-./01234
56789:;<=>?@ABCDEFGHIJKLMNOPQRSTUVWXYZ[\]^ 'abcdefghijklmnopqrstuvwxyz{¦}~àèùòì˚£
¡¿Ññ¤₧Ååç§ßÆæØø¨ÄÖÜäöüÉé¥ !"#$%&'()*+,-./0123456789:;<=>?@ABCDEFGHIJKLMNOPQRSTUVW
XYZ[\]^ 'abcdefghijklmnopqrstuvwxyz{¦}~
```

```
!"#$%&'()*+,-./0123456789:;<=>?@ABCDEFGHIJKLMNOPQRSTUVWXYZ[\]^ `abcdefghijklmnopqrstuvwxyz{¦}~àèùòì˚£¡¿Ññ¤₧Ååç§ßÆæØø¨ÄÖÜäöüÉé¥ !
"#$%&'()*+,-./0123456789:;<=>?@ABCDEFGHIJKLMNOPQRSTUVWXYZ[\]^ `abcdefghijklmnopqrstuvwxyz{¦}~ !"#$%&'()*+,-./0123456789:;<=>?@ABC
DEFGHIJKLMNOPQRSTUVWXYZ[\]^ `abcdefghijklmnopqrstuvwxyz{¦}~àèùòì˚£¡¿Ññ¤₧Ååç§ßÆæØø¨ÄÖÜäöüÉé¥ !"#$%&'()*+,-./0123456789:;<=>?@ABCDE
FGHIJKLMNOPQRSTUVWXYZ[\]^ `abcdefghijklmnopqrstuvwxyz{¦}~
```

```
 !"#$%&'()*+,-./0123456789:;<=>?@ABCDEFGHIJKLMNOPQRSTUVWXYZ[\]^_`abcdefghijklmnop
qrstuvwxyz{¦}~àèùòì˚£¡¿Ññ¤₧Ååç§ßÆæØø¨ÄÖÜäöüÉé¥ !"#$%&'()*+,-./0123456789:;<=>?@AB
CDEFGHIJKLMNOPQRSTUVWXYZ[\]^_`abcdefghijklmnopqrstuvwxyz{¦}~ !"#$%&'()*+,-./01234
56789:;<=>?@ABCDEFGHIJKLMNOPQRSTUVWXYZ[\]^_`abcdefghijklmnopqrstuvwxyz{¦}~àèùòì˚£
¡¿Ññ¤₧Ååç§ßÆæØø¨ÄÖÜäöüÉé¥ !"#$%&'()*+,-./0123456789:;<=>?@ABCDEFGHIJKLMNOPQRSTUVW
XYZ[\]^_`abcdefghijklmnopqrstuvwxyz{¦}~
```

```
!"#$%&'()*+,-./0123456789:;<=>?@ABCDEFGHIJKLMNOPQRSTUVWXYZ[\]^_`abcdefghijklmnopqrstuvwxyz{¦}~àèùòì˚£¡¿Ññ¤₧Ååç§ßÆæØø¨ÄÖÜäöüÉé¥ !
"#$%&'()*+,-./0123456789:;<=>?@ABCDEFGHIJKLMNOPQRSTUVWXYZ[\]^_`abcdefghijklmnopqrstuvwxyz{¦}~ !"#$%&'()*+,-./0123456789:;<=>?@ABC
DEFGHIJKLMNOPQRSTUVWXYZ[\]^_`abcdefghijklmnopqrstuvwxyz{¦}~àèùòì˚£¡¿Ññ¤₧Ååç§ßÆæØø¨ÄÖÜäöüÉé¥ !"#$%&'()*+,-./0123456789:;<=>?@ABCDE
FGHIJKLMNOPQRSTUVWXYZ[\]^_`abcdefghijklmnopqrstuvwxyz{¦}~
```

Figure 16-10 Diconix 150/P self-test results.

Table 16-2. Diconix 150/S DIP Switch SW 1-7 through SW 1-9 (Alphabet Selection) Settings

SW 1-7	SW 1-8	SW 1-9	Alphabet Selection
Off	Off	Off	American English
On	On	Off	European English
Off	On	Off	German
On	Off	Off	French
On	Off	On	Swedish
Off	On	On	Italian
On	On	On	Spanish
Off	Off	On	Danish

Table 16-3. Diconix 150/S Serial DIP Switch Function Details

Switch	Function	On/Up	Off/Down	US-Mac/GDT-Driver Setting
1	Baud rate	See Table 16-4		Off
2	Baud rate	See Table 16-4		Off
3	Baud rate	See Table 16-4		Off
4	Data bits	8 bits	7 bits	Off
5	Parity	See Table 16-5		Off
6	Parity	See Table 16-5		Off
7	Handshaking	See Table 16-6		Off
8	Handshaking	See Table 16-6		Off
1	CD line	Disabled	Enabled	On
2	CTS line	Disabled	Enabled	On
3	DSR line	Disabled	Enabled	On

Table 16-4. Diconix 150\S Serial DIP Switch Baud-Rate Settings

1	2	3	Baud-Rate	Stop Bits
Off	Off	Off	9600 baud	1
Off	Off	On	4800 baud	1
Off	On	Off	2400 baud	1
Off	On	On	1200 baud	1
On	Off	Off	600 baud	1
On	Off	On	300 baud	1
On	On	Off	300 baud	2
On	On	On	110 baud	2

Table 16-5. Diconix 150/S Serial DIP Switch Parity Settings

5	6	Parity
Off	Off	None
Off	On	Even
On	Off	Odd
On	On	Not Used

Table 16-6. Diconix 150/S Serial DIP Switch Handshaking Settings

7	8	Handshaking
Off	Off	Ready/busy
Off	On	X-ON/X-OFF
On	Off	ETX/ACK
On	On	Not Used

Diconix 150/S Setup Secrets

As explained in Chapter 3, the standard graphics resolution on a 9-pin ImageWriter printer is 72 × 72 dpi, the same as the Macintosh computer display. Since the standard graphics resolution on a 12-jet Diconix 150 is 96 × 96 dpi, text and graphics are printed at 33% higher resolution (96 dpi ÷ 72 dpi = 1.33) but at 75% reduction (72 dpi ÷ 96 dpi = 0.75). For the fastest-possible print speed, the GDT driver does not rescale the bit map. Instead, you have to compensate manually, by increasing the font size and adjusting the page setup. The procedure is logical, but not obvious.

Font Size and Page Setup... for Use with Desktop Macs Best results on a standard-size 512 × 342 dpi (7.11 × 4.75-inch) Macintosh display are obtained using the Geneva 14 font (not Geneva 12). When printed at 75% reduction, Geneva 14 output is very close to normal-size Geneva 12.

For a 1-inch top margin, enter 0.8 inches (not 0.75 inches) in the Page Setup... dialog box. The 0.05-inch difference has to do with the printer's hardware margin. The bottom margin should be set to 1.3 inches. Anything less, and footers may not print properly.

Centering requires a 1.9-inch left margin and a 0.0-inch right margin. The left indent marker on the document ruler should be set to 0. The right indent marker should be set to 6.5 inches.

Given this page setup, 4⅞-inches of body text (6.5-inch ruler width × 0.75 reduction = 4.875 inches) is nicely centered on a page with 1$^{13}/_{16}$ -inch left and right margins. The top and bottom margins both work out to approximately 1 inch. Headers and footers print fine. The document looks fine, like it was formatted in 12-point Geneva, and printed full size in Faster quality using an ImageWriter II.

Font Size and Page Setup... for Use with Laptop Macs Best results on a extended-size 640 × 480 dpi (8.89 × 6.67-inch) Macintosh display are also obtained using the Geneva 14 font. When printed at 75% reduction, Geneva 14 output is very close to normal-size Geneva 12.

For a 1-inch top margin, enter 0.8 inches (not 0.75 inches) in the Page Setup... dialog box. The 0.05-inch difference has to do with the printer's hardware margin. The bottom margin should be set to 1.3 inches. Anything less, and footers may not print properly.

Centering requires a 1.2-inch left margin and a 0.0 inch right margin. The left indent marker on the document ruler should be set to 0. The right indent marker should be set to 8.5 inches.

Given this page setup, 6⅜ inches of body text (8.5-inch ruler width × 0.75 reduction = 6.375 inches) is nicely centered on a page with 1$^{1}/_{16}$ -inch left and right margins. The top and bottom margins both work out to approximately 1 inch. Headers and footers print fine. The document looks fine, like it was formatted in 12-point Geneva, and printed full size, in Faster quality using an ImageWriter II.

Print... Options for Use with all Macs Unlike the driver bundled with the M150 Plus which uses ATM-outline fonts, and the ImageWriter driver which uses 1× or 2× bitmapped fonts, GDT's Diconix 150 Macintosh driver uses 1× bitmapped fonts only. It doesn't benefit from ATM and it doesn't matter whether or not a 2× bitmapped font is installed in the System file. The only font used for both standard and double-quality printing is the 1× font. This cuts down on image processing and results in very fast printing.

Compared to the M150 Plus driver (running on an M150 Plus), GDT's driver (running on a 150/S) is *much* faster. In addition, printing starts immediately, without delay. Resolution is lower, so the output is lighter. Really dark printing is possible, but only for bold type styles.

Next we'll look at a 50-jet printer, the Hewlett-Packard DeskWriter.

Hewlett-Packard DeskWriter

As shown in Figure 16-11, the Hewlett-Packard (HP) DeskWriter is a compact-size, ink-jet printer with an 9-inch-wide carriage.

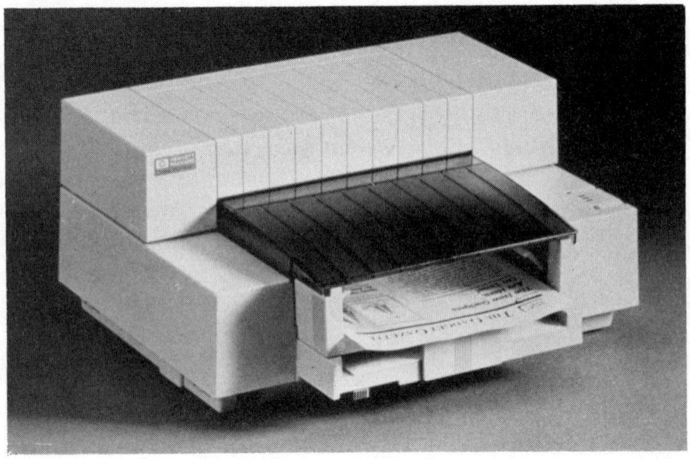

Figure 16-11 Hewlett-Packard DeskWriter. *(Courtesy Hewlett-Packard.)*

Compact size means that the printer is smaller than a LaserWriter and lighter than an ImageWriter. At 14⅓ pounds, the DeskWriter is 24 pounds lighter than an ImageWriter LQ, and 10 pounds lighter than an ImageWriter II.

Ink-jet describes the print head. The DeskWriter's print head has 50 nozzles which draw liquid ink from a reservoir and *shoot* it onto the paper. The ink-jets are like tiny water pistols. All you hear is a soft sound as the carrier mechanism moves the print head back and forth.

Hewlett-Packard DeskWriter Printer-Driver Requirements

Figures 16-12 and 16-13 show the Page Setup... and Print... dialog boxes from the factory bundled DeskWriter printer driver. Factory bundled means that the driver is packed with the printer. You don't have to buy it separately.

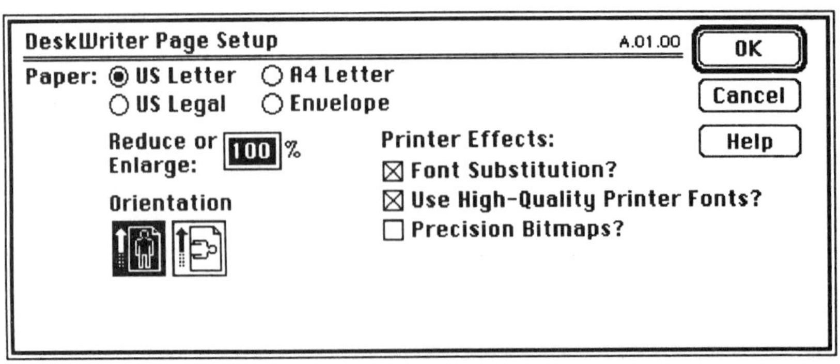

Figure 16-12 Page Setup... dialog box from the Hewlett-Packard DeskWriter printer driver.

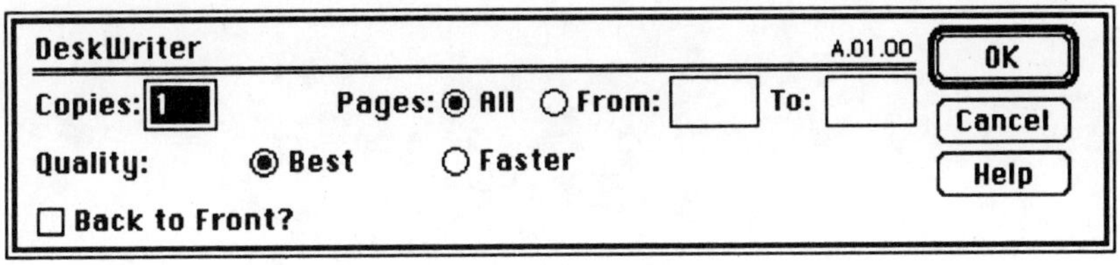

Figure 16-13 Print... dialog box from the Hewlett-Packard DeskWriter printer driver.

The bundled driver is supplied with 13 AGFA-Compugraphic outline fonts, including CS Courier, CS Times, CS Triumvirate (Helvetica), and CS Symbol. The driver also works with Adobe Type Manager software and is able to scale 4× bitmapped fonts, just like the LaserWriter IISC.

Everything about the driver works exactly as you'd expect it to work. Headers, footers, and margins print perfectly. Best quality pages take about a minute to print, which also compares to a LaserWriter IISC.

Hewlett-Packard DeskWriter Print-Head Requirements

DeskWriter print heads (also known as cartridges) have a finite shelf life. Factory sealed cartridges last up to 18 months. Once opened, they only last 90 days, whether you use them or not.

Cartridge packages are normally stamped with an expiration date. The cartridge itself is normally stamped with an 8-character manufacturing code just above the contacts indicated by the plastic wand in Figure 16-14.

The first number of the manufacturing code (third digit from the left) identifies the year of manufacture. The next two numbers of the manufacturing code (fourth and fifth digits from the left) identify the month of manufacture. The next two digits (six and seventh digits from the left) identify the day. Deciphering from right to left, a cartridge marked "AX91110A-3" indicates that it was manufactured 10/11/89. The anticipated expiration date would be 18 months later, or 4/11/91.

When unwrapping and installing the DeskWriter print head, it's important to stay away from the copper contacts. The contacts aren't *particularly* fragile, but oil and/or scratches on the contacts can stop one or more of the ink jets from working.

Hewlett-Packard DeskWriter Paper Requirements

In Best quality, the DeskWriter produces great-looking 300 × 300-dpi output, at 1 page per minute, regardless of paper. Some papers work better than others, but the paper selection *is not* critical. Copy paper is

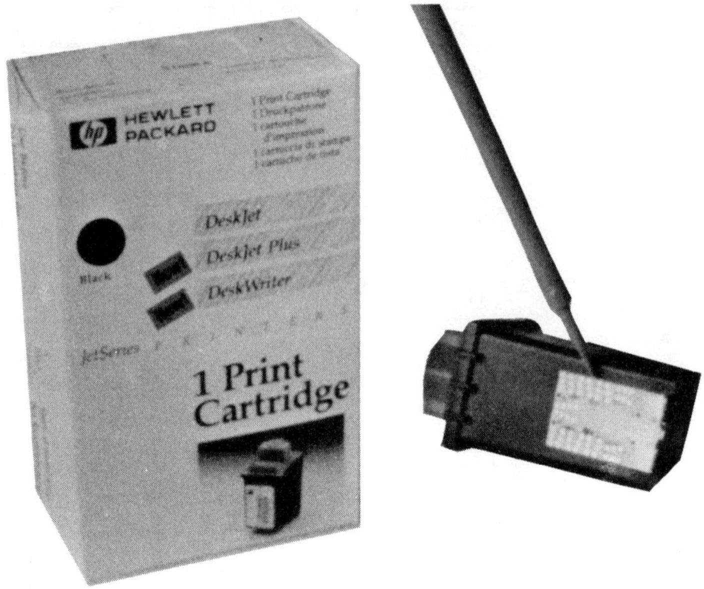

Figure 16-14 Hewlett-Packard DeskWriter print head.

fine. Letterhead stationery is fine. Anything that works in an ImageWriter II sheet feeder is fine.

DeskWriter 300 × 300 dpi output is virtually indistinguishable from LaserWriter IISC output. In Faster quality, resolution drops to 150 × 150 dpi, but speed doubles to 2 pages per minute. The 150 × 150 dpi is comparable to Best quality ImageWriter II output, except that the pages come out *much* faster and the printer makes *much* less noise.

The DeskWriter is not equipped with tractors. The paper tray is designed for cut sheets and envelopes only, just like a laser printer.

Hewlett-Packard DeskWriter Self-Tests

The DeskWriter is equipped with three built-in self-tests. The first test checks general mechanical and electrical fitness. This test runs automatically every time you turn the printer on. If the test fails, all of the keyboard (control panel) lights blink on and off. If the test passes, any paper that might have been in the mechanism is ejected, and the printer brings itself on line.

The second test checks the ink supply and the print head. To run the print-head self-test:

1. Turn the printer off, if necessary.
2. Hold down the *select* button and, while keeping it down, turn the printer on.

Typical results are shown in Figure 16-15.

```
ID H

2278 - 1.112   89/03/10
```

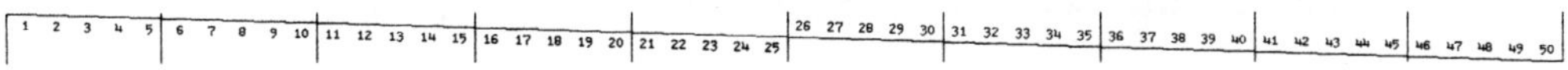

Figure 16-15 Hewlett-Packard DeskWriter print-head self-test results.

As shown in the test pattern, the individual ink-jets are numbered from 1 to 50. Malfunctioning jets (when applicable) are indicated by gaps in the diagonal line. The numbers of the malfunctioning jets (when applicable) are printed just in front of the print-head ID.

The third test checks the DeskWriter's RS-422A serial-interface. This test requires a mini-8 DIN loopback plug. Wiring details are given in Chapter 11, Figure 11-37. To run the loopback test:

1. Turn the printer off, if necessary.
2. Disconnect the Mac-to-DeskWriter cable from the bottom of the printer, if necessary.
3. Insert a properly constructed, mini-8 DIN loopback plug into the printer cable socket.
4. Hold down the *prime* button and the *select* button and while keeping them down, turn the printer on.

Typical results are shown in Figure 16-16.

If the printer fails this test, assuming the loopback plug is correctly wired and securely attached, there's probably something wrong with the printer's logic board. If the printer passes this test, but fails to print when connected to a Macintosh, there's either something wrong with the cable, the printer driver, or the Macintosh logic board. Most likely you have loose connections, or the Chooser desk accessory (DA) needs to be informed about the DeskWriter printer resource. The Chooser desk accessory is described in Chapter 1. The Macintosh logic board can be cleared by running TCG's loopback test described in Chapter 11.

Hewlett-Packard DeskWriter Interface Requirements

The DeskWriter is factory bundled with an Apple-compatible System/Peripheral-8 cable, wired exactly the same as the cable shown in Chapter 10, Figure 10-19. Other requirements are enhanced (Mac Plus or better) ROMs, 1 Mb RAM, two 800K drives (or one 800K drive and a hard drive), and System 4.1 (or later). The printer has no DIP switches and no font-cartridge slots.

Figure 16-16 Hewlett-Packard DeskWriter loopback test results.

The size of the built-in communications buffer is 12 kilobytes. The serial interface meets the RS-422A (not RS-232C) standard. Data-terminal-ready (DTR) handshaking is assumed. Baud rate (data-transfer speed) is fixed at 57.6 kilobaud. By way of comparison, the fastest the ImageWriter LQ can transfer data is 19.2 kilobaud. The fastest the ImageWriter II can transfer data is 9.6 kilobaud.

Hewlett-Packard DeskWriter Setup Secrets

The DeskWriter has a dual-purpose paper loader designed strictly for use with cut-sheet paper and business-size envelopes. Table 16-7 lists the supported paper sizes.

Table 16-7. Hewlett-Packard DeskWriter-Supported Paper Sizes

Stock	Paper Size	Page Size (Printable Area)
U.S. Letter	8.5 × 11.0 inches	8.0 × 10.15 inches
U.S. Legal	8.5 × 14.0 inches	8.0 × 13.15 inches
A4	210 × 297 millimeter	203 × 334 millimeter
No.10 envelope	4.12 × 9.5 inches	3.69 × 8.0 inches

The input tray capacity is 100 sheets. Paper weight is 16 to 24 pounds. Cut sheets feed automatically; envelopes have to be hand fed, just like a LaserWriter IISC. Since it takes a few seconds for the ink to dry, it's important that printed pages be allowed to drop into the output tray. If you pull them out of the printer before they drop, it might cause a smear.

Hewlett-Packard DeskJet and DeskJet Plus Printers

With a different control panel and logic board, this very same printer is sold into the PC-compatible market as a DeskJet Plus. An earlier model was simply called the DeskJet (no Plus). Both printers are designed to work with **font cartridges**, which contain the hardware equivalent of high-resolution software fonts. Two font cartridges alongside a DeskJet Plus are shown in Figure 16-17.

Since an ever-increasing number of Mac owners are investing in PC-compatible computers as well as Macs, this section shows how to connect PC-compatible DeskJet and PC-compatible DeskJet Plus printers to a Macintosh.

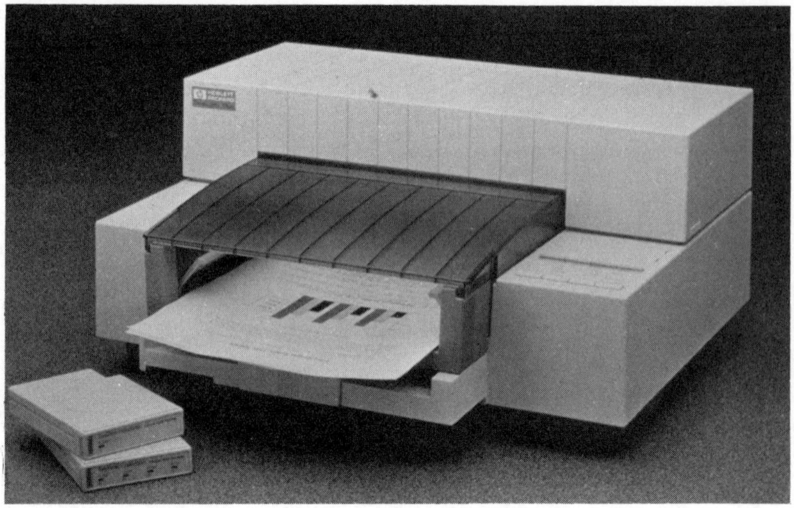

Figure 16-17 Hewlett-Packard DeskJet Plus. *(Courtesy Hewlett-Packard.)*

Since an ever-increasing number of Mac owners are investing in PC-compatible computers as well as Macs, this section shows how to connect PC-compatible DeskJet and PC-compatible DeskJet Plus printers to a Macintosh.

Hewlett-Packard DeskJet and DeskJet Plus Printer-Driver Requirements

Familiar-looking Page Setup... and Print... dialog boxes from the JetLink Express, a DeskJet/DeskJet Plus/DeskWriter-compatible Macintosh printer driver developed by GDT Softworks are shown in Figures 16-18 and 16-21. Figures 16-19 and 16-20 show the Page Setup... Options and Page Setup... Help dialog boxes. Figure 16-22 shows the Print... Help dialog box.

The GDT driver is supplied with 13 outline fonts, including Courier, Courier.B, Courier.BI, Courier.I, GDT Helv, GDT Helv.B, GDT Helv.BI, GDT Helv.I, GDT Tvmes, GDT Tvmes.B, GDT Tvmes.BI, GDT Tvmes.I, and Symbol. These fonts correspond to the Courier, Helvetica, Times, and Symbol bitmapped fonts generally supplied with Macintosh System software. The driver also works with Adobe Type Manager software.

As shown in Figures 16-19 through 16-22, JetLink Express version 1.0.2 supports four graphics resolutions (not just two), optional font cartridges, and bitmapped font substitution. The baud rate is also selectable. Holding down the option key while clicking the Help button in the Page Setup... dialog box returns the communications dialog box shown in Figure 16-23.

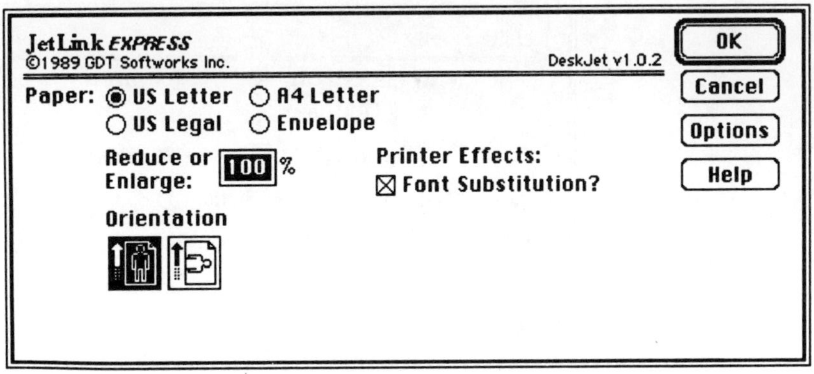

Figure 16-18 Page Setup... dialog box from GDT Softworks' JetLink Express Macintosh printer driver, version 1.0.2.

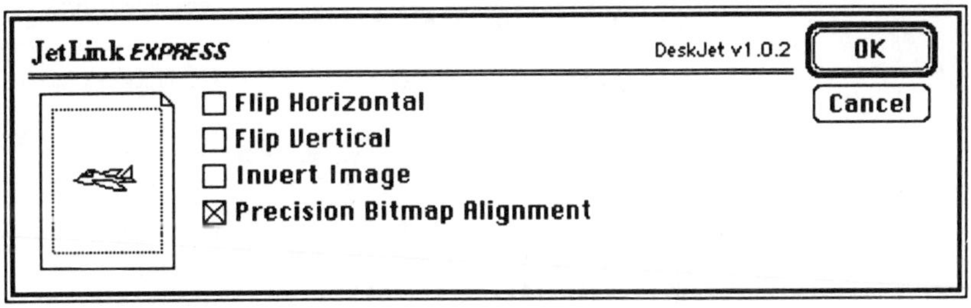

Figure 16-19 Page Setup... Options dialog box from GDT Softworks' JetLink Express Macintosh printer driver, version 1.0.2.

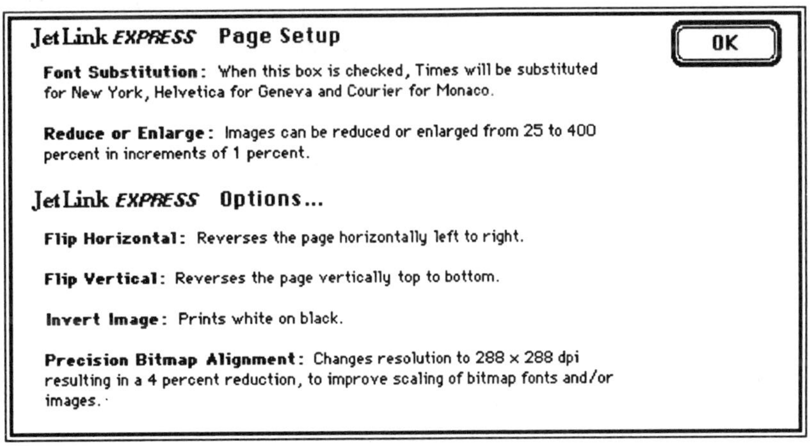

Figure 16-20 Page Setup... Help dialog box from GDT Softworks' JetLink Express Macintosh printer driver, version 1.0.2.

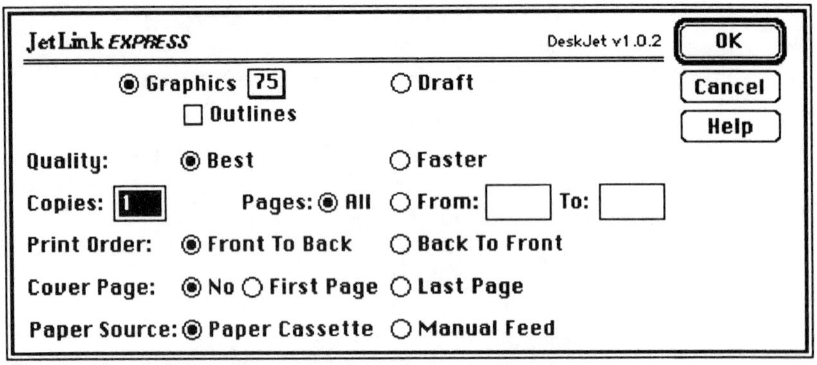

Figure 16-21 Print... dialog box from GDT Softworks' JetLink Express Macintosh printer driver, version 1.0.2.

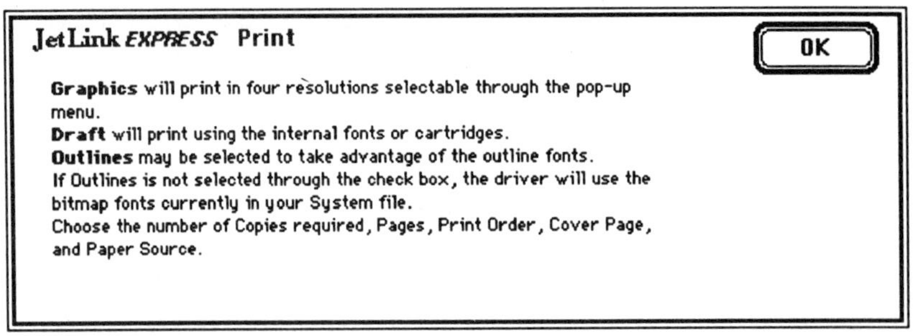

Figure 16-22 Print... Help dialog box from GDT Softworks' JetLink Express Macintosh printer driver, version 1.0.2.

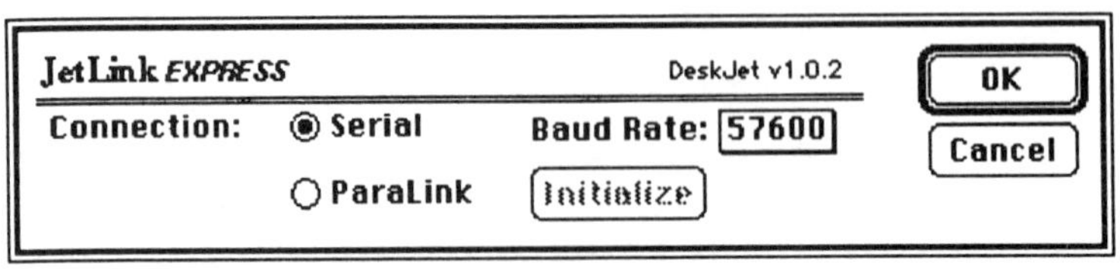

Figure 16-23 Communications dialog box from GDT Softworks' JetLink Express Macintosh printer driver, version 1.0.2.

As shown in Chapter 15, Figure 15-14, clicking on the currently selected baud rate returns a pop-up menu. The default baud rate, 9600, matches the factory setting for DeskJet and DeskJet Plus printers. An optional baud rate, 19,200, matches the optional 19,200-baud DIP switch setting for DeskJet and DeskJet Plus printers. The fastest baud rate, 57,600, matches the factory setting for DeskWriters. By correctly matching the driver's baud rate to the printer's baud rate (9600, 19,200, or

57,600), you can use the GDT driver with both DeskJets and DeskWriters. In contrast, the bundled DeskWriter driver *only* works with DeskWriters. Other requirements are similar. Both drivers require Mac Plus (or better) ROMs, 1 Mb RAM, two 800K drives (or one 800K drive and a hard drive), and System 4.1 (or later). Neither driver works with original-equipment 512K Macs, Lisas, and Mac XLs running under earlier System software.

Alternate DeskJet/DeskJet Plus Printer Drivers

Figures 16-24 and 16-25 show the Page Setup... and Print... dialog boxes from the Printer Interface III, a DeskJet/DeskJet Plus-compatible Macintosh printer driver developed by DataPak Software. Figure 16-26 shows the Print... Options dialog box.

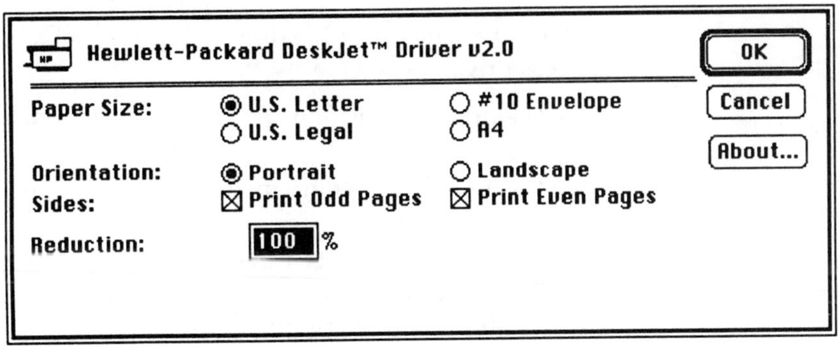

Figure 16-24 Page Setup... dialog box from DataPak Software's Printer Interface III, HP-DeskJet driver v2.0.

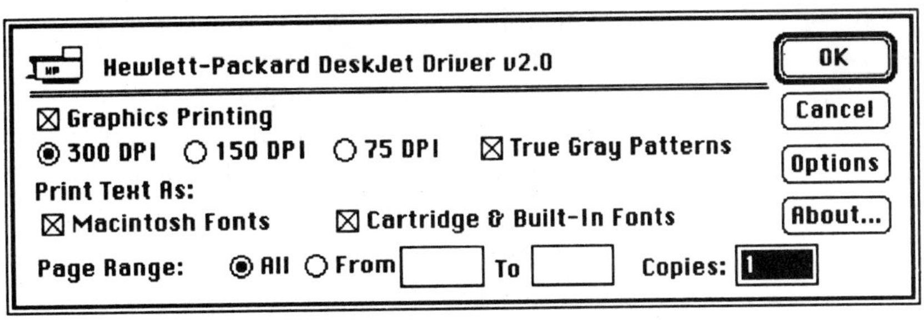

Figure 16-25 Print... dialog box from DataPak Software's Printer Interface III, HP-DeskJet driver v2.0.

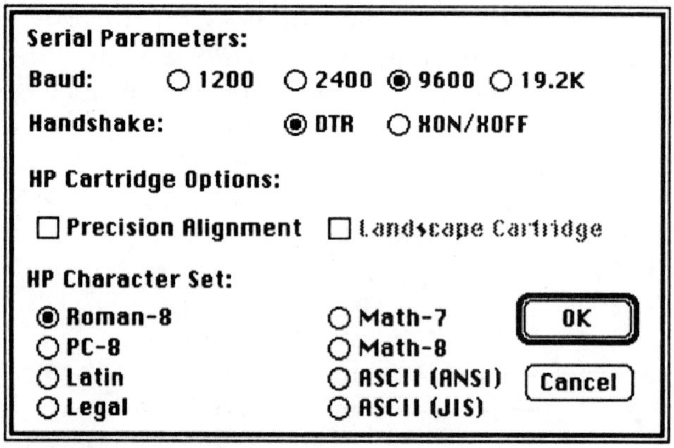

Figure 16-26 Print... Options dialog box from DataPak Software's Printer Interface III, HP-DeskJet driver v2.0.

Printer Interface III differs from the DeskWriter and JetLink-Express drivers in several ways:

1. The driver size is only 27 kilobytes, about half the size of the other drivers.
2. The minimum requirements are 512K of memory and one 400K disk drive.
3. The driver supports three graphics resolutions (75, 150, and 300 dpi), built-in fonts, and optional font cartridges. Bitmapped font substitution (using font cartridges, not outline fonts) is automatic. If there's no font cartridge to match the screen font, the driver automatically scales 4× bitmapped fonts, just like a LaserWriter IISC. If 4× bitmapped fonts are unavailable, the driver automatically scales 2× bitmapped fonts, just like an ImageWriter II. If neither 4× nor 2× bitmapped fonts are available, the driver uses 1x bitmapped fonts. 4× scaling results in 300 dpi; 2× scaling results in 150 dpi; 1× without scaling results in 75 dpi. Without ATM, outline fonts *are not* supported.
4. DTR *as well as* X-ON/X-OFF handshaking is supported. The baud rate is selectable from 1200 baud to 19.2 kilobaud.
5. When used with the DeskJet's built-in fonts and/or with optional font cartridges at 19.2 kilobaud, 300-dpi throughput is better than 2 pages per minute, *twice as fast* as a DeskWriter, which relies on outline fonts at 57.6 kilobaud.

Another difference has to do with printer compatibility. The factory bundled DeskWriter driver is only compatible with the DeskWriter. The Printer Interface III is only compatible with the DeskJet and the DeskJet Plus. The JetLink Express is compatible with both DeskJet printers and with the DeskWriter.

The point we're trying to make here is that there are even more DeskJet printer-driver choices than there are ImageWriter printer-driver choices. All three drivers are 100% satisfactory.

Hewlett-Packard DeskJet and DeskJet Plus Interface Requirements

All HP DeskJets, whether suffixed with Plus or not, are compatible with the Mac-to-serial-printer cables given in Chapter 15, Figures 15-5 through 15-7. They're also compatible with Mac-to-Imagewriter (Standard and Wide) cables and with Centronics-compatible parallel cables. Interface switching (from serial to parallel) is automatic. Just by connecting both cables, the printer can be shared between a Macintosh and a PC-compatible unit. Line switchboxes are not necessary!

The size of the built-in communications buffer is 12 kilobytes. The serial interface meets the RS-232C (not RS-422A) standard. Both transmission-on/transmission-off (X-ON/X-OFF) and data-terminal-ready (DTR) handshaking are supported. Baud rate is adjustable from 1.2 to 19.2 kilobaud.

Tables 16-8 through 16-13 contain DIP switch function details for the DeskJet and the DeskJet Plus and give recommended settings for use with JetLink Express and/or Printer Interface III. The DIP switches are located just under the input tray, as shown in Figure 16-27.

Table 16-8. Hewlett-Packard DeskJet Plus DIP Switch A Function Details

Switch	Function	Up	Down	US/Mac Setting
A-1	Character Set	See Table 16-9		Up
A-2	Character Set	See Table 16-9		Down
A-3	Character Set	See Table 16-9		Up
A-4	Character Set	See Table 16-9		Down
A-5	Paper Size	See Table 16-10		Down
A-6	Paper Size	See Table 16-10		Down
A-7	CR code	CR = CR + LF	CR = CR	Down
A-8	Perf. Skip	Don't Skip	Skip	Up

Table 16-9. Hewlett-Packard DeskJet Plus DIP Switch A-1 Through A-4 (Character-Set Selection) Settings

A-1	A-2	A-3	A-4	Character Set
Down	Down	Down	Down	PC-8
Down	Down	Down	Up	Roman-8
Down	Down	Up	Down	PC-8 D/N
Down	Down	Up	Up	ISO United Kingdom
Down	Up	Down	Down	ISO Germany
Down	Up	Down	Up	ISO France
Down	Up	Up	Down	ISO Italy
Down	Up	Up	Up	ISO Norway
Up	Down	Down	Down	ISO Sweden
Up	Down	Down	Up	ISO Spain
Up	Down	Up	Down	ASCII
Up	Down	Up	Up	ISO Portugal
Up	Up	Down	Down	PC-850
Up	Up	Down	Up	ECMA 94 Latin 1
Up	Up	Up	Down	Legal
Up	Up	Up	Up	Default to font cartridge

Table 16-10. Hewlett-Packard DeskJet Plus DIP Switch A-5 and A-6 (Paper-Size) Settings

A-5	A-6	Paper Size
Down	Down	U.S. Letter (8.5 × 11 inch)
Down	Up	A4 (210 × 297 millimeter)
Up	Down	U.S. Legal (8.5 × 14 inch)
Up	Up	Envelope (4.125 × 9.5 inch)

Table 16-11. Hewlett-Packard DeskJet Plus DIP Switch B Function Details

Switch	Function	Up	Down	US/Mac Setting
B-1	Text scale	66 lines	Disabled	Down
B-2	Resolution	300 ppi	75 ppi	Down
B-3	Terminal-mode	Enabled	Disabled	Down
B-4	Baud rate	See Table 16-12		Down

(continued)

Table 16-11. *(continued)*

Switch	Function	Up	Down	US/Mac Setting
B-5	Baud rate	See Table 16-12		Up
B-6	Parity/data	See Table 16-13		Down
B-7	Parity/data	See Table 16-13		Down
B-8	Handshaking	DTR	DTR & X-ON/X-OFF	Up

Table 16-12. Hewlett-Packard DeskJet Plus DIP Switch B-4 and B-5 (Baud-Rate) Settings

B-4	B-5	Baud Rate
Down	Down	9600 Baud
Down	Up	19,200 Baud
Up	Down	2400 Baud
Up	Up	1200 Baud

Table 16-13. Hewlett-Packard DeskJet Plus DIP Switch B-6 and B-7 (Parity and Data Bits) Settings

B-6	B-7	Parity	Data Bits
Down	Down	None	8 Data bits
Down	Up	Odd parity	7 Data bits
Up	Down	Even parity	7 Data bits
Up	Up	None	8 Data bits

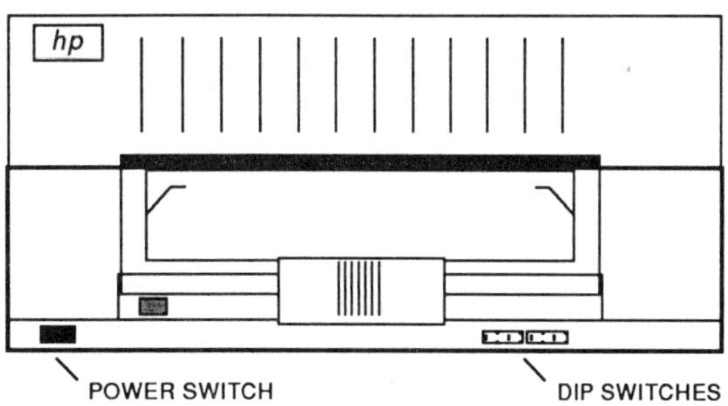

Figure 16-27 Hewlett-Packard DeskJet and DeskJet Plus DIP switch location.

The settings recommended here differ slightly from the PC-compatible factory settings. Specifically, the ASCII character set has been selected and the default 9600-baud data-transfer rate has been increased to 19,200 baud, in order to take full advantage of the printer's built-in 12-kilobyte communications buffer.

Hewlett-Packard DeskJet and DeskJet Plus Self-Tests

The DeskJet Plus is equipped with two built-in self-tests. The first test checks general mechanical and electrical fitness. This test runs automatically every time you turn the printer on. If the test fails, one or more of the keyboard (control panel) lights flash. If the test passes, any paper that might have been in the mechanism is ejected, and the printer brings itself on line.

The second test checks the ink supply and the print head. To run the print-head self-test:

1. Turn the printer off, if necessary.
2. Hold down the FF key and, while keeping it down, turn the printer on.

Typical results are similar to those shown in Figure 16-16, except the built-in character sets are identified by name. Actual results vary depending on whether you have a DeskJet or a DeskJet Plus.

Hewlett-Packard DeskJet, DeskJet Plus, and DeskWriter Electrical Requirements

One of the most remarkable aspects of ink-jet printers, in general, is their low-power requirement. DeskJets only consume 8 watts in standby and 25 watts in service. At 8 watts, turning on a DeskJet is equivalent to switching on a small night light. At 25 watts, printing is exactly the same as switching on a 25-watt table lamp.

By contrast, the LaserWriter IISC consumes 170 watts in standby and *900 watts* in service. That is comparable to running a window-mounted air conditioner. In most cases, to avoid blinking the room lights, you need a dedicated electrical circuit.

As a result of their low power requirements, all HP DeskJet/Desk-Writer models come with external power transformers, similar to the wall-mount transformers used by the Kodak Diconix printers examined earlier in this chapter. A 120-V AC, 60-Hz transformer is standard equipment. International 100-V AC, 50/60-Hz; 220-V AC, 50-Hz; and 240-V AC, 50-Hz transformers are optional. With the correct power transformer, you can connect DeskJets (and DeskJet Plus printers) to almost any computer (not just Macs) to produce 300-dpi documents anywhere in the world.

That's it for Kodak and HP ink-jet printers. Next, we'll look at a 24-pin color printer from Toshiba, the P321SLC.

Toshiba P321SLC

As shown in Figure 16-28, the Toshiba P321SLC is a 24-pin color printer with an 11-inch (not 10-inch) wide carriage.

Figure 16-28 Toshiba P321SLC. *(Courtesy Toshiba America.)*

The Toshiba P321SL (no C) is a monochrome version of the P321SLC. The Toshiba P341SL is a monochrome version with a 15-inch carriage. Given those differences, the information in this section applies to all three printers. In addition, all three use ribbons compatible with Radio Shack's DMP-2100 printer.

Toshiba P321SLC/P321SL/P341SL Printer-Driver Needs

Figures 16-29 and 16-31 show the Page Setup... and Print... dialog boxes from the factory bundled Toshiba printer driver. Figures 16-30 and 16-32 show the Page Setup... and Print... Options dialog boxes.

The driver is supplied with 13 outline fonts, including Courier, Courier.B, Courier.BI, Courier.I, Helvet, Helvet.B, Helvet.BI, Helvet.I, Tms Roman, Tms Roman.B, Tms Roman.BI, Tms Roman.I, and Symbol. These fonts correspond to the Courier, Helvetica, Times, and Symbol bitmapped fonts generally supplied with Macintosh System software. The driver also works with Adobe Type Manager software.

The driver is also supplied with three bitmapped screen fonts: 12-point ToshCourier, 10-point ToshDraft, and 10-point ToshElite. These fonts correspond to the printer's built-in character sets. Unlike Monaco 10 (which corresponds to the ImageWriter II's built-in NLQ character set) the Tosh fonts are legible. By selecting these fonts from the Font menu, perfectly spaced 10- and 12-point text documents can be printed

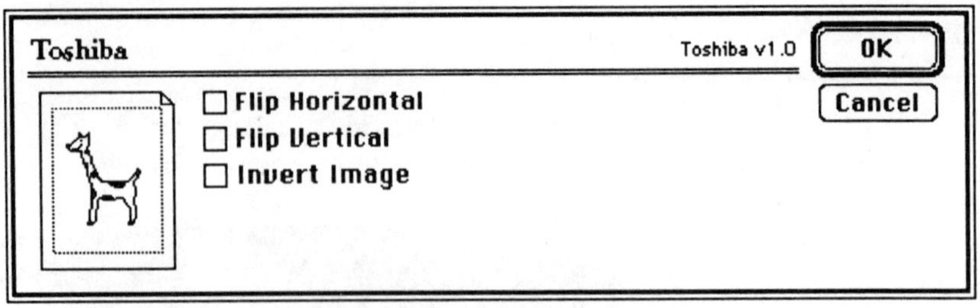

Figure 16-29 Page Setup... dialog box from the Toshiba P321SLC printer driver, version 1.0.

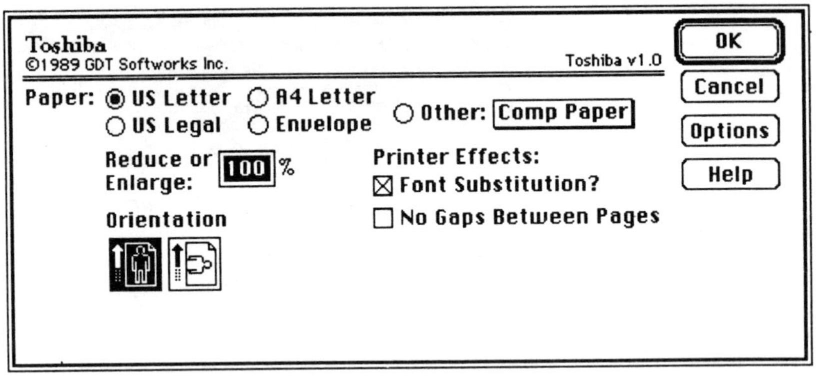

Figure 16-30 Page Setup... Options dialog box from the Toshiba P321SLC printer driver, version 1.0.

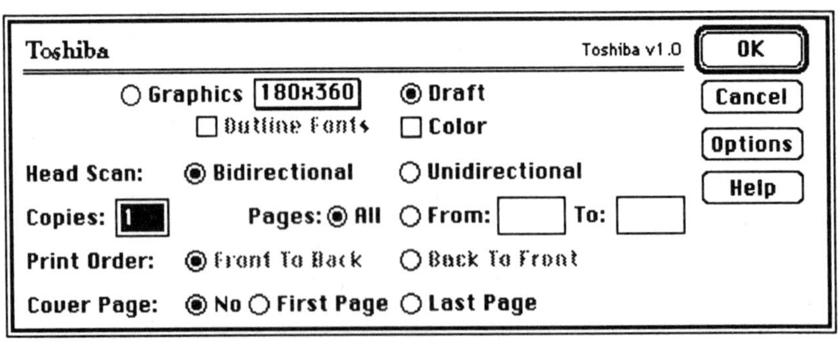

Figure 16-31 Print... dialog box from the Toshiba P321SLC printer driver, version 1.0.

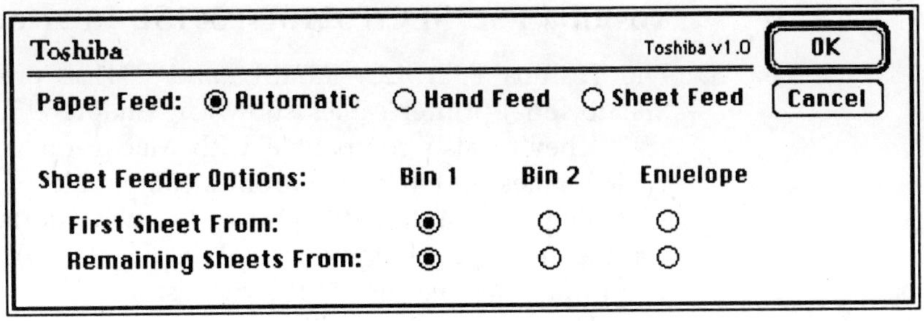

Figure 16-32 Print... Options dialog box from the Toshiba P321SLC printer driver, version 1.0.

in draft mode at very high speeds. ToshDraft is the fastest. ToshCourier and ToshElite are much faster than the equivalent outline fonts printed at the same (maximum) resolution.

As indicated in Figures 16-29 and 16-31, the driver also supports three graphics resolutions (180 × 180, 180 × 360, and 360 × 360), optional font cartridges, and bitmapped font substitution.

The baud rate is also selectable. Holding down the option key, while clicking the Options button in the Page Setup... dialog box, returns the communications dialog box shown in Figure 16-33.

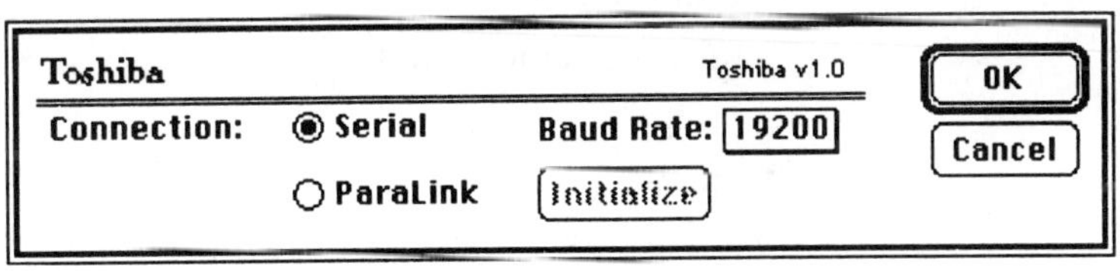

Figure 16-33 Communications dialog box from the Toshiba P321SLC printer driver, version 1.0.

As shown in Chapter 15, Figure 15-14, clicking on the currently selected baud rate returns a pop-up menu. The 19,200 default baud rate is the factory recommended setting for use with P321SL, P321SLC, and P341SL printers. The other rates support additional Toshiba printers, including the Expresswriter 311, when used with an optional serial-to-parallel converter. Serial-to-parallel converters are discussed in Chapter 15.

Other driver requirements include Mac Plus (or better) ROMs, 1 Mb RAM, two 800K (drives or one 800K drive and a hard drive), and System 6.0 (or later). The driver *does not* work with original equipment 512K Macs, Lisas, and Mac XLs running earlier System software.

Toshiba P321SLC/P321SL/P341SL Interface Requirements

The Toshiba P321SLC, P321SL, and P341SL are compatible with the Mac-to-serial-printer cables shown in Chapter 15, Figures 15-5 through 15-7. They're also compatible with Mac-to-Imagewriter (Standard and Wide) cables and with Centronics-compatible parallel cables. Interface switching *is not* automatic. One of the two interfaces has to be selected via the front-panel liquid-crystal-display (LCD) configurations menu. The printer *does not* use DIP switches.

The size of the built-in communications buffer is 32 kilobytes, enough to hold 16 pages of text. The serial interface meets the RS-232C (not RS-422A) standard. X-ON/X-OFF, ETX/ACK, and Rdy/Bsy handshaking are all supported. Baud rate is adjustable from 110 baud to 19.2 kilobaud.

To match the factory bundled Macintosh printer driver shown in Figures 16-29 through 16-33, the printer should be configured for:

1. Toshiba/Qume emulation (not IBM).
2. Serial interface (not parallel).
3. 19.2 kilobaud (not 9600 baud).
4. 8 data bits (not 7).
5. No parity.
6. 1 stop bit (not 2).
7. Rdy/Bsy handshaking.
8. 12 cpi.

These settings disagree with those given on page T6/7 of the *Toshiba P321SLC User's Manual*; nevertheless, they are correct for use with version 1.0 of the factory bundled driver.

Toshiba P321SLC Self-Tests

The Toshiba P321SLC is equipped with a unique built-in self-test. This test demonstrates various printer features and even prints a color-bar chart. To run the self (demonstration) test:

1. Turn the printer off, if necessary.
2. Hold down the EJECT button and, while keeping it down, turn the printer on.
3. Continue holding down the EJECT button until the self-test begins.
4. Let up the EJECT button.

Typical results are shown in Figure 16-34.

TOSHIBA P321SL AND P321SLC

To: One Printer User

From: Another

Subject: Toshiba P321SL and P321SLC

****

After evaluating dozens of models, looking at 9-pin and 24-pin versions, I discovered the Toshiba P321SL and P321SLC -- and let me show you what I got!

HIGH QUALITY - AND SPEED TO MATCH

72 characters per second in letter quality mode.

216 cps in draft mode, one of the fastest printers around.

CONVENIENT, WITH ENHANCED PAPER HANDLING, including fanfold bypass, built-in tractor, tear bar -- and

EASY TO USE, WITH FRONT-PANEL SELECTION of fonts, pitch, emulation, etc. - and NO dip switches!

HIGH RESOLUTION GRAPHICS in black and in color with the P321SLC

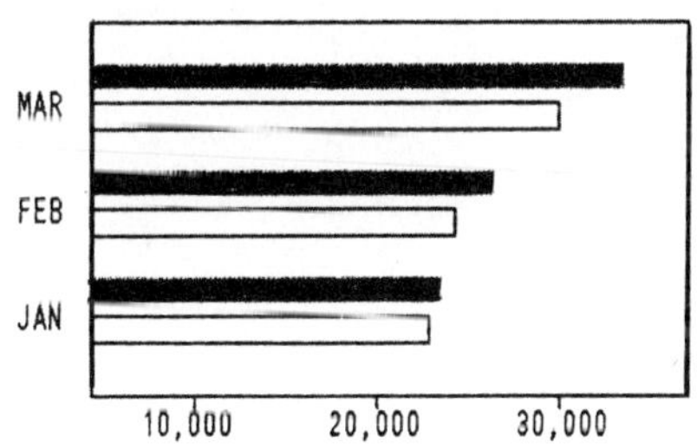

EXPENSES	JAN	FEB	MAR
Rent	4200	4200	4200
Utilities	1706	1110	1015
Maintenance	1435	1435	1435
Salaries	12959	18176	20233
TOTAL	22030	26599	28561

COMPATIBILITY

With convenient font and emulation cards, I have both compatibility with all of my favorite software packages and font flexibility.

I have to close now. For more facts, just ask your sales representative. By the way, the price is amazing -- so close to a basic 9-pin printer that you're in for a pleasant surprise!!

Just sign me . . .

Another Satisfied Toshiba Buyer

Figure 16-34 Toshiba P321SLC self-test results.

Other tests that can be selected via the front-panel configurations menu include a traditional self-test and a bidirectional alignment test.

All tests repeat until you stop them, or until you run out of paper. To stop any test in progress, press the SELECT button.

In Conclusion...

The Toshiba P321SLC supports 360 × 360-dpi *color* graphics, two built-in letter-quality character sets, built-in high-speed draft printing, and outline fonts. It has a built-in parallel port, a built-in serial port, and both *PC and Macintosh compatibility*.... That's an incredible list of features compared to comparably priced ImageWriter printers!

Study Figure 16-34 very carefully. More than any other graphic in the book, it proves our basic premise. With the correct communications settings, a properly constructed serial cable, and the right printer driver, you can have any printer you like on a Macintosh—any printer, any Macintosh.

APPENDIX

A

Glossary

A Size—refers to US letter-size paper measuring 8.5 × 11 inches.

A4 Letter—refers to European letter-size paper measuring 210 × 297 millimeters.

A4 Size—refers to European letter-size paper measuring 210 × 297 millimeters.

AC—an acronym for alternating current. In the United States, the polarity of the line voltage alternates 60 times a second. Different from direct current, where the polarity of the line voltage always stays the same.

Acronym—a term formed by combining the first letter (or letters) of the words in a popular expression. "What you see is what you get" becomes WYSIWYG.

Adobe Type Manager—a CDEV (control device) that adds outline-font technology to *existing* Macintosh System software (versions 6.0.2 to 6.0.4) and to *existing* Macintosh printer drivers.

Apple-Compatible—refers to any printer designed to respond properly to Apple control codes.

Apple Control Codes—a series of printer instructions understood by Apple-compatible printer ROMs.

AppleTalk—the networking protocol built into every Macintosh.

Ascent—the height of the tallest character in a font. Ascent is measured from the baseline up.

ASCII—an acronym for American Standard Code for Information Interchange (pronounced ASK-ee).

ATM—an acronym for Adobe Type Manager.

Baseline—the invisible plane from which all uppercase characters ascend.

Baud Rate—the speed at which binary digits (1s and 0s) are sent down the printer cable. Named for data communications pioneer, Emile Baudot.

Bidirectional Printing—printing which takes place in two directions. Even-numbered passes print from left to right. Odd-numbered passes print from right to left. Faster than unidirectional printing.

Binary Numbering System—a numbering system built on a base of only two digits. All digits are either 1s or 0s. Places increment by powers of 2 instead of by powers of 10.

Bit—a contraction of **bi**nary digi**t**. There are 8 bits in a byte; there are two bytes (16 bits) in a word.

Bit Map—a connect-the-dot coordinate system whereby text and graphics are filled in (printed) dot-by-dot using binary numbers. Each set of coordinates is marked with a 1 or a 0. A 1 means fill in (or print) the dot. A 0 means don't fill in (or don't print) the dot. Bit maps are useful for displaying (and printing) text and graphics, but they limit resolution and require several bytes per character. Bit maps are much slower and much less efficient than ASCII text, where each character is represented by a single byte.

BOB—an acronym for breakout box, a device used to jumper serial connections.

Boldface Printing—all dots are printed twice for greater intensity. Differs from double-strike printing in that the second strike takes place horizontally. Characters get wider and darker, but not any taller.

Buffer—the printer's random-access memory (RAM), measured in kilobytes. Since computer chips can transfer data much faster than mechanical printer mechanisms can reproduce it, small buffers are generally inserted between the two, to keep the data flow in check. Without a buffer, data transfers would generally have to take place between 300 and 1200 baud. Standard 2K buffers support 9600 baud, which significantly decreases print job time.

Byte—an 8-bit binary number which generally represents an alphanumeric character, a piece of a graphic, a control code, or some other computer instruction.

Carrier Rod—a steel bar which supports or carries the ribbon-cartridge deck.

CDEV—an acronym for control device.

Character—a dot arrangement that resembles a letter, a number, or some other symbolic communication.

Character Deviation—the alignment difference which sometimes results when text and graphics are printed bidirectionally.

Character Rectangle—a nonprinting box that limits the height and width of each character.

Chassis—the metal frames of machines and electrical devices.

Choose Printer—an early version of the Chooser desk accessory used to select Macintosh printer drivers and to indicate the selected printer port.

Chooser—a desk accessory used to select Macintosh printer drivers and to indicate the selected printer port.

Clear to Send—Under RS-232, pin 5 of the DB-25 connector is used to indicate that the modem has connected and enabled its carrier.

Closed—an abbreviation for closed circuit. A closed circuit is said to be ON. Different from an open circuit, which is said to be OFF.

Communications Buffer—the printer's random-access memory (RAM), measured in kilobytes. Since computer chips can transfer data bytes much faster than mechanical printer mechanisms can reproduce them, small buffers are generally inserted between the two to keep the data flow in check. Without a buffer, data transfers would generally have to take place at between 300 and 1200 baud. Standard 2K buffers support 9600 baud, which significantly decreases print-job time.

Control Codes—nonprinting computer instructions like carriage return, line feed, etc.

Cpi—an acronym for characters per inch. Each and every character in the Pica-10 character set measures 1⁄10-inch wide, resulting in 10 characters per inch. Each and every character in the Elite-12 character set measures 1⁄12-inch wide, resulting in 12 characters per inch. Cpi is synonymous with pitch.

Cps—in theory, an acronym for characters per second. In practice, cps often represents characters per fractional second. Running a 3-minute mile is not the same as running 20 miles per hour.

CTS—an acronym for clear to send.

Current—refers to the flow of electricity in the same way that it refers to the flow of water.

Data Bits—the 7 or 8 binary digits within a byte. Different from start bits or stop bits which are inserted between bytes.

Data Set—in reference to RS-232 devices, a synonym for modem.

Data Set Ready—DSR Under RS-232, pin 6 of the DB-25 connector is used by modems to indicate they are powered up and ready.

Data Terminal—in reference to RS-232 devices, a synonym for computer or printer.

Data Terminal Ready—DTR Under RS-232, pin 20 of the DB-25 connector is used by computers and printers to indicate they are powered up and ready. Also, a type of hardware handshaking which relies on a connection to pin 20. Some ImageWriter cables were built without that connection, which caused all kinds of problems.

DB-9 Shell—the metal or plastic housing for a DB-9 connector.

DB-9F Connector—a DB-9 female connector has 9 holes or sockets. Same as a DB-9S. Different from a DB-9 male connector which has 9 plugs or pins.

DB-9M Connector—a DB-9 male connector has 9 plugs or pins. Same as a DB-9P. Different from a DB-9 female connector which has 9 holes or sockets.

DB-25 Shell—the metal or plastic housing for a DB-25 connector.

DB-25F Connector—a DB-25 female connector has 25 holes or sockets. Same as a DB-25S. Different from a DB-25 male connector which has 25 plugs or pins.

DB-25M Connector—a DB-25 male connector has 25 plugs or pins. Same as a DB-25P. Different from a DB-25 female connector which has 25 holes or sockets.

DC—an acronym for direct current. Different from alternating current. In a DC power supply, alternating current is rectified and filtered so that the polarity of the output voltage never changes.

DC1/DC3—an acronym for data-control 1/data-control 3, the ASCII X-ON/X-OFF signals used in software handshaking.

Decimal—a numbering system built on a base of ten (dec) digits. Places increment by powers of 10.

Descent—the depth of the lowest character in a font. Descent is measured from the baseline down.

Deselected—indicates that the printer is not ready to receive data. It may be off, or out of paper. Deselected is synonymous with off-line.

Detent—a physical depression which serves to detain or stop a switch. The paper-thickness switch on early ImageWriter IIs had 4 detents. Later models have switches with 6 detents.

DIP—an acronym for dual in-line package. Refers to small devices such as switches with two (dual) lines of pins.

Dots—circular impressions made by cylindrical striker wires or pins in the printer's type head.

Double-Strike Printing—all dots are printed twice for greater intensity. Differs from boldface printing in that the second strike takes place vertically. Characters get taller and darker, but not any wider.

Download Character—an external character which is assigned an 8-bit ASCII code and downloaded by the program or the printer driver prior to printing. Once downloaded, these characters supersede the printer's built-in character assignments. Download characters are often required to make printers (including ImageWriter printers) 100% compatible with Macintosh System software. If the printer's communications buffer doesn't support download characters, or if the download DIP switch is disabled, the commence-download instruction causes the printer to malfunction.

DPI—an acronym for dots per inch. All 9-inch Macs display 72 dots per inch horizontally × 72 dots per inch vertically.

DSR—an acronym for data set ready.

DTR—an acronym for data terminal ready.

EIA—the abbreviation for Electronics Industries Association.

Elite—refers to 12-cpi printing.

Epson-Compatible—refers to any printer capable of understanding Epson control codes.

Epson Control Codes—a series of printer instructions understood by Epson-compatible printer ROMs.

Expansion Slot—an internal connector designed to accept option cards. The ImageWriter II and the ImageWriter LQ each have one expansion slot. The Imagewriter (Standard and Wide) has no expansion slots.

FG—an acronym for frame ground.

FOND Resources—a font's fractional-width tables and kerning information.

Font—refers to a complete alphabet of similarly designed characters in a single type *size*. Geneva 9 is a 9-point font. Other Geneva fonts are Geneva 10, Geneva 12, etc. Each is a different font, because each is a different size.

Fontastic Plus—a commercial font editor distributed by Altsys Corporation, which is used to add missing characters to existing fonts, to modify existing fonts, and to create entirely new fonts from scratch.

Font/DAM—an early version of Font/DA Mover supplied with System version 2.0, dated April, 1985. Superseded by Font / DA Mover version 3.2, which was supplied with System version 3.2, dated 1986.

Font/DA Mover—a standard Macintosh utility program used to move fonts and desk accessories in and out of System files.

Font Editor—a tool for viewing individual character matrixes or changing the way a whole font looks.

FontMover—an early Macintosh utility program used to move fonts in and out of original Macintosh System files.

Font Width—the space between the left and right boundary of the character rectangle.

Frame Ground (FG)—indicates that the chassis or frame of an electrical device is connected to electrical ground. Synonymous with protective ground.

Framing Errors—during a transmission, data bits (representing characters and other instructions) are framed by start bits and stop bits. If these are misinterpreted, a framing error results, which indicates the data bits were misunderstood.

Gender Changer—a connector which converts cable endings. Gender changers come in plug-to-plug (male-to-male), which converts female connections to male connections, and socket-to-socket (female-to-female), which converts male connections to female connections.

Handshaking—refers to the controlled movement of bits between a computer and a printer. The bits are like automobile traffic. Handshaking is similar to the stop-and-go rules of the road.

Hexadecimal—a numbering system built on a base of sixteen digits. 6 (hex) plus (a) 10 (dec) numerals (imals). Hexadecimal places increment by powers of 16 instead of by powers of 10.

Hexadecimal-Dump—a printer's built-in debug mode.

HFS—an acronym for hierarchical file system.

Hierarchical File System—abbreviated HFS. Allows a root directory and a hierarchy of multiple subdirectories. Different from MFS, the original Macintosh file system, which allows only one directory.

Ink-Jet—refers to a disposable print head which draws liquid ink from a self-contained reservoir. The ink is sprayed onto the paper through tiny, jet-like nozzles.

Interface—the cables, connectors, and electrical circuits which allow communication between computers and printers.

JetLink Express—a collection of high-speed Hewlett-Packard-compatible Macintosh printer drivers developed by GDT Softworks.

Jumper—a piece of wire used to short (close) two connections.

Leading—pronounced "led-ing," the space between lines. Originally referred to pieces of lead used between lines of type to prevent one line from descending into the next.

Least-Significant Bit (LSB)—the first or rightmost bit in a byte.

LED—an acronym for light-emitting diode, a type of lamp.

LocalTalk—generally refers to the cables and connectors that make the AppleTalk network functional.

Logic 0—a serial interface condition synonymous with ON, space, spacing, high, true, and positive voltage. Logic 0 means data are being sent. On an RS-232C mini-tester, the line LED usually glows red.

Logic 1—a serial interface condition synonymous with OFF, mark, marking, low, false, and negative voltage. Logic 1 means data are not being sent. On an RS-232C mini-tester, the line LED usually glows green.

LPM—an acronym for lines per minute, which tends to be an honest measurement of printer speed. LPM and throughput are generally synonymous.

LQ—an acronym for letter quality.

LSB—an acronym for least-significant bit; the first, or rightmost bit, in a byte.

Macintosh File System—the original Macintosh file system. All files are kept in the root directory. Different from HFS (hierarchical file system), which allows a hierarchy of subdirectories.

MacMatrix—a Mac-to-Toshiba printer-accessory package containing outline fonts, a printer driver, and a serial cable.

MacTable—an ergonomically designed work station for Macintosh computer systems. Developed and manufactured by ScanCo.

Matrix—the pattern which defines the horizontal and vertical limits of each character.

MFS—an acronym for the original Macintosh file system. All files are kept in the root directory. Different from HFS (hierarchical file system), which allows multiple subdirectories.

Monochrome—refers to a one-color ribbon or a one-color monitor. From the Greek roots monos, meaning one, and chroma, meaning color. Monochrome can mean any color you like, as long as it doesn't mean more than one color at a time.

Monospaced—refers to font with only one character width. From the Greek root monos, meaning one. Monospaced fonts can be as wide as you like, as long as each and every character (with the space around it) consumes exactly the same width.

Most-Significant Bit—the eighth, or leftmost, bit in a byte.

MSB—an acronym for most-significant bit; the eighth, or leftmost, bit in a byte.

NFNT—an acronym for new font numbering table.

NLQ—an acronym for near-letter quality. Frequently synonymous with wishful thinking.

OEM—an acronym for original equipment manufacturer. TEC is the OEM of Imagewriter (Standard and Wide) and ImageWriter II printers.

Off-Line—indicates that the printer is not ready to receive data. It may be off, or out of paper. Off-line is synonymous with deselected.

Offset—space between the origin and the left boundary of the character rectangle.

On-Line—indicates that the printer is turned on, loaded with paper, and ready to receive data. On-line is synonymous with selected.

Open—an abbreviation for open circuit. An open circuit is said to be OFF. Different from a closed circuit or a short circuit. When a circuit opens, the flow of electricity is stopped.

Option Card—a circuit board designed to plug into an expansion slot.

Origin—the left boundary of a character.

Outline Fonts—a type of printing that relies on mathematical font definitions which are stored in special outline-font files on the startup disk.

Paper Bail—a spring-loaded roller-shaft assembly used to hold paper against a platen.

Paper-Thickness Lever—a printer part which moves the carrier rod closer to and farther away from the platen to allow clearance for various paper thicknesses.

Parallel Interface—a printer interface designed to handle data in parallel fashion, 8 bits (1 byte) at a time. Standard equipment for PC-compatible computers and Epson-compatible printers. Cables require 7 more wires than serial-interface cables, which transmit data one bit at a time.

Parity Bit—a way of marking the eighth bit in a data byte so that 7-bit ASCII characters between 0 and 127 are received correctly. There are three kinds of parity: odd, even, and none.

Phillips—spelled with two l's, refers to Phillips-head screws or the screwdriver used with these screws.

Pica—refers to 10-cpi printing.

Pitch—refers to the number of characters per inch. In Pica 10, Pica is the typeface, 10 is the pitch. Each Pica 10 character measures 1⁄10-inch wide, resulting in 10 characters to the inch.

Pixels—a shortened term for picture elements, which refers to the luminous dots displayed on a computer monitor. Pixels are two dimensional. They have variable-size length and width.

Platen—the heavy-duty black-rubber roller used with all dot matrix printers.

Point—a unit of measurement equal to 0.0138 inches, or approximately 1⁄72 of an inch. Points are one-dimensional. They have length but not width.

PPI—an acronym for pixels per inch.

Printer Driver—software designed for communications between a computer and printer.

Printer Resources—a Mac-specific synonym for printer driver.

PrintLink Collection—a collection of Kodak Diconix-compatible and Epson-compatible Macintosh printer drivers developed by GDT Softworks.

Proportional—refers to a font with variable character width. Narrow characters have less width than wide characters. Pitch, the number of characters per inch, varies from inch to inch, according to word combinations.

Protocol—refers to an agreed set of communications options, including baud rate, parity, start bits, stop bits, etc.

RAM—an acronym for random-access memory.

RD—an acronym for receive data.

Ready/Busy—a type of handshaking.

Receive Data (RD)—under RS-232, serial data is received on pin 3 of the DB-25 connector and transmitted on pin 2.

Request to Send (RTS)—under RS-232, pin 4 of the DB-25 connector is used with modems to indicate that the computer is ready to send.

Resolution—on a printer, the number of circular impressions (dots) per square inch made by the cylindrical striker wires in the printer's type head. On a monitor, the number of luminous pixels per square inch.

Ribbon-Cartridge Deck—a platform which supports the ribbon cartridge.

ROM—an acronym for read-only memory.

RS-232—the recommended standard for serial-communications interfaces that was drafted in the 1960s by the Electronics Industries Association (EIA).

RS-232C—the latest revision of RS-232.

RS-232C Mini-Tester—an instrument used to monitor the logic level in a serial communications interface. Red lights generally indicate logic 0. Green lights generally indicate logic 1.

RTS—an acronym for request to send.

Selected—indicates that the printer is turned on, loaded with paper, and ready to receive data. Selected is synonymous with on-line.

Serial Interface—a printer interface designed to handle data in serial fashion, one bit at a time. Standard equipment for Macintosh computers and ImageWriter printers.

SG—an acronym for signal ground.

Shorting Blocks—jumper wires used to select communications settings.

Signal Ground—under RS-232, all signals are referenced to pin 7 which is the signal ground on a DB-25 connector.

Start Bits—leading bits which indicate that a data byte is about to be transmitted.

Stop Bits—trailing bits which indicate that a data byte has just been transmitted.

Striker Wire—a synonym for a print-head pin, as in 9-pin dot-matrix printer.

TCG—an acronym for Test Character Generator, the diagnostics program included with this book.

TD—an acronym for transmit data.

Test Character Generator (TCG)—the diagnostics program included with this book.

Throughput—a synonym for lines per minute, which tends to be an honest measurement of printer speed.

TIAT—an acronym for "This is a test."

TOF—an acronym for top of form.

Transmission-ON/Transmission-OFF (X-ON/X-OFF)—a type of software handshaking.

Transmit Data (TD)—under RS-232, serial data is transmitted on pin 2 of the DB-25 connector and received on pin 3.

Typeface—a complete set of fonts. All available sizes of Geneva make up the Geneva typeface.

Type Styles—variations of a typeface, such as bold, italic, and outline make up various type styles.

Unidirectional Printing—printing which takes place in one direction. Even-numbered passes print from left to right. Odd-numbered passes are carriage returns.

US Legal—United States legal-size paper measuring 8.5 × 14 inches.

US Letter—United States letter-size paper measuring 8.5 × 11 inches.

Voltage—refers to electrical pressure. Used in the same sense as water pressure.

VOM—an acronym for volt-ohmmeter. Generally refers to inexpensive pocket meters.

WYSIWYG—an acronym for "What you see is what you get."

X—a symbolic abbreviation for cross, crossing, or transmission, which literally means crossing over.

X-ON/X-OFF—an acronym for transmission-ON/transmission-OFF, a type of handshaking.

APPENDIX

B

Dealer/Manufacturer Addresses

Adobe Systems
(Adobe Type Manager—call for nearest dealer)
1585 Charleston Road
Post Office Box 7900
Mountain View, California 94039-7900
(800) 344-8335

Altex Electronics
(Apple-compatible System/peripheral-8 cables, DB-9 gender changers, DB-25 gender changers, Mac 128K/512K to Imagewriter cables, Mac 128K/512K to ImageWriter II/LQ cables, Mac Plus/SE/Mac II to ImageWriter II/LQ cables, minicircular 8-pin plugs {mini DIN-8 plugs}, minicircular 8-pin plug {mini DIN-8 plug} to open end cables, minicircular 8-pin {mini DIN-8} line switchboxes, PC AT to PC/XT adapters, PC/XT to PC AT adapters, RS-232 mini-testers, standard DB-25 line switchboxes, universal {serial to parallel} interface converters—call for a catalog)
300 Breesport
San Antonio, Texas 78216
(800) 531-5369

Altsys Corporation
(FONTastic Plus bitmapped-font editor, bitmapped fonts)
720 Avenue F, Suite 109
Plano, Texas 75074
(214) 424-4888

Casady & Greene
(Fluent {bitmapped} Fonts for the Macintosh and ImageWriter)
P.O. Box 223779
Carmel, California 93922
(800) 359-4920

C.Itoh Electronics
(OEM parts for C.Itoh 8510a, and C.Itoh C310R—call for nearest parts reseller)
2500 White Road
Irvine, California 92714
(800) 524-8338

DataPak Software
(Printer Interface III {Mac to HP DeskJet} printer driver)
14011 Ventura Boulevard, Suite 507
Sherman Oaks, California 91423
(800) 327-6703

Eastman Kodak Company
(Kodak Diconix M150 Plus printer—call for nearest dealer)
901 Elmgrove Road
Rochester, New York 14653-6304
(800) 255-3434

Electronic Industries Association
(Technical documentation on the RS-232 interface)
2001 Eye Street Northwest
Washington, DC 20006
(202) 457-4966

GDT Softworks
(PrintLink Mac-to-Epson drivers, PrintLink Mac-to-Diconix 150/300 drivers, Mac Daisy Link univeral Mac-to-serial printer driver, JetLink Mac-to-HP-DeskJet outline-font printer driver, universal serial-to-parallel interface converters)
Suite 188, 4664 Lougheed Highway
Burnaby, British Columbia
Canada V5C 6B7
(604) 291-9121

Hewlett-Packard Company
(HP DeskJet, HP DeskJet PLUS, and HP DeskWriter printers—call for nearest dealer)
Post Office Box 8906
Vancouver, Washington 98668-8906
(800) 752-0900

Howard W. Sams & Company
(CP8-COMPUTERFACTS service folder on Apple {Imagewriter} model A9M0303, CP10-COMPUTERFACTS service folder on NEC model PC-8023A-N, CP12-COMPUTERFACTS service folder on C.Itoh model M-8510AP, CP27-COMPUTERFACTS service folder on Apple ImageWriter II model A9M0310, CP33-COMPUTERFACTS service folder on C.Itoh model C310R)
2647 Waterfront Pky, E. Dr.
Indianapolis, Indiana 46214
(800) 428-SAMS

SAMS/Macmillan Computer Publishing
(Books, including *Macintosh Repair & Upgrade Secrets*, ISBN 0-672-48452-8 and *Microcomputer Troubleshooting & Repair*, ISBN 0-672-22629-4)
11711 N. College Ave.
Carmel, Indiana 46032
(317) 573-2500

IMPACT Printhead Refurbishing
(Mail-order ImageWriter print-head repair service—call for flat-rate price and repair/return-authorization number)
8701 Crosspark Drive
Suite 101
Austin, Texas 78754
(800) 777-4323; (512) 832-9151

Jameco Electronics
(Apple compatible System/peripheral-8 Cables, AppleTalk-compatible network cables, Apple II, II+, IIe-compatible parallel-printer cards and super-serial cards, DB-25 gender changers, ImageWriter-compatible AC power cords, LocalTalk-compatible network cables, Mac-to-Imagewriter printer cables, Mac-to-ImageWriter-II printer cables, minicircular 8-pin sockets {8-pin mini DIN female sockets}, miscellaneous OEM parts, printer stands, printout paper trimmers, RS-232 mini-testers, RS-232 breakout boxes, standard DB-25 line switchboxes, soldering equipment, test equipment—call for a catalog)
1355 Shoreway Road
Belmont, California 94002
(415) 592-8097

James River Paper Company
(Pro-Tech laser bond cut-sheet paper for use with ink-jet printers, laser printers, and ImageWriter sheet feeders—call for a sample pack)
P.O. Box 3402
Wallingford, Connecticut 06494
(800) 521-5035

JDR Microdevices
(Apple-compatible System/peripheral-8 Cables, DB-25 gender-changers, Mac to Imagewriter printer cables, Mac-to-ImageWriter II printer cables, miscellaneous OEM parts, RS-232 mini-testers, RS-232 breakout boxes, standard DB-25 line switchboxes, soldering equipment, test equipment, universal {serial-to-parallel} interface converters—call for a catalog)
2233 Branham Lane
San Jose, California 95124
(408) 559-1200

MEI/Micro Center
(4-color ImageWriter II ribbons, black Imagewriter ribbons, black Olympia NP 30 APL {Epson LX 80/90} ribbons, black Seikosha SP-1000AP ribbons, black Toshiba P321 ribbons, 9.5-inch × 11-inch business white laser-edge pin-feed computer paper, 14.875-inch × 11-inch green-bar pin-feed computer paper, universal printer stands—call for a catalog)
1100 Steelwood Road
Columbus, Ohio 43212
(800) 634-3478

Misco
(DEC-style {Apple-compatible} null-modem adapters, platen-cleaning chemicals—call for a catalog)
1 Misco Plaza
Holmdel, New Jersey 07733
(800) 876-4726

Nakajima All Precision Company
(Original equipment manufacturer of Fortis, Laser, and Olympia brands of Apple-compatible printers)
25-7 Hakozaki-Cho, Nihonbashi,
Chuo-Ku, Tokyo, 103. Japan
(03) 669-2431

Nakajima U.S.A.
(Original equipment manufacturer of Fortis, Laser, and Olympia brands of Apple-compatible printers)
625 Plainfield Road
Willowbrook, Illinois 60521
(312) 655-0277

NEC
(OEM parts for PC-8023A-N)
159 Swanson Road
Boxborough, Massachusetts 01719
(800) 325-5500

Olympia USA
(NP 30 APL printer—call for nearest dealer)
Route 22 & Orr Drive
Somerville, New Jersey 08876-0022
(800) 526-3843

Radio Shack
(Monochrome Seikosha SP-1000AP {DMP130} ribbon cartridges, RS232 troubleshooter boxes {mini-testers}, soldering equipment, test equipment). Over 700 stores coast-to-coast listed in the phone book under: "Electronic Equipment & Supplies"

ScanCo Scandinavian Computer Furniture
(MacTable, Macintosh-specific workstation)
P. O. Box 3217
Redmond, Washington 98073-3217
(800) 722-6263

SBF Computer
(Mac 128K/512K to Imagewriter cables, Mac 128K/512K to ImageWriter II/LQ cables, Mac Plus/SE/Mac II to Imagewriter cables, Mac Plus/SE/Mac II to ImageWriter II/ImageWriter LQ cables, minicircular 8-pin {8PIN MINIDIN} line switchboxes {DATASWITCHES}, standard DB-25 line switchboxes {DATASWITCHES})
22 Sheridan Avenue
Mount Vernon, New York 10552
(914) 664-3930

Seikosha Company Limited
(Original equipment manufacturer of Seikosha and some Tandy brands of dot-matrix printers)
4-1-1 Taihei,
Sumida-Ku, Tokyo, 130. Japan

Seikosha America
(Seikosha SP1000AP printer—call for nearest dealer)
1111 MacArthur Boulevard
Mahwah, New Jersey 07340
(800) 422-7768

Shreve Systems
(New and used ImageWriter parts—call for a catalog)
2421 Malcolm Street
Shreveport, Louisiana 71108
(318) 635-1121

Sun Remarketing
(ImageWriter parts and upgrades—call for a catalog)
Post Office Box 4059
Logan, Utah 84321
(800) 821-3221

Toshiba America Information Systems
Computer Systems Division
(MacMatrix printer driver, P321SLC 24-pin color printer—call for nearest dealer)
9740 Irvine Boulevard
Irvine, California 92718
(800) 334-3445

William F. Nye Oil Company
(Electronic-servicing specialty lubricants, Nyoil-brand lubricant does not contain rust inhibitors)
12 Howland Road
Fairhaven, Massachusetts 02719
(508) 996-6721

Larry P.'s Guide to Mail-order Sanity:

1. If there's no address and/or no phone number in a magazine advertisement, it means the company positively does not want to talk to you. Don't waste your time. Shop elsewhere!
2. Avoid ordering from any catalog with a misplaced index. Locating misplaced indexes is a hassle. If management misplaced their own index, imagine what they're going to do with your order!
3. Avoid ordering from any catalog printed on high glare paper. If the printed presentation glares, you can bet the personal service will glare even more.
4. Don't discuss. Don't ask. Know what you want before you pick up the phone.
5. Observing these strategies will help you avoid incompetent mail-order firms, but you could still receive unsatisfactory goods. In that case, please call the company that filled your order. This address list is not an endorsement. The author cannot guarantee your satisfaction.

APPENDIX

C

Imagewriter Control Codes

Hexadecimal	Meaning
04	Stop downloading custom characters
08	Backspace
09	Move to next horizontal tab
0A	Line feed
0B	Vertical tab
0C	Form feed
0D	Carriage return
0E	Turn on double width (headline mode)
0F	Turn off double width (headline mode)
18	Cancel all unprinted text
1B n	Set n dots between Elite-proportional characters (n = 1 to 6)
1B 21	Turn on bold
1B 22	Turn off bold
1B 24	Switch to standard ASCII characters
1B 27	Switch to downloaded ASCII (27 to 126, 160 to 139) characters
1B 28 a b — n.	Set horizontal tab line
1B 29 a b — n.	Clear selected horizontal tabs

Hexadecimal	Meaning
1B 2A	Switch to high-ASCII (160 to 239) downloaded characters (valid for 7-bit mode)
1B 2B	Maximum width of download character is 16 dots
1B 2D	Maximum width of download character is 8 dots
1B 30	Clear all tabs
1B 3C	Turn on bidirectional printing
1B 3E	Turn on unidirectional printing
1B 41	Set line-feed pitch to ⅙ inch
1B 42	Set line-feed pitch to ⅛ inch
1B 44 00 01	Turn on slashed zeros
1B 44 00 20	Recognize 7-bit data bytes, ignore 8th bit
1B 44 01 00	Turn on Italian alphabet
1B 44 02 00	American-English alphabet
1B 44 03 00	Turn on European-English alphabet
1B 44 04 00	Turn on German alphabet
1B 44 05 00	Turn on Swedish alphabet
1B 44 06 00	Turn on French alphabet
1B 44 07 00	Turn on Spanish alphabet
1B 44 20 00	Add line feed when line is full
1B 44 40 00	CR, LF, VT, FF all signal end-of-line
1B 44 80 00	CR = CR + LF
1B 45	Turn on Elite (12 cpi, 96 dpi)
1B 46 nnnn	Move print head to a position nnnn dot columns from the left margin
1B 47 nnnn	Print line of nnnn data bytes
1B 49	Start downloading custom characters
1B 4C nnn	Set left margin at column nnn
1B 4D	Turn on near-letter quality
1B 4E	Turn on Pica (10 cpi, 80 dpi)
1B 4F	Turn off paper-out detection
1B 50	Turn on Elite proportional (160 dpi)
1B 51	Turn on ultracondensed (17 cpi, 136 dpi)

Hexadecimal	Meaning
1B 52 nnn c	Print nnn repetitions of character c (nnn = 1 to 99)
1B 53 nnnn	Print line of nnnn data bytes
1B 54 nn	Set line height to nn/144 inch (nn = 01 to 99)
1B 56 nnnn x	Print nnnn repetitions of the dot column x
1B 58	Turn on underline
1B 59	Turn off underline
1B 5A 00 01	Turn on unslashed zeros
1B 5A 00 20	Recognize 8-bit data bytes
1B 5A 01 00	Turn on French alphabet
1B 5A 02 00	Turn on Swedish alphabet
1B 5A 03 00	Turn on German alphabet
1B 5A 04 00	Turn on European-English alphabet
1B 5A 05 00	Turn on American-English alphabet
1B 5A 06 00	Turn on Italian alphabet
1B 5A 07 00	Turn on American-English alphabet
1B 5A 20 00	Don't add line feed when line is full
1B 5A 40 00	Only CR signals end-of-line
1B 5A 80 00	CR = CR
1B 63	Initialize printer
1B 65	Turn on semicondensed (13.4 cpi, 107 dpi)
1B 66	Turn on forward line feeding
1B 67 nnn	Print line of nnn × 8 data bytes
1B 6C 30	LF = CR + LF; FF = CR + FF
1B 6C 31	LF = LF; FF = FF
1B 6E	Turn on extended (9 cpi, 72 dpi)
1B 6D	Turn on correspondence quality
1B 6F	Turn on paper-out detection
1B 70	Turn on Pica proportional (144 dpi)
1B 71	Turn on condensed (15 cpi, 120 dpi)
1B 72	Turn on reverse line feeding
1B 73 n	Set spacing between proportional characters to n dots (n = 0 to 9)
1B 75 nnn	Set additional horizontal tab at column nnn

Hexadecimal	Meaning
1B 76	Set TOF to current position
1D 30	Initialize vertical tabs and set TOF
1D 41 40	Set top of form (TOF)
1F 41	Drop to next TOF or BOF
1F 42	Drop to next vertical tab
1F 43	Drop to next vertical tab
1F 44	Drop to next vertical tab
1F 45	Drop to next vertical tab
1F 46	Drop to next vertical tab
1F n	Feed 1 to 15 lines of blank paper (n = 1,2,3,4,5,6,7,8,9,:,;,<,=,.,?)
41 ... 50	Width code when using top 8 wires
41 40 1E	Set TOF of next form
43 40	Set bottom of form (BOF)
61 ... 70	Width code when using bottom 8 wires

APPENDIX

D

ImageWriter II Control Codes

Hexadecimal	Meaning
04	Stop downloading custom characters
08	Backspace
09	Move to next horizontal tab
0A	Line feed
0B	Vertical tab
0C	Form feed
0D	Carriage return
0E	Turn on double width (headline mode)
0F	Turn off double width (headline mode)
11	Select printer
13	Deselect printer
18	Cancel current line
1B n	Set n dots between Elite-proportional characters (n = 1 to 6)
1B 21	Turn on bold
1B 22	Turn off bold
1B 24	Switch to standard ASCII characters
1B 26	Map MouseText to low-ASCII (64 to 95) characters

Hexadecimal	Meaning
1B 27	Switch to downloaded ASCII (27 to 126, 160 to 139) characters
1B 28 a b — n.	Set horizontal tab line
1B 29 a b — n.	Clear selected horizontal tabs
1B 2A	Switch to downloaded high-ASCII (160 to 239) characters (valid for 7-bit mode)
1B 2B	Maximum width of download character is 16 dots
1B 2D	Maximum width of download character is 8 dots
1B 30	Clear all tabs
1B 3C	Turn on bidirectional printing
1B 3E	Turn on unidirectional printing
1B 3F	Send ID string
1B 41	Set line feed pitch to 1/6 inch
1B 42	Set line feed pitch to 1/8 inch
1B 44 00 01	Turn on slashed zeros
1B 44 00 04	Turn off perforation skip
1B 44 00 20	Recognize 7-bit data bytes, ignore 8th bit
1B 44 01 00	Turn on Italian alphabet
1B 44 02 00	Turn on Danish alphabet
1B 44 03 00	Turn on European-English alphabet
1B 44 04 00	Turn on German alphabet
1B 44 05 00	Turn on Swedish alphabet
1B 44 06 00	Turn on French alphabet
1B 44 07 00	Turn on Spanish alphabet
1B 44 20 00	Add line feed when line is full
1B 44 40 00	CR, LF, VT, FF all signal end-of-line
1B 44 80 00	CR = CR + LF
1B 44 10 00	Turn off software select
1B 45	Turn on Elite (12 cpi, 96 dpi)
1B 46 nnnn	Move print head to a position nnnn dot columns from the left margin
1B 47 nnnn	Print line of nnnn data bytes
1B 48 nnnn	Set page length to nnnn/144 inch (nnnn = 0001 to 9999)

Hexadecimal	Meaning
1B 49	Start downloading custom characters
1B 4B 30	Turn on black color
1B 4B 31	Turn on yellow color
1B 4B 32	Turn on magenta color
1B 4B 33	Turn on cyan color
1B 4B 34	Turn on orange (yellow and magenta) color
1B 4B 35	Turn on green (yellow and cyan) color
1B 4B 36	Turn on purple (magenta and cyan) color
1B 4C nnn	Set left margin at column nnn
1B 4D	Turn on near-letter quality
1B 4E	Turn on Pica (10 cpi, 80 dpi)
1B 4F	Turn off paper-out detection
1B 50	Turn on Elite proportional (160 dpi)
1B 51	Turn on ultracondensed (17 cpi, 136 dpi)
1B 52 nnn c	Print nnn repetitions of character c (nnn = 1 to 99)
1B 53 nnnn	Print line of nnnn data bytes
1B 54 nn	Set line height to nn/144 inch (nn = 01 to 99)
1B 56 nnnn x	Print nnnn repetitions of the dot column x
1B 57	Turn off half-height text
1B 58	Turn on underline
1B 59	Turn off underline
1B 5A 00 01	Turn on unslashed zeros
1B 5A 00 04	Turn on perforation skip
1B 5A 00 20	Recognize 8-bit data bytes
1B 5A 01 00	Turn on French alphabet
1B 5A 02 00	Turn on Swedish alphabet
1B 5A 03 00	Turn on German alphabet
1B 5A 04 00	Turn on European-English alphabet
1B 5A 05 00	Turn on Danish alphabet
1B 5A 06 00	Turn on Italian alphabet
1B 5A 07 00	Turn on American-English alphabet
1B 5A 10 00	Turn on software select
1B 5A 20 00	Don't add line feed when line is full

Hexadecimal	Meaning
1B 5A 40 00	Only CR signals end-of-line
1B 5A 80 00	CR = CR
1B 61 30	Turn on correspondence quality
1B 61 31	Turn on data-processing quality
1B 61 32	Turn on near-letter quality
1B 63	Initialize printer
1B 65	Turn on semicondensed (13.4 cpi, 107 dpi)
1B 66	Turn on forward line feeding
1B 67 nnn	Print line of nnn × 8 data bytes
1B 6C 30	LF = CR + LF; FF = CR + FF
1B 6C 31	LF = LF; FF = FF
1B 6E	Turn on extended (9 cpi, 72 dpi)
1B 6D	Turn on correspondence quality
1B 6F	Turn on paper-out detection
1B 70	Turn on Pica proportional (144 dpi)
1B 71	Turn on condensed (15 cpi, 120 dpi)
1B 72	Turn on reverse line feeding
1B 73 n	Set spacing between proportionally printed characters to n dots (n = 0 to 9)
1B 75 nnn	Set additional horizontal tab at column nnn
1B 76	Set TOF to current position
1B 77	Turn on half-height text
1B 78	Turn on superscript
1B 79	Turn on subscript
1B 7A	Turn off superscript and/or subscript

APPENDIX

E

ImageWriter LQ Control Codes

Hexadecimal	Meaning
08	Backspace
09	Move to next horizontal tab
0A	Line feed
0B	Vertical tab
0C	Form feed
0D	Carriage return
0E	Turn on double width (headline mode)
0F	Turn off double width (headline mode)
18	Cancel current line
1B n	Set n dots between characters
1B 21	Turn on bold
1B 22	Turn off bold
1B 28 a b — n.	Set horizontal tab line
1B 29 a b — n.	Clear selected horizontal tabs
1B 30	Clear all tabs
1B 3C	Turn on bidirectional printing
1B 3D 30	Send name of near-letter quality font
1B 3D 31	Send name of data-processing font

Hexadecimal	Meaning
1B 3D 32	Send name of near-letter quality font
1B 3D 33	Send name of letter quality font
1B 3D 39	Send name of optional ROM font
1B 3E	Turn on unidirectional printing
1B 3F	Send ID string
1B 40 30	Get paper from first bin
1B 40 31	Get paper from second bin
1B 40 32	Get paper from third bin
1B 41	Set line feed pitch to ⅙ inch
1B 42	Set line feed pitch to ⅛ inch
1B 43 nnnn	Print line of nnnn × 3 data bytes in high resolution
1B 44 nn	Turn on software switches
1B 44 00 01	Turn on slashed zeros
1B 44 00 02	Turn off color-ribbon sensor
1B 44 00 04	Turn off perforation skip
1B 44 01 00	Turn on Italian alphabet
1B 44 02 00	Turn on Danish alphabet
1B 44 03 00	Turn on European-English alphabet
1B 44 04 00	Turn on German alphabet
1B 44 05 00	Turn on Swedish alphabet
1B 44 06 00	Turn on French alphabet
1B 44 07 00	Turn on Spanish alphabet
1B 44 20 00	Add line feed when line is full
1B 44 40 00	CR, LF, VT, FF all signal end-of-line
1B 44 80 00	CR = CR + LF
1B 44 10 00	Turn off software select
1B 45	Turn on Elite (12 cpi, 96 or 192 dpi)
1B 46 nnnn	Move print head to a position nnnn standard resolution dot columns from the left margin
1B 47 nnnn	Print line of nnnn data bytes in standard resolution
1B 48 nnnn	Set page length to nnnn/144 inch (nnnn = 0001 to 9999)
1B 4B 30	Turn on black color

Hexadecimal	Meaning
1B 4B 31	Turn on yellow color
1B 4B 32	Turn on magenta color
1B 4B 33	Turn on cyan color
1B 4B 34	Turn on orange (yellow and magenta) color
1B 4B 35	Turn on green (yellow and cyan) color
1B 4B 36	Turn on purple (magenta and cyan) color
1B 4C n	Move down n/216 inch
1B 4C nnn	Set left margin at column nnn
1B 4E	Turn on Pica (10 cpi, 80 or 160 dpi)
1B 4F	Turn off paper out detection
1B 50	Turn on Elite proportional (160 or 320 dpi)
1B 51	Turn on ultracondensed (17 cpi, 136 or 272 dpi)
1B 52 nnn c	Print nnn repetitions of character c (nnn = 001 to 99)
1B 53 nnnn	Print line of nnnn data bytes in standard resolution
1B 54 nn	Set line height to nn/144 inch (nn = 01 to 99)
1B 55 nnnn xxx	Print nnnn repetitions of the dot column xxx in high resolution
1B 56 nnnn x	Print nnnn repetitions of the dot column x in standard resolution
1B 57	Turn off half-height text
1B 58	Turn on underline
1B 59	Turn off underline
1B 5A nn	Turn off software switches
1B 5A 00 01	Turn on unslashed zeros
1B 5A 00 02	Turn on color-ribbon sensor
1B 5A 00 04	Turn on perforation skip
1B 5A 01 00	Turn on French alphabet
1B 5A 02 00	Turn on Swedish alphabet
1B 5A 03 00	Turn on German alphabet
1B 5A 04 00	Turn on European-English alphabet
1B 5A 05 00	Turn on Danish alphabet
1B 5A 06 00	Turn on Italian alphabet

Hexadecimal	Meaning
1B 5A 07 00	Turn on American-English alphabet
1B 5A 10 00	Turn on software select
1B 5A 20 00	Don't add line feed when line is full
1B 5A 40 00	Only CR signals end-of-line
1B 5A 80 00	CR = CR
1B 61 30	Turn on near-letter quality
1B 61 31	Turn on data-processing quality
1B 61 32	Turn on near-letter quality
1B 61 33	Turn on letter quality
1B 63	Initialize printer
1B 65	Turn on semicondensed (13.4 cpi, 108 or 216 dpi)
1B 66	Turn on forward line feeding
1B 67 nnn	Print line of nnn × 8 data bytes in standard resolution
1B 68 nnnn	Move print head to a position nnnn high resolution dot columns from the left margin
1B 6B	Turn on optional ROM-chip character set
1B 6C 30	LF = CR + LF; FF = CR + FF
1B 6C 31	LF = LF; FF = FF
1B 6E	Turn on extended (9 cpi, 72 or 144 dpi)
1B 6F	Turn on paper-out detection
1B 70	Turn on Pica proportional (144 or 288 dpi)
1B 71	Turn on condensed (15 cpi, 120 or 240 dpi)
1B 72	Turn on reverse line feeding
1B 73 n	Set spacing between characters to n dots (n = 0 to 9)
1B 75 nnn	Set additional horizontal tab at column nnn
1B 76	Set TOF to current position
1B 77	Turn on half-height text
1B 78	Turn on superscript
1B 79	Turn on subscript
1B 7A	Turn off superscript and/or subscript

APPENDIX

F

Epson Control Codes

Hexadecimal	Meaning
07	Beep
08	Back space
09	Move to next horizontal tab
0A	Line feed plus carriage return
0B	Vertical tab
0C	Form feed
0D	Carriage return or CR plus line feed
0E	Turn on double width for the present line
0F	Turn on condensed (17 or 20 cpi)
11	Select printer
12	Turn off condensed
13	Deselect printer
14	Turn off double width for the present line
18	Clear internal buffer
1B 0E	Turn on double width for the present line
1B 0F	Turn on condensed
1B 19 30	Turn off cut-sheet feeder (CSF) mode
1B 19 34	Turn on cut-sheet feeder (CSF) mode
1B 19 52	Eject cut sheet

Hexadecimal	Meaning
1B 20 n	Set number of dots between characters
1B 21 n	Turn on multiple print mode
1B 23	Recognize 8-bit data bytes
1B 24 n1 n2	Set absolute dot position
1B 25 00 00	Switch to built-in ROM characters
1B 25 01 00	Switch to download characters in RAM
1B 26	Define download characters
1B 2A m n1 n2	Turn on various graphic modes
1B 2D 30	Turn off underline
1B 2D 31	Turn on underline
1B 2F m	Select vertical-tab channel mode
1B 30	Set line feed pitch to 1/8 inch
1B 31	Set line feed pitch to 7/72 inch
1B 32	Set line feed pitch to 1/6 inch
1B 33 n	Set line feed pitch to n/216 or n/144 inch
1B 34	Turn on italic
1B 35	Turn off italic
1B 35 30	CR = CR only
1B 35 31	CR = CR + LF
1B 36	Switch to alternate character set or IBM 2
1B 37	Clear alternate set or switch to IBM 1
1B 38	Turn off paper-out detection
1B 39	Turn on paper-out detection
1B 3A 00 00 00	Copy the built-in ROM characters to RAM
1B 3C	Home print head
1B 3D	Turn on MSB is always 0
1B 3E	Turn on MSB is always 1
1B 3F n m	Reassign 8-bit graphic modes
1B 40	Initialize printer
1B 41 n	Set line-feed pitch to n/72 inch
1B 42	Set vertical tab
1B 43 00 n	Set number of inches per page
1B 43 n	Set number of lines per page
1B 44 ... 00	Set horizontal tab
1B 45	Turn on bold

Hexadecimal	Meaning
1B 46	Turn off bold
1B 47	Turn on double-strike
1B 48	Turn off double-strike
1B 49 30	Clear character set in low-ASCII control area
1B 49 31	Use character set in the lower control area
1B 4A n	n/144 or n/216-inch line feed after printing
1B 4B n1 n2	Turn on standard-density graphic mode
1B 4C n1 n2	Turn on double-density graphic mode
1B 4D	Turn on Elite (12 cpi)
1B 4E n	Skip n lines at perforation
1B 4F	Turn off skip n lines at perforation
1B 50	Turn on Pica (10 cpi)
1B 51 n	Set right margin
1B 52	Initialize default tab settings
1B 52 n	Use international characters
1B 53 30	Turn on superscript
1B 53 31	Turn on subscript
1B 54	Turn off superscript/subscript
1B 55 30	Turn on bidirectional printing
1B 55 31	Turn on unidirectional printing
1B 57 30	Turn off double-width for all lines
1B 57 31	Turn on double-width for all lines
1B 58 n1 n2	Set left and right margin
1B 59 n1 n2	Turn on double-speed double-density graphics
1B 5A n1 n2	Turn on quadruple-density graphics
1B 5C n1 n2	Set relative dot position
1B 5E a n1 n2	Turn on 9-pin graphics mode
1B 62	Set vertical tabs in channels
1B 69 30	Turn off immediate printing
1B 69 31	Turn on immediate printing
1B 6A n	n/144- or n/216-inch reverse LF after printing
1B 6C n	Set left margin
1B 70 30	Turn off proportional

Hexadecimal	Meaning
1B 70 31	Turn on proportional
1B 78 30	Turn off near-letter quality
1B 78 31	Turn on near-letter quality
7F	Delete 1 character
FF	Delete 1 character

Index

J

K

R

S

T

By opening this package, you are agreeing to be bound by the following agreement.